TRANSNATIONAL SOCIAL MOVEMENTS AND GLOBAL POLITICS

Syracuse Studies on Peace and Conflict Resolution

Harriet Hyman Alonso, Charles Chatfield, *and* Louis Kriesberg

Series Editors

TRANSNATIONAL SOCIAL MOVEMENTS AND GLOBAL POLITICS

SOLIDARITY BEYOND THE STATE

Edited by
JACKIE SMITH, CHARLES CHATFIELD,
and RON PAGNUCCO

With a Foreword by
ELISE BOULDING

Syracuse University Press

First Edition 1997
01 02   6 5 4 3

The paper used in this publication meets the minimum requirements
of American National Standard for Information Sciences—Permanence of
Paper for Printed Library Materials, ANSI Z39.48-1984. ∞™

Library of Congress Cataloging-in-Publication Data

Transnational social movements and global politics: solidarity beyond the state /
edited by Jackie Smith, Charles Chatfield, and Ron Pagnucco :
with a foreword by Elise Boulding. — 1st ed.
  p.   cm.—(Syracuse studies on peace and conflict resolution)
Includes bibliographical references and index.
ISBN 0-8156-2742-4 (cloth : alk. paper).—ISBN 0-8156-2743-2
(pbk. : alk. paper)
1. Social movements—Case studies. 2. Non-governmental
organizations—Case studies. I. Smith, Jackie G., 1968– .
II. Chatfield, Charles, 1934– . III. Pagnucco, Ron. IV. Series.
HN18.T72 1997
303.48′4—dc21   97-18716

Manufactured in the United States of America

CONTENTS

ILLUSTRATIONS

Figures

Tables

FOREWORD

Elise Boulding

The complex set of transnational social movements beginning in the latter part of the nineteenth century, oriented toward solving the problems of war, economic and social justice, and human rights, led to the great flowering of international nongovernmental organizations (INGOs) in this century—and it is that flowering that this book is about. The social movement perspective, with its focus on the passion for human betterment for the planet as a whole, gives a sense of the powerful dynamics at work in a phenomenon that has cried out for more adequate documentation as this century draws to a close. These movements originated in the West but soon included every continent. In today's emerging global civic culture, one overriding problem complicates transnational collaboration of peoples: the West's premature formulation of universal civic values before there had been sufficient intercultural discourse to establish an authentic consensus about such values, particularly in relation to individual rights versus group rights. This book lays the groundwork for dealing with that problem, but much work lies ahead.

We are in a strange transition period when the legacy of centuries of colonial expansion and technological development has saturated all continents with weapons and supporting military infrastructures, overwhelming traditional conflict resolution capacities as well as traditional knowledge of the ecology of local habitats. Transnational social movements have a very special role to play in countering cultural homogenization and in assisting the recovery of the damaged peace cultures on every continent. I would note especially the growing role of transnational indigenous peoples' movements in the INGO world and the two-way learning process this makes possible. Two-way learning means continuing cultural development for traditional as well as industrialized societies, and such development is very different from destruction of cultures. Perhaps the day will come when we can value each human language, each set of cultural lifeways, as much as we value endangered species of plants and animals.

Because states are becoming increasingly helpless to handle multiplying ethnic conflicts, as is the UN itself, we must look to the INGO community to help evolve new constitutive orders that allow for the cultural diversity and autonomy that states as presently constituted deny their people. The peace and justice INGOs that have worked on this problem for much of this century now have a new set of potential collaborators, ethnic INGOs. This category of transnational associations—with their complex and widely dispersed diasporas and with social goals of bettering the life of their peoples in the context of a commitment to a peaceful world order, a basic requirement for consultative status at the UN—has grown more than fivefold in the period from 1970 to 1994, to a total of 544 now registered with the Union of International Associations. Another category, transnational networks of communities of faith, has doubled since 1970, to a total of 3,228, many of the newer ones interfaith peace INGOs.* Although not all the ethnic and religious INGOs are committed to nonviolent conflict resolution, many are, and these represent resources badly needed by overburdened fellow INGOs, to say nothing of the needs of overarmed and underskilled states.

The essays brought together in this book are beautifully organized to give, first, an overview of the transnational movement phenomenon, and next, case studies on the mobilization of transnational resources in national conflicts, which provide striking examples of courageous work of transnational social movement organizations (TSMOs) in conflict arenas. A useful examination of the difficulties of linking grassroots activism transnationally focuses on the successes and failures of disarmament movements. The chapters on how TSMOs work with and influence, reshape or fail to reshape international institutions and their policies are of great importance, as are the closing theoretical reflections. Both the potentialities and the limitations of TSMOs are carefully and empathically analyzed.

In a time of great discouragement with how the world is going, it is good to be able to sit back with the authors of this book and consider how the capacity for global civic action is developing, however slowly, and with however many setbacks. The media give us the bad news, and we may almost lose the sense of vision of a humane and more just future world that this century began with at the Hague Peace Conference. But just as the convening of the Hague Conference and

---

* Information from the computerized data base of the Union of Transnational Associations, Brussels, Belgium.

the subsequent forming of the League of Nations and then the United Nations were all helped into existence by the transnational activists of the last decades of the nineteenth century, so new structures that will bring more peaceful lifeways to peoples and the biosphere we inhabit may eventually come into being from the new understandings and the new undertakings of the transnational activists of the closing decades of this century.

INTRODUCTION

What Is the Subject of This Book?

"NGOs: They're everywhere, but what are they?"* That question, posed in a public forum, is generating a large and rapidly growing scholarly literature. Nongovernmental organizations (NGOs)—and specifically, the international ones (INGOs)—are the subject of this book. More specifically still, this book is about those INGOs that promote institutional and policy changes in the international order. Borrowing from sociological scholarship on social movements, we refer to these associations as transnational social movement organizations (TSMOs). The subject of this book is not only discrete organizations but also the broader, more ephemeral social movements of which they are a part and the processes through which those organizations and movements relate to both national and intergovernmental decision making.

The underlying assumption of this volume—and, indeed, of the mushrooming literature on INGOs—is that nonstate actors have become significant international actors and will increase in importance as the world stage becomes more complex and integrated. The increased importance of INGOs affects, in turn, how various groupings of people within and across national boundaries exert influence on decision making.

The classic image of world government was a federation or union of nation-states under some universal authority. Now, however, a much more complex model is coming into view. The state, although still an essential component, cannot be viewed as a unitary actor but rather as a complex process within an international context of contending and cooperating associations, while intergovernmental organizations are not so much higher, supranational authorities as reflections of a global political process. In this model, nongovernmental associa-

---

* Carole Collins, *National Catholic Reporter*, 19 May 1995, 7.

tions on all levels of jurisdiction are part of the international relations process. Beyond all their differences and conflicts, they link the common interests of people across national boundaries and provide an interface between the more formal elements of politics. This is more than a vision: it is the present political reality to which the title of this volume points: Solidarity beyond the State.

How Might This Book Be Used?

The authors and editors of this book represent several academic disciplines and some activist networks. Our approach is broadly interdisciplinary, drawing upon analytical concepts from sociology and international relations and upon the historical record. The volume combines a historical overview and specific cases of transnational social movement activity with an original and yet grounded theoretical framework of interpretation. The book is designed for use as a supplementary text in undergraduate courses in international relations and social movements and as a primary text for advanced study. We hope both to introduce the subject to nonspecialists and to facilitate the integration of specialized scholarly analyses.

How Is the Book Organized?

Part 1 introduces TSMOs as a continuing phenomenon. Chapter 1 introduces TSMOs in the context of transformations in twentieth-century world society. Chapter 2 documents their rise prior to 1945, with particular attention to the relationship between nongovernmental organizations and intergovernmental ones (IGOs, such as the League of Nations and the UN). Chapter 3 documents the development and salient characteristics of TSMOs since midcentury, particularly in relation to IGOs.

Chapter 4 offers a theoretical framework for the TSMO phenomenon. Our analysis borrows from the sociological theory of social movements, but it also modifies and adapts that theory in the light of international relations theory and of historical experience. This analytical chapter provides, therefore, a conceptual bridge from the first three chapters to the case studies in part 2.

Parts 2, 3, and 4 together consist of nine case studies. They are grouped in terms of three broad strategies through which TSMOs act in the international arena: *mobilizing transnational resources,* such as memberships and organization coalitions, to influence the outcome of national policy; *generating constituencies* in support of specific multilateral policies; and *targeting intergovernmental institutions* in order to generate multinational policy. We should note, however, that each case study relates to more than one strategy and often to several processes of interaction.

The reader will observe that the case studies are grouped in terms of various processes of TSMO activity rather than along issues of common concern. Admittedly, it can be very useful to identify transnational social movements and organizations in terms of the global issues that denominate them—issues relating to the environment, for example, or economic development, women's liberation, indigenous peoples, human rights, peace, and international law, to mention but a few. Referred to as "issue networks," those groupings help to clarify the relationships among the transnational organizations and other components of broad social movements. The case studies in this book relate to several issue networks, but they are not a balanced representation of issues. Rather, they are examples of the ways that TSMOs act and interact with one another, with national movements and governments, and with intergovernmental agencies, as they seek to influence policy formation on those various levels.

The case studies, then, enable the reader to experiment with the analytical framework of chapter 4: to test, modify, and expand that model in a set of concrete instances.

What are the implications of the TSMO phenomenon, the specific case studies, and our analytical framework for the fields of international relations and social movement theory? That question is the focus of part 5, the last two chapters of the book.

Although not designed to be comprehensive, the list of works cited is a useful introduction to the bibliography of the field and the issues reflected in the case studies.

How Did This Book Come About?

Each of the editors brings to *Solidarity Beyond the State* a long-standing interest in movements for social change and in the roles of international nongovernmental organizations. All of us are grateful for the contributions made to our understanding by colleagues and friends. The idea for this book emerged, however, directly from a workshop at the University of Notre Dame on International Institutions and Transnational Social Movement Organizations. We appreciate the support the Kroc Institute for International Peace Studies and the Social Science Research Council provided for the workshop. Editors Smith and Pagnucco are grateful to Janie Leatherman for her collaboration in the initial workshop and for her contributions to their thinking about transnational social movements and international institutions. The workshop demonstrated the need to bridge various disciplines, and the book project was a reasonable next step.

Each case study and chapter of this book, including our own writing, has been subjected to editorial review by all three editors. Jackie Smith did the primary writing for the theoretical chapter, although its conceptualization and structure is the result of extensive discussion among the editors, and she did most of the final editing. Support from the University of Notre Dame's Kroc Institute for International Peace Studies and Department of Government and International Studies allowed her to devote a considerable amount of time to this book. All of the editors thank our families and friends, who have supported our work in countless ways. Finally, we appreciate the meticulously professional copyediting of Bettie McDavid Mason.

As a participant in the Notre Dame workshop, I was pleased to join Smith and Pagnucco in this project. It has been a significant intellectual challenge to me, a historian, to learn something of the political science and sociological approaches and the literature with which my two colleagues are so very familiar; but it has been a personal and a professional pleasure, too.

It would have been appropriate to add a third chapter to part 5, one that would address the implications of this project for history. In the course of this collaboration, it has become ever more clear that the national-transnational peace movement I have studied, like other social causes that are the subject of discrete histories, is most fully appreciated as an issue network among other networks. Together and independently, their activity informs a growing solidarity beyond the state, which has become institutionalized in the twentieth century. That, I believe, is the broad history yet to be written. To envision it requires analytical paradigms drawn from sociology and political science. For this especially I am indebted to my colleagues.

Springfield, Ohio   Charles Chatfield
September 1996

CONTRIBUTORS

Chadwick F. Alger is affiliated with the Mershon Center for International Studies and Department of Political Science at Ohio State University. He is coeditor of *The United Nations and Policies of Member States* (1995) and author of numerous articles on the role of NGOs in the UN system and on participation of local people in world affairs.

David Atwood is the former general secretary of the International Fellowship of Reconciliation and currently works in Geneva as associate representative for disarmament and peace at the Quaker United Nations Office. His Ph.D. dissertation from the University of North Carolina at Chapel Hill analyzes the role of NGOs at the First UN Special Session on Disarmament. His work has appeared in edited books and in *Peace Review*.

Charles Chatfield is a professor of history at Wittenberg University. A long-time student of peace movements, he is the author of *For Peace and Justice: Pacifism in America 1914–1941* and *The American Peace Movement: Ideals and Political Activism*. He coedited *Peace Movements and Political Cultures*, completed *An American Ordeal: The Antiwar Movement of the Vietnam Era* for the late Charles DeBenedetti, and coedited with Ruzanna Ilukhina *Peace/Mir: An Anthology of Historic Alternatives to War*, the result of collaboration among U.S. and Russian historians.

David Cortright is president of the Fourth Freedom Forum and a visiting fellow at the Joan B. Kroc Institute for International Peace Studies at the University of Notre Dame. His most recent publications include *Peace Works: The Citizen's Role in Ending the Cold War* and the coedited books, *Economic Sanctions: Panacea or Peacebuilding in a Post — Cold War World* and *India and the Bomb: Public Opinion and Nuclear Options*.

Patrick Coy is assistant professor of political science at Kent State University, teaching in the Center for Applied Conflict Management.

He is the editor of *A Revolution of the Heart: Essays on the Catholic Worker.*

William DeMars is assistant professor of political science at the American University in Cairo. He is currently writing a book, *Inadvertent Power: Humanitarianism, War, and Statebuilding in Africa,* on the politics of international humanitarian action in the Ethiopia/Eritrea war.

Michael W. Hovey is coordinator of peace and justice education and adjunct assistant professor of religious studies at Iona College in New Rochelle, New York. He has served as a nongovernmental organization (NGO) representative of Pax Christi International at the United Nations Commission on Human Rights.

Louis Kriesberg is professor of sociology, the Maxwell professor of social conflict studies, and the former director of the Program on the Analysis and Resolution of Social Conflicts at Syracuse University. He is the author of *International Conflict Resolution* and *Social Conflicts* and is editor or coeditor of several books on conflict resolution.

Ralph B. Levering is professor of history at Davidson College. He is author or coauthor of six books, including *The Public and American Foreign Policy, 1918–1978, The Cold War: A Post-Cold War History,* and *Citizen Action for Global Change: The Neptune Group and Law of the Sea* (forthcoming).

John D. McCarthy is Ordinary professor of sociology and a member of the Life Cycle Institute at the Catholic University of America in Washington, D.C. He is coauthor of *Power Organizing* (forthcoming) and is coeditor of *Comparative Perspectives on Social Movements.*

Ron Pagnucco is assistant professor of sociology at Mt. St. Mary's College in Emmitsburg, Maryland. His essays have appeared in several journals, research volumes, and edited collections, including *Sociological Inquiry, Peace and Change, Research on Democracy and Society,* and *Research in Social Movements, Conflict and Change.*

Dieter Rucht is a senior researcher at the Wissenschaftszentrum Berlin für Sozialforschung in Germany. He is editor of *Research on Social Movements: The State of the Art in Western Europe and the USA* and the author of *Modernisierung und neue soziale Bewegungen: Deutschland, Frankreich und USA im Vergleich.*

Jackie Smith is assistant professor of sociology at the State University of New York at Stony Brook. Her research on transnational social movements has appeared in *Research in Social Movements, Conflict, and Change, Voluntas,* and *Peace Review.*

ABBREVIATIONS

AFOR	American Fellowship of Reconciliation
AFSC	American Friends Service Committee
AI	Amnesty International
AIUSA	Amnesty International USA
AOSIS	Alliance of Small Island States
CAN	Climate Action Network
CEAT	Coordination Européene des Amis de la Terre [European Coordinating Committee of Friends of the Earth]
CHR '78	Campaign Human Rights '78
CLAT	Confederación Latinoamericana de Trabajadores (Latin American Confederation of Workers)
CND	Campaign for Nuclear Disarmament
CO	Conscientious objector
CORE	Congress on Racial Equality
CRM	Civil Rights Movement [Sri Lanka]
CSCE	Conference on Security and Cooperation in Europe
EC	European Community
ECOSOC	Economic and Social Council (UN)
ECU	European Currency Unit
EEB	European Environmental Bureau
EFTA	European Free Trade Association
END	European Nuclear Disarmament
EPDP	Eelam People's Democratic Party
ERA	Eritrean Relief Association
ERD	Emergency Relief Desk

ERN	Emergency Response Network
EU	European Union
G77	"Group of 77"
GEF	Global Environment Facility
IACHR	Inter-American Commission on Human Rights
IAPL	International Association for the Protection of Labor
ICC	International Chamber of Commerce
ICRC	International Committee of the Red Cross
IFOR	International Fellowship of Reconciliation
IGO	Intergovernmental organization
ILO	International Labor Organization
IMfS	International Mobilization for Survival
INCD	Intergovernmental Negotiating Committee for a Convention to Combat Desertification
INF	Intermediate-Range Nuclear Forces
INGO	International nongovernmental organization
ISA	International Seabed Authority
ISB	International Socialist Bureau
ITTA	International Tropical Timber Council
JVP	Janatha Vimukthi Permuna
KUPO	Kotogoda United People's Organization
LTTE	Liberation Tigers of Tamil Eelam
MNC	Multinational Corporation
NCC	National Council of Churches
NGO	Nongovernmental organization
NSMs	New social movements
NUPO	Negombo United People's Organization
NWFC	Nuclear Weapons Freeze Campaign
OAS	Organization of American States
OEP	Ocean Education Project
OIHP	Office international d'Hygine publique
PBI	Peace Brigades International

QUNO	Quaker United Nations Office
REST	Relief Society of Tigray
SANE	Committee for a Sane Nuclear Policy
SCLC	Southern Christian Leadership Conference
SERPAJ	Service for Peace and Justice
SIPRI	Stockholm International Peace Research Institute
SMI	Social movement industry
SMO	Social movement organization
SMS	Social movement sector
SNCC	Student Nonviolent Coordinating Committee
SSD	Special Session on Disarmament (UN)
START	Strategic Arms Reduction Treaty
TSM	Transnational social movement
TSMI	Transnational social movement industry
TSMO	Transnational social movement organization
TSMS	Trasnational social movement sector
UMLSP	United Methodist Law of the Sea Project
UN	United Nations
UNCED	UN Conference on Environment and Development
UNCHE	UN Conference on the Human Environment
UNCLOS	UN Conference on Law of the Sea
UNDP	UN Development Programme
UNEP	United Nations Environment Programme
UNICEF	United Nations Children's Emergency Fund
USAID	United States Agency for International Development
WOLA	Washington Office on Latin America
WOW	War on Want
WRI	War Resisters International
WWF	World Wide Fund for Nature

PART ONE

The Phenomenon of
Transnational Social Movements

1

SOCIAL MOVEMENTS
AND GLOBAL TRANSFORMATION

Louis Kriesberg

Abstract

Transnational social movement organizations (TSMOs) are interactive components of a world currently in the process of rapid transformation. This chapter examines four major trends are transforming the world and providing the context for TSMOs' activities: growing democratization, increasing global integration, converging and diffusing values, and proliferating transnational organizations. In many ways, TSMOs can and do affect transnational policies; contributing to the development of global civic society through contentious as well as cooperative relations.

The world is changing in ways that foster the growth of transnational social movement organizations (TSMOs) and increase their significance. TSMOs, in turn, contribute to these global changes by directly influencing particular policies and by affecting the context in which they are made. Those influences are mapped out in this chapter, and attention is given to global developments that constrain, as well as foster, the work of TSMOs.

TSMOs should be considered in the context of the more loosely bounded transnational social movements (TSMs) of which they are a part and in the context of the changing global system, because these form the environment in which TSMOs function. Furthermore, we are in a period of turbulence and transition, with old national and international structures being transformed (Rosenau 1990; Commission on Global Governance 1995). In such periods of flux, the little shifts in direction that TSMOs help bring about can have large, long-run effects.

Global changes involve powerful, large-scale social forces, and even shifts that appear abrupt are typically products of slowly evolving changes that develop largely undetected. Even efforts by powerful persons or organizations generally make only marginal—and rarely wholly intended—differences. For example, the end of the Cold War and the dissolution of the Soviet Union contributed in part to the recent surge in the establishment of TSMOs. The end of the Cold War and of the Soviet Union were triggered by actions initiated by Mikhail Gorbachev; but those actions and their unforseen effects can be explained only by profound global changes underway for many years. Furthermore, the activities of TSMOs in the areas of human rights and peace movements contributed to the transforming changes in Eastern Europe and the Soviet Union (Kriesberg and Segal 1992; Stokes 1993).

Major Trends Providing the Context for TSMO Activities

Four interactive trends shaping the contemporary world have profound implications for TSMOs: growing democratization, increasing global integration, converging and diffusing values, and proliferating transnational institutions. Each tends to support the formation and growth of nongovernmental organizations (NGOs), including TSMOs, and each also affects the nature of TSMO activities. The trends, however, do not all move steadily in the same direction; indeed, in some ways they contradict each other.

Growing Democratization

For more than two hundred years, the world has been undergoing fundamental democratization. More people are able to participate in the political process in more societies as suffrage has gradually been extended to men without property and to others who had been disenfranchised because of their race, ethnicity, sex, or social status.

Democratization is also manifested in the increasing freedom that individuals and collectivities have from control or interference by governments, as is evident in the growing legitimacy and protection of human and civil rights. Because it eroded the credibility and legitimacy of authoritarian rule, the dissolution of the Soviet Union provided a further boost for democratization in both the region controlled by the former Soviet Union and elsewhere in the world. Nevertheless, according to Freedom House estimates, in 1995 only 20 percent of the world's population lived in free countries; 40 percent lived in partly free countries, and 40 percent lived in closed or repressive countries. Compared to 1985 statistics, these trends represent progress, but they are reversals of gains made up to 1993. Thus, while there is reason for optimism about democratic expansion, threats of renewed authoritarianism remain.

The democratization trend is evident in social systems at the organizational, community, national, and global levels. Three of the developments from which it derives are particularly notable: extending supportive norms, improving means of communication, and increasing material surplus.

Extending supportive norms. Increased democratization results in part from changes in what people regard as moral and legitimate. Thus, the spread of ideas supporting individualism and the rights of every person to free expression also contributes to democratization, as may be seen in the growing acceptance of the norm, if not the reality, of universal human and civil rights.

Democratization is also supported by the legitimacy often accorded claims by ethnic or other communal groups to the right to use their language, practice their religion, and otherwise express their cultural traditions. This legitimacy may be seen in the decay and even active rejection of expressions of racism. At the same time, however, a rise in violent resistance against immigrants and other minorities threatens this democratic norm in some places.

Norms that uphold the value of an individual's participation in decisions affecting his or her life have spread within every society and across the world. One sign of this trend is the almost universal participation of people in elections, even if some elections allow little room for choice.

Indicators of normative support for these rights may be seen in the actions taken by the United Nations. The UN General Assembly approved the Universal Declaration of Human Rights in December 1948, and the international community built upon this Declaration and reinforced it with two legally binding International Covenants on Human Rights that entered into force in 1976. More recently, the UN has intervened (even militarily) to promote democratic elections within countries and to promote humanitarian objectives in internal conflicts.

The current widespread occurrence of ethnic and other communal conflicts, some of which have been genocidal, seem to belie the above observations. However, the ethno-nationalist claims for sovereignty and exclusiveness are assertions—admittedly extreme ones—of the collective rights that otherwise are seen as progressive and democratic. Furthermore, the international condemnation of large-scale human rights violations and the recent interventions to stop the violations reflect the existence of international norms against the suppression of one people's rights by the violent imposition of another people's. However, when perpetrators are strong, interests of possible defenders of the norm are not engaged, and when a high level of international consensus is not mobilized, the existence of norms is often insufficient to assure governments' compliance with them.

Improving means of communication. Rapidly improving technology and communication facilitates popular participation in collective decision making. Movies, telephones, television, audio and video tape cassettes, fax, and electronic mail provide multiple sources of information, and that information can be immediately transmitted. Until recently much of this information was sent from one person or organization to others who lacked the ability to respond. What is particularly striking about the recent innovations is that they make rapid exchanges and sustained social interaction possible.

Increases in people's ability to use these means of rapid communication also profoundly affect transnational mobilizing possibilities. One of these changes is the expansion in the numbers of people who have the skills to use both the old and the new means of communication; for example, the increase in literacy means that the printed means of communication are increasingly accessible. Another change is the increase in the ability of people to afford to use the improved technology. Because both the old and the new means of communication and transportation cost considerably less than they once did, more people are able to organize to advance their interests domestically and internationally.

Increasing material surplus. The material standard of living for most people has been improving over the last few centuries. The resources thus made available allow people in more countries of the world to use the newer technologies and be in communication with their counterparts elsewhere in the world. They also provide greater opportunities for people to form associations and participate in public life. Citizens are thus better able to mobilize themselves to express their dissatisfactions, and they sometimes obtain satisfaction.

This long-term increasing standard of living, however, is far from universal and is not steadily rising: for instance, the per capita Gross National Product (GNP) in 1994 was $37,500 in Switzerland, $25,510 in the United States, $730 in Egypt, and $150 in Chad (Sivard 1996). Some countries have had devastating collapses in the people's living standards, particularly those plagued by internal or cross-border wars. Even without such calamities, many countries suffer from economic recessions, and in the last few decades from stagnation and decline in wages.

Countering the potential for democratization are gross inequalities in technological and material growth. Many people undoubtedly have a higher standard of living than did previous generations, but many people in every society still live quite poorly and have little access to the resources needed to be active socially and politically. Large economic and social inequalities persist not only between different countries but also within countries.

Those inequalities limit democratization insofar as they give people different degrees of protection from control by others and different levels of participation in collective decision making. For example, within the United States electoral activity varies greatly among different income strata and ethnic groups; those of lower income and education levels vote and participate in politics much less than richer and more highly educated individuals. Moreover, there is increasing inequality in developed countries; this is most evident in countries formerly governed by the Communist parties, but it is also present within the United States.

Global inequalities in access to modern means of communication are immense. For example, in 1993 the number of television receivers per 1,000 people ranged from 16 in Ghana to 40 in India and 816 in the United States (American Almanac 1996–97, table 1342). Even more fundamental are literacy rates, which vary greatly among countries, and within countries by social differences such as gender. Thus, while in the United States literacy rates for both females and males is reported to be 99 percent, in Egypt it is 39 and 64 percent, respectively; and in India 38 and 66 percent (Sivard 1996; table 3).

The absence of social and economic conditions that support democracy inhibits its rapid expansion, perhaps even resulting in regressions from the most recent democratic advances.[1] As in the past waves of democratization, some regressions are likely. But for the reasons indicated, many will endure to secure one more incremental step toward greater global democracy.

Increasing Global Integration

Humans are believed to have originated in East Africa and migrated to all parts of the earth, living in relative isolation for many thousands of years. During the last few thousand years, however, human beings are becoming increasingly reintegrated. In recent decades that has been an exponential increase in social exchanges, and the human species

1. Karl and Schmitter (1994), for example, analyze the sources and duration of the wave of democratization starting in 1974, referring to it as the fourth wave of democratization. Huntington (1991) refers to the current wave as the third wave of democratization.

increasingly recognizes that its members share a common fate, whatever that may be. Rapidly growing social integration is manifested in several developments, most notably, increasing economic interdependence, growing information exchange, and ever more challenging global problems.

Signs of increasing global economic interdependence abound in what we wear, eat, and see. The expansion of the global market and the attendant growth of international trade, foreign investments, and the transnational movement of labor reflect this interdependence. As a consequence of this economic integration, what happens in one economy greatly affects people in many others. Immigration flows, remittances, and investment transfers all occur transnationally, impacting locally on employment, wages, and the prices of commodities. Yet governments are increasingly limited in their ability to control these developments, which are shaped by decisions made by multinational corporations and intergovernmental organizations (IGOs).

The increasing diffusion and exchange of information and cultural products, important aspects of global integration, are most evident in the realm of popular culture. Music, film, and television from the United States or other first world countries are routinely transferred to many other countries. Less frequently, music or other elements of popular culture from countries in the third world become known around the globe.

Many problems are global or regional, unconstrained by state borders. For example, air and water pollution and resource exhaustion impact entire regions or even the whole world, as is evident in the effects on the ozone level and the warming of the earth.

In addition, population growth and the resulting increased demands on limited resources have impacts beyond a particular country or region, for example, by producing refugee flows. These problems require transnational responses and therefore stimulate the formation of TSMOs.

These multiple problems do not impact all peoples of the world with the same urgency, as witnessed by the varying priority given to environmental protection and economic development in the countries of the North and of the South. This derives in part from the immense economic and social inequalities in the world. Those inequalities also compound the difficulties associated with the increasing penetration of the global market. For these and other reasons, global inequalities constitute a major problem challenging all peoples.

Many problems that were formerly invisible or were considered local have become transnational as they have been made visible on television. Such has been the case with the plight of victims of famines and epidemics. Whether caused by natural disasters, by internal or international wars, or by various combinations of sources, these problems generate and sustain humanitarian and other TSMOs, which in turn help arouse popular attention.

Although global integration may encourage transnational cooperation, it may also bring more peoples into conflict with each other, for example, regarding migration and trade. Such conflicts may foster TSMOs, because new TSMOs often are formed to oppose or to differentiate themselves from those already established (cf. Zald and McCarthy 1980). Consequently, they may appear to negate each other's efforts, but such competition and conflict can provide better solutions than would have been found by any single actor.

These developments undermine state power. Many citizens are coming to believe that their national governments cannot solve their problems, that the forces operating are beyond the power of the state. Some people believe the solution is to strengthen state controls (on, for example, immigration); others suggest reducing state efforts and opening the economies further to free market forces. Increasingly, however, many citizens are beginning to see transnational efforts as necessary responses to the global developments that impact their lives. The vehicles for such efforts, however, are still in early experimental stages.

Converging and Diffusing Values

Increasingly, values and norms are widely shared. Some people see this tendency as the diffusion of Western and particularly U.S. ideas, a kind of hegemony. But the movement is not unidirectional. Challenges to the apparent Western cultural domination are evident in the growth of ethnic and religious particularism.

But long-term trends in the world move people toward shared values. The dissolution of the Soviet Union and the rejection of the Communist parties in the former Soviet bloc countries have discredited that alternative ideology. As a result, at least, for the present, we see greater international consensus on many values than had previously been evident.

As was discussed above, the recognition of basic human rights is another widely held value that helps underpin broad acceptance of the desirability of democracy and the value of tolerance of social and cultural differences. The promotion of and support for tolerance of diversity in particular has many of the qualities of an international social movement.

The convergence and diffusion of many values is widely (but not universally) discernible. Consumerism, the high priority many people give to having goods and services for consumption and enjoyment, has spread throughout the world. The current widespread faith in "free market forces" as the most effective way of producing consumer items exacerbates inequalities and conflicts about them.

The diffusion of some of these values helps create discrepancies between the expectations people have regarding what they should have and what they actually have. The gap between their actual conditions and their standards generates dissatisfaction. This dissatisfaction is a crucial element in the emergence of social movements to correct the unsatisfactory conditions.

Widespread elite and mass reactions against many modernizing trends must also be recognized. Particularistic claims are made in the name of an ethnic community, for example, as members of an ethnic community seek to advance the interests of their people relative to others. These particularistic claims may take the form of nationalist claims for political independence. Also, members of a particular religion or ethnicity or self-attributed social race may reject the value of tolerance and seek to give membership in their social category a privileged position in society.

Everywhere there are signs of diversity of values as well as commonalities. For example, many people express their concern about the importance of community solidarity over rampant individualism. Such views are expressed by persons of both the left and the right. Many people also react against consumerism and economic development, instead supporting environmental protection and policies that limit economic development.

Proliferating Transnational Institutions

The growing number and scope of transnational nongovernmental and governmental organizations has been remarkable. Governmental and nongovernmental organizations often oppose one another's policies, but some cooperate and interpenetrate each other. For example, certain NGOs at times have been substantially controlled by governments.

The United Nations and its specialized agencies have grown by expanding their membership and by increasing their functions and operations. This growth is important because the UN system is global and has many features that provide a basis for the formation and influence of INGOs, including TSMOs.

The UN gives citizen groups limited access to influence policymaking at the global level. Article 71 of the UN Charter provides that "The

Economic and Social Council may make suitable arrangements for consultation with non-governmental organizations." The purpose of those consultations is to enable the Council "to secure expert information or advice from organizations having special competence . . . and, . . . to enable organizations which represent important elements of public opinion to express their views" (Lador-Lederer 1963, 71–72). For some groups, such as women's groups that are often excluded from political activities in their countries, Article 71 provides access not available at the national level.

The large ad hoc UN conferences, beginning with the UN Conference on the Human Environment (UNCHE) in Stockholm in 1972, represent the major platform for TSMO access to UN decision making (Stephenson, 1995). Nongovernmental forums following the form established largely at UNCHE now parallel all major intergovernmental conferences.

Regional international governmental organizations are important forums within which international nongovernmental organizations (INGOs) function (Taylor 1984). This is especially true in Europe. Beginning with the establishment of the European Coal and Steel Community in 1952, numerous organizations were founded to address economic and other matters. These include, for instance, the European Economic Community and the European Atomic Energy Community, which were established in 1957. Despite setbacks in regional organization, such as the European Defense Community, the overall trend has been the expansion of the matters under European Community jurisdiction and the increase in membership beyond the original six countries.

The growth of regional IGOs, which can give citizens access to policymakers that they may not have in national arenas, fosters the formation of INGOs (Haas 1958; Kriesberg 1960). This tendency is evident in the rapid increase of international NGOs in Europe, paralleling the establishment of European intergovernmental institutions.

The evolution of the Conference on Security and Cooperation in Europe (CSCE) exemplifies the complex interaction between a major regional IGO and TSMs (Leatherman 1993). CSCE negotiations concluded in 1975 with the Helsinki Final Act, signed by thirty-five participating states. The CSCE's provisions for confidence-building measures and the protection of human rights was supported by peace and human rights national and transnational social movements, and those movements were, in turn, fostered and strengthened by the CSCE, (now the Organization for Security and Cooperation in Europe, or OSCE). Together, they contributed to the fundamental transformation in East-West relations (Thomas 1994).

International Nongovernmental Organizations (INGOs) include a wide variety of organizations with members from several countries.[2] Members are typically national associations but often also include individuals. They are generally organized to provide services and advance the interests of their members, for example, occupations and industries. The number of INGOs has been increasing and in 1993 totaled 4,830 (Union of International Associations 1993, 1698). The higher density of national nongovernmental organizations within the relatively well-to-do countries means that people from those countries are likely to have disproportionate influence on the work of INGOs. This impression is reinforced by the fact that most of the INGOS are headquartered in the United States or Western Europe.

Many INGOs reflect and reinforce the status quo. Sometimes, powerful and well-to-do persons and groups in various countries form transnational organizations to formulate policies that they believe will benefit their interests and values. The Trilateral Commission, founded in 1973 by North American, Western European, and Japanese business, labor, and political elites, reflects this tendency, developing policy prescriptions targeting common economic concerns (Sklar 1980).

TSMOs, in contrast, are INGOs, such as Greenpeace or Amnesty International, that seek to bring about a change in the status quo. TSMOs work for progressive change in the areas of the environment, human rights, and development as well as for conservative goals like opposition to family planning or immigration. Figure 1 illustrates the relationships between NGOs, INGOs, and TSMOs. The largest inclusive category consists of all NGOs, national and international, organized for religious, recreational, political, or functional purposes. SMOs are that subset of NGOs working to "[change] some elements of the social structure and/or reward distribution of society" (McCarthy and Zald 1977,1212). INGOs are those NGOs whose memberships transcend national boundaries. At the intersection of SMOs and INGOs are transnational social movement organizations. In other words, TSMOs are INGOs that work specifically for some social or political change and operate an international office or secretariat to serve a membership active in more than two states.

Because they facilitate international communication and cooperation and cultivate organizational skills, INGOs contribute to the development of TSMOs. Many INGOs, for instance, provide networks or social infrastructures that can process conflicts among different people and generate consensus about global problems and their solutions,

---

2. For discussions of international NGOs, see Lador-Lederer (1963), Kriesberg (1972), Feld (1972), and Taylor (1984).

FIGURE 1.1.

Distinctions among Nongovernmental Organizations

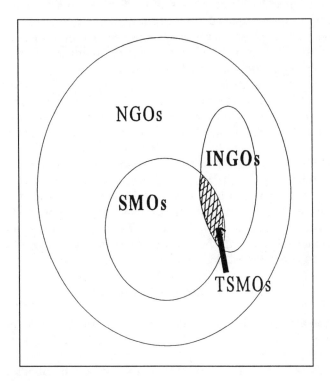

Figure not drawn to scale

thus facilitating the formation and growth of transnational social movements. In other words, some INGOs that have members from countries with diverse and even conflicting interests may indirectly provide channels for constructing options that help bridge antagonistic differences and contribute to peacebuilding (Kriesberg 1972).

Although INGOs often represent people who would otherwise be excluded from participation in transnational governance, many TSMOs and INGOs are not accountable to broad constituencies. Some are controlled by their managerial or charismatic leadership. Certainly multinational corporations are not controlled by the citizens at large, or even by their millions of shareholders; rather, their managers and major investors make policy.

In the past some INGOs were supported or assisted through covert government actions, such as those of the Central Intelligence Agency of the United States and the KGB or Communist Party of the Soviet Union. The involvement of the Soviet and Russian side has certainly decreased since the disintegration of the Soviet Union; and now there is an opportunity for a reduction from the United States side as well. However, other governments, such as those of Iran, Libya, and Syria have assisted TSMOs that help wage national liberation struggles, and they probably continue to assist them.

Developments such as the end of the Cold War and technological advances reinforce the conditions that make transnational social movement action possible. More people in more places in the world have the capability of communicating with each other and organizing. Second, they often provide incentives to form TSMOs, even making certain TSMOs essential. Particular environmental problems require transnational responses (Princen and Finger 1994). Finally, contentions among different actors in the world are vital for global democracy, giving expression to different perspectives, providing alternative solutions, and encouraging new syntheses. TSMOs often make the added contribution of reducing the dominance of the more powerful actors in a world characterized by immense inequalities.

TSMOs as Agents Affecting the Trends

As the cases in this volume demonstrate, TSMOs can be important agents of global change. The identities and organizations functioning in the subglobal domains may be barriers to forming broader global identities or organizations. TSMOs are fostered by the trends we have surveyed and, in turn, affect those trends. TSMOs tend to reinforce the trends by:

1. supporting networks of social relations that are the social infrastructures for action

2. cultivating constituencies for intergovernmental organizations

3. providing reservoirs of resources and redistributing those resources

4. fostering new transnational identities and

5. stimulating one another to attack transnational sources of common problems.

TSMOs help transmit information by providing a network of relations for the diffusion of ideas and practices, thereby facilitating mobilization for movement goals. They also help diffuse norms and values about participation in policymaking and execution and serve as constituencies for other NGOs and for IGOs, thus fostering democratization.

TSMOs provide reservoirs of resources because members in one country or region may have great wealth that can be drawn upon by

TSMOs and other INGOs in countries or regions with fewer resources. Moreover, as people work together to advance a particular goal, they strengthen their bonds and shared identity. That identity is likely to transcend identification with any single country. In the case of INGOs, that may mean a broader and stronger identity as a member of a particular profession. In the case of a TSMO, it may mean an identity as a human rights advocate.

The activities of some TSMOs foster the growth of other TSMOs because they sometimes arouse competition or even opposition. This phenomenon occurs at both the regional and global levels. For example, persons engaged in social movements to improve the position of women or to protect the environment differ in their analyses of the problem and in the strategies to be pursued to solve it. They are likely to form a variety of organizations reflecting those differences.

These activities tend to reinforce many aspects of the global trends previously described. Furthermore, they tend to do so in ways that foster continued growth of TSMOs. This does not mean that the world will become harmonious or that the TSMOs and the transnational social movements within which they function will work in harmony. Conflicts will continue to erupt, some of them pursued in destructive ways.

The multiplicity of TSMOs and INGOs is likely to mitigate conflicts insofar as the organizations cross-cut each other.[3] Conversely, when the organizations are based on coinciding lines of cleavage, interests, and identities, they make conflicts across those lines more intense and difficult to resolve. TSMOs and INGOs by definition cross-cut state borders; and they also are likely to cross-cut many other lines of cleavage, because they are based on many different interests, values, and identities.

Effects of TSMOs on Transnational Policies

Global and regional activities are shaped by many kinds of intentional policies. These include declarations of principles, the establishment of intergovernmental institutions, placing different people in decision-making offices, and providing particular goods or services through the market place or through public or private nonprofit organizations.

TSMOs affect particular regional and global policies in several ways. A discussion of how they effectively influence global policies must also recognize some of the factors constraining them. First, it

---

3. The significance of cross-cutting ties for preventing the eruption of conflicts and for limiting their destructive pursuit has been posited and tested by research by many analysts. See, for example, Ross (1920), Dahrendorf (1959), and Kriesberg (1982).

should be noted that operating internationally raises transaction costs and therefore sometimes inhibits action. Second, TSMOs sometimes block each other. Third, there are many difficulties in implementing international coordination.

Finally, TSMOs are only one of many global actors, and they are often relatively powerless when compared to other global actors such as governments, multinational corporations, and international banking institutions. Clearly, despite all these developments described above, states—particularly large, economically developed ones—remain very powerful global actors.

TSMOs nevertheless possess many capabilities that give them unique roles in global political processes and strengthen their influence on transnational policies. Those capabilities include operating at many levels and having complementary components. TSMOs help shape transnational policies in ways such as mobilizing support, broadening participation, sustaining activity, framing issues, and implementing policies.

TSMO Capabilities

As other chapters of this book reveal, TSMOs have many capabilities that give them particular advantages in bringing about changes in the status quo. Two in particular are related to the transnational character of TSMOs.

TSMOs Work at Many Levels. They can work by trying to influence IGOS and other INGOs by direct contacts. They often try to affect the views of the attentive public and of elites, at the regional or global level. In addition, they usually also work at the national level to influence officials, national organizations, and the public at large.

TSMOs Can Complement One Another. Members in different countries have varying kinds of resources, and therefore organizations in several countries can complement each other. For example, a TSMO can include people who speak out in one country even if members are silenced in another. The work of Amnesty International is based on that principle. Thus, although people in one country may be intimidated and endangered by protesting the wrongful imprisonment of individuals in their country, protests can be effectively mounted in other countries.

TSMOs provide safe havens and external bases in one country from which campaigns can be launched in another. There may also be a division of tasks, for example, having fighters in one country and fund raisers in another. This has often been the case for organizations waging national liberation struggles, during which members in exile or in the diaspora sustain the struggle by providing funds and a base for those engaged in resistance in the homeland. A division of labor also occurs in TSMOs with members from relatively more economically developed countries of the North complementing the efforts of persons from less developed countries of the South (see chaps. 5 and 7).

Methods of Shaping Global Policy

TSMOs affect global policies through a great variety of methods, which other chapters in this book document. Described below are five general ways various TSMOs attempt to alter the status quo.

TSMOs Help Mobilize Support for Particular Policies. Because many problems are difficult to solve within one country, transnational action is much more effective. For instance, the nineteenth-century campaign to end the slave trade was necessarily an international one. More recently, international campaigns on environmental issues reflect the growing realization of the need to develop transnational responses to global problems.

TSMOs Help Widen Public Participation in International Policy Processes. International policies are formed by agreements and actions of government representatives from several countries. Those representatives may consult with or otherwise take into account some of their constituents who may be affected by the policy change under consideration. The views of the constituents are filtered through their representatives, who have their own perceptions, values, and interests. In any case, these constituents tend to be from a narrow group with strong ties to government representatives.

TSMOs provide avenues for broader participation in policy-making. They offer a direct channel of communication between persons with similar concerns in different countries. Once established, they often develop offices for educating members and the public and for lobbying national representatives and IGOs.

TSMOs Help Sustain Attention on Critical Global Problems. Governments, particularly democratic ones, have short attention spans. Particular issues become salient and action seems necessary, but then attention wanes and another issue suddenly claims attention. TSMOs help keep the attention of the public and policymakers focused on the issues of concern to them. A TSMO therefore often provides continuity of action and develops expertise that can be utilized by persons in governments, international agencies, and the media when their attention turns (however briefly) to concerns of social movements.

TSMOs Help Frame Issues and Set the Policy Agenda. As international organizations, they are often in a better position to receive mass media attention than if they were an organization of only a single nation.

They can discuss and propose new options from a variety of national perspectives. For example, high-ranking physicists and others from the United States, the Soviet Union, and the United Kingdom, meeting in a group called Pugwash, discussed ways to monitor underground nuclear weapons testing and arrived at shared understandings that were used in official negotiations about limiting nuclear weapons testing (Pentz and Slovo 1981).

Some TSMOs and Other INGOs Carry Out Transnational Policies. This procedure is common in the human rights field, as TSMOs and other NGOs provide data on governments' compliance with or violations of human rights agreements. And in the early 1980s, a coalition of organizations initiated a global boycott of the Nestlé Corporation to bring about its compliance with new standards for the marketing of baby food (Sikkink 1986).

Conclusions

TSMOs contribute much to the shaping of policies at the global and regional level and will do more. They will continue to do so, however, within a system where their goals challenge or compete with the interests of powerful actors such as states and multinational corporations.

Many TSMOs seek to challenge the great inequalities in the world. The immense differences in wealth, power, and status within and among countries are oppressive for those people who have little. But the TSMOs can never be wholly outside or above those structured inequalities. Moreover, some TSMOs may pursue policies or reproduce leadership patterns that relatively disadvantaged persons view as supporting and reinforcing the inequalities.

A homogeneous, tightly ordered world is not to be expected or desired. Diversity is needed and, in any case, will always remain. TSMOs arise from that diversity and contribute to its flourishing. The multiplicity of TSMOs is a source of significant cross-cutting ties that help mitigate destructive conflicts. As a totality, TSMOs help form global civil society. For a legitimate, egalitarian, and democratic international system to exist, underlying pluralistic social groupings must develop. Alexis de Tocqueville (1945), in celebrating American democracy, stressed the importance of the many public associations in America for the maintenance of freedom against tyrannies by the government or by the majority of the people. Perhaps in the future someone can celebrate a global democracy sustained by the proliferation of transnational associations.

2

INTERGOVERNMENTAL AND NONGOVERNMENTAL ASSOCIATIONS TO 1945

Charles Chatfield

Abstract

International nongovernmental organizations (INGOs) were often catalysts for the emergence and innovation of intergovernmental organizations (IGOs) and regimes. By 1945 both kinds of associations had matured in dynamic interaction, and among the nongovernmental groups there were some that qualify as transnational social movement organizations (TSMOs). The structures and activities of most INGOs were similar, but the TSMOs among them had distinctive goals. Their strategies included generating constituencies for multinational programs, mobilizing transnational pressures on national policy, and attempting to influence international negotiations and IGOs. In the process, they contributed to the development of intergovernmental agencies and regimes. INGO (and TSMO) activity, conditioned as it was by state and interstate decision-making, introduced new variables into the international system.

Histories of the twentieth century are dominated by wars and revolutions—by violence on a massive scale. We dare not deny the horrendous realities in that view of history, lest we repeat them. But there is another reality, a nurturing one. This century has experienced a revolutionary growth of peace-oriented concepts and institutions: a broad spectrum of intergovernmental organizations and transnational citizen movements; accepted procedures for bilateral and multilateral consultation, arbitration, mediation, second-track diplomacy, peacekeeping, and even disarmament; passive resistance and nonviolent action in Finland, India, Brazil, South Africa, the United States, and elsewhere; a panoply of procedures for resolving conflict within nations; religious ecumenism; international regimes regarding health, development, humanitarian aid; and widely accepted norms of human rights. This quiet revolution has become highly visible in the second half of the twentieth century, notably at the end of the Cold War.

Why should we be surprised? After all, for thousands of years human collaboration—in the arts, religion, science, economic exchange, communications, social reform, and even political experience —has transcended the arbitrary lines of political boundaries. If we are surprised now by the extent of transnational cooperation, perhaps that is because we have attended inordinately to inter-nation relations, neglecting the processes through which transnational relationships have became so fully institutionalized.

The international sector is traditionally described as comprising intergovernmental and nongovernmental organizations. The former, IGOs, are said to reflect the maturation of the modern system of nation-states. In the nineteenth century the dominant European states held occasional summits to deal with crises over political and territorial security, and they also set up a few multigovernment agencies to deal with health, commercial, communications, and technological concerns. The invention of such IGOs enabled nations to delegate limited jurisdiction in specific areas without surrendering the principle of sovereignty. They multiplied dramatically in the twentieth century. Perhaps 12 of them had been created by 1874, 37 by 1914, 92 by 1944 (Lyons 1963, 14; and see fig. 2.1).[1]

Intergovernmental institutions were not, however, merely the product of interstate arrangements. Historically, they also reflect forces that were concurrently restructuring national states, often through the agency of voluntary associations and social movements.

International *nongovernmental* organizations (INGOs) grew even more rapidly than intergovernmental ones in the nineteenth and twentieth centuries (fig. 2.1). As states became increasingly constitutional

---

1. Lyons adapts estimates by G. P. Speeckaert (1951, 270), favorably comparing them with previous estimates by Paul S. Reinsch and Leonard Woolf, among others. The figures in table 2.1 follow Speeckaert's later inventory (1957, viii), adjusted to begin in 1815 instead of 1693, in line with Lyons, but continue past Lyons's 1914 cutoff date. Wallace and Singer's 1970 estimate corresponds to Speeckaert's, as does Skjelsbaek's (1971), and they discuss the difficulties of quantifying the data. Independently, in 1934, Potter estimated 750 INGOs (9, n.1). See also Jacobson (1979, 10–11) and Feld's comparison of IGO and NGO growth (1972).

FIGURE 2.1.

Growth of IGOs and INGOs 1849–1954

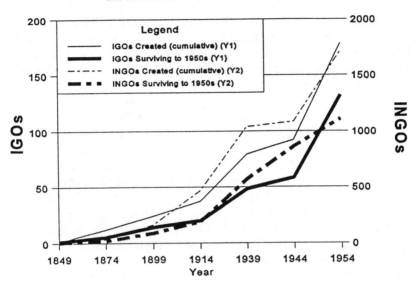

and their societies became ever more complex and formal, citizen participation was channeled into voluntary associations. Some of them became linked across national boundaries to form networks and formal organizations as diverse as the Anti-Slavery Society (1839), the International Typographical Union (1852), the International Association of Geodesy (1862), the World Alliance of Young Men's Christian Associations (1855), and the International Committee of the Red Cross (1863). These were early INGOs (by convention, NGOs are distinguished from transnational profit-making, or business associations). Perhaps 32 had been formed by 1874, 466 by 1914, and 1083 by 1944, although not all survived (fig. 2.1).

People formed INGOs in response to shared interests and the forces of growing interdependence. They were often motivated, too, by their need for allies in their struggle for democratic and participatory power, whether on class or national lines, and in their attempt to mitigate interstate conflict. Accordingly, international associations were formed around causes such as antislavery, organized labor, temperance, anti-imperialism, women's suffrage, and peace. These were the prototype transnational social movement organizations, or TSMOs.

Together with other nongovernmental associations and intergovernmental ones, they played dynamic and interactive roles in the developing international system. They pushed for and advanced international cooperation. They worked to prevent interstate conflict, to create international organizations, and to cultivate broader institutions and routines that would make cooperation across national boundaries routine. Here at work were the nonterritorial actors that came to constitute what Johan Galtung has aptly called a "sixth continent" in the world order (1975, 158).[2]

TSMOs and the Emergence of Intergovernmental Organizations

At several critical junctures INGOs (notably TMSOs) contributed impetus, concepts, and public support to the formation of international institutions. Paul Reinsch wrote that the "public unions," or IGOs of his time had advanced mostly "through the associated efforts of private individuals" (1911, 148). A half century later, F. S. L. Lyons observed about the same period, "It would be natural, but misleading," to assume that governments normally initiated intergovernmental bodies. "Sometimes, it is true, governments did take the lead, but . . . usually what happened was that associations of private individuals pursuing similar aims in different countries began to hold international conferences and to form international associations" that eventuated in intergovernmental bodies (1963, 20).

True, the extraordinary efforts of the individual Swiss businessman Henry Dunant resulted in both the International Red Cross (1863) and the intergovernmental "Convention on the Amelioration of the Wounded in Armies of the Field" (Geneva 1864), which institutionalized an international law of war. But Dunant was effective for the long run because he set in motion an international network of national Red

---

2. Until recently, treatments of INGOs tended to describe them or categorize them. Thus, Galtung placed them within his overall schema of direct and structural violence, dissociative and associative peace, whereas Judge and Skjelsbaek classified them with respect to the principle of authorization (e.g., by treaty), the principle statutory meeting and other structural characteristics, leadership and membership, geographical distribution, and specific issues or activities. Feld, Mander, and Lyons write narrative or descriptive histories of INGOs and IGOs but rarely of their interaction. Those authors who do approach nongovernmental associations analytically, in the context of a dynamic international system (Feld and Willetts are especially insightful), tend to ignore the pre-1945 period or treat it as merely preliminary to the system under study. It is interesting, therefore, that early INGOs were appreciated by contemporaneous observers like Paul Reinsch, Leonard Woolf, and Lyman White as parts of an interactive system.

Cross societies that, in turn, helped to implement and sustain the regime anticipated in the interstate conventions on war.

To build constituencies for international programs; to bring transnational pressure on governments; to influence international negotiations and IGOs were all strategic influences that well before 1945 characterized transnational movements for changes in the distribution of goods and services, rights and power—changes in social and international norms. All of these strategies were applied at one time or another by the international peace movement, which was the most wide-ranging TSM to originate in the nineteenth century. The peace movement is, therefore, a useful model with which to introduce TSMO-IGO interaction prior to the League of Nations.

The Peace and Arbitration Campaign

The goal of mobilizing concern for peace and opposing militaristic nationalism stimulated the formation of the earliest peace societies in the United States and England (1815), and it characterized international peace congresses in Europe sporadically from 1843 to 1850, and annually from 1889 to 1914 (Cooper 1991; van der Linden 1987; Grossi 1994). By then there were peace societies in most European nations and also transnational peace associations.[3] Within each peace society and among them there were significant differences in constituency, philosophy, and emphasis. Some worked for international exchanges and understanding; one for a universal language; others against imperialism, economic nationalism, and arms races, or for international law. Prior to 1914, however, the arbitration of intergovernmental disputes provided a common denominator for the movement, which mobilized pressure on governments.

Leaders of the American Peace Society (1828) introduced arbitration resolutions into the U.S. Congress while Richard Cobden and fellow free-traders approached the British Parliament. Arbitration was included in the 1848 Treaty of Guadalup Hildalgo and was used to resolve the U.S. *Alabama* claims against Great Britain in 1871. By then it had been pressed upon governments. In England it was promoted by a citizen coalition led by Randal Cremer of the Workingmen's Peace Association and Henry Richard of the London Peace Society. Leaders in Switzerland and France pressed for bilateral arbitration treaties with the United States. The American Peace Society and (after 1882) the

---

3. The Ligue international de la paix par la justice, the Ligue international de la paix et de la liberté, and the Inter-Parliamentary Union.

National Arbitration League applauded the endorsement of arbitration in principle in the 1884 Republican platform, and subsequently by both parties and the Congress. The effort to create constituencies for the program crested in the 1890s, when the Universal Peace Congress movement created a detailed plan for an international tribunal of arbitration that was endorsed by national NGOs comprising educators, lawyers, businessmen, and government officials.

Then came Tzar Nicholas II's call for an international meeting to deal with problems of war and armaments. That First Hague Conference (1899) opened an opportunity to influence international negotiations. European governments frantically headed off any significant constraints on armaments, war, or sovereignty; but a transnational citizens movement generated public pressure in the form of petitions, demonstrations, and proposals. Women in particular organized a concerted international campaign. At The Hague, peace advocates created a salon where citizen internationalists mixed with diplomats, and they operated the only available press service. Public pressure ensured that the diplomats had to produce something, and the arbitration movement provided readily accessible information and proposals to which the delegates turned as a fallback position from disarmament (Kuehl 1969, 43, 45; Cooper 1991, 103). Although they rejected compulsory arbitration, and their so-called Permanent Court of Arbitration was no more than a panel of judges on call, they legitimated the principle in a Convention for the Pacific Settlement of International Disputes (Davis 1962; Scott 1909). The Hague negotiators made arbitration a salient issue and that, in turn, reinvigorated the international peace movement.

Fresh momentum was channeled through the Peace Congresses and the rapidly growing Interparliamentary Union (an association of legislators, 1889) A number of U.S. congressmen were enlisted, and there were arbitration caucuses in the British and French legislatures (Douglas 1975). Peace societies mushroomed in the first decade of the century, and public pressure, especially in the United States, Britain, and France, provided the impetus for the Second Hague Conference of 1907. Seven years later, World War I made peace an overwhelmingly salient issue, and the advocates of arbitration made the proposed League of Nations the venue for their reform. At that historic juncture, the League's charter acquired provisions for periodic international congresses, compulsory arbitration, sanctions, and an arbitral court— concepts that had gained international currency and legitimacy through the long arbitration campaign and the larger peace movement of which it was a part.

Unquestionably, a transnational coalition of private associations helped to define basic elements of the Covenant of the League and to generate popular pressure for its adoption.[4] That, in turn, affected the negotiating positions of Wilson and the European leaders (Latané 1932).

The formation of the League of Nations embodied two different versions of internationalism. At the outset a dominant concern with interstate security was institutionalized in the League, notably in its Council. Gradually, a pervasive if fragile vision of transnational community became institutionalized through the convergence of INGOs and specialized intergovernmental agencies that was encouraged by the League's Secretariat.

The League Era

Article 24 of the League charter provided that "there shall be placed under the direction of the League all international bureaus already established by general treaties if the parties to such treaties consent. All such international bureaus and all communications for the regulation of matters of international interest hereafter constituted shall be placed under the direction of the League." That mandate applied only to intergovernmental agencies, and it was not fully implemented. Nonetheless, the League gradually formed working relations with some 40 specialized IGOs and had routine contacts with over 450 INGOs, about half of those contacts being "active and close and constant." (Potter 1934, 10).

Concurrently with the League, and mandated by its charter, there was formed the International Labor Organization (ILO). Its creation owed very substantially to the prewar precedent of negotiated conventions on working conditions (notably by the International Association for the Protection of Labour [1901]), to proposals and pressure from international organized labor during the war, and in some measure to independent internationalists. Contributing, too, was the desire of the U.S., British, and French governments to undercut the appeal of Bolshevism. The governing body of the ILO was designed to represent equally labor, management, and governments. Labor had the advantage of the very large and powerful International Federation of Trade Unions (1901, 1919), whereas employers had *to create* an umbrella

---

4. The NGOs most important in forging the League were the following: in the United States, the League to Enforce Peace, League of Free Nations Association, World's Court League, and Carnegie Endowment for International Peace; in Great Britain, the Fabian Society, League of Free Nations Association, League of Nations Union, Independent Labour Party, and Bryce Committee.

INGO, the International Organization of Industrial Employers (1919) in order to coordinate and organize their presence in the international body. The interaction of governmental and nongovernmental sectors that was formalized in the ILO took place more informally under the auspices of the League.

Perhaps the greatest legacy of the League of Nations was the network of cooperation that it facilitated in the interwar era, when advances in knowledge, technology, and communications, together with commercial and political developments, contributed to a sharp increase in the number of IGOs and INGOs. Despite the fact that the League, like the later UN, was designed as an agency of national governments, primarily to stabilize the interstate order, it cultivated a transnational civil service and role for itself. It was officially subject to a consensus of national policymakers, but in fact its first secretary-general, Sir Eric Drummond, adroitly created networks of complex interaction between the specialized ministries of governments and the special offices of the League, as Martin Dubin has shown (1983). League sections, even those that were virtually sidelined by internation stalemates, maintained continuous contacts with government ministries and INGOs (and, through them, with domestic NGOs), so that *the intergovernmental organization deliberately cultivated a transnational process.*

Since NGOs helped government ministries relate to private professional and technical communities within their countries, it was only natural that INGOs, would be included on the level of League consultation. Occasionally the League convened INGOs; often it was represented at their meetings. Sometimes it solicited and even contracted for their expertise; at other times it made its own technical services available to them. Even TSMOs were accommodated internationally much as SMOs were integrated into national political processes. League sections were in more or less close contact with the relevant IGOs, INGOs, and government agencies, so that each one constituted a node within a complex web of international relationships. Moreover, as a contemporary observer noted, "through their relations with the League these organizations are able to maintain contacts with each other better than they otherwise could" (Potter 1934, 14).

The international web of associations was not only interconnected; it was dynamic and interactive. A few INGOs were formed as a result of the League's existence, and sometimes on its initiative.[5] Thus the

5. Examples are the International Institute of Statistics, the International Agricultural Co-ordination Committee, the Joint Committee of the Major International Associations, and Committee of International Students' Organizations (White 1951, 248).

International Federation of League of Nation Societies (1919) popular-
ized the League, gave it a direct conduit to the peoples, and reinforced
national support for its policies. With societies in most nations, the
Federation became involved in League politics, notably the debates
over collective security measures in the face of fascism and aggression.
Similarly, the Committee on Intellectual Cooperation was a League-
related agency with considerable autonomy, owing in part to the
French government's interest in Paris being an international center. It
had a large constituency among INGOs and had, in fact, some of the
activist characteristics of a TSMO.

Some IGOs, on the other hand, owed their formation to INGO initiative and activity.[6] Eric Nansen's so-called International Office for Refugees, for example, dealt with famine, disease, and displaced persons
during and after World War I. It resulted from both intergovernmental
and private initiatives and worked with multiple organizations. Even
when it was more or less incorporated in the League system (1930–
1931), the Nansen Office depended heavily on INGOs for funds and
services.

The United Nations

Unfortunately, the League's initial strong cooperation with INGOs
waned as the international system became ever more politicized in
the 1930s (White 1951, 252–55; Dubin 1983). Still, the experience and
networks upon which the League drew for two decades were tapped
in forming the United Nations Organization and the related specialized agencies. The World Health Organization, for example, built upon
the experience of the League's Health Organization, just as the UN
Relief and Reconstruction Agency had a precedent in the Nansen Office and its successors, or as the Trusteeship Council was in some
measure anticipated in the Mandates Commission. What the UN ab-
sorbed from the League was not merely an organizational scheme, but
rather a network of functioning IGO-INGO relationships.

In the United States a national consensus for the United Nations
Organization was produced largely by an aggressive coalition of civic,
church, business, and professional associations that worked with the
administration's explicit encouragement. Backed by that coalition,

6. Examples are the International Bureau of Education, the Institute of Refrigeration,
the International Sugar Office, the International Tin Committee, the International Union
for the Protection of Literary and Artistic Works, the International Union for the Protection of Industrial Property, the International Relief Union, and the already noted International Institute of Agriculture (White 1951, 245–47).

NGO leaders and their counterparts in other nations contributed to several features of the UN charter: its educational and cultural components, its economic and social orientation, its explicit commitment to human rights (Eichelberger 1977; Divine 1967; Robins 1971), and specifically Article 71, which legitimated a consultative relationship between the UN and INGOs. That provision was a kind of recognition of the fact that international nongovernmental organizations were de facto elements of a complex world order and TSMOs a source of transnational change within it.

INGOs and TSMOs—Structures and Roles

In 1933, Lyman White showed that INGOs, though hardly noticed in the grand scale of international affairs then, had developed quite mature characteristics of organizational structure, membership, funding, and programs.[7] Indeed, they looked very much like their counterparts in the 1970s, and the sequence of their development was quite similar to that of early IGOs (Lyons 1963, 29–35). Transnational social movement organizations had distinctive goals and strategies, but structurally they developed along the lines of all INGOs.[8]

TSMOs mainly began as informal networks of people who shared common concerns, often in national associations. Sometimes individuals from one country would proselytize in another (as in the peace, women's, and labor movements, for example, or the International Law Association [1873]). A network might become formalized as a political and goal-oriented coalition such as the campaign for arbitration, which never developed a truly central organization. It might be institutionalized on the initiative of a sponsoring donor, as was the Carnegie Endowment for International Peace and the Rockefeller Foundation.

Commonly, though, informal networks gave rise to *congresses*— large international meetings to exchange information and opinion,

---

7. White distinguished fully transnational and active institutions from the loose associations among those INGOs tabulated by the Secretariat of the League of Nations four years earlier. After analyzing structure, membership, and activities, he reduced the organizational entries from 478 to 37 for the purpose of close, comparative analysis (White 1933, 17–18).

8. Early TSMOs included the Interparliamentary Union, the Institute of International Law, the International Chamber of Commerce, the World Alliance of Young Men's Christian Associations, international trade unions (e.g., International Federation of Trade Unions), the Women's International League for Peace and Freedom, the Universal Esperanto Association and related groups, the (World) Zionist Organization, the International Red Cross, temperance groups, and the International Federation of League of Nations Societies.

heighten motivation, solidify and extend the network. Periodic congresses were succeeded, in turn, by *conferences* that had some jurisdictional authority (White 1933, 17–19). These were forums for acting on issues of internal organization and expressing collective opinion on public policy. Conferences usually met annually or biennially, and they evolved into the main jurisdictional authority for most INGOs. They required significant advance preparation, and, although a hosting national group usually handled logistical matters, the international supervised the conference program. For that purpose, the most active INGOs (including almost all those that would qualify as TSMOs) evolved committee systems.

Study committees were formed on various subjects, though typically an executive committee was created with a jurisdiction limited to what was expressly authorized by the governing body that supervised the preparation of conferences and had executive jurisdiction between them. Usually, too, a general secretary was appointed, with duties that varied according to the size and functions of the organization. Most importantly, the secretariat represented the group to other INGOs, IGOs, and governments.

Although some transnational movements remained informal networks of organizations, the predominant form was a federation of national or local groups (e.g., the League of Red Cross Societies). Some INGOs, but not TSMOs, were based on the direct membership of individuals (e.g., the Institute of International Law and the International Olympic Committee). And some TSMOs combined an international federation with a provision for direct membership (e.g., the International Federation of League of Nations Societies, the International Red Cross, the World's Alliance of YMCAs, and the Jewish Agency for Palestine). The financial resources of INGOs in 1933 ranged from $556 to nearly $4,000,000 annually, mainly from membership dues, but also from gifts, legacies, and subventions (White 1933, 56ff).

Even though those nationals with the largest memberships usually were U.S.-based, the individual membership of INGOs was overwhelmingly European. Secretariats were almost exclusively located in Europe or (for 4 percent) the United States (White 1933, 129). The largest source of funding for INGOs was the United States, with Great Britain, France, and Canada constituting a second tier of support, and other European countries plus Japan, South Africa, British and French dependencies, and China comprising a third. Although the INGO system was clearly Eurocentric, its TSMO component generated strong pressures to modify and abolish empires and colonies, contributing to the mandate and trusteeship systems that ended much territorial imperialism.

By the mid-1930s several international organizations constituted an important set of exceptions to the organizational structure described above because they were effectively, though often covertly, dominated by the Soviet Union. In that respect they were not legitimate nongovernmental organizations, although to the extent that they attained public legitimacy and subsumed authentically national social movements, they had the accouterments of INGOs and the goals of TSMOs.[9]

The activites of INGOs can be distinguished between those mobilizing an organization's own constituency and those also targeting a larger public (White 1933, 30–31):

TABLE 2.1.

Types of INGO Activities by Target

INGO Members	INGO Members and the Public
Interchange of ideas	Education and propaganda
Promotion of member interests	Research and collection of information
Coordination and regulation of member activities	Determination and registration of facts
Social fellowship	Humanitarian activities
Finance and recruitment	
Organization of meetings	

TSMOs were distinguished from other INGOs primarily by the fact that their goals, humanitarian or otherwise, involved members in mobilizing public pressure for political and social change. The individual members of social movements were not necessarily politically active. They could be important as a base of financial support, to be sure, but more than that, they were the basis of the networking that was the raison d'être of all INGOs, and they were the defining, cause-oriented *constituencies* characteristic of TSMOs.

The *public*, for politically active INGOs, comprised those sectors that they sought to influence. In the case of transnational SMOs, as of national ones, it is useful to distinguish *elite publics* from the *public-at-large*. Elite publics formed the decision-making establishment, includ-

9. Thus Feld deals with communist labor organizations and has a category of "transnational political groups" that includes parties, liberation movements, churches, and foundations in addition to what he calls "traditional" NGOs. Willetts also makes a case for including transnational political movements among NGOs, or what he calls broadly, "pressure groups" (1982, 6–8).

ing (but not exclusively) government leaders who were the ultimate target of SMO efforts. The public-at-large represented popular opinion, which was the proximate target of SMO efforts on the assumption that it could influence elites. Following the First World War, there was a shift in TSMO strategy from elite publics toward the public-at-large.

Strategies

INGOs were able to flourish within the nation-state system precisely because states were, in fact, composites of social, cultural, ethnic, and economic groupings. INGOs (including TSMOs) formed transnational links among various constituencies. It did not take significant size to do that. It did not necessarily require the mobilization of large blocs of people. It did not always require that issues have broad salience. It did require establishing issue-specific networks and responding to political opportunities.

Accordingly, it is useful to identify pre-1945 INGOs in terms of the issues, or areas, of their primary concern. It is also difficult to do so, as various attempts illustrate (see esp. Speekaert 1957, viii; Judge 1978; Skjelsbaek 1971, 429; and Willetts 1982a, 2–8). We can reasonably conclude at least that the largest single blocs of INGOs have comprised groups with economic and professional concerns. To those we can add recreational and avocational associations. Beyond them are groups that Peter Willetts calls "promotional." These include welfare agencies (that provide relief services), religious organizations (that promote values), and communal groups (that promote a group identity and status). If those border on being transnational social movements, a second cluster, "specific-issue, promotional groups" (such as those that promoted arbitration or, later, those that opposed nuclear arms or apartheid in South Africa), clearly are TSMOs.

The advantage of Willetts's approach is that it categorizes groups in terms of their *purposes*—what they mobilize to do. There are difficulties in his schema: for instance, important women's organizations were organized to mobilize women on public as well as constituent issues. But the difficulties only validate Willetts's insistence that the purposes of many INGOs were mixed, contributing to complex interactions along a broad range of issues. In any case, already at mid-century White observed that INGOs—whether they promoted group and professional interests, performed specific tasks, advanced research and knowledge, or promoted a social movement—were international actors whose roles included being sources of understanding (including information and analysis), molders of opinion, and advocates of change (1951, 10–14).

TSMOs mostly challenged the legitimacy of traditional social and political arrangements by popularizing knowledge, information, alternative concepts, or civic activity; but sometimes they tried to influence specific governmental decisions by mobilizing elite and popular publics. They targeted political action more or less consciously in relation to the priority of their goals—whether their immediate object was legitimizing their views and values or was seeking authorization for specific political decisions and programs.[10]

Rarely were strategic alternatives clear. Often mobilization was an ad hoc matter of reaching anyone who would listen. Nonetheless, citizen activists did align for change across boundaries. In the nineteenth century they campaigned against the slave trade, commerce in prostitutes, imperialism, and war; for the causes of labor and women, alcoholic temperance, the humane treatment of prisoners of war, and democratic republicanism, to mention only some outstanding campaigns. Other causes were added in the twentieth century.

Pre-1945 transnational social movements used several strategies, which can be illustrated from their varied experience. They sought to generate constituencies for multinational programs, to mobilize transnational pressure on national governments, and to influence international negotiations and IGOs. These approaches sometimes overlapped, depending on the character of TSMO organization and the political opportunities of any given time. Each choice of strategy more or less consciously reflected an association's purpose, and the practical consequences of that choice defined an INGO's international role.

Generating Constituencies for Multinational Programs

The well-known International Committee of the Red Cross obtained recognition by international convention, both as an INGO and also for its operating principles (exempting civilians and prisoners of war from the arbitrary use of force). It developed an active program that necessitated modifications of military behavior without challenging political or military policy per se. Essentially, the ICRC was granted political space in which to operate as a nongovernmental advocate for those imprisoned and wounded in war. Following World War I, a similar recognition was accorded the relief efforts of the League of Red Cross Societies (1919), while the Nansen Office marshaled succor for displaced persons.

---

10. In this respect it is helpful to distinguish between the relative goals of authority and legitimacy in decision making. See Willetts (1982a, 21–24) and also Ernst Haas (1990, esp. 87–88).

Many other INGOs originated for the promotion of humanitarian multinational programs. Often they constituted epistemic communities—professional and disciplinary groups that, in the sense of Ernst Haas, "share a commitment to a common causal model and a common set of political values. They are united by a belief in the truth of their model and by a commitment to translate this truth into public policy, in the conviction that human welfare will be enhanced as a result" (Haas 1990, 41). In that sense, political values distinguish members of epistemic communities from merely professional or intellectual associations. Such were the people concerned with relief for the poor and disadvantaged, who first met internationally in 1856 and then gathered frequently from 1889 to 1914 as the Congress of Public and Private Charity. Their meetings generated so much professional respect that they attracted official observers from governments, and their 1907 Bureau of Information and Studies was recognized by the French government as a public utility (Lyons 1963, 264). There were similar associations in mental illness, blindness and deafness, child care, and the treatment of the criminally imprisoned, the latter two concerns resulting in organizations with designated headquarters. The more cohesive these international communities became, of course, the more they sought to influence public policy, if not through collective action, then by empowering their members and the public with information.

Other kinds of transnational communities were formed. Within the women's movement, for example, the International Council of Women (1888) sought to heighten women's consciousness of and competence in social issues: by 1911 it comprised twenty national councils (Lyons 1963, 272–73). World War I spawned the Women's International League for Peace and Freedom (1915, 1919), a TSMO with headquarters in Geneva, where it monitored League affairs, provided its national branches with excellent information, and mobilized international expressions of women's opinion on key issues—most dramatically on the Disarmament Conference of 1932.

The movement to deal with alcoholism aligned professional and religious reformers, although it divided along the lines of temperance and prohibition, each approach generating INGOs with large international memberships. Both lines targeted individual alcoholics for personal regeneration, although the prohibition movement also sought to influence local and national legislation. Similarly, the campaign against prostitution—so-called white slavery—was mobilized by reformers who demonstrated that prostitution was an international commerce and coordinated efforts to rescue women and children across political boundaries, notably through the large membership of the Union Internationale des Amies de la Jeune Fille (1877). Aware of the limitations of private action, the movement targeted national policy-making. That was a general pattern: humanitarian concerns often led to political action, whether by member societies and individuals or by the INGO itself.

A particularly interesting example of mobilizing constituencies for a multinational program was the resurgence of an idea that had been proclaimed by Victor Hugo in 1848 as a "United States of Europe." After World War I, as fears of unfettered nationalism rose, the notion of European unity claimed some distinguished advocates among industrialists, intellectuals, and statesmen. In the mid-twenties it acquired a substantial organizational base in the International Committee for a European Customs Union, the Paneuropean Union, and the League for European Cooperation (Pegg 1983).

In some measure, European unity was an official French strategy for national security in the absence of U.S. or British guarantees, but the positive response of Germans and others, notably social democrats, gave the notion a larger significance. It was taken to the League of Nations Assembly by French foreign minister Aristide Briand, who was authorized to solicit reactions from European governments. Official responses were generous in principle but negative on specifics, and the concept languished as the world plunged into the Great Depression. Its time would come only after Europe was radically restructured by World War II.

Mobilizing Transnational Pressures on National Policy

Most international movements focused initially on national policy, even if they shifted their approach later in response to new opportunities. For some the national approach remained defining. For example, the campaigns against slavery and the slave trade depended on enforcement by England and other states, even though they forged transnational networks. Similarly, reformers challenging international commerce in prostitution promoted changes in national laws, such as those defining the age of consent.

The vigorous movement for women's suffrage, although broadly transnational, necessarily focused on constitutional reform in specific nations, as did the international temperance movement. An interesting variation was the Evangelical Alliance (1846), an interdenominational Protestant association located in London, for which the central concern was religion: the Alliance came to the aid of Christians persecuted in various countries insofar as it could engage Foreign Office support (Lyons 1963, 254).

Few international movements tried to intervene in inter-nation conflict, but it is instructive to note the experience of the socialist internationals in Austria before World War I and throughout Europe in the 1930s.

An exploding arms race and impending general war became salient issues for socialists in the years between the First International (1864–76) and the Second International Association of the Working Man (1889). By the early twentieth century, meetings of the Second International reflected workers' tension between nationalism and class solidarity. The organization was, after all, a loose federation of socialist parties, each of which tried to put down roots in a nation on which its political existence depended. It held periodic meetings and had an executive agency with limited jurisdiction, the International Socialist Bureau (ISB), which was the link for Austrian socialists.

Given the instability of its ethnically diverse empire, the Habsburg regime was highly sensitive to both the threat of Serbian expansion on its southern border and to social unrest within it. That gave some leverage to socialists, who were relatively well organized in Austria and had considerable worker support. On the other hand, socialists depended on the state for political opportunity. They wanted to avoid a general war for many reasons, not least its propensity to strengthen autocratic power. Accordingly, they tried to localize the Balkan wars of 1912–1913 (as they had done during Italy's 1906 Balkan intervention).

Austrian socialists negotiated with the empire while also initiating parliamentary challenges and public rallies. Through the ISB they coordinated their efforts with other socialists who launched massive rallies throughout Europe, effectively mobilized public opinion against intervention, and helped restrain the militant elites (Wank 1988, 51). Operative in this situation was the juncture of socialist solidarity, apprehensive public opinion, vulnerability of key governments, division within foreign policy elites, and a still fluid diplomatic context. Sadly, socialists failed to achieve the same force in 1914. Thereafter, the mobilization of workers to prevent war remained an unachievable goal.

The Second International disintegrated under the pressures of wartime nationalism and conflicting socialist positions on the war. Its place was taken by the International Trade Union Federation (1919) and the Labor and Socialist International (1923), essentially federations of autonomous national and international organizations. Competing with them in the wake of the Bolshevik Revolution were the Communist International (1919) and the Red Trade Union International (1921). These had roots in various nations, and to that extent they channeled indigenous social protest; but they were controlled from Moscow as extensions of Soviet foreign policy making. Their combination of bottom-up social forces with top-down policy control produced great tension in some national sections (the standard history is Braunthal 1967).

The socialist-labor and communist internationals were surely the largest and most aggressive TSMOs of the 1920s and 1930s. Both of them attempted to form political coalitions with other SMOs through which to mobilize public opinion on foreign policy, while waging internecine campaigns against each other. Their conflict was particularly rife in the unstable Weimar Republic of Germany. After the 1933 Nazi takeover there, however, the Communist International began to endorse a "United Front" with social democrats and bourgeois peace advocates, while urging strong collective security measures against German and Italian aggression. Even so, the left remained bitterly split. When Stalin and Hitler negotiated a nonaggression pact in 1939, the Communist International reversed itself again to appease Nazi aggression in Poland—until Germany attacked Russia in 1941 and the Soviets once more called for a united front.

The conflict between socialist and communist TSMOs (indeed, the Soviet manufacture of a TSMO to serve its own policy interests) weakened European solidarity and collective security in the face of fascist aggression. It destabilized domestic politics for major European decision makers. Sadly, it showed how Byzantine ideological battles and national interests among select TSMOs helped undercut a multilateral policy like collective security.

Influencing Intergovernmental Negotiations and Agencies

Sometimes governments were spurred to international action by the very formation of professional and humanitarian constituencies (as of economic ones), by the quality of their work and the intrinsic relationship of transnational to national issues. In the cases of traffic in women and children, the treatment of imprisoned criminals and persons imprisoned or wounded in war, private actions stimulated governmental negotiations, which led to international conventions or treaties. In other cases, INGOs mobilized to initiate and participate in intergovernmental negotiations, as in the case of international labor conventions.

Given competitive national economies, the regulation of factory conditions of labor had an international dimension. Private initiatives led to private international congresses, from which came proposals for intergovernmental regulation. Eventually, an intergovernmental congress was held in Berlin (1890), at which the principle of regulation was legitimized but international controls were rejected. That impasse was broken with the formation of the International Association for the Protection of Labor (IAPL, 1900), a federation of national societies for labor legislation. Its international congresses attracted governmental participation, which led in turn to a series of intergovernmental conferences (1905–1912). With the bureau of the IAPL providing the staff work, those conferences resulted in several labor treaties and conventions (Lyons 1963, 138–56). The structure of negotiated conventions became the foundation on which the International Labor Organization was built.

Representing business and consciously targeting intergovernmental negotiations in relation to other venues of support was the International Chamber of Commerce (ICC, 1920). It was anticipated by a network of local and national Chambers of Commerce in the latter half of the nineteenth century, and it emerged from the First World War as a conference-based federation of national chambers, with a secretariat in Paris and a system of specialized committees on virtually every aspect of economic activity. In the interwar period it challenged the conventional economic wisdom of economic nationalism while promoting both the economic reconstruction of Europe and a more open economic order.

The ICC assumed multiple roles. It was designed to facilitate international business and, since the business leadership was deeply divided over economic issues during the interwar period, it also functioned to reconcile opposing views within its international membership. It self-consciously promoted economic internationalism within the larger business and political sectors of the industrial nations. In this last sense the ICC thought of itself as not only a business bureau but "a world movement with the dynamics of a party commanding loyalty and demanding action" (Ridgeway 1938, 4).

ICC leaders Charles C. Dawes and Owen Young negotiated the restructuring of reparations, incorporating approaches worked out in ICC meetings. The organization used the negotiation of international conventions as occasions to present technical reports to the Postal Union, the International Telegraph Union, and other IGOs. Its technical committees established consultative relationships with League sections and the ILO, presenting themselves as the voices of world business. With the International Law Association, the ICC produced a draft shipping code, the Hague Rules (1921) that was largely written into international law by a diplomatic conference. Similarly, it created and operated a service of arbitration and conciliation in commercial disputes, a procedure that was validated by a 1923 protocol of the League Assembly and subsequently incorporated into an international convention (Ridgeway 1938, 1959).

In such ways the ICC contributed a base of expertise and influence that helped, during the Second World War, to institutionalize the vision of an international economy responding to market forces under inter-governmental supervision and with established procedures for the ne-gotiation, conciliation, and arbitration of differences. It not only targeted intergovernmental negotiations but also generated constitu-encies for institutions like the later International Monetary Fund and the General Agreement on Trade and Tariffs.

Although it may seem difficult to think of a business agency as a social movement organization, the ICC in its early years was compara-ble to international labor in seeking to change the distribution of rights and goods through changes in institutionalized practice and power, and on behalf of a broadly based constituency. If, having secured space in the system, it increasingly acted like a vested interest group or specialized bureaucracy, that but suggests that its role changed over time relative to international norms and institutions. Indeed, whereas early social movement theory identified challenges to the status quo with the organization of various underclasses, it now seems likely that pressure to change public norms and institutions is also generated by associations for which class is not an organizing principle (although questions of distributive justice are of course inextricably woven into all public interest questions).

TSMOs and the Emergence of International Regimes

Seeking changes in the distribution of goods and services, rights and power, social and international norms, TSMOs cultivated support for international programs, mobilized international pressure on gov-ernments, and lobbied international negotiations and agencies. They were in that measure prototypes of later transnational social move-ments and issue-oriented networks. To the extent that they were suc-cessful, TSMOs contributed both to the development of IGOs and also to newly institutionalized norms, or regimes.

Thanks to the research of Martin Dubin, we have a full account of the formation of an international regime in health care (Dubin 1991; 1993; 1995). The creation of a modern health regime during the in-terwar period was achieved by a global epistemic community of bio-medical scientists and public health officials, facilitated by private agencies like the Rockefeller Foundation and by the League of Nations. The story illustrates the dynamic interaction of INGOs and IGOs and the strategic approaches typical of TSMOs. Whereas the peace and arbitration movement illustrates the role of social movements in form-ing IGOs, the origin of the modern health regime illustrates the interactive role of private and public sectors in forming and strengthening an international norm.

Health-related intergovernmental conventions and agencies prior to World War I were designed to prevent the spread of epidemic diseases. That approach was epitomized in a 1907 convention (Rome) and the creation of a supervising IGO, the Office international d'Hygine publique (OIHP, Paris). By that time, as Dubin observes, "the expanding horizons of the biomedical community were accompanied by a shift in the underlying normative principle making it legitimate for governments to assume new levels of responsibility for assisting scientific discovery and improving public health administration in the interest of entire populations" (1993, 23).

The new approach was institutionalized in some public health offices, in the Rockefeller Foundation (founded in 1913 expressly to reduce disease by increasing medical knowledge and services), and in the wartime work of the Inter-Allied Sanitary Commission and several Red Cross societies. Following the war, a League of Red Cross Societies was formed with a broad mandate, incorporated in Article 25 of the League of Nations charter, to work for "the prevention of disease and the mitigation of suffering throughout the world." The League's charter also provided for a health committee. For political reasons the semiautonomous OIHP acquired that role. In fact, initiative passed to the League's medical director, Dr. Ludwik W. Rajchman, who was also the secretary of its health committee.

Under Rajchman's astute leadership, the health organization amassed an impressive record: a central system for reporting epidemic diseases; a worldwide, standardized epidemiological database; an international exchange program for public health officers; the empirical standardization of biological agents; systematic studies of environmental factors in health; assistance with health surveys and services; and responses to epidemics and other technical problems, especially in less developed countries (Dubin 1993, 28–32). The Rockefeller-funded interchange of health personnel across boundaries generated the nongovernmental International Society of Public Health Medical Officers, which in turn reinforced the governmental constituency for the new public health vision.

Those activities built close-knit networks among funding agencies like Rockefeller, research institutes, private medical associations, and national public health services throughout the world. The League's health secretariat completed an interactive circuit among these constituencies, whose combined efforts institutionalized the biomedical/public health community and the modern health norm that it promoted. In this respect, Dubin concludes, the interwar health regime was "not simply an intervening variable between the epistemic community and states, but an independent variable that had a distinct role in developing new knowledge and in reshaping both itself and transborder networks, and state institutions" (Dubin 1993, 42). The regime institutionalized both a modern norm for public health and the transnational community that promoted it.

There were other regimes, other "islands of order" (Dubin 1993, 1) prior to World War II. A norm regarding the treatment of workers was identified with the ILO in the language of its constitution: "labor should not be regarded merely as a commodity or article of commerce." Recognition of the rights of prisoners of war, wounded, and civilians to be treated as noncombatant victims of war was promoted and monitored by the International Red Cross. Some areas of transnational consensus were bounded by international conventions, such as those prohibiting slavery and slave trade, or guaranteeing freedom of commerce and transit on international waterways.

Even international law owed much to private initiatives, as did the proscription of slavery. Voluntary association was beginning to define as yet incipient regimes: women's rights to full participation, for example, the application of arbitration and conciliation in many areas of conflict, and the principle of inalienable human rights (that owed much to the interwar community of international lawyers in the Americas [Jones 1991]). Such developments as these had multiple causes, but transnational social movements were among the agents of change.

Conclusion

Certainly there were mature transnational social movement organizations well before the middle of the twentieth century. They developed and were structured like other INGOs, with which they shared many kinds of activities. They were distinguished mainly by their purposes—to change the status quo in the interest of some assumed public good—and by the strategies they used. That they are sometimes difficult to distinguish from other international nongovernmental associations is perhaps due in part to changing roles within a fluid international system.

TSMOs and other INGOs intersected with states to create intergovernmental organizations, to shape them, and to complement their transnational orientation. In varying measure, they interacted with IGOs to influence international norms. On occasion TSMOs and coalitions of them mobilized their minimal resources to change the distribution of goods, rights, and power in the international order.

Surely those early nongovernmental networks were historically significant. But the *kinds* of their significance—the outcomes of their efforts—depended on two sets of variables: coincidental decisions made on state and international levels, and (in Charles Tilly's phrase) "big structures, large processes" in the international order. Not the least of the large processes that have affected nonterritorial actors throughout this century is that quiet revolution of which they themselves have been a part. They also were variables, after all, and introducing them into the international system changed it. Indeed, the very process of institutionalizing them at various points probably affected the potential of both the system and their roles in it at other junctures. In that measure the dynamic quality of the system, of which we also are a part, also conditions our analysis of it.

3

CHARACTERISTICS OF THE MODERN TRANSNATIONAL SOCIAL MOVEMENT SECTOR

Jackie Smith

Abstract

Contemporary protest movements have become globalized. Data drawn from the *Yearbook of International Organizations*, for example, show rapid growth in transnational social movement organizations (TSMOs), mostly in the areas of human rights, environment, womens' rights, peace, and development. Transnational networks have also become stronger: there has been significant growth in the formal and informal links between TSMOs, intergovernmental organizations, and other nongovernmental organizations (NGOs). Also, their geographic distribution has become more balanced between industrialized and developing regions.

Transnational social movement organizations, or TSMOs, are a subset of social movement organizations operating in more than two states.[1] The transnational structures of these organizations provide them with resources essential for addressing interdependent global problems and allow them greater access to intergovernmental institutions. In the preceding chapter, Chatfield illustrated how particular TSMOs helped

1. I am grateful to John Boli, Charles Chatfield, William Gamson, Robert Johansen, Sam Marullo, John McCarthy, Ron Pagnucco, and Dieter Rucht for their comments on earlier drafts and for their thoughtful suggestions and insights about organizing this dataset. Any errors remaining are my responsibility.

inaugurate and shape the development of these intergovernmental institutions. While recognizing this initiating role, this chapter assumes that, once established, intergovernmental institutions affect the ongoing political opportunity structures available to social movements and the organizations that further them. The interactions among both governmental and nongovernmental actors, moreover, further shape intergovernmental institutions and law within the existing institutional frameworks.

The growth in intergovernmental institutions has brought with it needs for new skills and knowledge on the part of activists (Archer 1983; Atwood 1982; Brysk 1992; Epstein 1993; Mansbach and Vasquez 1980; Wiseberg 1992). Mansbach and Vasquez noted that, "[a]ccess to a system requires an understanding of the rules of the game in that system, a willingness to follow them, and the skill to do so—assets that can only be acquired with experience" (1980, 97). TSMO structures and operations help activists become familiar with intergovernmental institutions and develop their skills for working effectively in such contexts. Regional and global meetings of TSMOs familiarize national and local leaders with transnational political processes and help them make strategic connections between national and transnational political activities. TSMO structures foster a division of labor between national and transnational levels of the organization that may be integral to effectiveness in movement attempts to influence state behavior: they allow the movement to expand its activities in intergovernmental and transgovernmental policy arenas while not decreasing its efforts in national political contexts. Indeed, the transnational perspective and coordination provided by an international headquarters may enhance some national movement campaigns.

As formal movement actors, TSMOs serve as movement focal points. TSMOs cultivate relationships with officials in intergovernmental organizations (IGOs) and national delegations, monitor progress on given issues, and devise and implement means of advancing movement goals when progress is stalled. Thus, as the cases studies in later chapters demonstrate, TSMOs play driving roles to advance particular goals through global political processes. They help to define and raise issues to the political agenda, draft proposals for resolutions or legal conventions for consideration by national delegations to IGOs, coordinate the efforts of national social movement organizations (SMOs) to support government passage of international conventions or legislation, and publicize and monitor states' compliance with intergovernmental agreements.

All TSMOs do not perform all of these activities, and looking across different movements, one usually finds an informal division of labor among TSMOs, in which some have the expertise to focus on certain aspects of the political process, such as drafting legal conventions, while others aim primarily to educate a broader population about the issues or to monitor local level compliance with global norms (see, for instance, chapter 5, on Peace Brigades International). Carrying out these activities, TSMOs often rely on the cooperation of other TSMOs as well as informal and formal mobilizing structures.

Where significant numbers of formal movement organizations are present, more attempts to influence the decisions of intergovernmental institutions are likely, and these attempts are probably more formally coordinated transnationally. Such movements should also produce more organized national activity, since transnational consultation generates common interpretations of problems and helps disseminate complementary mobilizing and action frames. In contrast, for issues where transnational movement organizations are scarce, more nationally divergent activity around the issue and little coordinated movement activity in IGOs are expected. In such cases, any activity on the issue within IGOs will probably be met with uncoordinated and weak movement pressure, if any (see, for instance, the differences chapter 8 describes between the 1978 and later nuclear disarmament mobilizations as well as the discussion in chapter 9 of the failure of the U.S. Freeze movement to generate transnational action).

The two previous chapters presented a few illustrations of the kinds

TABLE 3.1.

**Examples of TSMO Tactics 1983–1993
(by target of activity*)**

Individuals	National Governments	Intergovermental Institutions
Education	Letter-writing campaign	Draft int'l conventions
Citizen exchanges	Fact-finding missions	Document violations of int'l law
Work camps	Protest demonstrations	Early warning activities
Speakers bureau	Direct actions	Promote "internat'l" days
Legal aid	Lobby nat'l policymakers	Advise IGO officials
Alternative marketing	Petitions	Lobby delegates
Networking	Observer missions	Monitor transnat'l corp.
Nonviolence training	Advise national govts.	Monitor int'l agencies
Technical training	Draft nat'l legislation	Political socialization
Media campaigns		

* Categories are illustrative, not necessarily mutually exclusive of activities TSMOs carry out. Clearly the range of activities is vast, although it can be clustered in terms of three major targets of activity: individuals, national governments, and intergovernmental institutions. Table 3.1 displays examples of the range of tactics TSMOs use to influence global politics. While not an exhaustive summary of the transnational tactical repertoire, the list demonstrates some of the variation in TSMO activities. Many tactics listed in table 3.1 mirror those used by national and local SMOs: a key difference is that many TSMO tactics are carried out within a global or regional strategic framework. In other words, they ultimately aim to shape intergovernmental and transgovernmental political processes. The transnational structures of TSMOs make them best suited for accessing decision makers and institutions at the transnational level as well as strategically coordinating national and local efforts. The work of TSMOs helps develop important links between individuals and international institutions.

Activities such as human rights education help disseminate information on international legal standards. Moving in the other direction (e.g., from individuals and localities to IGOs), local level ties allow TSMOs to monitor and aggregate individuals' demands for change and to monitor government compliance with these standards. Moreover, because of their international focus and expertise, the international staff of TSMOs can research issues of popular concern and raise them onto the global agenda. Their activities in intergovernmental institutions, combined with their contacts with local constituencies, make some TSMOs attractive allies to IGO bureaucrats and to some national delegations at intergovernmental negotiations. Clearly, too, the various activities described here require very different kinds of material and political resources, and, therefore, one should expect to find a division of labor among TSMOs similar to that observed among national SMOs (Zald and McCarthy 1980).

Characteristics of TSMOs, 1973–93

Methods and Data

Data for this study come from the *Yearbook of International Organizations* (Union of International Associations), the most complete census of international organizations, which includes information on organizations' founding dates, goals, memberships, and interorganizational ties. The Union of International Associations uses UN records on nongovernmental organizations (NGOs), self-reports, referrals, and the media to identify organizations and to compile organizational profiles for the *Yearbook*. Editors consistently check this reported information against other sources, such as periodicals, official documents, and the media (Union of International Associations 1993, ix; A. Judge, 1993).

In order to determine which international organizations were indeed TSMOs, each page of organizational entries in the 1974, 1983/4, and 1993/4 volumes of the *Yearbook* was reviewed and every nongovernmental organization whose primary aims included some form of social change (broadly defined) was coded.[2] In addition to these three separate reviews of the *Yearbook* volumes, TSMOs identified for each year were cross-checked with other years.[3]

These data show that the transnational social movement sector is quite large and diverse and that it has grown dramatically in recent years. More than sixty percent of all TSMOs active in 1993 were formed after 1970, and their average age declined over the two decades from 33 to 25 years. The oldest active TSMO, the Anti-Slavery Society for the Protection of Human Rights, was formed in 1839, but the vast majority of TSMOs emerged in the latter half of the twentieth century. Key aspects of the TSMO population are summarized below as a backdrop for the case studies to follow.

Movement Issues

Displayed below are several dimensions of the transnational social movement sector and changes in it between 1973 and 1993. A central question is, What issues motivate transnational social movement activity? Presumably, transnational clusters of movement organizations and individuals working for a particular social change goal, called transnational social movement industries (TSMIs), are reflected in national movements, although their relative sizes and emphases vary (cf. McCarthy and Zald 1977). For instance, while TSMOs working for human

---

2. The organization's name and reported "Aims" were used to determine the organization's goals. Rigorous criteria for defining which groups to include were developed, and a codebook is available from the author.

3. Data for 1973 were collected in collaboration with Kathryn Sikkink. Reliability checks were carried out on two dimensions of the data collection: selection of TSMOs for inclusion and codebook reliability. In order to assess the reliability of the original selection of cases for inclusion, the 1993 *Yearbook* was read through a second time and the names of groups selected as TSMOs were recorded. The comparison of this list with the original selection resulted in a 0.89 reliability estimate (this estimate is relevant only to the replicability of the study, since new groups identified through this second reading were added to the dataset). A random 10 percent of the organizations in the 1993 listing were coded by a second coder, and comparison of results yielded a 0.97 reliability estimate. For more information on methodology, contact the author.

rights help form the largest TSMI, the human rights social movement industry (SMI) is a comparatively small one in relatively open, democratic states.

TABLE 3.2.

Transnational Social Movement Industries

TSMI	1973	1983	1993
	N = 183	N = 348	N = 631
Human Rights	23%	23%	27%
Environment	6	7	14
Women's Rights	9	7	10
Peace	8	6	9
World Order/Multi-Issue	7	9	8
Development	4	4	5
Self-Determination/Ethnic	10	11	5

Source: Yearbook of International Organizations, 1973, 1983, 1993

Table 3.2 displays the most populous transnational social movement industries between 1973 and 1993, when the number of TSMOs doubled from just under 200 to more than 600 organizations. A surprising variety of issues has attracted international activism. Some of the oldest TSMOs are involved in human rights or the promotion of the use of the international language Esperanto. Others promote animal rights, white supremacy, and the international regulation of transnational corporations. The largest TSMIs include the human rights, environment, women's rights, peace, development, ethnic nationalist, and world order TSMIs. These seven TSMIs in table 3.2 account for between 67 and 78 percent of all TSMOs in each year.[4] The human rights industry, which makes up the largest segment of the transnational social movement sector, doubled in size over the decades from 41 to 168 organizations. By far the fastest growing segment, the environmental TSMI

4. No other industry made up more than 3 percent of the cases except for groups promoting the international language Esperanto, which were 8.5 percent of the TSMO population in 1993. These groups have been excluded from the table because they do not appear to be as active politically. Nearly all of these groups had small numbers of individual members and only three indicated relationships with an intergovernmental organization. Other TSMIs were those promoting animal rights, international law, consumers' rights, violent revolution, consumer protection (e.g., vs. transnational corporations) and population issues.

expanded from 10 TSMOs in 1973 to 90 groups in 1993. That 42 percent of all environmental TSMOs active in 1993 were formed after 1985, and 80 percent were formed after 1970, indicates the relative newness of this expansion of transnational environmental activism. Some of this growth might be the result (or even the partial cause) of UN meetings on the environment in 1972 and 1992 and a UN commission report on the environment and development in the mid-1980s.[5] Some of the growth may also be due to the increasing ability of intergovernmental organizations to address issues related to North/South tension —especially environmental degradation and development tradeoffs— since the decline of Cold War tensions.

TSMOs working for women's rights—including the enhancement of women's roles in economic development, gender equality, and the promotion of "wages for housework" (economic restructuring to account for women's unpaid labor)—also multiplied over the decade. Peace and development TSMOs doubled their numbers. The "world order" TSMI—including groups working for multiple interrelated goals of peace, human rights, international law, economic justice, and environmental protection—grew from 12 groups in 1973 to 48 in 1993. Some of the growth in this particular industry may be the result of frame modifications made to respond to post-Cold War realities that make peace seem less dependent on resolving problems like arms races and more contingent on cultivating more equitable economic situations—or at least stronger multilateral institutions for conflict resolution.

The ethnic unity/self-determination industry was the only industry that remained stagnant over the decade. This lack of growth may indicate a shift in the nature of transnational ethnic mobilization, towards more violent forms. While the use of violence would not eliminate them from inclusion as TSMOs, such groups are unlikely to be included in the *Yearbook,* as few of these would have formal associations with the United Nations agencies and most would not wish to have information on their organizations published in this forum.[6] Another possibility is that such groups have begun to emphasize the protection of human rights as opposed to separatism. One plausible rationale for this argument is that changes in the international opportunity structure affecting these groups included an increasing willing-

5. This commission report was published as *Our Common Future* by the World Commission on Environment and Development.

6. Only one TSMO explicitly promoting violent revolution (in Latin America) appeared in the *Yearbook* volumes used in this study.

ness of the international community to be more proactive in defending minority rights. This greater proactivity is most clearly evidenced in recent UN efforts in the early 1990s to protect Kurds in Iraq after the Persian Gulf war as well as the progress, however limited, in establishing an international tribunal to prosecute war criminals in the former Yugoslavia, and the establishment of a High Commissioner for Human Rights. Apparent global responsiveness to human rights issues might have led to a decline of ethnic liberation organizations in favor of groups espousing more internationally recognized human rights goals.

TSMOs and Their Environments

The theoretical assumptions guiding this book are that TSMOs have extensive and growing amounts of contact with intergovernmental organizations. Literature on the work of nongovernmental organizations within IGOs shows that effectiveness in this arena requires cooperation and coordination between different nongovernmental organizations (Weiss and Gordenker 1996; Willetts 1996).

Groups can be most effective as advocates in global political institutions if they can claim to represent a truly global constituency. This is particularly true in universal forums such as the United Nations. But critics of TSMOs and other INGOs frequently point out that these groups are based disproportionately in the North and that they overrepresent northern constituencies. Figure 3.1, which illustrates the geographic distribution of TSMO memberships between 1983 and 1993, shows that while this criticism of TSMOs is true, changes in recent years are leading to somewhat more geographically balanced TSMO memberships. Western democratic states are likely to be the most frequent sites of TSMO activities, because these states are typically wealthier and their citizens freer to engage in political associations than are most people of the Southern Hemisphere (Skjelsbaek 1971). However, figure 3.1 shows that although western Europeans and North Americans are still disproportionately represented in TSMO memberships, people from most regions of the developing world are becoming increasingly integrated into transnational social movement efforts. Overall, the percentage of TSMOs reporting members in developing countries grew from 46 percent in 1983 to 61 percent in 1993. At the same time, more TSMO headquarters are located in developing countries: whereas in 1983 only 17 percent of all TSMOs had their international offices in the Southern Hemisphere, by 1993 this figure rose to 24 percent. Thus, although the integration of Southern memberships has been slow, TSMO memberships are increasingly more bal-

FIGURE 3.1

Geography of TSMO Memberships

Number of TSMOs with Members in Region

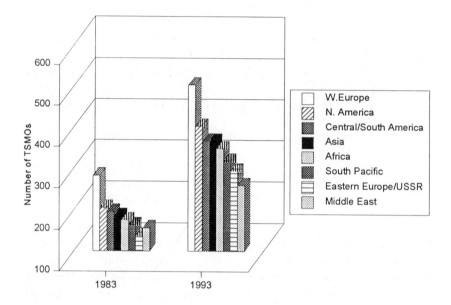

anced in terms of geographic representation; this does not mean, however, that TSMOs here succeeded in overcoming discrepancies in representation across class divisions.

While geographic representation is critical for most transnational social movements, another important TSMO strategy is the cultivation of ties with other NGOs and with intergovernmental agencies. Table 3.3 rates changes in the extensiveness of the links of TSMOs with other actors in their environments,[7] as well as changes in the numbers of countries represented in memberships of the TSMOs. The figures in table 3.3 show a trend since 1983 towards more extensive networking between TSMOs and other international actors. Between 1983 and 1993, the percentage of groups reporting no links with IGOs declined from 52 to 42 percent, while the percentage reporting five or more such links doubled from 8 to 16 percent. Also, although TSMO-contact is growing, it is clear that, for a substantial number of TSMOs, intergov-

---

7. Links with IGOs are *Yearbook* reports of formal consultative ties as well as less formal contacts with intergovernmental organizations. Relations with other NGOs are reported by the organizations themselves and are cross-referenced in the *Yearbook.*

ernmental activity does not constitute the central focus of the organizations' work.

TABLE 3.3.

Density of External Networks of TSMOs

	1973	1983	1993
#IGO Contacts			
0	49%	52%	42%
1–4	40	40	42
5 or >	11	8	16
(N)	(160)	(262)	(555)
#NGO Contacts			
0	56%	51%	20%
1–4	42	45	49
5 or >	2	4	31
(N)	(160)	(251)	(558)
Mean Country			
Memberships	33.89	31.02	33.57
Median	28	23	23
(N)	(153)	(233)	(483)

Source: Yearbook of International Organizations, 1973, 1983, 1993

Although the percentage changes look quite small, the actual changes in the numbers of organizations are fairly large, as the population of TSMOs doubled in this time period. The density of contacts between TSMOs and other NGOs has grown even more dramatically: the percentage of TSMOs reporting no other contact with other NGOs fell from more than half to just 20 percent, and the percentage of TSMOs reporting five or more contacts grew more than tenfold. These changes have implications for global governance and institution building, although it is uncertain whether the further proliferation of TSMOs and their contacts with IGOs facilitates or further complicates international negotiation and problem-solving efforts (see, e.g., Stanley Foundation 1995).

In short, indicators of the density of TSMOs' networks with their environment show increasing—although not necessarily extensive—contacts among TSMOs and IGOs and NGOs. Between 1983 and 1993 there was also a slight expansion in the number of countries in which

TSMOs have members, which suggests a possible trend towards an increased global integration of social movements.[8] The overall number of member countries is also surprisingly large, given the obstacles to such extensive transnational organization. The median, 23 countries, demonstrates that many TSMOs are not merely regional transnational organizations but instead typically span an average of more than four continents.

TSMO Structures and Mobilization Patterns

As research on national movements has shown, SMOs can take a number of organizational forms, and these forms can affect what the organizations are able to do (McCarthy and Wolfson 1996). While these data do not allow for very elaborate comparisons of organizational forms, the structure of membership can be used to indicate variation in organizational form, since this factor is likely to affect how organizational tasks are performed. The four general categories are individual members, professional members, organizations of organizations (coalitions), and federated structures, which are TSMOs with national and / or local branches (e.g., Amnesty International).[9] Table 3.4 summarizes the membership structures of TSMOs. The majority of TSMOs are organized as coalitions or as federations of national or regional sections. A surprising number of TSMOs, however, maintain individual memberships—despite the apparent obstacles one might anticipate in sustaining a transnational individual-based membership (cf. Olson 1968). A significant percentage of TSMOs are organized around professional groupings; Médicins Sans Frontières (Doctors Without Borders), International Physicians for the Prevention of Nuclear War, and the Union of Esperantist Railwaymen are examples of this form. While

8. While there was a proliferation of the number of states between 1988 and 1993, this is not likely to have significant effects on these results, given an apparent lag in the reporting of memberships in these new states: Few new states were listed in organizational entries and old names of states remained.

9. What I call federated organizations are equivalent to McCarthy and Wolfson's (1996) "Franchise" groups, or local chapters of a national organization. D. Young (1991) includes in his definition of federations both organizations of autonomous local organizations and differentiated, decentralized international organizations. I think it appropriate, however, to distinguish between the two at least until we know more about decision making procedures within forms. Decentralized international organizations typically have tiers of decision making: Amnesty International USA meets annually to pass resolutions that its delegates then raise at the AI international convention. Coalitions, on the other hand, are likely to have different methods for incorporating more autonomous members' interests into collective decision making procedures.

some of these groups may have individual rather than organizational members, they are distinguished by the fact that the professional identities of their members imply more formally structured relationships.[10] Members of such groups are likely to have contact with each other as part of their professional work and therefore face lower transaction costs for collective action than do groups of individuals organized outside professional networks.

TABLE 3.4.

Membership Structures and Age Cohorts of TSMOs

| | 1973 | 1993 | 1993 | | |
| | All | All | > 20 | 10–20 | < 10 |
Membership	TSMOs	TSMOs	Yrs. Old	Yrs. Old	Yrs. Old
Federations (Nat'l sectn.)	50%	29%	42%	18%	20%
Coalition (Org'l members)	25	40	33	42	48
Individual members	20	22	18	28	25
Professional members	2	7	7	9	6
N	183	477	215	130	114

Source: Yearbook of International Organizations, 1973, 1993

The right-hand columns in table 3.5 show variation in organizational forms of TSMOs according to when they were founded. Among the organizations established within the past ten years, a very small percentage have adopted federated structures, although this is the most common form for groups formed before 1973. Most new TSMOs are coalitions (48 percent) or have individual membership bases (25 percent). The percentage of professional membership organizations remained fairly constant across age cohorts. This finding reflects the changes in communications technologies and reduced transaction costs. With higher communication and transportation costs, federated organizations' multiple tiers of authority helped to reduce costs and heighten efficiency: locals report to national sections, national sections send delegates to international meetings. Because electronic mail, faxes, and other communication technologies are now more readily available, as is transnational transportation, it is feasible for more de-

10. Some of these groups are actually organized into national level sections, but this information cannot always be determined from their *Yearbook* entries.

centralized organizations to operate. These data alone cannot allow us to tell whether certain forms are better at integrating members in the sense of maintaining active participation of individuals and of preserving membership roles in decision making. Future work might investigate variation in membership integration across organization forms.

Table 3.5 indicates that TSMOs with different organizational forms vary in the extent to which they attract broad networks of IGOs and NGOs, and in how geographically dispersed their membership are. These two measures of interconnectivity between TSMOs and other actors, moreover, indicate to some degree how successful an organization is. The logic of global political strategy, for instance, suggests that organizations with more extensive links with IGOs and NGOs and with broader geographic diversity will be most effective politically. In multinational institutional contexts, such organizations appeal to the interests of national delegates because they are viewed as representatives of broad constituencies. Examined below is the question of which organizational forms appear most capable of fostering these linkages. Organizations of organizations (be they autonomous organizations or national sections of transnational organizations) are likely most networked in intergovernmental forums, given that their memberships are likely to be more expansive and geographically diverse. This dynamic may limit the ability of such organizations to develop extensive ties with NGOs. Individual member organizations may be less attractive to IGOs and likewise to NGOs because of the more narrow constituencies they represent.

International Position and Survival

Table 3.5 reveals the relationships between IGO, and NGO, and country links and TSMO membership structure and survival, displaying the means for TSMOs that survived past the ten-year survival threshold[11] and for TSMOs that disbanded between 1988 and 1993. A recent study of U.S. peace movement organizations suggests that those SMOs with more extensive external networks are most likely to survive (Edwards and Marullo 1995). Organizations with more ties with other NGOs and IGOs as well as with more expansive memberships are likely to be ones that are most widely respected and accepted by external actors. Such acceptance is necessary if an organization is to

11. TSMOs that were 10 years old or younger were significantly more likely to disband than were older groups. The mean age of groups that died in this period was 16, as compared with a mean of 25 for all other groups.

effectively mobilize other resources necessary for survival.[12] Table 3.5 shows that federated TSMOs had significantly more dense networks with IGOs and NGOs and that they had broader membership scopes than did TSMOs with other structures, possibly because of their comparative longevity. Organizations with individual members were, however, significantly less integrated into external networks of NGOs and IGOs. That coalitions were not significantly less able to build ties with other organizations, suggests that these organizations may retain authority (or even a mandate) to expand their international networks on behalf of their memberships.

TABLE 3.5.

Network Density, Membership Structures, and Survival of TSMOs

	#IGO Contacts	t	#NGO Contacts	t	#Member Countries	t
Membership Structure						
Federation	3.80	4.12 **	7.92	5.40 **	37.63	1.87
Org. Coalition	2.49	0.18	5.08	0.19	28.32	−1.37
Individuals	0.81	−4.10 **	1.60	−5.13 **	32.41	−0.44
Professionals	1.53	−1.17	2.21	−2.16 *	32.27	−0.26
Survival						
Age >10	2.99	4.78 **	5.65	2.45 *	38.96	6.01 **
Death (1988–1993)	0.22	−3.15 **	1.15	−2.78 **	17.35	−3.02 **

* p(t) <.05   ** p(t) <.01

Source: Yearbook of International Organizations, 1988, 1993

Finally, as expected, TSMOs with more dense external networks were more likely to survive. The mean score of IGO contacts for groups surviving past ten years was ten times that of groups that disbanded between 1988 and 1993. Similarly, surviving groups had nearly four

---

12. I treat survival as a proxy measure for organizational success, following Minkoff (1995). As the Gamson/Goldstone exchange (Gamson 1990) emphasized, organizations must survive for long periods if they are ever to see their own victories through. Those organizations that survive are therefore successful in the sense that they are around to continue the struggle. While antislavery and anti-apartheid groups may disband after largely achieving their goals, most TSMOs are not likely to see their goals achieved in the near future.

times as many NGO links, on the average, and nearly twice as many countries of membership as groups that did not survive. This finding supports a similar one reported by Edwards and Marullo (1995) in their study of U.S. peace movement organizational deaths. Variations in external networks across movement industries show that environmental and development TSMOs experienced the most dramatic growth in number of ties with IGOs and NGOs, perhaps reflecting new institutional opportunities in this area that may stem from the 1992 UN Conference on Environment and Development.[13] That movement industry had little relation to organizational death rates, however, suggests that structural factors are more important for organizational survival than are factors such as the salience of issue: environmental degradation may be an extremely important issue for a large public, but if environmental SMOs fail to develop organizational structures capable of sustaining necessary human and material resources, their organizations will not survive.

Conclusions

Over the past decade the transnational social movement sector has grown quite dramatically, and it has developed more extensive links with intergovernmental organizations and with other nongovernmental organizations. At the same time, a more balanced geographical range of organizations and individuals are represented among TSMO memberships.

TSMOs are relatively new actors in a complex and rapidly changing political environment, but the following chapters present evidence demonstrating how activists within these organizations are learning to play politics in global political arenas. The transnational social movement sector brings a new dimension to the study of social movements. On the one hand, it reveals a global political process with its own logic that is subject to the pressure of organized, non-state collective actors. On the other hand, by building ties with national and local movement organizations (some of whom are members of TSMOs), this sector also

13. Groups attending the UN Conference on Environment and Development may be more likely to be reported in the *Yearbook* than other groups because the Union of International Associations has a mandate from the UN to assemble this list of organizations and therefore has access to all UN registries of nongovernmental organizations. This is not likely to unduly bias the data because the Union has developed—over several decades—a deliberate and diversified strategy for identifying transnational organizations. Thus, most organizations that are even minimally active are not likely to be omitted for long, and organizations that are politically active are even less likely to be long unreported.

may help link national and even localized movements to global political processes.

The data presented here illustrate the broad dimensions of the sector, and they suggest at least six hypotheses that merit further investigation.

Hypothesis 1: *Transnational movement organizations will form around issues for which national political opportunity structures are relatively closed, or for which purely national solutions are inappropriate.* Movements attempting to promote the protection of human rights, womens' rights, and self determination—movements that essentially assert the political rights of excluded groups—are among the top transnational movement industries. Peace and world order industries, which deal with foreign policy issues, are movements also facing rather constrained opportunities to affect national policy, at least in contrast to movements targeting domestic issues (Pagnucco and Smith 1993). Although the environmental movement may have relatively open opportunities within national political structures (at least compared to other movements), environmental issues are increasingly out of national governments' control, and attempts to protect environmental resources must target multiple governments simultaneously.

Hypothesis 2: *Favorable international political opportunity structures, including new institutional opportunities within IGOs, contribute to the emergence of new TSMOs and other forms of transnational movement cooperation.* The growth in the number of environmental TSMOs in the aftermaths of two world environmental conferences supports this hypothesis.

Hypothesis 3: *Greater cooperation among TSMOs, IGOs, and NGOs can be expected as these actors increase their appreciation of the global nature of many problems and cultivate better understandings of multilateral political dynamics.* The overall tripling in the average number of TSMO links with IGOs and NGOs suggests a learning curve in transnational activism: Activists appear increasingly to recognize the global nature of the problems they address as well as the political need to coordinate social change efforts. Whether such ties will continue to fuel new organizational growth is yet unclear, but they clearly have implications for the strategies TSMOs adopt.

Hypothesis 4: *TSMOs' experiences should lead to more politically saavy global social movement action.* One manifestation of this is the expanded cooperation among TSMOs and other NGOs for common political goals. But political learning on the global stage should produce new conceptualizations of politics and appropriate strategies of influence, just as national activism has transformed movement strategies and tactics historically. Politics in the UN system often defy intuition: typically one must study or participate in them in order to understand their logics and avoid their many pitfalls. As TSMO organizers attempt to further their goals through global activism, they learn more about the formal and informal politics involved transnational mobilization and UN operations. We can therefore expect these groups to further modify their strategies both within and outside this complex institution.

Hypothesis 5: *As the field of transnational movement organizations working on a given issue expands, there will be greater competition for members and resources and slower growth or even organizational decline.* This hypothesis extrapolates more from research on national social movement sectors (Zald and McCarthy 1980) than from the transnational data presented here. But clearly the growth patterns outlined in this chapter will be shaped by dynamics internal to the transnational social movement sector itself, as well as by resource and political constraints from the environment.

Hypothesis 6: *TSMOs are becoming more decentralized as their memberships become increasingly localized (or grass-roots based) and as new technologies facilitate greater scope of participation in organizational decisions.* The organizational forms chosen by newer TSMOs differ from those of older generations, and groups formed within the last ten years were more likely to be coalitions or organizations of individuals than were older organizations. The advancement of communication and transportation technologies has made more decentralized organizational structures viable. These more decentralized structures, which allow for more intensive, two-way communication within transnational organizations, may contribute to more integrated and democratic participation in TSMOs.

Federated structures, while not the most commonly selected organizational form, were most able to cultivate ties with IGOs and NGOs, and they also enjoyed the most extensive numbers of countries of membership. In general, organizations of organizations were far more able than individual and professional organizations to cultivate these ties. Understandings of global political processes, moreover, suggest that such organizations will be most influential on global policy, and the preceding data show that they are more likely to survive. However, more detailed analyses—such as those in the following chapters—can expand understandings of transnational social movements' interactive role in global politics.

4

SOCIAL MOVEMENTS AND WORLD POLITICS

A Theoretical Framework

Jackie Smith, Ron Pagnucco, and Charles Chatfield

Abstract

Transnational social movements are efforts by clusters of relatively marginalized actors to promote some form of social or political change. Transnational social movement organizations have increasingly emerged to advance social movement goals. Movements promoting different goals not only vary in the actors they mobilize and in their degree of formal coordination but also face different political opportunities in national, intergovernmental, and transgovernmental decision-making arenas, and these factors influence the strategic choices they make. The intervention of transnational social movements in national, intergovernmental, and transgovernmental political processes alters decision makers' perceptions of problems and of the costs and benefits associated with different policy choices. Although social movements do not often realize their specific goals, they clearly impact global policy.

Social Movements in Global Environments

Social movements result when networks of actors relatively excluded from routine decision-making processes engage in collective attempts to change "some elements of the social structure and/or reward distribution of society" (McCarthy and Zald 1977, 1217).[1] Social movements

---

1. This chapter draws substantially from Smith's dissertation research (J. Smith 1995b).

may be said to be transnational when they involve conscious efforts to build transnational cooperation around shared goals that include social change. Through regular communication, organizations and activists are able to share technical and strategic information, coordinate parallel activities, or even to mount truly transnational collective action. Like national social movements, transnational ones incorporate a range of political actors, including individuals, church groups, professional associations, and other social groups. Movements are distinguished by the actors and resources they mobilize and in the extent to which they communicate, consult, coordinate, and cooperate in the international arena.

Previous chapters have described some of the sources of transnational social movements, relating them to new technological capabilities for mobilization as well as to increasing interdependencies among nation-states and to growing recognition of the need to address global problems cooperatively. Political scientists, especially those of the so-called realist tradition, have emphasized the obstacles to intergovernmental cooperation and the failures of intergovernmental organizations (IGOs) to resolve most global crises, but other scholars have observed the formation of large numbers of nongovernmental organizations (NGOs) and intergovernmental organizations (INGOs), including transnational social movement organizations (TSMOs), that promote international cooperation. A major theme of this book is that while some aspects of the international system hinder cooperation, transnational social movements and their organizations contribute various forms of political leverage needed to overcome systemic barriers to global problem solving. The impact of social movements on the political process is conditioned by their mobilizing structures; by the political opportunities inherent in national, intergovernmental, and nongovernmental contexts; and by strategies to mobilize resources to act.

Mobilizing Structures

Social movement organizations (SMOs) are those formal groups explicitly designed to promote specific social changes.[2] They are the principal carriers of social movements insofar as they mobilize new human and material resources, activating and coordinating strategic action throughout ebbs and flows of movement energy. They may link vari-

---

2. SMOs vary in their degree of *formalization*, or formally defined roles, rules and criterion of membership, and *centralization*, or the degree of concentration of decision-making power (see Gamson 1990).

ous elements of social movements, although their effectiveness in coordinating movement activities varies greatly according to patterns of organization and participation. For instance, individuals may participate in a social movement without being formally associated with an SMO, and professionals such as lawyers and scholars, whether or not they are affiliated with a movement organization, often play important roles in advancing goals of the movement or in focusing efforts of the movement on specific policy prescriptions. Organizations that are not formally established to work for movement aims may also become important—if transitory—parts of social movements, particularly during peaks of movement mobilization.

In contrast to social movement organizations within nation-states, transnational SMOs (TSMOs) incorporate members from more than two countries, have some formal structure, and coordinate strategy through an international secretariat. Their transnational membership structures facilitate communication and action across national borders as well as in intergovernmental institutions. Often they address issues that governments cannot resolve alone or in concert.

Typically, a movement seeks to involve large numbers of individuals and groups that are not routinely working for its goals. Accordingly, the possibilities for influence are defined by the social and political characteristics of the domestic or transnational society within which a movement operates. In chapter 1, Kriesberg described some of the critical changes in transnational society that have shaped transnational social movements. In addition, distinctly national patterns of social relations affect how resources and people are aggregated, coordinated, and activated for specific social changes. Although they are similar for all movements in a given society, some elements of them may be more appropriate than others to specific movements; and given the shifting salience of issues, some may be more active at some times than at others. These fundamental infrastructures that support and condition citizen mobilization are called movement *mobilizing structures*.

Table 4.1 draws from McCarthy (1996) to show the variety of different mobilizing structures that can contribute to transnational social movement activity. The first cell of the table displays a range of *informal, nonmovement* structures through which transnational movements can mobilize influence. National mobilizing structures are likely to include friendship and professional networks, or informal collections of individuals and / or organizations that because of social or work routines have either incidental or deliberate contact on a regular basis. However, their transnational importance has expanded with the expansion of travel and communication. In addition, officials in inter-

TABLE 4.1.

Dimensions of Transnational Movement Mobilizing Structures

	Nonmovement	Movement
Informal	Friendship networks	Activist networks
	Professional networks	Affinity groups
	Expatriate networks	Refugee networks
	Individuals in IGO bureaucracies or national delegations	
Formal	Churches	TSMOs
	Unions	SMOs (national)
	Professional associations	Protest committees
	Regional cooperative assoc.	Transnational NGO coalitions
	Service organizations	"Challenger" research institutes
	IGO bureaucracies	
	National delegations	
	Foundations	

Adapted from McCarthy 1996, 145.

governmental agencies and delegates on national missions to IGOs can be important channels of transnational mobilization. There are also distinctly transnational networks of people likely to be responsive to movement goals, such as refugees and émigré students or workers, who might bring pressure on their state of occupancy to modify policies vis-à-vis their home states (Cuban refugees in the United States, for example).

The *formal, nonmovement* cell in table 4.1 lists societal organizations likely to support nascent movements or to join broader campaigns. Some of them have grown out of earlier social movements (like unions and women's organizations, as Chatfield notes in chapter 2). Such formal organizations may be seen as sites for what Oberschall calls "block recruitment" for movements (1980; see also McCarthy 1996). When they support or join broader movement campaigns, they can bring large constituencies whose activism may enhance a movement's political impact. Moreover, churches, unions, and professional associations may at times provide protection from government repression or lend legitimacy to the movement.

Also, the aims of some intergovernmental organizational bureaucracies frequently overlap with those of social movements, and thus these structures may be fairly accessible for movement mobilization. The UN Human Rights Commission and High Commissioner for Refugees, for example, rely heavily on the work of human rights TSMOs to protect populations subject to human rights abuses. Although IGO structures do not carry a large base of popular support, cooperation with IGO bureaucracies can help advance movement aims by helping promote intergovernmental agreements on movement issues, transmitting political information to TSMOs, or ensuring nongovernmental organizations' access to world conferences. National delegations can often be mobilized as advocates for particular issues in intergovernmental organizations. For instance, chapter 12 shows the Dutch government's role in promoting the right to conscientious objection. Often, too, activists from TSMOs are asked to serve on their national delegations, and from these positions they can provide important access and information to their TSMO colleagues,[3] as is shown in chapter 7, below, which illustrates how the appointment of civil rights activists to the Carter administration's UN delegation helped advance human rights concerns in that forum.

The *informal, movement* dimension of mobilizing structures shown in table 4.1 consists of networks of activists or like-minded individuals. These networks are more readily mobilized because such individuals typically have common understandings of the relevant issues at stake and of appropriate actions, and they often have extensive contacts. Thus refugee networks, or links among political exiles, can be an important base of movement activity. As chapters 5 and 7 show, dissidents driven from their home countries may bring their struggle to a transnational context through TSMOs. Networks and organizations, whether informal or formal, tend to be linked to social movements and intergovernmental agencies in terms of congruent issues. Accordingly, some scholars group INGOs and TSMOs with IGOs as issue-oriented networks.

Formal movement structures consist of TSMOs, national SMOs (which may form temporary alliances with TSMOs or with SMOs from other countries), and transnational coalitions of NGOs designed to advance a particular movement goal, such as disarmament. Other formal movement structures include committees of other nongovernmental organizations that may be formed specifically to carry out a movement's

3. A considerable number of individuals move between IGO or government and social movement positions, bringing with them the expertise, professional contacts, and diplomatic knowledge and skills they cultivated in prior positions.

aims, as when a women's professional organization forms a special committee to protest abuses of women's rights. Challenger research institutes, designed to carry out research that provides a knowledge base that social change movements can use in their efforts to change government policies and popular practices, are another formal element of transnational movements' mobilizing structures. These research organizations produce scientific justifications for movement claims and technical background information for TSMOs' education campaigns. They may also help educate TSMO activists about intergovernmental political processes and issues, thereby providing them with technically appropriate policy proposals and other political ammunition for intergovernmental lobbying campaigns. Given the complexities of global social change issues and the political processes and interests surrounding these issues, such organizations may be essential movement allies.

Social movements vary dramatically in their *mobilizing structural configurations*, the number and strength of the actors they incorporate and the extent to which they are coordinated (McCarthy 1996). Some movements are represented by strong national (or transnational) umbrella organizations that help to coordinate action and provide a unified image of the movement. But the influence of a single organization on a movement varies over time, and it is rare that any organization will retain undisputed leadership. In some movements the actors are arrayed in such a way that they are less able to unite under a common organizational banner. Such movements remain more diffuse or reticulate in structure than do movements with strong centralizing organizations.

Another critical variable is the amount and combination of human, material, and political resources that movements bring to their efforts for social change. Money and members alone usually will not translate into political influence. Neither will the presence of political allies without the financial resources and activists to generate sustained political pressure. In addition, social movements often challenge the interests of other social groups, and they can generate opposition from countermovements. The strength and organization of the opposition to a social movement influences that movement's potential for political impact.[4] All such variables affect the impacts of social movements on global political processes.

4. Transnational social movements and the organizations that comprise them are not merely political lobbies: They are forums for generating intrasociety debate and consensus around the definition of a problem and its appropriate solution.

Issue Networks

The collection of actors involved in social movement efforts may be more or less tightly integrated through informal social networks and routines. Technologies that facilitate international communication and transportation have contributed to the development of transnational social movements and "issue networks" (Sikkink and Keck in press; Sikkink 1993). In Sikkink's definition, issue networks form from clusters of activists and movement organizations, policymakers, intergovernmental officials, media, and foundations pursuing a common, principled goal. Linked by a common interest in advancing a particular value, these networks aid communication and strategic coordination, thereby facilitating movement activity.

Sometimes actors in networks choose to create formal organizations, or coalitions, serving on either an ad hoc, temporary basis or a permanent basis to facilitate routine communication and to coordinate members' (usually organizations') activities. Coalitions may be formed to focus the actions of diverse organizations and to enhance the movement's efficient use of resources. At the same time, serious obstacles to long-term coalition work may result from disagreements about strategy and resource allocations, as well as from coalition members' own resource limitations (Kleidman 1993; Staggenborg 1986). Coalitions typically form around campaigns, which are deliberate efforts to coordinate movement actions around a particular policy or event and thereby to extend the movement's message beyond its elite and informed publics to a more general audience (Chatfield 1992). Chatfield (1969), for instance, describes such coalitional efforts in his analysis of U.S. pacifist organizations in the interwar period. By creating structured communication links between movements and other societal organizations, coalitions help to disseminate movement frames, or definitions of problems and proposed solutions, into more general public debate, thereby shaping evolving public opinion on a particular issue.

The concept of issue networks is attracting attention among international relations scholars, and it is especially useful for linking social movement organizations with allied elites in governmental and intergovernmental agencies, in the media, or in business. Contributors to this volume focus on transnational social movements and their agencies (TSMs and TSMOs), however, because these concepts problematize the dynamic interactions *within* issue networks. All actors in a network are concerned about their relative strength and independence; for example; all bring to their common issue area distinct constituencies and other resources; and many have other agendas as well. Consequently their respective strategies may complement or contest one another.

Structures of Opportunity

The social and political environments in which movements operate are characterized by a variety of "opportunity structures," factors that facilitate or constrain social change efforts. For instance, the extent to which human rights to political expression and association are respected within a country affects the risks and costs, and therefore the possibilities, for mobilization (Tarrow 1994; Wiltfang and McAdam 1991); national tax laws affect groups' mobilizing potential, as they affect fundraising possibilities (McCarthy et al. 1991; McCarthy and Zald 1973); and rules of access and state enforcement procedures further define the possibilities for movements to affect policy (Kitschelt 1986; Kriesi et al. 1995; Risse-Kappen 1995). Finally, broader cultural themes and social values condition the possible appeal of movements' social change frameworks (Snow and Benford 1988; Johnston and Klandermans 1995). Movement actors must respond to these opportunity structures even as they work to alter them.

It is necessary to consider the factors that define the opportunities for collective political action in three distinct but clearly related arenas: the national, intergovernmental, and transgovernmental. Although social movement scholars have elaborated frameworks for thinking about national "structures of political opportunity," and a few have considered broader cultural and social opportunities (e.g., Rucht 1996; Pagnucco and McCarthy 1992), they have not accounted for the role of international political processes in social movement activity.

Studies of national movements are limited to examinations of institutions and influence patterns characterizing national policymaking processes. When we attempt to explain global policy processes, however, we must account not only for national but also for intergovernmental decision-making structures and cultural contexts, which may involve procedures, rules of access, constellations of allies and adversaries, and systems of meaning and value that are very different from those in national arenas. And because social movements also target nongovernmental actors, the social and political contexts of transnational movements themselves are also relevant.

Three major political settings for decision making—the national, the intergovernmental, and the transgovernmental arenas—structure the opportunities to institutionalize social movement action. National political arenas shape definitions of national interest such as governmental positions in bilateral and multilateral negotiations, and on decisions regarding the implementation of international agreements. Intergovernmental arenas are the venue of multilateral negotiations and international agencies. Here, mainly, is where formal multinational agreements and operational programs are negotiated. Here also is the primary source of international regimes, those broadly assumed norms of collective behavior and institutions that structure the relations and communications among governments.

By *transgovernmental arenas* we mean the contribution to decision making and policy formation that comes from the bureaucracies of intergovernmental agencies as they interact with experts and interest groups in and outside of governments.[5] Decision makers in this arena are typically intergovernmental and national bureaucrats charged with implementing (or stonewalling) international agreements. Although bureaucrats are formally under instructions from higher political authorities, the technical nature of their jobs often allows them some freedom in performing their tasks. They develop relationships with relevant experts or interest groups possessing information and constituencies that can help them with their official duties (see McCarthy and Wolfson 1992, also see chaps. 11 and 13 below). Accordingly, although IGOs are the agents of governments, they are at the same time transnational agencies largely independent of any single government.

These interrelated decision points represent nodes of international decision-making webs rather than peaks of a hierarchical policymaking process. Although interdependent, each of these arenas manifests a unique set of access rules, political alliances, elite interests, and norms, and each therefore demands different approaches by movements seeking to influence it. Thus, movement strategies should vary according to the political arena(s) they target, and each strategy will likely demand different kinds of resources and skills (Burstein et al. 1995). Movements may, at various times, target one or more of these arenas in attempting to influence governments' definitions of international policy (see chap. 10), shape international agendas or the dynamics of bilateral or multilateral negotiations themselves (see chaps. 8, 12, and 13), or foster compliance with intergovernmental agreements by, for instance, monitoring and reporting on governments' behavior (see chaps. 5, 6, and 7).

Within each political arena, several factors affect movement poten-

5. We use the term *transgovernmental arena* to emphasize the decision-making role of intergovernmental agencies and also to include the role of nongovernmental ones, rather than strictly relations among elements of national governments and of IGOs. Our use of the term is consistent with that of Keohane and Nye (1972, 382).

tial for influence, including the institutions that define formal and informal access to policymaking, the stability of broad political alignments, the presence or absence of influential allies or support groups in the environment, splits in the governing elite, and changing norms (Tarrow 1988). As the following case studies show, the ability of social movement actors to take advantage of openings in national, intergovernmental, and transgovernmental opportunity structures varies across issue and time.

National Arenas

Increasing global interdependence, coupled with the emergence of institutions that move decisions of relevance further from local populations, forces social movements and other actors to target political arenas beyond those of single states. Many TSMOs work to foster the convergence of national decisions around certain goals by coordinating national pressure for a desired policy. For instance, Amnesty International sometimes organizes simultaneous demonstrations at the embassies of a government that abuses human rights in order to press other governments to take some action against it.

Transnational action is complicated by the fact that different national contexts offer varying opportunities for, and constraints on, social movement mobilization and political action. Each, for instance, requires that activists adapt to distinctive patterns of elite conflicts, potential alliances, institutional access, and changes in social norms. But national contexts can also be influenced by governments' awareness of movement pressures on other governments. This was true in the 1980s mobilizations in Western Europe against new NATO deployments of intermediate range nuclear weapons, which somewhat limited Reagan's ability to define West European security needs and reinforced the aims of the nuclear freeze movement in the United States (Cortright 1993). By coordinating pressures on national governments, movements also seek to bolster a government's confidence that other governments will pursue policies similar to its own. For instance, the broad transnational mobilization in defense of Nigerian playwright and environmental justice leader Ken Saro-Wiwa very likely played a role in generating the almost unanimous and immediate international condemnation of his execution.

Intergovernmental Arenas

Intergovernmental relations are increasingly characterized by an interrelated system of institutions that govern interactions among states and facilitate collective problem solving. Routine forums such as the United Nations General Assembly or the European Parliament provide regular means for governments to bring attention to problems requiring international action and to initiate collective attempts to resolve them. As chapter 8 shows, special global conferences present opportunities for movements to influence multilateral negotiations by at least heightening the sense of urgency on issues such as disarmament. Treaty mandated review conferences and regular meetings of specialized intergovernmental agencies such as the UN Human Rights Commission also provide opportunities for TSMOs to draw attention to the issues they seek to influence and to alter governments' perceptions of the costs and benefits associated with inaction.

The structure and purpose of intergovernmental organizations has meant that actors within IGOs value transnational organizations for their ability to aggregate interests across national boundaries and to help generate options for resolving conflicts, thus facilitating intergovernmental policymaking (Streek and Schmitter 1991). To further their own global conflict resolution work, IGOs such as the United Nations have established formal mechanisms to facilitate cooperation with TSMOs and other nongovernmental organizations. The task of serving a global constituency is simplified when the interests of citizens are organized (Andersen and Eliassen 1991; Bomberg 1993; McLaughlin et al. 1993). Therefore, the more a movement can aggregate popular interests into concrete policy demands, the more effective it should be at coordinating global strategy and utilizing the political opportunities created by intergovernmental institutions. Chapters 12 and 13 especially illustrate the close relationships between some TSMOs and IGOs; chapter 9, in contrast, shows how bilateral antagonism between the United States and Soviet Union may have inhibited transnational movement efforts focused on multilateral institutions. Intergovernmental organizations can also be structured in ways that limit TSMO intervention in multilateral political processes, as chapter 11 shows in the case of the environmental movement and the European Union.

Intergovernmental institutions, although the locus of multilateral decision making, typically lack reliable mechanisms for enforcing international agreements. By serving as monitors or as direct providers of humanitarian assistance, TSMOs are the eyes, ears, and hands of some intergovernmental agencies. As such, they report states' violations of human rights norms and help ensure that human needs are met. Chapters 5 and 7 illustrate the former task by describing how human rights TSMOs utilized international reporting mechanisms to bring international pressure on countries violating human rights norms. Chapter 6 shows how the ability of TSMOs to reach threatened populations and even the dynamics of the Ethiopian civil war during the 1980s were affected by differences in TSMO definitions of neutrality.

Extra-Institutional Contexts

In sum, political opportunity for TSMOs is structured by the national, intergovernmental, and transgovernmental arenas in which they operate. Beyond these institutional contexts, however, and in each arena, the potential for influence is affected by social and cultural contexts (Rucht 1996)—including even values, beliefs, and patterns of behavior that movements seek to change. Thus it makes a difference whether or not a movement's goals are consistent with values widely shared in the population it seeks to mobilize (Snow and Benford 1988). Patterns of association affect a movement's capacity to activate adherents (McPhail and Tucker 1968). Local and national structures of association and the operational procedures of the media affect opportunities to influence public and political agendas (McCarthy et al. 1996). Opportunity for TSMOs is relative to multiple contexts, both institutional and cultural.

In a similar vein, Wapner shows that environmental movement efforts at local—as opposed to governmental—levels of human activity can be

> rooted in the actual experiences of people, as a form of governance. It can alter the way people interact with each other and their environment, literally to change the way they live their lives. To the degree that such efforts have ramifications for wider arenas of social interaction—including states and other actors—they have world political significance (1995, 336).

Thus, while many studies—including several in this volume—emphasize the "high politics" of transnational social movement activity in explicitly political arenas, the "deep politics" of shaping individuals' thinking and actions on environmental, peace, development, and other issues clearly occupy much, if not most, social movement energies.

Movement Strategies and Frames

Movement mobilizing structures and opportunity structures determine the general contexts for movement action, but within these parameters, movement actors face a range of strategic choices that may have consequences for global policy processes and political outcomes.

Should they focus on an imminent policy decision on the intergovernmental agenda, for example, or attempt to raise new issues onto the
table? Should they lobby decision-making elites or mobilize popular
political pressure? An important purpose of this book is to document
some of the various strategies that movements have generated while
working within (and in some cases outside of) rapidly evolving intergovernmental institutional and normative frameworks.

Movement strategies are designed to maximize the effectiveness of
collective efforts to affect policy processes or to otherwise alter the
political environment. In carrying out their political goals, SMOs must
employ two distinct strategic programs, namely, a mobilizing strategy
and an action strategy. Mobilizing strategies attempt to attract new
activists and resources for the cause or to energize existing adherents
and resources. These strategies focus on maintaining the resources and
organizational procedures essential for generating collective political
action.

In order to mobilize and activate adherents, social movement actors
must devise interpretive frames that process political information, interpreting certain conditions as problems in need of attention and
conveying the need and potential efficacy of collective attempts to
address the problem (Snow et al. 1986; Johnston and Klandermans
1995). Indeed, many social movement activities, including public education and media campaigns, leafletting and public demonstrations
can be considered "frame dissemination tactics" aimed at attracting
new adherents or activating passive sympathizers (McCarthy et al.
1995). Chapter 6, below, dramatizes how the different ways that
TSMOs "framed" neutrality influenced their abilities to retain donor
constituents, their strategies, and their effectiveness in the field.

Action strategies, on the other hand, are the activities that social
movements employ in order to influence policy. For instance,
Greenpeace's mobilizing strategy involves dramatizing the plight of
endangered animal species in order to attract and motivate members
and to generate financial support for political action work. Its action
strategy, however, frequently targets issues only indirectly related to
wildlife preservation. And groups like Amnesty International spend
much effort to recruit and educate members as they engage them in
actions pressing governments to observe international human rights
standards.

A critical component of movement action strategies is what Tilly
(1984) has labelled "repertoires of contention," or standard collections
of tactics that a given population recognizes as possible means of influencing political or other authorities. Clearly, the trends described by
Kriesberg in chapter 1 have contributed to the emergence of a globally

recognized repertoire of contention, even as some tactics, such as letter writing or petitioning, apparently are irrelevant in some national
contexts.

Most TSMOs have minimal or no contact with intergovernmental
agencies, as chapter 3 indicates. Such organizations often find their
aims better met through noninstitutional efforts to change social beliefs, values, or practices. They may choose such a strategy, moreover,
because it is deemed a more effective way to meet group aims, because
the group lacks the skills, knowledge, or other resources needed to
work in intergovernmental arenas, or because these institutions do not
present opportunities to affect the changes the group seeks. Indeed,
many TSMOs carry out activities such as promoting dialogue among
nongovernmental actors from many states and otherwise sharing and
processing ideas and action strategies. And even those groups attending international conferences such as the "Earth Summit," held in
Rio in 1992, do so more to network and learn from other NGOs in the
nongovernmental segment of the conference than to try to influence
the formal proceedings (see Quizon 1991, 205–6).

In this sense, a primary goal of many TSMOs may be to build
transnational solidarity beyond state boundaries—in other words, to
give people a global, trans-state identity in which a higher loyalty (e.g.,
to a TSMO's membership or to global priorities generally) prevails.
For instance, environmental groups may try to change patterns of
consumption and disposal rather than hope for changes in the economic or policy arena to protect the environment. And groups like
War Resisters International (WRI) promote goals that directly challenge state authority: encouraging people to refuse to fight for their
state, WRI supports nonviolent noncooperation predicated on the notion that if enough people refuse to fight there will be no more wars.
Regular communication among like-minded people from different
countries, which can check ethnocentric interpretations of events, cultivate a sensitivity to the needs and experiences of persons from different regions, and provide alternative sources of information. TSMOs,
then, serve as vehicles for the diffusion of values, frames, tactics, and
practices among different national populations. Such diffusion is,
moreover, an action strategy difficult for most governments to control.

Coupled with a growth in transnational social movements' organizational strength is a rise in the number of failed or challenged states
whose authority is resisted, often by violent means. Two such cases—
Ethiopia and Sri Lanka—appear among the studies in this book. Such
conditions present new challenges to human rights groups, many of
which are organized to insure that governments protect individual
human rights and other values. Such groups are now faced with the

question of how to hold nongovernmental actors accountable to international norms. For some of these human rights groups, autonomy from governments provides access to parties in conflicts that would otherwise be denied. This was the case, for instance, in Somalia, where the Mennonite Central Committee's conciliation team was able to build ties to local leaders largely because it was not seen as part of other international governmental interventions (Lederach 1995).

Thus, although the following case studies focus (disproportionately perhaps) on how transnational social movement actors intervene in institutionalized global politics, we note that many groups do not utilize IGOs or even national governments in their efforts for social change. If they see governments as nonresponsive or intergovernmental agencies as too complex or difficult to reach, organizers often choose alternative paths to the changes they seek. Instead, such groups focus on changing people's views and behaviors and directly pressing economic actors to change their practices (see Wapner 1995).

Those TSMOs that do choose to pursue institutionalized politics as a path toward change face a number of choices as well. Because multilateral politics is essentially composed of multiple layers of decision making, TSMOs seeking to influence it can target a variety of national, intergovernmental, and transgovernmental political arenas. The structure of an organization and the resources available to it will condition its range of choices.

Roles and Impacts of Transnational Social Movements

Emerging research suggests that movements are important actors in global politics. The cases examined in this volume contribute to this understanding, demonstrating how social movement actors intervene in national, intergovernmental, and transgovernmental political arenas to influence the practices of governments. Few social movements are successful if by "success" is meant that they achieved specific policy changes. However, there are several ways transnational social movements can and do influence the outcomes of international political decisions. First, movements focus the attention of elites and the general public on important global concerns. By facilitating transnational communication, TSMOs help to generate consensus around particular frames, or interpretations of global problems and their solutions. This consensus may help governments to modify their policies and endorse multilateral programs.

Second, TSMOs help governments learn about a problem, or at least about the political costs of failing to act on it. Intervening in national, intergovernmental, and transgovernmental political arenas, some

TSMOs provide political information to delegates about the nature of a problem and possible responses to it, about public opinion on the issue, or about the negotiations themselves. Utilizing their transnational communication networks, TSMOs can assemble information critical to verifying government compliance with agreements.

Third, the presence of TSMOs in global political processes enhances government accountability. Because few governments—even democratic ones—allow for broad public participation in their foreign policy processes, most international decision making occurs with little public accountability. As the following case studies demonstrate, it is increasingly clear that transnational social movements influence the outcomes of international relations at least by interacting in and shaping the *political processes* that generate global policy.

Social Movements and Global Politics

With this anthology the editors attempt to apply concepts from political sociology to the study of global political processes. Our approach therefore owes an intellectual debt to scholars who have enhanced our understanding of international and transnational politics. In contrast to classical, state-centric approaches to international relations theory, our approach builds on the following core assumptions to develop a framework of global politics that helps to account for the presence of transnational social movements. We understand that states are complex institutions that hardly fit a conception of them as unitary actors. We assume that domestic and international political processes are increasingly related, making rigid distinctions between them inappropriate. Finally, we emphasize the increasingly obvious point that states do not monopolize global political processes. Rather, they interact with a range of other actors and are influenced by institutional processes.

Work in the early 1970s, particularly that of Keohane and Nye (1972) and of Feld (1972), highlighted the fact that transnational actors "contaminated" international relations models to such an extent that international policy outcomes could often not be explained without accounting for them (Keohane and Nye 1972, xxv). Both of these studies graphically displayed notions of patterns of international and transnational interactions, as in Feld's adaptation of Keohane and Nye's diagram below (1972, 13). This model illustrates the interactive dynamics within societies and between them as well as those between social, governmental, and intergovernmental actors. Classical interpretations of international relations account for only the upper part of the diagram, namely interactions between governments and IGOs. The recog-

FIGURE 4.1.

Network of Transnational and Intranational Relations and Interactions Involving Nongovernmental and Governmental Actors

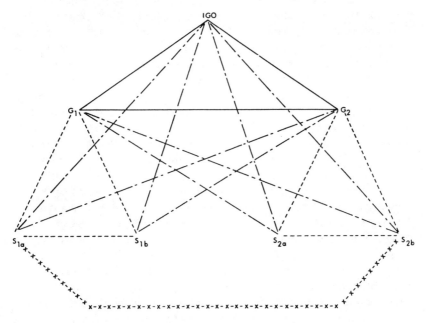

International relations and interactions - - - - - - -
Classical intergovernmental relations and interactions ————
Transnational relations and interactions between
    nongovernmental actors and governmental actors — · — · — · —
Transnational relations and interactions between
    nongovernmental actors x - x - x - x

From Feld 1972, 13.

nition that nongovernmental and transnational actors intervene in international and multilateral relations expands the interactive network considerably.

Beginning in the 1970s, international relations scholars focused increasingly on the institutional arrangements and informal practices that conditioned interactions among governments and transnational or other nonstate actors. They realized that much of international relations was indeed orderly, patterned, and predictable, despite the absence of a force that could govern relations among governments.

Scholars focusing on international regimes (see, e.g., Krasner 1983; Keohane 1984; Haggard and Simmons 1987; Young 1989) saw the increasing prevalence of "sets of implicit or explicit principles, norms, rules, and decision-making procedures around which actors' expectations converge in a given area of international relations" (Krasner 1983, 2). These are manifest in intergovernmental agencies and less formal institutions such as ad hoc intergovernmental conferences, as well as in multilateral treaties, conventions, and resolutions.

Functional theorists, including Mitrany (1966, 1975) and Taylor (1975, 1991), also have developed an understanding of international political processes that subordinates states' predominant role to more complex interactive processes evolving from task-specific international cooperative efforts. Scholars like E. Haas (1964), avoided the normative emphases of earlier functionalists, focusing primarily on the organizational dynamics of IGOs and their impacts on states' perceptions and policy choices. This perspective implicitly recognized what early "interdependence" theorists (e.g., Keohane 1977) made explicit: namely, that some global issues demanded cooperative international efforts and reduced government autonomy. Moreover, interdependence assumes that developments in technology, the environment, and the economy will make international coordination and cooperation ever more imperative.

A second assumption of our framework is that states themselves represent aggregations of a variety of contrasting interests and should not be treated merely as unitary actors in global politics. Pressure groups acting in national political arenas press political leaders and administrators to favor certain policies over others, and increasingly they bring pressure on national decision makers to adopt particular positions on intergovernmental policy choices.

Putnam (1988) partly accounted for this dynamic with his notion of multilateral politics as a "two-level game," in which international and national policymaking contexts are affected by interdependent national and multilateral decision-making processes.[6] Each state comes to the international decision-making "game" with a position (more or less clearly and firmly articulated) on the issue at stake in the respective intergovernmental negotiations. This position, which frequently constrains governments' negotiating space, is largely the outcome of struggles at the national level over appropriate policy choices. A number of TSMOs attempt to influence governmental decisions by building

---

6. Putnam's (1989) model exaggerates the independence of multilateral decision-making processes from nonstate pressures (see also Knopf 1993; Risse-Kappen 1995a, 16).

transnational cooperation to support dissident positions within a country, by bringing pressure from citizens outside a country on that government, or by linking national groups or individuals in a network of information exchange that facilitates their struggles to shape their nation's international policies (see Risse-Kappen 1995).

Our third core assumption is that domestic and international political processes are increasingly interdependent. As arrangements develop for regional economic integration, such as the European Union or the North American Free Trade Agreement, what once were purely "domestic" decisions will have increasing international significance, and vice versa. Thus, national and transnational actors can be seen making more attempts to influence decision-making processes.

The following case studies discuss the impacts of transnational social movements on global political processes. The first cluster of cases illustrates how movements mobilize transnational resources to influence national conflicts. By building ties with transnational actors, national social movement actors in these cases altered their political leverage vis-à-vis governments. The most immediate consequence of such transnational mobilization was the greater protection of activists from further human rights abuses. A second set of cases examines how transnational social movements worked to mobilize new constituencies into multilateral policy processes. Finally, a third group of cases highlights direct attempts of transnational social movements to influence multilateral decision-making processes. These cases emphasize the relationships among TSMOs and intergovernmental institutions, exploring the extent to which movements can exert various forms of leverage on the international system.

PART TWO

Mobilizing Transnational Resources
in National Conflicts

5

COOPERATIVE ACCOMPANIMENT AND PEACE BRIGADES INTERNATIONAL IN SRI LANKA

Patrick Coy

Abstract

International nonviolent protective accompaniment is a technique used by Peace Brigades International (PBI) to protect threatened human rights activists in Sri Lanka. PBI's accompaniment in two different cases shows how the strategic use of information by PBI helped to increase the safety of local activists. One case, that of an individual human rights activist, demonstrates the importance of coordination and networking as a threatened human rights activist fashioned working relationships with human rights organizations. Another case, that of members of a grassroots organization promoting nonviolent change shows that international networking and protective accompaniment extended the choices available to members of a grassroots group under threat, making it more possible for exiled leaders of the group to return to Sri Lanka and continue working for social and political change.

Human rights and nonviolent activists face a dizzying array of threats to their well-being.[1] Although astute activists may know how to exploit the political dynamics of these threats and turn them to their advantage, they may not always be able or choose to do so. Although

1. I gratefully acknowledge the support of the Albert Einstein Institution Fellows Program in the research and writing of this paper and in a broader project on Peace Brigades International. The findings and opinions expressed herein are mine alone and not necessarily those of the Institution. I also thank Steven Burgess, the editors of this anthology, and especially Ed Kinane for helpful comments.

structural remedies that address the roots of political violence are the preferred long-term solution, some short-term tactical responses that may facilitate the eventual implementation of structural solutions. International nonviolent protective accompaniment, one such technique, rests on the idea that the presence of unarmed international escorts alongside local activists can deter attacks. Violence and threats directed at foreign nationals, or those they are escorting, often result in higher political costs for the transgressors than the same actions directed at unaccompanied local citizens.

When members of a clan accompanied each other to the local watering hole for protection thousands of years ago, they were using simple protective accompaniment tactics. Like so much else in the early history of nonviolent action, these first applications were likely spontaneous and intuitive developments (Sharp 1973, 101). But accompaniment tactics evolved, becoming more complicated as human interactions grew and as people gradually learned more about the technique. Social movement history reveals that today's nonviolent tactics are often modifications or revivals of previously popular tactics (Oliver 1989). In the twentieth century, social movements committed to nonviolence began refining protective accompaniment techniques in a variety of contexts. Some of the most prominent examples come from the U.S. civil rights movement.

In the 1947 Journey of Reconciliation, for instance, eight blacks accompanied by eight whites rode buses through the Upper South to test a 1946 Supreme Court decision outlawing segregated seating on interstate travel. Sponsored by the Fellowship of Reconciliation and the Congress on Racial Equality, it was a forerunner of the more famous "Freedom Rides" through the Deep South in 1961, testing integrated seating on interstate bus travel and the integration of bus terminal facilities (Farmer 1985). The Freedom Summer of 1964, organized by the Student Nonviolent Coordinating Committee (SNCC), brought nearly one thousand young white volunteers from the North to Mississippi to work alongside the mostly black SNCC fieldworkers attempting to register blacks to vote. The organizers calculated that the presence of whites would decrease the likelihood of violence and make it easier to turn to their advantage any violence that did occur (Sitkoff 1981).

Escorting opposition politicians or human rights activists from exile back to their home countries is not uncommon. Well-known examples include the violence-marked return of Benigno Aquino to the Philippines in 1983, and of Kim Dae Jung to South Korea in 1985 (Weston 1985). Peace Brigades International (PBI) escorted Rigoberta Menchu to Guatemala on five occasions prior to her receipt of the Nobel Peace

Prize in 1992. More generally, PBI's team in Guatemala has helped increase the political space necessary for dissident groups to grow and flourish, especially in the case of the Mutual Support Group for the Disappeared (Coy 1993; Mahony and Eguren 1997). Witness for Peace placed foreign nationals around Jalapa and throughout Nicaragua in the 1980s, attempting to deter an invasion of Nicaragua by counterrevolutionary forces or by the United States (Griffin-Nolan 1991). Weber (1993) concluded that small-scale initiatives like these hold great promise for relevancy and effectiveness.

Accompaniment forms vary, going beyond simply escorting threatened individuals. The International Committee of the Red Cross (ICRC) visits political detainees to provide them with international visibility and protection from abuse while imprisoned (Blondel 1987). Amnesty International, and the International Committee of Jurists send international observers to trials where the rights of the accused are likely to be abrogated, or where human rights violations are raised (Ray and Taylor 1977; Weissbrodt 1982). Newmann and Weissbrodt (1990) claim that these visits can have a substantial impact on fair treatment being accorded the defendant.

Yet another variant of the accompaniment tactic is used by international organizations like the United Nations (UN) and the Organization of American States (OAS), which send international observers to oversee elections where political intimidation, violence, or election rigging is probable. Sometimes, as in Haiti in 1993, these observer missions are not tied directly to elections, but rather they monitor human rights, opening space for political activity and facilitating the return of exiled political leaders like the deposed president Aristide. The UN and OAS abruptly removed their observers from Haiti in mid-October, 1993 in the face of rampant violence and repeated failures of the initiatives of international governmental organizations. That left the observers from Cry for Justice (a coalition of NGOs that included PBI) as the only international presence in large areas of the countryside.

Sri Lanka's parliamentary election period of July-August 1994 was marked by heavy levels of political violence and intimidation, including thousands of violent incidents and over twenty election-related murders (Inform 1994; Perera 1994). In response, Sri Lankan nongovernmental organizations (NGOs) set up a grassroots citizens' poll watch, with cooperation from the International Human Rights Law Group and PBI, who provided international observers and escorts to accompany the local monitoring teams (Coy 1994; International Human Rights Law Group 1994).

Peace Brigades International is a TSMO specializing in international protective accompaniment. It was founded in 1981 by Gandhians and Quakers long active in international peace efforts. Significant deployments of PBI teams include Guatemala (1983-present), El Salvador (1987–1992), Sri Lanka (1989-present), Canada (1993-present), Colombia (1994-present) and Haiti (1995-present). PBI teams usually enter a region upon the invitation of an organization engaged in nonviolent struggle. Operating where political space is contested and democratic freedoms are compromised, PBI adopts a stance of nonpartisanship as it aids local activists attempting to secure political space within which human rights and nonviolent struggle may be more safely exercised. The organization has pioneered a model of nonviolent protective accompaniment by volunteer foreign nationals (Wiseberg 1991; Coy 1993, 1995).[2]

Functioning as international observers, PBI escorts are committed to and trained in nonviolence. Armed with cameras, notebooks, and sometimes cellular phones, they accompany only those who disavow the use of violence.[3] Their presence may reduce the potential for violence and, in any event, allows PBI to publicize eyewitness accounts of violent incidents. The eyewitness nature of the accounts increases their credibility and significance: to be able to say, "We were there and we saw . . ." amplifies a message considerably (Weissbrodt and McCarthy 1981).

Typical recipients of PBI accompaniment include journalists, trade unionists, human rights workers, indigenous peoples, health workers, refugee communities, religious figures, opposition politicians, and local NGOs under threat from governments or parastate organizations as a result of their nonviolent activities.

Protective accompaniment by PBI takes many forms, depending on the social and political dynamics of the conflict, the nature of the perceived threat, the recipient's preferences, and PBI's resources in the field. PBI's international escorts may provide constant, twenty-four-hour accompaniment. In other cases, they may be present only when a local activist engages in public actions and feels under increased threat. Or PBI personnel may simply make conspicuous visits to an organization's offices or an activist's home. These unpredictable visits are designed to heighten the international visibility of the local activist, thereby increasing the safe political space within which the activist can operate.

The deterrent value of the accompaniment depends upon clear and

2. Other NGOs, especially the Shanti Sena in India, have long done similar nonviolent interventionary work, but largely in a domestic context relying on local activists (see Weber 1993).

3. A grant from the European-based NGO Forum supporting PBI's escorting of election monitors in Sri Lanka allowed it to introduce cellular phones to its nonviolent action toolkit.

regular communications between PBI and governments, police and military forces, or paramilitary groups thought to be somehow responsible for the threat (Eguren 1994; Mahony 1997). Potential violators of human rights must understand that adverse publicity generated by PBI can bring increased domestic and international political costs in response to an attack.[4]

Like most transnational social movement organizations (TSMOs), PBI utilizes a number of institutional mechanisms to enhance its influence in the global political arena. The organization publishes a sixteen-page *Project Bulletin* ten times each year. Written by PBI teams in the field, it reports on their work while analyzing the politics and state of human rights in the countries where they are operating. Just as important may be the *Bulletin's* regular profiles of and interviews with local activists, which give voice to activists in the global South whose political struggles are often ignored by an international media dominated by Northern interests (Muzaffar 1992).

PBI has built an Emergency Response Network (ERN) consisting of about six thousand people across the globe who are linked through computer and telephone networks. ERN members receive action requests about threats and violent incidents facing PBI teams or those with whom they work. They then send letters, telexes, faxes and phone calls to government officials and others, calling for the correction of the perceived injustices. These communications tell perpetrators of political violence, "The eyes of the world are upon you."

A useful response network must be regularly maintained and updated, have clear commitments from its members to respond, and use the latest in computer technology, automated fax and telex generation, and delivery services. The availability of this technology is one of the reasons for the increased power and influence wielded by some TSMOs in global politics (Dorsey 1993).

Human Rights and Accompaniment in Sri Lanka

Long-running ethnic tensions in Sri Lanka exploded into overt civil conflict in 1983. The mainly Hindu Tamil minority (17 percent) came under severe attack by the largely Buddhist Sinhalese majority (74 percent) in July 1983. The rage ran its course in less than a month, leaving over 3,000 Tamils dead and turning close to 150,000 into refugees.

4. One of the most violent police attacks on PBI clients in Sri Lanka's Free Trade Zone (a frequent site of labor unrest and PBI escorting) resulted at least partly from the failure of the PBI team to directly communicate with and explain its mission to police officials in the Zone (Coy 1995).

Before July 1983, only small sectors of the Tamil community—primarily in the north and the east of the island—worked for an independent Tamil state in Sri Lanka. Some, particularly the Liberation Tigers of Tamil Eelam (LTTE), embraced armed insurrection. After the 1983 ethnic riots, however, much larger numbers of Sri Lankan Tamils agitated for an independent or semi-independent homeland, and many accepted armed struggle and terror tactics as a means of obtaining this goal (Hoole et al. 1992; UTHR 1992). In response, the Sinhalese-dominated government instituted a series of repressive internal security measures aimed primarily at the Tamil minority.

Meanwhile, a second front was opened up in the south against the embattled government by Sinhalese nationalists known as the Janatha Vimukthi Permuna (JVP). Revolutionary Marxism mixed with Buddhist-Sinhalese chauvinism in the JVP to create a peculiar political force bent on revolution. An Indo-Lanka Peace Accord was signed between Sri Lanka and India in July 1987, introducing an Indian peacekeeping force in the Tamil-dominated north. The JVP exploited anti-India and anti-accord sentiments in the Sinhalese population and stepped up their revolutionary activities, including assassination, intimidation, torture, and other terror tactics (Chandraprema 1991).

In response to the twin threats it faced, the Sri Lankan government and its agents employed tactics that Sloan (1984) has called "enforcement terrorism," including summary executions, disappearances, secret arrests, torture, and prolonged imprisonment without trial.[5] Many reliable estimates put the dead and disappeared related to the JVP rebellion at around 30,000.

The JVP rebellion was largely crushed by 1991, but the government's war with the LTTE continued unabated into 1995. Emergency Regulations and the Prevention of Terrorism Act are still in place, severely curtailing civil liberties (Hyndman et al. 1994, 48–64). Secret arrests and unlawful detention, combined with extortion and torture, are widely experienced by the Tamil minority at the hands of the Sinhalese-dominated police and military (Amnesty International 1994;

---

5. For international reports on general human rights conditions in Sri Lanka, see the reports of Amnesty International and Asia Watch. Also helpful is the Report of the UN Working Group on Enforced or Involuntary Disappearances, wherein the situation in Sri Lanka was termed the "worst ever" in the records of the Working Group (UN Working Group on Disappearances 1992). For domestic documents, see the reports of the nongovernmental groups INFORM and the Civil Rights Movement and the governmental Human Rights Task Force. An illuminating documentation of a significant case from this period is Batty Weerakoon's booklet, *The Xtra-judicial Xecution of Richard de Soysa* (1991, Colombo, Sri Lanka, self-published).

UTHR 1993). And although the number of disappearances has dropped significantly, they were still occurring as of 1995.

When PBI was first invited to Sri Lanka in 1989, very little political space existed there. The term *little political space* means that those who engage in even minimal oppositional political activity, human rights documentation and promotion, independent and critical media activities, trade union organizing, or other grass roots organizing are persecuted and under threat. It may also mean that those who simply express opinions critical of the governing regime risk violations of their fundamental civil and political liberties.

In Sri Lanka in 1989 human rights organizing was so suspect and political space was so closed that lawyers who were merely filing habeas corpus cases for the families of the disappeared and the arrested were themselves threatened and even disappeared. The Sri Lanka Bar Association invited PBI to provide accompaniment for those few lawyers still willing to take on fundamental human rights cases.

Governments repressing their own populations are reluctant to permit entry to groups seeking to expose and mitigate human rights violations. Therefore, PBI often sends its staff into countries under tourist visas, without identifying their organizational connections. Once in the country, and after establishing broad contacts among diplomats and domestic and international NGOs, PBI then approaches the local government with its organizational mandate, only then negotiating official status and terms of entry and residency.

This process may take months or years, during which time PBI continues its work in an unofficial, and at times even semiclandestine manner. Every situation is different, but relevant factors influencing whether and when a TSMO gains official status include the degree of governmental repression, the government's experience with international human rights monitoring, the status and prestige of the particular TSMO, the government's dependence upon and vulnerability to trade partner and donor nation pressures; the specific international human rights norms signed by the host nation and the degree to which the nation is "nested" (Meyer 1994) within international norms and institutions, and the degree of bureaucratic inefficiency (this may also be used as a foil for government foot-dragging in dealing with requests for official status).[6]

6. The PBI Central American Project, for example, only received the formal edict for the official status of its Guatemala team in March, 1995, despite having had a team there continuously since 1983. The lack of a formalized, official agreement regarding a team's status can work in favor of a TSMO, resulting in increased freedom for its teams. But it

The PBI exploratory team entered Sri Lanka in 1989 under tourist visas, as did the first members of the permanent team who soon followed. Although the team met with a number of top government officials in the summer of 1990, no agreement was reached on the team's official status. In fact, PBI did not seek formal status or register as an INGO until team members were denied extensions on their six-month tourist visas in the spring of 1991. At that time, international pressure orchestrated through PBI's Emergency Response Network helped advance negotiations of official visa and work arrangements between PBI and the government.

In 1997, PBI continued to provide protective accompaniment to threatened individuals and organizations as well as international observers for demonstrations and other public functions. In response to the mid-1995 escalation of the government's war with the LTTE, the PBI team began more intensive work in the war zone of the island's Eastern Province.

In what follows, PBI's work with two different parties is explored, providing a window into the role PBI's presence may sometimes play in the decisions taken by local activists. The first case concerns an individual human rights activist; the second focuses on a grassroots social movement organization.[7]

Protecting the Individual Activist

Tharmalingam Selvakumar is a Tamil who claims he was abducted, tortured, and detained for six days in January 1993 by the Eelam People's Democratic Party (EPDP). He further claims that the EPDP attempted to extort one million rupees from his family in return for his

---

is even more likely to have the opposite effect. In fact, lack of official status and relations may compromise the deterrent dynamic of accompaniment by reducing the flow of information between the TSMO and the government. It may also constrain the teams, underscore the tenuous nature of their situation, and make them more timid and less prone to take risks that the work actually requires.

7. Much of the information on these cases was obtained during a participant observation study with the PBI team in Sri Lanka. In June 1993, I joined the team for three months, living in the PBI house in Colombo with the team of international volunteers and functioning as a member of the team. Utilizing standard qualitative research methods (Bogdan and Biklen 1992), I collected field notes based on my daily experiences and observations as a team member and on the many "informal interviews" that naturally occurred in my role as a participant observer. Formal, recorded interviews with recipients of PBI services, members of collegial organizations, diplomats, and police officials were conducted after I left the team. I returned to Sri Lanka and to the PBI team for one month in August 1994, continuing my participant observation research.

release (about $21,000 in U.S. dollars). He says the EPDP turned him over to the police, who held him without charges. Selvakumar's family managed to pressure the government through a few high-ranking Tamil politicians, and he was released without charges after twenty-two days (Jabhar 1993).

A militant Tamil group with close ties to the Premadasa regime, the EPDP aided the Sinhalese-dominated government in its war with the separatist LTTE. The EPDP is known to use a variety of intimidation tactics against the civilian Tamil population, including extortion, occupation of homes, and forced recruitment (Oberst 1994). As recently as June 1993, armed groups of EPDP cadres operated openly in Colombo with the support of the government (many claimed that these armed groups were used by the government as a form of social control of the minority ethnic population of Tamils), ostensibly looking for LTTE "suspects" who came to Colombo from the LTTE-controlled north. Instances of kidnapping, extortion, and torture of these "suspects" by both the security forces and the EPDP were common in the Colombo Tamil community at this time (Amnesty International 1993).

A former EPDP sympathizer, Selvakumar let the EPDP use a family home in Madras, India. His EPDP interest may have been in reaction to troubles he had with the LTTE over the sale of some property in the north of Sri Lanka. In any event, he chose to disassociate himself from the EPDP; and it was then that he was allegedly kidnapped, tortured, and held illegally while the EPDP attempted to extort money from his family.

Selvakumar filed a fundamental human rights case in the Supreme Court of Sri Lanka against the police, the attorney general of Sri Lanka, and Douglas Devananda, the EPDP leader who Selvakumar claims was driving the van used in his abduction. Upon filing the suit, Selvakumar claims to have received death threats from the EPDP and offers of bribes from both the EPDP and police officials to drop the case. He also says that the police official named in the suit threatened to bring charges against him, publicly alleging links with the LTTE, unless he withdrew.

R. K. W. Goonesekara, a leading fundamental human rights lawyer in the country and former principal of the Colombo Law College, took up the case. Many in the diplomatic community and in the staffs of domestic and international NGOs thought Selvakumar's case had significant ramifications for the overall human rights climate in the country.

It was the first attempt to make clear in the courts the close cooperation between the government and paramilitary groups and political parties in violating an individual's rights. Goonesekara claimed it was important as part of a larger legal effort to get the Supreme Court to extend the boundaries of liability beyond the state for the violation of fundamental freedoms:

> It is nonstate persons, like Devananda, or parastate organizations, like the EPDP, who really are the instigators of what we think of as state violations. . . . What about the man who is at the back of it, who makes use of state apparatus to do some wrong to his political enemies? We had succeeded in some of these cases, and Selvakumar's case would have been another opportunity. (Goonesekara 1994)

Selvakumar added that his case "not only involves me, but a lot of young Tamil boys and businessmen who are taken by the EPDP under the cover of arresting LTTE suspects. Then they demand millions of rupees for their release."

Many in Sri Lanka speak of a "fear psychosis," the fruit of massive political violence, that severely dampens social and political activism. The level of fear in Colombo is manifest in the fact that, although Selvakumar was abducted on New Year's Eve in view of a hundred witnesses, he convinced only two people to sign affidavits regarding the abduction. This fear psychosis is also a function of what Gamson (1988) calls the "legitimating frames" that regimes use to justify abuses and keep the citizenry in line. The Sri Lankan government repeatedly invoked the frame of "national security" to legitimate and defend abuses against the Tamil minority. Selvakumar's public challenge to that frame was an important element in a series of events that eventually caused the government to bring the EPDP forces in Colombo under greater control.

PBI provided protective accompaniment for Selvakumar from April 1993 through August 1993, when he fled the country with PBI's assistance. It included overnight stays at the family home almost every night, regular daytime visits to the home, and escorts when he traveled the city on business related to his case. During periods when the danger was thought to be especially high, the PBI team provided twenty-four-hour accompaniment.[8] Their effectiveness was enhanced, moreover, by a *network* of civil rights organizations.

---

8. International protective accompaniment is often used for those whose life or liberty is threatened by their own government. Governments, as signatories to international human rights norms, and as participants in an increasingly globalized economy, are particularly susceptible to outside pressures regarding internal human rights violations. Since the pressure points for nonstate actors are not as clear, we know less about the effects of international accompaniment when the source of the threat is not directly tied to or accountable to a government. But the intimate, highly public nature of the

The international human rights organization field consists of a patchwork of over 1,000 groups (Shelley 1989). Many have emerged in response to specific forms of oppression, producing distinctive mandates (Steiner 1991, 5–15; Wiseberg 1992, 372). Their impressive but sometimes confusing array of activities has produced at least five functionally-based typologies (Claude and Weston 1992; Ray and Taylor 1977; Scoble and Wiseberg 1974; Shestack 1978; Wiseberg 1992). Their areas of specialization sometimes complement and other times overlap each other (Eide 1986).

Because there is such a large variety of specialized human rights groups, negotiating the maze of organizations can be difficult. It thus took Selvakumar over two months to find the right match, and in the end it was with four separate organizations, three international and one domestic. The International Committee of the Red Cross (ICRC) was one of them.

Prison visitation and interviewing of political detainees, followed by *confidential* reporting and lobbying of the host government, is central to the mission of the ICRC (Blondel 1987; Forsythe 1990). The high levels of access that the ICRC obtains may be attributed partly to the fact that when it finds governments in violation of international human rights norms, it does not publicize those findings. ICRC's recommendations for change are made privately, and usually only to the government in question. This procedure helps ensure that there is little public loss of face for the transgressors and thus may make it easier for them to change their policies.[9]

Amnesty International (AI), also involved in Selvakumar's case, employs a vastly different method. Like PBI, AI relies on the *public* exposure of real and potential human rights violations and on the power of international lobbying through the letter writing of ordinary citizens and elites. Elizabeth Nissan, a staff member of the Asia Desk at AI in London contrasts the different approaches.

> We are not there, we are not going in and out of prisons every day of the week, monitoring conditions and raising concerns with the government privately. But we are publicizing our findings. And it seems to me that these are two sides of the same process that can not be done by the same organization. . . . You can't threaten [a government's international

---

EPDP's ties to the Sri Lankan government at the time of this case seemed to increase the likelihood of accompaniment having a beneficial effect.

9. Despite repeated requests from the ICRC, Sri Lankan NGOs, and UN agencies, the Sri Lankan government refused to allow the ICRC to work in Sri Lanka from 1983 to 89. For the complicated but revealing history of the Sri Lankan government's political maneuvering vis-à-vis the ICRC, see Civil Rights Movement (1990).

image] in the way that we probably do and expect to have everyday access on the ground. So the roles are different, but quite complementary. In different countries one of our public objectives might be for other human rights organizations to have access as a beginning protection on the ground. (Nissan 1993)

The ICRC visited Selvakumar while he was imprisoned and documented his case. But as Selvakumar soon found out, once a detainee is released, the ICRC is not likely to provide much more assistance. Upon his release from prison, he paid the ICRC a visit.

When I told the ICRC that I was filing a case and that the EPDP was trying to get me and kill me, I asked them if they could help me. They told me they were not in a position to help me. . . . I wrote to Amnesty International and to all these other organizations, too. Very few even answered me. I was so desperate. Finally I had several meetings with a local human rights organization [Civil Rights Movement] and I was told there was an organization [PBI] that could give shadow protection. (Selvakumar 1993)

The international office of Amnesty International in London contacted PBI in Sri Lanka by electronic mail and provided background data on Selvakumar, suggesting that PBI visit him to gather more information on his case for both PBI and AI. The Civil Rights Movement (CRM), one of the leading domestic human rights organizations in Sri Lanka, and the corecipient of the 1990 Carter-Menil prize for human rights, eventually arranged a meeting with PBI and Selvakumar to determine his security needs and compatibility with PBI's mandate.[10]

AI sent out an Urgent Action appeal on behalf of Selvakumar in April 1993 and helped place a number of stories about his case in the major daily newspapers in Colombo and elsewhere. Both AI and Selvakumar assumed that his heightened visibility would also increase his security. At the same time, PBI began providing nonviolent protective accompaniment to Selvakumar and his family, attempting to extend the political space within which he could operate safely.

Once Selvakumar found a match between his needs and TSMO mandates, the three organizations worked together in an exercise of "cooperative accompaniment." They channeled information to each

10. The granting of high-profile prizes by foreign organizations to human rights activists whose work has endangered them in their own country is one of many nonviolent tactics used to increase their international visibility and decrease the threat level facing them (Wiseberg 1991; also, see chap. 7 in this volume).

other as Selvakumar's case developed in the courts and as they aided him in his attempt to flee the country until his case was resolved. It was not unusual for Selvakumar to have specific needs that one organization, because of its mandate or resource limitations, could not meet. But it was also not unusual for one of the other organizations to step in and fill the gap.[11]

This sort of information sharing and task sharing is a typical activity in the NGO world, especially among TSMOs like PBI and AI (Smith et al. 1994, 15; Willetts 1982b, 184). By drawing on each organization's unique resources, a threatened activist may stitch together a patchwork quilt of increased safety.

Selvakumar was initially skeptical of the usefulness of the protective accompaniment technique because of PBI's commitment to nonviolence and its unwillingness to testify in court.[12] But he later credited PBI's presence with reducing the levels of surveillance and harassment of him and his family by the police and the EPDP. He interpreted the working relationships this way: "I sincerely believe that I have been safe this long owing to PBI's presence. Amnesty International brought my case more to light and it was published in the papers through their Urgent Action Network, but the physical presence of PBI was very helpful."

Other activists, stymied by a lack of resources or the complexity of the task, may fail to fashion a protective quilt out of the maze of TSMO mandates. To negotiate a series of politically sensitive working relationships, those seeking protection must often have European language skills, access to transportation or communication, and the means to overcome cultural barriers. Lacking these or the time to investigate and initiate appropriate connections, many give up in frustration. Selvakumar was one of the lucky ones. Fluent in a number of languages, he benefited from family money, broad intercultural experiences, political astuteness, and a tenacious commitment to his cause.

The expansion of human rights TSMOs is a trend that is likely to continue in the near future. As the case of Selvakumar suggests, there are two sides to this coin. The expanding volume of organizations can

11. What I am calling *cooperative accompaniment* has been used many times. In 1989, PBI freed up one of its El Salvador team members to help escort the outspoken Lutheran Bishop Medardo Gomez, a key player in the peace process there. The escorts were an ad hoc group of foreign nationals and church workers from various organizations, coordinated out of an independent office in Chicago (Kinane 1995).

12. The PBI team in Sri Lanka at the time decided that testifying in court on behalf of those it accompanied would violate the team's nonpartisan status and mandate. What constitutes partisan activity is often a contentious issue on PBI teams (see MacQuarrie 1993).

lead to confusion, poorly informed referrals, or fatal delays, but it may also help meet the wide range of needs of different human rights victims and activists. A positive outcome often requires awareness of the particular mandates and services offered by individual organizations and informed coordination among them. Although this networking is not wholly uncommon, broader application of the cooperative accompaniment approach is much needed. The revolution in communications technology that is rapidly expanding and speeding the flow of information between organizations may be a positive force in this regard.[13]

Information is the lifeblood of the human rights movement: collecting, analyzing, and distributing it is a chief function of most human rights NGOs (Claude and Weston 1992, 364; Willetts 1982a, 16–87). Without timely and accurate data, human rights promotion and protection by governments, international organizations, NGOs, and even individual citizens would come to a virtual standstill. And each of these four sectors relies heavily on the information provided by the NGOs working in the field (van Boven 1984; Weissbrodt 1982).

Although technological changes may have expanded human rights information campaigns to a more general audience, most information that human rights TSMOs gather is still directed at policy elites, including governmental and intergovernmental officials, and the diplomatic community (Scoble and Wiseberg 1974). One of the tactics used by the PBI team in Sri Lanka is to maintain what Galtung (1988) calls "strategic linkages" across various domains of power. PBI does this through regular meetings with a broad base of local government officials, diplomats, funding agency officials, and influential international and domestic NGOs. PBI selectively informs these influential contacts about its teams' activities and the dangers facing local activists, and that knowledge and influence may then be tapped later if needed. As one team member put it, "We try to cast our protective net as widely as possible, including using our diplomatic contacts. We inform and when necessary involve others in the cases we are working on." Using the "insider status" (Willetts 1982b, 181) that PBI had cultivated through its regular meetings with "influential allies" (Tarrow 1994, 88) in the diplomatic community was an important tactic in Selvakumar's case.

PBI team members arranged a number of meetings in the embassy of a western European country with the official handling Selvakumar's

13. According to Narayan Desai, founder of the Shanti Sena and a PBI founder, the absence of accessible and efficient mechanisms for international consultation and communication was one of the reasons for the demise of the World Peace Brigade, PBI's predecessor organization (Walker 1988).

request for a visa and political refugee status. They provided the official with detailed information on Selvakumar and his case. When asked for the team's assessment of the threats he faced, they discussed the team's political analysis of those threats. PBI team members explained what they and some of their Sri Lankan contacts took to be the broader significance of the case, describing the cooperative accompaniment effort that emerged among the three human rights organizations, all of which were providing information to the embassy.

The official said that it is "crucial that we be able to forward to our home office the assessment of human rights nongovernmental organizations with intimate knowledge of the case. . . . PBI's assessment, reflected in your accompaniment record, combined with AI's ongoing interest in the case, should go a long way to securing the visa." The official also directly noted the involvement of the Civil Rights Movement, saying that she knew CRM to be "very careful and astute about getting involved in individual cases," and that its involvement indicated "both a high level of threat and the importance of the case overall." Not long thereafter, the visa arrived and PBI escorted Selvakumar to the airport.[14] He now has political asylum status in a western European country and is pursuing a law degree.[15]

Selvakumar's attempt to flee Sri Lanka in the summer of 1993 occurred concurrently with a move throughout Western nation-states to constrict the flow of refugees into their territories. Moreover, the repatriation of Sri Lankan Tamil refugees was increasingly supported even though they would be returning to face significant dangers (Asia Watch 1993). It is reasonable to assume that intervention and advocacy

14. The PBI Guatemala team has also regularly helped threatened activists go into exile. But PBI teams do not always do so. In El Salvador in 1989, the PBI team agreed to a request from contacts in the popular movement not to use PBI resources to facilitate local activists' going into exile. The team was told that some in the movement had made a covenant with each other that they would stay in the country and continue organizing, and they wanted PBI to honor the covenant (Kinane 1995). A prominent human rights organizer in Sri Lanka, speaking from personal experience, thinks that the availability of protective accompaniment in the days immediately preceding an activist's' flight into exile is one of the most critical and helpful services TSMOs like PBI can provide (Kandasamy 1993).

15. On 13 July 1994, the Sri Lankan Supreme Court ruled in Selvakumar's favor and against the police saying that they "blatantly disregarded every consitutional safeguard against the arbitrary deprivation of liberty." The individual officers and, even more significantly, the state itself were all ordered to pay damages to Selvakumar. The court also directed the nation's attorney general to issue "precise and detailed instruction to all officers in charge of Police Stations as to their duties . . . to respect, secure and advance the fundamental rights guaranteed by the Constitution." However, the court dismissed the complaint against Devananda and the EPDP for their alleged role in the abduction, citing lack of sufficient evidence.

by the four human rights groups was at least a contributing factor when Selvakumar successfully obtained his visa. Moreover, among the factors that influenced his decision about where to apply for a visa was PBI's advice, based on its inside information about which embassies were known to be especially sensitive to human rights concerns and with which PBI had good working relationships. The strategic flow of information and influence from PBI to the embassy regarding Selvakumar's status exemplifies how TSMOs can affect individual cases.

Bridging National and International Organizations

The second case explores the working relationship between PBI and a social movement organization (SMO) engaged in domestic organizing and international networking, the Center for Conscientization.

Social movements working for local and global transformation through nonviolence are a key element in the political climate of the late twentieth century (Falk 1992; Walker 1988). Despite the political violence that marks Sri Lanka, and in some cases because of it, Sri Lanka is home to SMOs that work collaboratively to redefine political action, exploiting whatever pockets of safe political space they find or can fashion with the cooperation of TSMOs. That social movements tend to operate via broad movement networks has long been recognized (Gerlach and Hine 1970). International networking is important for many Sri Lankan SMOs; in a dangerous political climate it may even function as a kind of informal organizational accompaniment.

Janawaboda Kendraya (Center for Conscientization) is a nongovernmental organization whose members work with two grassroots people's empowerment projects named after the communities in which they are located: the Negombo United People's Organization (NUPO) and the Kotogoda United People's Organization (KUPO).

Inspired by liberation theology and Paulo Freire's work in developing critical social awareness, the Center for Conscientization members (largely Sinhalese and Catholic) began to organize and animate traditionally disempowered and oppressed groups in 1983. They worked with the landless in a land squatting effort, set up community theaters as vehicles for social expression and political dissent, and organized in the garment factories in the Free Trade Zones then springing up in Sri Lanka and within which organizing was restricted. The Center also promoted a radical critique of Sri Lanka's participation in the international political economy. These activities did not endear the group to a government under violent siege from the JVP and the LTTE. The group's founders felt threatened in 1989 and 1990 during the height of terror surrounding the government's response to the JVP rebellion. Accused of being JVP, the group sent four founders into exile in the Philippines, India, and England.

Others stayed behind and continued their work amid ongoing death threats. In response, they cultivated more contacts with TSMOs, turning to PBI for protective accompaniment in 1990. One member explained that international networking is critical not only for security reasons, but as a step toward unified, structural solutions to what are seen as structural problems.

> It is important for us to be able to work with international groups. . . . One incident here can now go all over the world. So every incident has an impact in other places and situations. . . . I see that solidarity among the local groups, national groups, and international groups is an important counter to these present structural problems. . . . All problems are linked with other problems and structures.

The PBI team's work with the Center was varied, and it was evaluated and renegotiated on a regular basis. NUPO members received individual escort and overnight presences, and PBI often provided the group with international observers for demonstrations or marches. But the primary tactic employed by PBI was a regular presence at the offices of NUPO and KUPO. This presence was still being maintained, albeit in reduced form, in late 1993.

The all-day visits by PBI were scheduled on those days when one of the community groups that NUPO or KUPO animates were meeting at the centers. This strategy sent a double message: one of deterrence that was directed at the perceived source of threat and one of hope and confidence building that was directed at the local activists.

The presence of international observers amid the grassroots group was intended to send a message to the government or to paramilitary groups that harassing or attacking this group would be costly. It was likely to make visible behavior the government would rather keep hidden in order to convince aid-donor nations that Sri Lanka was curbing human rights abuses and to persuade corporate investors that it was a stable investment site.[16]

16. Government officials openly acknowledge that they were forced by international pressure into setting up task forces and commissions designed to protect human rights (Jayaweera 1991). That most of these mechanisms have largely failed is another matter. That the Sri Lanka government acts with care and circumspection regarding human rights abuses in the periods preceding important aid-and investment-related meetings has long been evident (Abeysekera 1992). The Scandinavian countries have been especially active in human rights promotion in Sri Lanka, including using aid and trade pressures (Counterpoint 1994).

For groups like NUPO and KUPO that organize locally, the presence of an international third party like PBI is both a symbolic and a concrete expression of the concern that part of the international community has for their rights. According to one member of the Center, it not only can defuse the paralysis of fear but also can affect the way local organizers perceive their own work and its importance:

> When PBI is here with us, it decreases our fear and the fear of the people who come to the center with the groups we animate. The violence here has gotten inside people; it does not just operate on the outside, just kill the body. It also operates on the inside through fear and kills the spirit of the people. But we see that we are not alone in our struggle, and that helps us overcome that fear. . . . The people see that this work is important and that others care about it.

Whereas PBI offered protection for Selvakumar to prosecute his case and helped him leave when the risks seemed too high, in the case of the Center for Conscientization, PBI's role was reversed. Here PBI's presence was a factor in the decisions exiled leaders made to return and resume their organizing work.

Vincent Bulathsinghala, is the coordinator of the Center, is one of the founders who went into exile. On the anniversary of the disappearance of his brother, he said:

> I was convinced by others after my brother disappeared that I must leave. I had done nothing wrong, or nothing illegal in my work, so it was difficult for me to see why I must go. . . . There is no rule of law in Sri Lanka, but the government and the police respect the outsider, especially those with white skin. It is not good; it is an imperialist attitude, but it is true here. So the presence of an international group like PBI gave our group strength.[17] (Bulathsinghala 1993)

Rev. Ben Wasantha (an assumed name) is a Catholic priest long active in nonviolent empowerment projects. A founder of the Center for Conscientization, he also fled Sri Lanka after being threatened by federal Security Forces. When he and his colleagues thought it might be safe for him to return in late 1992, the availability of PBI accompaniment was a factor in his deliberations (Wasantha 1993).

A PBI escort accompanied Wasantha from England to his home village in Sri Lanka for a family visit, and then to his new residence,

---

17. The roles that ethnicity, skin color, and nation-state citizenship play in PBI's work in Sri Lanka and elsewhere is complex, and problematic for many within PBI. For analysis of these issues, see Coy (1995, 1997).

where he received twenty-four hour accompaniment for two weeks. "It made a tremendous difference for me," he said. "I did not know what to expect, exactly what I would be returning to. So having PBI's escort helped me to deal with the unknown and to keep my fears in check. I felt much safer" (Wasantha 1993).

The Significance of Accompaniment

Assessing the effectiveness of nonviolent actions is difficult because of the complex array of factors that influence events and remain beyond the control of the researcher. Moreover, how success and failure is defined varies among the actors, who often operate with vague long-term goals and who do not always specify concrete objectives. Indeed, the notions of "success" and "failure" are not only vague and restrictive but also fail to exhaust the possible outcomes (McCarthy and Kruegler 1993, 27). PBI members typically lament the assessment dilemma that marks their work; as one team member remarked, "Obviously you can't know—you really can't know how effective you are because you don't know if something would have happened if you weren't there."

There are numerous examples of rough or violent treatment of a local citizen by police or military personnel changing dramatically upon the appearance of a PBI team member carrying a camera and notebook. Every former team member seems able to recount such an experience, and most attribute the behavior change to their presence as international observers. Still, for many the bottom line is whether or not those being accompanied believe that PBI's presence makes a difference in their situation and affects the choices they make.

The data offered here suggest that the Sri Lanka Project of Peace Brigades International, while not determining the behavior of nonviolent activists for human rights, serves to expand the range of choices available to them.[18] Bleiker (1993) has shown that a certain amount of "breathing space" free from the encroachment of the state is required for the expression of regime-critical opinions and their growth into

18. This approach remains incomplete as it does not address whether the escorted individuals know enough about the accompaniment technique and its likely effects in their situation to make solid assessments about the deterrent value of accompaniment. In other words, their increased sense of safety could be false and misplaced, because it depended upon their knowledge of the complex dynamics of accompaniment; how experienced the TSMO is in accompaniment; the foreign aid needs of the country; and whether those doing the threatening clearly understand the role of the escorting organization, including the amount and significance of the international pressure it can generate.

broader forms of popular dissent. Activists in social movement organizations like those profiled here share with social movements across the globe the goal to refashion politics and reclaim political space and relevancy (Falk 1992; Melucci 1989, 227–32). The protection of these activists, and the expansion of the choices available to them through the technique of nonviolent protective accompaniment, seems to bode well for a future marked by more humane forms of politics and governance. In the building of that future, TSMOs are sure to play a significant role.

Although transnational social movement organizations do not determine state behavior, they act within institutional contexts to constrain the range of choices available to states (Leatherman et al. 1993), and they change the decisional latitude of states (Dorsey 1993) by influencing the information environment within which states make decisions (Sikkink 1993). It is reasonable to assume that the role and function of TSMOs will continue to expand in the post-Cold War era. Previously constricted by the bipolar approach to global politics of the Cold War, TSMOs were more easily neutralized or dismissed as a tool of one camp or the other. Now, in the increasingly complex world of today's global politics, TSMO roles are formalized in international agreements. A prominent case in point is the 1992 agreement negotiated by Guatemalan refugees living in exile in Mexico regarding how they would return to Guatemala under the Central American Peace Accords. The refugees insisted that the international agreement stipulate their right to nonviolent protective accompaniment of their own choosing (PBI, Witness for Peace, and others).

Unarmed insurrection and nonviolent resistance against authoritarian regimes has increased dramatically in the past fifteen years (Zunes 1994). International protective accompaniment is only one of many nonviolent techniques that TSMOs and others are refining through manifold applications around the globe. TSMOs are demonstrating that governments may be constrained and dissidents sustained, sometimes in lifesaving ways. These experiments in nonviolence will result in the development of still more techniques useful for others who strive to reclaim their history and fashion their future in a manner less encumbered by the vagaries of violent repression. That is a prospect deserving of the best resources of transnational and domestic social movement organizations the world over.

6

CONTENDING NEUTRALITIES

Humanitarian Organizations and War in the Horn of Africa

William DeMars

Abstract

The Ethiopian conflict attracted humanitarian action by dozens of international organizations during the 1980s. The clandestine "cross-border operation" established a connection from rebel regions of Eritrea and Tigray, through Sudan, to the international humanitarian network. Without central coordination, the operation organized itself into three tracks, each of which represented a different model of humanitarian neutrality. The humanitarian wings created by the insurgents themselves interacted with three international agencies: the Emergency Relief Desk (ERD), War on Want (WOW), and the International Committee of the Red Cross (ICRC). ERD was a coalition of church-linked organizations which sought a balanced policy of providing emergency assistance to parties in the conflict. WOW, on the other hand, publicly advocated the legitimacy of the Eritrean and Tigrayan revolutions based upon universal humanitarian norms. The ICRC minimized the strategic consequences of humanitarian action by upholding its traditional policy of strict neutrality, which hinges on its operational acceptance by all warring parties. The negotiating strategies of the insurgents, the structures of the international organizations, and the priorities of Western donor governments all affected the dynamics of the cross-border operation.

Civil wars spawn the most serious international humanitarian crises of famine, human rights abuse, and refugee migration. This linkage has been unmistakable in recent internal conflicts—notably Somalia, Bosnia, and Rwanda—that attract the attention of international media, governments of major powers, and the United Nations precisely because they generate human suffering on such a large scale. Civil wars were frequent and destructive during the Cold War as well, but the scale of civilian abuse was often hidden from international scrutiny, and the victims of conflict were sometimes isolated from any access to international aid and protection. Although the international response to the human consequences of conflict is still unreliable, there is a greater likelihood in the 1990s than during any previous period that victims of internal wars will be visible on the international stage and that humanitarian efforts will be made on their behalf. The actors most responsible for this historical shift are humanitarian international nongovernmental organizations (NGOs).

Often, because international nongovernmental organizations (INGOs) whose primary emphasis is social service are drawn into social change advocacy in the course of their work, the boundary between transnational social movement organizations (TSMOs) and other NGOs working on humanitarian issues is blurred. Accordingly, the more inclusive term INGO is used throughout this chapter to refer to both humanitarian INGOs and TSMOs among them. The political context determines when an INGO is operationally a social movement agent.

Humanitarian INGOs are nonstate, nonprofit enterprises that take action to implement universal standards of human welfare or justice, and that neither pursue political power nor use violence. They include an enormous variety of organizations addressing issues such as hunger, economic development, refugees and displaced persons, and human rights. It is useful to analyze them together because the events that generate suffering on the largest scale—internal conflicts—attract large numbers of INGOs whose mandates cover this entire spectrum of humanitarian concerns. In conflict settings, humanitarian INGOs interact with each other and with the warring parties in surprising ways that are not revealed by analyzing a single organization or narrow issue area. Their efforts to aid victims of war in rebel-controlled regions of Ethiopia during the 1980s involved them in contention over alternative models of neutrality.

Although occupied by Italy from 1936 to 1941, Ethiopia was never colonized. Emperor Haile Selassie held his crown from 1930 until he was overthrown by his own military in 1974. Within three years Colonel Mengistu Haile Mariam assassinated his rivals and emerged as the strong man of the regime, which embraced Marxist-Leninist ideology and accepted Soviet military aid.

Two significant insurgent groups opposed the government during the 1980s. The Eritrean People's Liberation Front sought independence from Ethiopia for the former Italian colony of Eritrea on the Red Sea. The Tigray People's Liberation Front, based south of Eritrea in Tigray, fought to replace the Mengistu government in Ethiopia. Both rebel fronts occupied large rural areas with significant populations by 1980, leaving the government to control only major towns in Eritrea and Tigray. The insurgents used guerrilla hit-and-run military tactics to attack these garrison towns and to disrupt government transport of military, economic, and humanitarian supplies to them. The government launched destructive annual offensives, including massive attacks on rural peasants and their economic resources. Neither front received significant military or political support from outside governments.

International observers believed through the 1980s that neither side could win a military victory, but the rebels confounded this view by finally defeating the government. Following a year-long rebel offensive, Mengistu fled to Zimbabwe in May 1991, and the largest army in Tropical Africa collapsed. The victorious rebels established separate transitional governments in Eritrea and Ethiopia (Morrison 1992). After a referendum supervised by the United Nations, Eritrea became an internationally recognized, independent state in May 1993 (Pateman 1994).

The long war induced acute famine, widespread human rights violations, and massive refugee movements. It also attracted a large-scale humanitarian response to assist and protect victims of the war. Humanitarian NGOs formed a substantial part of that response by mounting a cross-border operation to bring relief and development supplies from northeast Sudan into rebel-controlled areas of Eritrea and Tigray. They undertook this effort illegally, without the consent of the Ethiopian government, and in the face of frequent attacks by the Ethiopian military. The cross-border operation was a precursor and model for the post-Cold War framework of humanitarian intervention in internal conflicts. It also illustrates the organizational tensions that permeate humanitarian policy.

Organizational Tensions of Humanitarian Action

NGO humanitarian action expresses and generates solidarity among societies. Any social movement organization may involve both "conscience constituents," who provide resources but do not directly benefit from organizational action, and "beneficiary constituents" (McCarthy and Zald 1977). In contrast to social movement organizations operating within a single country, humanitarian NGOs link conscience constituents in one country with beneficiary constituents in another.

Because the two groups almost never meet, their relationship is mediated by NGO professional staff, who hold the power and responsibility of managing complex international transfers of resources and information between societies.

Humanitarian INGOs operate under constant pressure to cultivate new projects and attract funding. Both the survival of each organization and its capacity to achieve the ideals for which it was created depend on entrepreneurial initiative. NGOs exhibit an enormous variety of specific tactics, yet all humanitarian action can be understood analytically as addressing two broad objectives: delivering material *assistance*, such as relief food, medicine, or development supplies (Anderson and Woodrow 1989), and securing *protection* from abusive treatment (Forsythe 1985, 265).

Humanitarian action in internal conflicts draws NGOs into a politically complex environment where building solidarity among societies requires making deals with governments and warring parties. In order to take action in internal conflicts, humanitarian NGOs must assemble five fundamental relationships into a coherent strategy. In addition to identifying the needs of a beneficiary constituency, INGOs must obtain resources and influence from conscience constituents, obtain acquiescence and sometimes resources from their home government, negotiate with warring party elites to gain access to the population, and manage their relations with other agencies active in the same crisis.

The last two of these relationships indicate that NGOs bargain with warring parties, and often compete with each other, for humanitarian access to the victims of war. Someone with a gun and a political agenda stands between the humanitarian agency and the population. To gain access to the population to deliver assistance or provide protection, humanitarian actors must obtain the consent of at least one of the warring parties.

The greatest resource for managing these organizational tensions is a discourse and practice of humanitarian neutrality. Each organization asserts that it is concerned only with the human needs and rights of the victims of conflict—not with influencing the political and military contest between the adversaries—and attempts to persuade donors, beneficiaries, and warring parties to accept its particular conception of neutrality.[1]

The claim of each responsible NGO to humanitarian neutrality is authentic in its own terms. Yet the multiple organizations seeking access to the population in each conflict present humanitarian neutrality in a plurality of forms. All these organizations operate "above poli-

---

1. See Finnemore (1993) on international organizations as "teachers" of norms.

tics," but they fashion different responses to the same reality, and the responses carry different political consequences for the adversaries in the conflict. Neutrality becomes plural, and multiple neutralities contend with each other in the form of humanitarian organizations bargaining for access to the victims of conflict.

Sources of the Cross-Border Operation

War and famine have been closely linked throughout Ethiopian history. Emperor Haile Selassie ignored the famine of 1974, and public exposure of his negligence contributed to his overthrow. The new military government established an official commission to warn of future famines but then cut off all international aid to the rebellious region of Eritrea (Shepherd 1975). The insurgents learned that they needed their own link with the international humanitarian network to counter the government's willingness to starve Eritrea as a counterinsurgency technique.

A small group of Eritrean intellectuals loyal to the Eritrean People's Liberation Front founded the Eritrean Relief Association (ERA) in 1975. ERA was the first of its kind—a "general purpose" humanitarian arm of a liberation front. As such, it could forge links not only with the international Red Cross movement but also with the expanding world of relief, development, and human rights NGOs.

The Tigray People's Liberation Front created the Relief Society of Tigray (REST) in 1978, after defeating rival rebel groups in Tigray (Tereke 1990, 141). The Eritrean Front later defeated its main rival; accordingly, by 1981 both ERA and REST held monopolies on humanitarian access to the respective rebel areas of Eritrea and Tigray. The extension of humanitarian activity by ERA and REST depended directly on the scope of territorial control by their military sponsors.

ERA and REST were distinct in personnel and budget from their parent fronts and functioned exclusively in civilian relief and development activities. These policies helped assure donors that international assistance was not feeding soldiers. At the same time, both ERA and REST cultivated a subtle ambiguity between their activities within Eritrea and Tigray and the face they presented to the outside world. Facing outward toward the international humanitarian network, ERA and REST acted as humanitarian *nongovernmental* organizations attempting to maximize both the flow of international resources to Eritrea and Tigray and the flow of information on the goals and successes of their revolutions to the world. Facing inward, however, they functioned as auxiliaries to the local *governmental* institutions established by the respective fronts. They provided health, education, hunger relief, and agricultural development services. The Eritrean and Tigray liberation fronts both developed "a political practice . . . which linked the provision of public welfare with mass political mobilization." (Duffield and Prendergast 1994, 9). ERA and REST incorporated famine relief and economic development into broader revolutionary projects.

The Eritreans and Tigrayans each pursued customized versions of Mao's "national democratic revolution" (DeMars 1993, 45–56). Both implemented land reforms that provided direct benefits to the majority of poor peasants while minimizing violence between classes. They created new structures for village-level democracy through mass organizations to mobilize workers, peasants, women, and students. These policies were designed to bring immediate gains in the material well-being of the peasants and to convey a promise of what the revolution could accomplish when the enemy was finally destroyed. Humanitarian programs were closely integrated with these revolutionary institutions. The lists of beneficiaries for famine relief from both ERA and REST were determined either by locally elected committees or by vote of all village members.

The Eritrean national struggle expressed a colonial conception of nationhood based on the history of Eritrea as an Italian colony from 1889 to 1941 (Bereket 1989). The rebels argued that the Eritrean people, who comprise at least nine distinct ethnic groups, are entitled to exercise their right to national self-determination with the option of independent statehood. ERA helped create an Eritrean national identity by providing its services to all ethnic groups without discrimination. In its international contacts, ERA asserted claims of human rights, including the collective right of the Eritrean people to national self-determination. The human rights component of international humanitarian discourse provided ERA with an opportunity to articulate Eritrean nationalism under a humanitarian mantle. In contrast to Eritrea, Tigray was never a European colony, and its ethnic composition is relatively homogeneous. REST advocated human rights issues to a lesser extent than did ERA (DeMars 1994).

ERA and REST were created by revolutionary African intellectuals who wove strands of Maoist politics and Western humanitarianism into a coherent whole. The organizations competently pursued authentic humanitarian goals of hunger relief, refugee prevention, human rights advocacy, and participatory economic development while simultaneously serving the political interests of their parent revolutions by mobilizing popular support. ERA and REST lobbied the humanitarian community with its own values. Revolutionary humanitarians in Eritrea and Tigray selectively engaged the NGO world to evolve a multitrack network of international linkages. This multitrack character can be exemplified by the tactics of three organizations, each of which defined and occupied a central position in a distinctive track, and each of which practiced a different form of humanitarian neutrality.

Humanitarian TSMOs in Ethiopia

Emergency Relief Desk (ERD) was both a coalition of church-linked donor NGOs and a distinct NGO operating in Khartoum. Between 1981 and 1991, ERD channeled about half of the international famine relief assistance that passed through the cross-border operation, supporting programs worth a total of $350 million (Duffield and Prendergast 1994, 13). ERD helped create a new model of international humanitarian policy toward internal wars that has become dominant since the end of the Cold War. In this approach neutrality means balance in the delivery of material assistance to populations on all sides of a conflict.

War on Want (WOW) was a small British NGO that worked alone to publicize human rights violations by the Ethiopian government, and, in consortia with other agencies, to channel infrastructure development assistance to Eritrea and Tigray. WOW constructed a model of humanitarian policy in which, paradoxically, neutrality means advocacy. WOW mounted a public campaign supporting the legitimacy of the Eritrean and Tigrayan revolutions that was based on their practical adherence to universal humanitarian standards.

The International Committee of the Red Cross (ICRC) was an early contributor to the cross-border operation but was frustrated in attempting to apply its traditional definition of neutrality. For the ICRC, neutrality means minimizing the consequences of its operations for the strategic interests of the adversaries. This was the road not taken in the cross-border operation, though it is discernible in a trail of unsuccessful negotiations between the ICRC and the revolutionaries. It is essential to trace that trail in order to understand the significance and innovation of the tracks pursued by ERD and WOW.

The stories of these three organizations illustrate how actors following different definitions of neutrality can respond differently to the same humanitarian reality, and how their contending neutralities can be used by warring parties to fashion an ensemble of international linkages that serve both humanitarian and political ends.

Building an International Network

By 1978, ERA and REST each had an office in Khartoum, a capacity to transport food aid from Sudan into areas of Eritrea or Tigray controlled by their parent liberation armies, and some links with European NGOs. For the next five years the cross-border operation extended to a broad web of transnational organizational relationships.

Lutheran NGOs based in Norway and Sweden moved cautiously to establish working relationships with ERA and REST in the 1970s. Responding to initial invitations from Eritrean Lutheran leaders of ERA, they raised funds from both private donations and their governments. The Swedes were drawn in through historical links with Lutheran churches in Eritrea (Arén 1978).

By 1980 the Scandinavians were joined in the cross-border operation by several other European church NGOs.[2] The growing interest created a problem because ERA and REST made separate aid appeals to each donor NGO, leaving contributors uncertain about the overall need. In response, the original Norwegian and Swedish NGOs formed Emergency Relief Desk.

The initiative began as a single desk and expatriate staff person in the Khartoum offices of the Sudan Council of Churches. It was a modest innovation that laid the basis for the massive expansion of the cross-border operation.

ERD supplied three elements that were essential for building confidence in ERA and REST among mainstream NGOs. First, to overcome the political sensitivity of the cross-border operation, ERD engendered personal trust between NGO expatriates and the leaders of ERA and REST. The first ERD Executive Secretary in Khartoum, for example, was Sture Normark, a Swedish Lutheran missionary with fifteen years' previous experience in Eritrea.

Second, ERD created a structure of formal accountability and reporting. The agency specialized exclusively in delivering relief assistance (primarily grain purchased in Sudan) to ERA and REST for cross-border transport. From its permanent office in Khartoum, ERD sent independent field monitors into Eritrea and Tigray to produce regular reports that circulated among international NGOs. For donor NGOs and governments, ERD provided integrated assessments of relief needs in all the rebel areas and placed a representative in Khartoum who worked with leaders of the rebel relief agencies on a daily basis. Through its Norwegian NGO connection, ERD participated in two overlapping international federations of Protestant church NGOs: the Lutheran World Federation and the World Council of Churches. Using these networks, Protestant NGOs throughout the world—and

2. These included Norwegian Church Aid, Swedish Evangelical Mission, Christian Aid of Britain, Dutch Interchurch Aid, and German Brot für die Welt (Bread for the World).

their national governments—could make discreet contributions to the cross-border operation.[3]

Third, ERD furnished an additional layer of political insulation for risk-averse NGOs unwilling to deal directly with ERA and REST. Before 1985, donors found political security in the covert nature of the cross-border operation. After 1985, when the operation became better known, donor NGOs could explain that they provided assistance only through "international NGOs" (referring to ERD) and "indigenous NGOs" (referring to ERA and REST).

ERD's clandestine profile also helped church NGOs manage the political tensions inherent in a policy of supporting aid projects on both sides of the war. Church-related bodies align their foreign policies with interests that lie in the structure of loyalty among affiliated national churches. In the political context of the Ethiopian conflict, therefore, a clandestine ERD was necessary to allow church NGOs to support both the cross-border operation and also humanitarian programs undertaken with Ethiopian churches on the government side.

During this stage of humanitarian action, when most international emergency aid flowed to the government side, ERD contributed to a larger process of redefining *neutrality as balance*. This concept, which legitimizes the delivery of emergency assistance to vulnerable populations on all sides of internal wars, has become dominant in humanitarian policy since 1990. However, as the tactics of other participants in the cross-border operation illustrate, it is not the only possible concept of neutrality.

The low profile of ERD was not entirely acceptable to ERA and REST, which lobbied NGO supporters to publicize Eritrea and Tigray in their home countries, to withdraw funding from programs on the government side, and to criticize human rights violations by the Ethiopian government. Ideally, the rebels sought an outflow of public information favorable to their diplomatic image to complement the inflow of international aid resources. ERD resisted this pressure, although the clash between rival humanitarian agendas set up considerable tension and debate within the ERD coalition (Duffield and Prendergast 1994). Despite their preference for publicity, ERA and REST pragmatically accepted the terms of ERD support. They forged another ensemble of international linkages—a second track of humanitarian engagement— to NGOs willing to work on the partisan edge of humanitarianism.

War on Want was a small, secular NGO with a membership in Britain that appealed to young, "New Liberal Left" readers of the

---

3. Catholic NGOs were also active on both sides of the Ethiopian conflict (DeMars 1993).

Guardian. When ERA established an office in London in 1975, WOW was the first NGO to help, providing office space and arranging contacts (Ghebrehiwot 1991). After distancing itself from such controversial causes for several years, WOW renewed a role in the cross-border operation during the early 1980s, sending representatives to both Eritrea and Tigray.

After 1982, WOW not only supported REST materially but also adopted a high public profile regarding Tigray. WOW published *The Hidden Revolution*, which articulated a three-level case combining strands of humanitarian and socialist ideology (Firebrace and Smith 1982). First, it praised the human rights record of the Tigrayan rebels and denounced gross abuses by the Ethiopian government. Second, it contrasted the participatory development work of REST with the government's coercive development schemes.[4] Third, it argued that in this war between two revolutionary projects, the Tigrayan insurgents represented true socialist ideals. WOW stopped short of explicitly endorsing the Tigrayan armed struggle, retaining thereby the identity of a humanitarian organization applying universal criteria.

When the Tigrayan rebel leadership appeared to veer sharply to the left in 1983, WOW sustained aid to REST but backed off from further public advocacy for the Tigrayan revolution. WOW then began presenting the humanitarian face of the Eritrean revolution. It sent WOW Programme Officer James Firebrace and Stuart Holland, British Labour Party Spokesman for Overseas Aid and Development, to Eritrean rebel areas in April 1984. In their report, published as *Never Kneel Down*, they championed the Eritrean right to national self-determination, the progressive social and economic revolution of the Eritrean front, and effective famine relief through ERA (Firebrace and Holland 1985). Without endorsing the armed struggle, they supported the rebel front's proposal for an internationally supervised referendum on the future of Eritrea.

WOW's willingness to balance on the edge of humanitarian legitimacy allowed it to play a unique role with two funding consortia of European agencies involved in Tigray and Eritrea. In spring 1983 several hundred thousand Tigrayan migrants were moving toward Sudan in search of food. Efforts to mount a large trucking operation to the interior were stymied by a truck shortage, poor roads, and weak maintenance capacity. A group of British agencies met in 1983 to form the Tigray Transport and Agriculture Consortium (Briottet 1990; TTAC

---

4. Other TSMOs, including the International Commission of Jurists and the International League for the Rights and Liberation of Peoples, reported on human rights violations by the Ethiopian government during the 1980s (DeMars 1994).

1987). The consortium funded garages and road building and bought eighty-three new trucks for REST by 1985. An overlapping group of European NGOs formed the Eritrea Inter-Agency Consortium in 1983. It funded only development programs and dealt exclusively with ERA (Briottet 1990; Firebrace 1991).

WOW became the "lead agency" for these NGO consortia, accepting administrative responsibility, greater public visibility, and an INGO role. This arrangement allowed some member NGOs to conceal their support for REST and ERA. At the same time, WOW was excluded from the Disasters Emergency Committee of large, mainstream British NGOs that had special arrangements with television networks for joint funding appeals. Although the mainstream agencies kept their distance from WOW in public, they relied on WOW to channel their support to politically sensitive operations in Tigray and Eritrea.

In contrast to ERD, which supported only emergency relief activities with ERA and REST, the two consortia coordinated by WOW funded an array of development projects with direct and significant consequences for the political interests of the Tigrayan and Eritrean revolutions. The grass roots agriculture and health projects of ERA and REST involved the poorest people as active participants in their own economic development precisely because they were thoroughly integrated into the structures of village democracy instituted by the insurgents as engines of revolutionary mobilization. Terracing eroded land was a political act in Eritrea and Tigray. Moreover, the Tigray consortium built roads and supplied trucks to REST—forms of infrastructure with potential political and military reverberations.

Thus, WOW worked the politically fertile fields of humanitarianism. In effect, WOW defined *neutrality as advocacy*. It measured each of the adversaries according to the same universal standards of human rights, participatory economic development, and famine relief and found the Ethiopian government wanting on all counts. In this way impartiality in the application of humanitarian standards laid an ideological base for advocacy of the rebel cause in public information and resource allocation. This is the paradox of impartiality that complicates humanitarian action in internal conflicts.

Secular NGOs dominated the membership of both the Eritrea and Tigray consortia. Unlike church NGOs, whose local partner organization is often the humanitarian wing of an indigenous church body, secular NGOs have no natural local partner. They must forge a partnership in each situation, perhaps with a local government institution, ministry of the national government, or local NGO. Being less rooted in local civil societies, secular NGOs may be more likely than church NGOs to take politically charged humanitarian positions.

Expanding the Cross-Border Network

International humanitarian NGOs spun a complex web of organizational ties with all three major adversaries in the Ethiopian conflict during the early 1980s. Yet Ethiopia did not command world attention or draw large flows of material assistance until October 1984. The trigger for the shift of international policy was migration. Drought and brutal Ethiopian government counterinsurgency policies combined to precipitate the displacement of nearly two million starving peasants from rebel-held areas of northern Ethiopia. They moved in two directions—toward Ethiopian government towns and toward Sudan.

After months of hiding the famine, the Ethiopian government allowed Western television coverage of the worst affected areas in and around Tigray. A British Broadcasting Company television report on famine victims in government towns stunned citizens of Western nations, who flooded relief agencies with donations and pressured their governments to take action. The surge of public interest precluded a half-hearted response by the United States and other donor governments. For relief operations on the government side, donors contributed over $1 billion in emergency assistance during 1985 and nearly as much in 1986.[5]

Massive migration was the catalyst for humanitarian action in the cross-border operation as well. More than 100,000 Eritreans and 200,000 Tigrayans poured into Sudan, overwhelming relief capacities. International support for cross-border relief soared in 1985, though it remained a small fraction of the aid showered on the government side. From 1983 to 1985 cash contributions to ERA and REST multiplied tenfold, and the annual income for the cross-border operation approached $100 million in 1985 (ERA 1986; REST 1986).

The impact of migration on the international relief network derived from a potent synergy of humanitarian and political agendas. Humanitarians were concerned because undernourished rural families forced to leave homes and crops are extremely vulnerable to hunger and disease. At the same time major donors, especially the United States and Britain, feared that a mass refugee exodus into Sudan could destabilize its government—then a Western ally against communist Ethiopia. Refugee prevention as a political and humanitarian goal powerfully reinforced ERD and its definition of neutrality as balance.

---

5. To place the scale of the Ethiopian relief operation in perspective, the country's annual gross national product was under $5 billion, and annual development assistance during the early 1980s ranged from $200 million to $400 million (Africa Watch 1991, 364; USAID 1987, 36; Jansson 1990, 45).

To increase the scale of cross-border assistance and prevent migration, Western donor governments had to forge a new level of cooperation with Eritrean and Tigrayan rebels, whose revolutionary goals they did not support. On the government side, humanitarian diplomacy between donor and recipient elites was orchestrated publicly by a series of United Nations special representatives (Kent 1989). But the UN had no contact with the rebels in the Ethiopian conflict, so the task of humanitarian diplomacy on the rebel side fell to an obscure NGO with no public identity and a small office in Khartoum—Emergency Relief Desk.

ERD expanded its operational scale while clinging to its traditional mandate. Using its links with networks of Protestant church NGOs, ERD conveyed information broadly while avoiding public attention to itself. Motivated by refugee prevention objectives, government donors looked to ERD for credible information on the magnitude of relief needs in rebel areas of Eritrea and Tigray.

The operational basis for ERD's expansion of scale was a new capacity in 1984 to receive international grain shipments through Port Sudan and to transport grain to positions on the Ethiopian border for transfer to ERA and REST (Hendrie 1989). This capacity positioned ERD to act as a conduit for relief contributions from the largest donor after 1984, the U.S. government. Lutheran World Relief is the American sister agency of the Scandinavian Lutheran NGOs that founded ERD. Its executive director in New York was so moved by confidential appeals from ERD in 1983 that he allocated nearly $1 million of privately raised funds to ERD (G. Smith 1990). When the Reagan administration initiated support for cross-border relief as a refugee prevention measure in 1984, the United States Agency for International Development (USAID) funneled the covert allocation through Lutheran World Relief and ERD. From 1985 until the war ended in 1991, this pipeline became the single largest source of international food assistance for both ERA and REST, providing 30 percent to 40 percent of the food they received from all sources.

The magnitude of ERD's accomplishment in portraying the cross-border operation as a single entity stands out more clearly in light of several forces acting to splinter and destroy the operation during 1985. First, the Ethiopian army launched separate ground offensives in Eritrea and Tigray, temporarily cutting both cross-border relief routes (Africa Watch 1991, 198). Second, REST lost its cross-border route through Eritrea from 1985 to 1988 due to a political rift between leaders of the Eritrean and Tigrayan rebels. Finally, a 1985 coup in Sudan brought a new government that temporarily banned the flow of relief aid into rebel Eritrea and Tigray. ERD sustained the image of unity in the cross-border operation, and donors sustained the reality of their contributions.

War On Want continued after 1985 to play a leadership role in the advocacy track of the cross-border network. The Tigray Transport and Agriculture Consortium helped REST and the Tigray front build an all-weather road deep into Tigray (TTAC 1987). Other NGOs supported ERA and REST development projects to conserve soil and water, replace animals and implements destroyed by the war, and improve health care at the village level. Each of these undertakings had a clear humanitarian rationale, but at the same time, they all enhanced the bond between the revolutionary elites and their mass base, strengthening them in relation to their enemy, the Ethiopian government.

The evolution of the cross-border operation was the result of independent tactical decisions by hundreds of actors who could not foresee the results of their actions. Yet ERA and REST powerfully shaped its ultimate architecture. They managed to place the plurality of Western humanitarian ideology and practice in the service of their revolutions by letting the humanitarian network organize itself into several tracks. These tracks represented rival conceptions of humanitarian neutrality that intensified their contest as the cross-border effort developed.

ERD contributed to forging a new norm of humanitarian neutrality as balance. The controlling factor in melding political and humanitarian support for such action is refugee prevention. In practice, this means getting food through, even if that enhances the strategic interests of political adversaries. If ERD reluctantly tolerated political consequences of its humanitarian operations, WOW actively stoked the fires of humanitarian partisanship. The INGO consortia it led provided transport and development that could enhance the strategic capacities of an adversary in a conflict. WOW also made a public case for the legitimacy of the Eritrea and Tigrayan revolutions, based on universal humanitarian standards. Hence, WOW implemented a model of neutrality as advocacy.

The cross-border operation encompassed yet a third humanitarian approach, that of the International Committee of the Red Cross. Unwilling to conform to either of the new models of neutrality, the ICRC found itself increasingly marginalized in the cross-border operation.

The Road Not Taken

The ICRC is part of the International Federation of Red Cross and Red Crescent Societies, an INGO formed in 1919 to include relief in natural disasters and other peacetime work. Officially, the federation includes the ICRC itself, the state signatories to the Geneva Conventions, their national societies, and a federation of them. The ICRC itself was established in 1863 as a private, Swiss humanitarian association. Its vision is to work with governments and military leaders to constrain the level of violence in war and ameliorate its consequences. Historically, the ICRC has pursued three major strategies. First, it became the primary promoter of humanitarian law by drawing states into negotiating and ratifying successive Geneva Conventions and Protocols. These treaties bind states to avoid indiscriminate violence in war and to respect and care for the wounded, sick, prisoners, and civilians. Second, the ICRC encouraged the founding of national Red Cross—and later Red Crescent—societies to serve as auxiliaries to national governments for treatment of the wounded during wartime.

The third major ICRC strategy, which is the focus of this profile, is a peculiar style of direct action in armed conflict, even where the parties to the conflict do not acknowledge the applicability of humanitarian law, which for internal wars is quite nebulous.[6] Consequently, the ICRC normally acts in internal conflicts with no explicit reference to humanitarian law (Forsythe 1993).

The International Committee collaborates with governments to develop humanitarian law, cooperates with the national societies, and takes direct action in conflict situations, but it keeps each sector of activity relatively independent of the others. This segmentation contrasts with the fluidity and permeability of relations among the components of humanitarian NGO networks.

In some ways, the ICRC is an anomaly among both INGOs and TSMOs. It is a nongovernmental Swiss association, but its most important links are with the government signatories of the Geneva Conventions and adversaries in war. It promotes a social movement for humanitarian law, but the parts of that movement most deeply embedded in civil society—the national societies—have relatively little power to govern the movement as a whole or to direct ICRC policy.

This structure, in contrast to the looser network structures of other humanitarian NGOs, allows the ICRC to operate as an independent,

---

6. The 1949 Geneva Conventions affirmed the applicability of humanitarian law to internal conflict but established only a thin infrastructure of implementation. Common Article 3 applies the basic principles of the conventions to "armed conflicts not of an international character," but does not precisely define this category (R. Abi-Saab 1986). States rarely acknowledge the applicability of Common Article 3, and when they do, the provisions for implementation are minimal. Thus, Common Article 3 permits, but does not require, a humanitarian response to particular internal wars (G. Abi-Saab 1988). The 1977 Protocol II to the Geneva conventions has never been recognized by a government as applicable to a noninternational conflict within its territory (Kooijmans 1991, 231).

unitary organization when it takes direct action in armed conflicts. It funds humanitarian action primarily with donations from governments and negotiates directly with the political and military elites of the adversaries in conflicts. When the ICRC conducts humanitarian action in an armed conflict, it works with elites on behalf of the interests of broader societies rather than mobilizing those societies for action.

The diverse field tactics of the ICRC are integrated by a conception of "neutral humanitarian intermediary" that defines its organizational ethos and interest. Thus, the ICRC emphasizes humanitarian mediation, not political mediation, to end a conflict (Forsythe 1985). In every action and negotiating position, ICRC delegates attempt to gain simultaneous acceptance from opposing adversaries to act in the midst of the war on behalf of its victims. Every action is designed to demonstrate that ICRC operations are not only humanitarian (concerned solely with the welfare of people removed from the fight) but also neutral. Neutrality for the ICRC means that each action generates *no significant strategic benefits* for any adversary in the conflict.

To maintain its reputation for this brand of neutrality, the ICRC follows two practices that distinguish it from most other humanitarian organizations operating side by side. First, it is extremely careful to directly supervise the needs assessment and distribution of material assistance such as food aid so that it serves people in need and not military or political purposes. Second, it conveys information on abuses of protected persons only discreetly and to the leaders responsible for curbing the abuse—it does not engage in public human rights advocacy. As the ICRC attempted to fashion a role in the cross-border operation during more than a decade, the latter practice ultimately impaired its acceptability in Eritrea and the former practice weakened its relevance in Tigray.

The ICRC was one of the first international supporters of the fledgling cross-border operation in 1976.[7] Humanitarian aid to rebels without the permission of the government was a significant tactical departure for the ICRC in Africa (Jacobs 1987, 181, 311). From 1978 to 1982 the ICRC provided about one-fourth of ERA's annual international relief aid. The ICRC delegate in Khartoum advised ERA on planning its relief transport but ruled out donating trucks because they could have enhanced the strategic capacity of the Eritrean rebel front. The ICRC maintained the operation despite Ethiopian military attacks on cross-border transport routes (Bacchetta 1990).

7. Operational details are drawn from documents furnished by ICRC officials in Geneva on the condition that they not be directly quoted.

Unlike other international agencies, including ERD and WOW, the ICRC established a direct negotiating relationship with the rebel military leadership. The major issue in these negotiations during the early 1980s was the fate of several thousand Ethiopian soldiers captured by the Eritrean front. Red Cross delegates sought permission to visit the prisoners in accordance with ICRC conventional procedures, which include access to all prisoners, visits without witnesses, the opportunity to register each prisoner, and repeat visits. Such visits are designed to convince the adversaries of the neutral and humanitarian character of the ICRC, and to lead to an exchange of prisoners with the ICRC as intermediary. Through years of negotiation with the Eritrean front, the ICRC never achieved private prisoner visits. It was limited to providing relief supplies for the prisoners and visiting them in the presence of rebel representatives (Nicod 1990; Küng 1991).

To understand the Red Cross model of neutrality, two questions must be addressed: Why did the negotiations fail? And why was gaining access for private prisoner visits so important to the ICRC? The Eritrean front repeatedly raised three sorts of objections (EPLF 1985, 7). First, it argued that the ICRC was a security risk, even claiming that delegates conducted intelligence-gathering activities in Eritrea. Second, the Eritreans were reluctant to allow full access without reciprocal ICRC access to their own captured rebel fighters. However, since the government denied the existence of both the war and the rebel fronts, ICRC delegates in Addis Ababa were blocked from discussing the issues. Third, the insurgents wanted to mount public international condemnation of the government for ignoring the existence of its own soldiers captured in Eritrea and for mistreating detained rebel fighters.

Of the three sorts of objections—security, reciprocity, and publicity—the last appears to have been decisive. Ultimately, the talks failed because the ICRC would not meet rebel demands to publicly denounce the Ethiopian government and draw attention to the cause of Eritrean independence.

The ICRC considered the cost of such an approach to be too high. A public human rights campaign would have threatened the government's strategic interests and therefore would have required the ICRC to abandon any hope of eventual acceptance by both sides as a neutral intermediary, the only issue that distinguished it from the growing number of NGOs getting involved in the cross-border operation.

If the ICRC failed to persuade the Eritrean front to incorporate a Red Cross model of humanitarian neutrality, the front also failed to sway the ICRC into public human rights advocacy on behalf of Eritrean national self-determination. These two streams of neutrality—both of which originated in the West—clashed in Eritrea.

In Tigray the ICRC faced the challenge of a different rival neutrality. It gained access to Tigray from both the government and the rebel sides for the first time in 1983. The immediate aim was to provide food on both sides of the war so migrants could choose to walk in either direction for relief. In contrast to the NGOs supporting Emergency Relief Desk, however, the ICRC was not satisfied to remain indefinitely in a strictly limited relief role. Its long-term strategy, therefore, was to work on each side as a base for gaining acceptance by both sides to act as a neutral humanitarian intermediary.[8]

The bottleneck for relief operations with REST was transport capacity, measured in trucks, passable roads, and security of transit. The Ethiopian Air Force directly attacked cross-border routes within Tigray. In 1985 the ICRC set up a transport operation, with 111 Red Cross trucks and its own repair shop, to deliver food deep into Tigray. The operation was independent of REST and sought to place an ICRC observer at each convoy and at each relief distribution in Tigray (Nicod 1990; Khüng 1991). Ironically, the Red Cross emblem—the powerful symbol of ICRC humanitarian neutrality—was not emblazoned on its trucks for fear of making them targets for government guns.

Concurrently on the government side of Tigray and Eritrea, the ICRC established a "landbridge" system that allowed peasants living in rebel-controlled areas to walk into government towns and pick up monthly food rations to carry home. The system expanded in scale during 1985 and was stabilized through secret coordination with the Tigrayan and Eritrean fronts. There was no contact across military lines, but Red Cross delegates passed information from the Ethiopian operation through headquarters in Geneva to the head delegate in Khartoum, who consulted with each front. He showed them maps indicating distribution points and asked them to respect the site and to send women and children for rations (Riedmatten 1990; Küng 1991).

The landbridge in Tigray was as close as the ICRC came to conducting a major action with the consent of both government and rebels. Rather than a true cross-line operation, in which the ICRC acts as a neutral intermediary accepted by both sides, it was largely an operation on the government side, with parallel coordination in Khartoum.

The cross-border component of ICRC strategy delivered food effectively into Tigray but did not endure. The autonomous operation generated high costs per ton of delivered grain. It made sense only as an

8. When the Tigrayan front captured Ethiopian soldiers, it held them only a few months and then released them in Tigray. The ICRC provided some relief supplies to REST for the prisoners but did not raise the issue of prisoner visits.

expression of Red Cross neutrality, which precludes enhancing the strategic interests of the adversaries. This model of neutrality was increasingly crowded in the cross-border operations during the 1980s by two rival models. Emergency Relief Desk expanded food assistance after 1984 according to an emerging model of neutrality as balance. The Tigray Transport and Agriculture Consortium, with War On Want as lead agency, modeled neutrality as advocacy by donating trucks to REST and building roads in rebel Tigray. In this context the elaborate and expensive Red Cross operation appeared increasingly irrelevant.

The realignment of contending neutralities was driven by the growing priority to prevent migration from Eritrea and Tigray, defined as both a humanitarian interest by international NGOs and a political interest by government donors. From the point of view of ERD and other relief NGOs, the ICRC was so meticulous in its efforts to minimize the strategic consequences of assistance that it could not deliver food in adequate volume to keep migrants in place. From the point of view of WOW and other advocacy NGOs, the ICRC was so careful not to take sides in the war that it did not publish information on the government human rights violations that were the root cause of the migration. These practical bulwarks of Red Cross neutrality became perceived as handicaps in the campaign to prevent migration.

In May 1987 the ICRC decided to withdraw entirely from the cross-border operation in both Tigray and Eritrea. Every initiative to make a unique contribution as a neutral intermediary was either redundant with respect to NGO operations or rebuffed by the insurgents. The famine emergency of 1984–1985 had apparently subsided, and ERA and REST could count on substantial relief and transport support from other sources, such as ERD and the twin consortia led by WOW. Moreover, ICRC nutritional assessments indicated that the populations in greatest danger resided in central Tigray, beyond the reach of the existing cross-border roads. The failure of the 1986 agreement with the Eritrean front to allow private prisoner visits also played a role in the decision. The ICRC could have remained in the cross-border operation by conforming to the relief model set by ERD or the advocacy model set by WOW, but it made little progress on the traditional Red Cross model of acting as a neutral intermediary.

The ICRC accomplished much for victims on both sides of the war in Ethiopia, and it pursued the widest variety of humanitarian tactics of all organizations involved in the conflict. Evaluated according to its own demanding standard, however, the ICRC failed to carry out a single action for which it had the consent of opposing elites to act as a neutral humanitarian intermediary.

The ICRC continued to work on the government side until it was expelled in 1988, though it renewed operations immediately after the rebel victory in 1991.⁹ In the cross-border operation through the end of the war, however, ERD became increasingly important as a conduit for international food assistance to expanding rebel territory. Thus, the model of neutrality as balance triumphed in the humanitarian contention of the cross-border operation.

Conclusion

The transnational humanitarian movement's cross-border operation to Eritrea and Tigray was a web of contentious and complementary organizational links and specializations. It was created through an accumulation of tactical choices made by hundreds of persons with no central coordination. In 1981, a decade before the end of the war, neither the existence nor the shape of the cross-border operation was firmly established. Working without a clear template for action, humanitarian personnel tailored responses to the shifting context.

In the process, the cross-border operation organized itself into an entity that was more than the sum of its parts. It displayed a structure that is intelligible as the intersection of the evolving interests of the Eritrean and Tigrayan fronts, international NGOs, and external government donors. The international humanitarian network eventually brought to the cross-border operation a full array of NGOs seeking access to the population and presenting humanitarian neutrality in several forms.

ERA and REST represented a brilliant melding of humanitarian and revolutionary agendas. Through these organizational innovations, the insurgents incorporated Western relief, development, and human rights practices into their Afro-Maoist revolutions. Portraying themselves as indigenous NGOs, ERA and REST negotiated links with a multitude of international organizations to attract attention and resources. On the basis of the case that they met international standards being violated by the Ethiopian government, they produced a humanitarian diplomacy to advocate the legitimacy of their revolutions in international forums and to gain acceptance in the club of states.

The International Committee of the Red Cross, War On Want, and the Scandinavian NGOs that launched Emergency Relief Desk all drew upon universal humanitarian principles. Yet they responded to the

---

9. When a coalition led by the Tigray People's Liberation Front took power in May 1991, REST leaders immediately asked the ICRC head delegate in Addis Ababa to handle the postwar humanitarian crisis of Ethiopian soldiers and civilian displaced from Eritrea south into Ethiopia (DeMars 1992).

same reality with different policies, which generated different political consequences for the adversaries in the conflict. Their responses can be seen in retrospect to represent distinct models of humanitarian neutrality that contended with each other for access to the victims and support from donors.

ERD represented an evolving conception of *neutrality as balance*. This conception, which has been institutionalized in UN and NGO policy since the end of the Cold War, holds that material assistance should be delivered to vulnerable populations on all sides of internal conflicts in order to prevent starvation and migration with their destabilizing political consequences. This model of neutrality is relatively tolerant —in practice, if not in theory—of policies that influence the strategic interests of the warring parties.

WOW, in contrast, followed a conception of *neutrality as advocacy*. This approach contains a paradox. Universal standards such as human rights and participatory development are applied impartially to measure the performance of all the adversaries in a conflict. If one side is found to meet standards that the other side violates, however, impartiality can lead to advocating the legitimacy of one side in the conflict. WOW operated on the edge of humanitarian partisanship by publicly endorsing the legitimacy of the Eritrean and Tigrayan revolutions and by leading NGO consortia that channeled resources cross-border for building rebel transport and agricultural infrastructure.

The ICRC could have achieved acceptance in the cross-border operation by conforming to either of these models. Instead, it attempted to maintain its traditional role as *neutral humanitarian intermediary* that would seek acceptance from all adversaries on the basis of a credible claim that its operations had no significant influence on their strategic interests. In order to avoid creating such an influence, the ICRC neither channeled resources into the cross-border operation with the liberality of ERD nor channeled information on government human rights practices to the international public with the forcefulness of WOW.

To understand why these organizations adhered to their specific models of neutrality, it is helpful to observe the comparative structures of the transnational social movements in which they were embedded. ERD was founded by, and composed exclusively of, NGOs linked with churches. It was also connected by its members with several overlapping global networks of church NGOs. The effective structure of this transnational social movement resides in the common loyalty of NGO professionals and governing boards to church bodies in both donor and recipient countries. Hence, church NGOs are part of a *symbiotic federation* rooted in church bodies. Church NGOs normally work in partnership with local churches and share their organizational interests. In Ethiopia and Eritrea, where churches had populations on all sides of the conflict, the organizational interests of church NGOs led them to support relief assistance on all sides of the conflict—to practice neutrality as balance.

In contrast to church NGOs, secular NGOs such as WOW and most members of the consortia for Eritrea and Tigray have no natural local partner organizations. Their transnational social movement structure is a *fluid federation* of ad hoc and potentially shifting alliances. As a result, secular NGOs operating in internal conflicts are more likely than church NGOs to take politically charged humanitarian positions. WOW found a role in the Ethiopian conflict by practicing neutrality as advocacy for the Eritrea and Tigrayan revolutions on the basis of universal humanitarian standards.

The ICRC participates in the global Red Cross and Red Crescent Movement, which has a complex federated structure. However, the ICRC segments its several forms of participation in the broader movement. When the ICRC engages in humanitarian action in armed conflicts, it functions as a *unitary organization* rather than as part of a federation. Its organizational interest, also rooted in its historical mission to promote humanitarian law and its unique relationship with the state system, is to act as a neutral humanitarian intermediary with the simultaneous consent of opposing adversaries. This aspiration leads the ICRC to strictly minimize the strategic consequences of its operations.

Ironically, the Red Cross model of neutral intermediary was marginalized in the cross-border operation by the intersection of the interests of the Maoist insurgents and Western government donors. The rebels chose to resist ICRC initiatives and strengthen the other two tracks of the cross-border operation, which generated benefits for themselves or costs for the Ethiopian government. Government donors, of which the largest was the United States, sought to prevent migration. They therefore promoted the model of neutrality as balance with its priority on delivering large-scale material assistance and its tolerance of strategic benefits for the adversaries.

Preventing migration is the humanitarian objective that has assumed a dominant position in international policy toward recent internal conflicts such as Bosnia, Rwanda, and Chechnya. The cross-border operation to Eritrea and Tigray constituted a crucial link in the historical origins of current policy. The cross-border operation also illuminates the reality of contending neutralities within the humanitarian network and shows how the political priorities of both adversary elites and external government donors can influence the specific mix of humanitarian policies that is operationalized in a particular conflict.

7

THE TRANSNATIONAL STRATEGIES OF THE SERVICE FOR PEACE AND JUSTICE IN LATIN AMERICA

Ron Pagnucco

Abstract

The Service for Peace and Justice (SERPAJ), a nonviolent human rights organization in Latin America, actively resisted the military dictatorships of the 1970s and 1980s. It was founded through transnational networks of Europeans, South Americans, and North Americans who continued to work together in the struggle for freedom. Under the constraints of very repressive regimes, SERPAJ tried to mobilize support for human rights through international institutions such as the Organization of American States (OAS) and the United Nations. Also, it cultivated links with such social movement organizations as the International Fellowship of Reconciliation (IFOR) and the U.S.-based Washington Office on Latin America (WOLA). In 1976, SERPAJ launched an International Campaign for Human Rights from its headquarters in Buenos Aires just as the military took power there. The Campaign educated and mobilized thousands of people in Latin America and in Europe on human rights issues and led to other international developments, including the bestowal in 1980 of the Nobel Peace Prize on the Campaign's founder, Adolfo Perez Esquivel. By heightening international awareness of the human rights situation in Latin America, the award of the prize to Perez Esquivel strengthened the human rights movement in Argentina and Latin America and contributed to the process of democratization.

Human rights and pro-democracy movements in authoritarian, repressive states have a special need for the help of transnational allies and institutions.[1] Serious constraints on organizing and mobilization, and the closure of points of institutional access such as democratic elections and the courts, have led many movement groups to look beyond the boundaries of their states for help. This has been especially true for human rights groups, which often are most crucial, if not most active, in repressive states. During the 1970s and 1980s, the global expansion of human rights groups, the incorporation of human rights concerns in the aid and trade policies of a number of Western states, and the development of international institutions and norms concerning human rights provided transnational political opportunities for those groups struggling against repressive regimes (see Pagnucco 1995; Smith 1995a; Brysk 1990). Human rights groups may also pursue transnational strategies because, in this modern age of global interdependence, repressive states often depend upon military and other international aid. Although the dependence of states on such foreign assistance varies, no state is completely autonomous in the modern world system. Thus, the struggle against repressive states often involves attempts to cut their aid from other states.

The Service for Peace and Justice (SERPAJ), a Latin American transnational social movement organization, utilized a transnational strategy in its struggle for human rights in the 1970s and 1980s. Headquartered in Buenos Aires during the height of state repression in Argentina, SERPAJ relied upon its transnational network of allies for help. It also attempted to use intergovernmental organizations (IGOs) in its efforts to restore respect for human rights in Argentina.

Latin America in the 1960s, 1970s and 1980s

The 1960s, 1970s, and 1980s were turbulent decades in Latin America. Political polarization and violence spread throughout the continent, and by the mid-1970s Argentina, Bolivia, Brazil, Chile, Ecuador, Paraguay, Peru, and Uruguay were under military rule. Many of these regimes remained in power into the 1980s. Although these regimes varied in their degrees of repressiveness, all imposed serious constraints on political participation and violated basic human rights.

1. Many thanks to Brady Tyson, Richard Chartier, Marty Deming, Creuza Maciel, Adolfo Perez Esquivel, Hildegard Goss-Mayr, John Howard Yoder, Jim Forest, Carlos Acuña, Tom Cornell, William Wipfler, Tom Quigley, Richard Deats, and Guillermo O'Donnell, who kindly shared their time to discuss with me their work and knowledge of SERPAJ, in addition to providing relevant documentation. Carlos Acuña commented on an earlier draft. Part of the research for and writing of this essay was conducted while I was a Visiting Faculty Fellow at the Kroc Institute for International Peace Studies, University of Notre Dame.

Some of the most brutal and repressive regimes known in Latin American history came to power during the 1960s and 1970s. Many took a new bureaucratic authoritarian form in which the military directly controlled the government and staffed many of its offices (see O'Donnell and Schmitter 1986). This structure of repression, combined with the militaries' strategy of demobilizing society, made these regimes especially difficult to dislodge.

During these decades the Catholic Church in Latin America also underwent some major changes that were very significant for the human rights movement. The Second General Conference of bishops, held in Medellin, Colombia, in 1968, stated that the church must make a "preferential option for the poor" and work for the human rights of all, especially the marginalized. The bishops committed resources and personnel to this effort, and in some countries the Church became the backbone of the opposition to authoritarian rule. However, in other countries the hierarchy actually supported the military regime (Argentina) or was not very active in opposing it (Uruguay). Nevertheless, after Medellin, human rights activists such as those in SERPAJ found important support in the Church in Latin America, where approximately 90 percent of the population was at least nominally Catholic.

The Service for Peace and Justice in Latin America developed out of a network of Roman Catholics and Protestants who were actively concerned with peace, nonviolence, and social justice. The religious pacifist International Fellowship of Reconciliation (IFOR), and its U.S. branch, the American Fellowship of Reconciliation (AFOR) were key groups in this network. The IFOR and AFOR organized the first Latin American Fellowship of Reconciliation (FOR) chapter in 1941 in Montevideo, Uruguay. Making extensive use of Methodist church networks in Latin America, including American missionaries such as Earl Smith and Richard Chartier, the FOR organized small chapters in Argentina, Brazil and, elsewhere during the 1940s and 1950s. However, the predominantly Protestant group had some difficulty organizing in a largely Roman Catholic continent.

In the early 1960s the IFOR sent two dynamic Roman Catholic organizers, Jean and Hildegard Goss-Mayr, on the first extensive organizing tour of the FOR in Latin America. The goal of the Goss-Mayrs was not necessarily to set up FOR chapters but to convert the Roman Catholic Church in Latin America to nonviolence. The philosophy and practice of nonviolence was virtually unknown in Roman Catholic circles, and even those few groups in Latin America that were committed to nonviolence (both Catholic and Protestant) tended to take a more passive, nonconfrontational, and spiritual view of nonviolence (Chartier 1984). The Goss-Mayrs traveled throughout the continent, talking to bishops, priests, nuns, and Catholic organizations of the right and left. They gave lectures and held training sessions on nonviolent action (Pagnucco and McCarthy 1992; J. and H. Goss-Meyer 1990).

In 1966 the Goss-Mayrs and Methodist missionary Earl Smith helped organize the first continental gathering of Latin American nonviolent activists. Later in the 1960s the Goss-Mayrs, Smith, and others used their transnational FOR network to bring FOR veterans and leading U.S. civil rights leaders like Glenn Smiley and James Lawson to Latin America to teach about nonviolence. In 1971 the Goss-Mayrs, Smith, and Smiley organized the second continental gathering of Latin American nonviolent activists, where "Service for Liberating Action in Latin America—Nonviolent Orientation" was created. At a third continental meeting in 1974, the Service for Liberating Action became the Service for Peace and Justice (SERPAJ), and Argentine activist Adolfo Perez Esquivel was named its Coordinator General. SERPAJ headquarters were established in Buenos Aires, and chapters soon emerged in several other countries, including Chile (1977), Brazil (1977), and Uruguay (1981), which were then under very repressive right-wing regimes (Pagnucco and McCarthy 1992; Perez Esquivel 1983).

The late 1960s and early 1970s also saw the development of transnational support networks in the United States and Western Europe. Representatives of churches and nonviolent organizations in Western Europe and the United States attended the Continental meetings in 1966, 1971, and 1974. By the late 1960s, Glenn Smiley and other FOR veterans of the civil rights movement, including Brady Tyson and Bernard Lafayette, formed "Justice-Action-Peace Latin America" to support the growing nonviolent movement in Latin America. By 1972 the Goss-Mayrs and others formed the European Groups Supporting Nonviolent Initiatives in Latin America, a West European network of groups including the FOR, the War Resisters International, and the Catholic peace group, Pax Christi, to support the movement. Thus, from the 1940s through the early 1970s, a transnational network of nonviolent activists committed to peace and justice developed within Latin America and among activists in Latin America, the United States, and Western Europe. This transnational network, out of which SERPAJ emerged, proved especially critical to SERPAJ in the 1970s and 1980s as it struggled against state repression.

The Transnational Strategy of SERPAJ

Founded to strengthen communication and coordination of action among isolated Latin American nonviolent groups and to educate and train people in the theory and practice of nonviolence, SERPAJ was not a mass membership organization, but a cadre "service" organization with a handful of staff members in each national branch. It saw its ties with groups outside of Latin America as valuable and important. After the Continental conference in 1974, for example, SERPAJ encouraged its European allies to protest the approaching French nuclear tests in the Pacific Ocean (Fabre 1974a, 1974b). However, the first major international campaign by SERPAJ focused on a situation in Latin America: the plight of indigenous peasants who were struggling for the right to purchase land for a just price in Llangahua Central, Ecuador. SERPAJ used its transnational networks to publicize the peasants' struggle and mobilize transnational protest. It circulated a statement written by the peasants themselves and encouraged its contacts to send telegrams and letters to the Ecuadoran president and Minister of Agriculture in Ecuador asking them to remedy the peasants' plight (Fabre 1974c,5). Although using a tactic similar to the one used by Amnesty International for nonviolent political prisoners, SERPAJ's concerns went beyond civil and political rights to include other issues and rights. Advancing these multifaceted goals, SERPAJ organized or supported local and transnational nonviolent direct action like fasts, demonstrations, and peasant land occupations (Pagnucco and McCarthy 1992; McManus and Schlabach 1991).

In the face of the growing repression in Latin America, SERPAJ issued a study document titled "Christian Reflections on the Universal Declaration of Human Rights" in 1975 (Veiga 1985). In 1976 it escalated its efforts by launching the large-scale International Campaign for Human Rights 1976–1978. Claiming that the upward spiral of violence required urgent reflection and action in defense of human rights, SERPAJ sought to mobilize governments, churches, international organizations, popular movements, peasant unions, workers, students, and others to press the United Nations to strengthen the observance of human rights throughout the world. Specifically, the Campaign sought the convening of a Special Session of the UN General Assembly addressing Human Rights and the establishment of an independent High Commissioner for Human Rights. SERPAJ proposed that for two years groups around the world engage in extensive organizing and study in preparation for a 1978 "Assembly of the Peoples in Defense of Human Rights." Here organizations and popular groups would meet to discuss human rights issues and propose their joint conclusions to a Special Session of the UN General Assembly.

On 29 March 1976, just three days after the military coup in Argentina, Adolfo Perez Esquivel began a four-month organizing tour of Latin America, the United States, Canada, and Europe. The IFOR helped organize the tour, which sought to further the International Campaign. Perez Esquivel traveled to Peru, Ecuador, Colombia, Panama, and Mexico, where he met with bishops, priests, ministers, church groups, and others working for human rights. He also traveled outside Latin America, visiting France, Belgium, Germany, Denmark, Holland, Austria, England, Spain, Italy, Switzerland, the United States, and Canada. In Europe, Perez Esquivel met with representatives of the UN Human Rights Commission and the International Labor Organization, as well as with officials of the European Common Market, members of the Danish parliament, and Austrian government officials. He also addressed many public meetings in Europe and the United States and met with a number of nongovernmental organizations (NGOs), including the World Council of Churches, the Institute for World Order, the World Federation of Workers, and the International Commission of Jurists (Perez Esquivel 1977).

AFOR member Richard Chartier accompanied Perez Esquivel during much of his tour in the United States. As a Methodist minister and FOR member in Buenos Aires in the late 1960s and early 1970s, Chartier influenced Perez Esquivel's thinking about nonviolence, and they developed a close friendship. When Chartier assumed a leadership role in the AFOR, he proved to be a very valuable ally for SERPAJ and Perez Esquivel during the darker days of repression. Perez Esquivel described his purpose for making this international tour:

> Our major objective is to draw together many countries and to work to make clearer the problems faced in Latin America, that the industrialized nations might come to see the situation in those countries and understand the relationship between the politics of their governments and the situation in which these countries find themselves. . . . What we are trying to do is to open all possible avenues of understanding and conscience and to take to international organizations those problems which are part of the life of our people. (quoted in Sanders 1978, 6–7)

Besides issuing a call to work for the implementation of the Universal Declaration of Human Rights, Perez Esquivel urged his Northern counterparts and international officials to direct more attention to conditions in Latin America to "spotlight repression which has already been institutionalized on the continent" (quoted in Sanders 1978, 7).

Perez Esquivel highlighted the need for transnational cooperative action, claiming, "[F]rom our experience we see that the work . . . should not be done only within Latin America. To be effective, it [must] be the joint effort of many groups and not the work of only one organization or one country" (quoted in Sanders 1978, 7). Clearly, transnational work was an essential part of SERPAJ's strategy. There were no purely domestic human rights movements in Latin America during the dictatorships of the 1960s, 1970s, and 1980s, just as there were no purely autarkic repressive regimes: many of these regimes collaborated with each other to repress dissidents and human rights activists, and all of these regimes received military assistance from the North.

The Latin American human rights movement found a growing number of allies in the U.S. during the later years of the Vietnam war. At that time, human rights concerns became an increasingly important basis for the expanding opposition to U.S. support for the South Vietnamese regime. By the time the United States ended its involvement in the war, antiwar groups, large segments of the public, and many members of Congress were calling for a U.S. foreign policy that respected international human rights norms and thus prevented future Vietnam wars. Other events, such as the U.S. supported overthrow of the democratically elected Chilean president Salvador Allende in 1973, contributed to the growing U.S. human rights movement, much of which focused on the abuse of human rights in Latin American states allied with the U.S.

In 1976 the Coalition for a New Foreign and Military Policy formed a Human Rights Working Group which soon attracted almost as many members as the Coalition itself (Livezey 1989). By 1974 the number of groups in Amnesty International USA (AIUSA) had grown to sixty, making it the fifth largest national section of Amnesty International. AIUSA was an effective ally of human rights activists in Latin America and helped to change some U.S. policies toward the region through its careful documentation and congressional testimony (see Ray and Taylor 1977). In 1974, Protestant and Catholic church agencies supported the formation of the Washington Office on Latin America (WOLA). WOLA promoted public education, testified at congressional hearings on the worsening situation in Latin America, and frequently brought human rights activists from the region to the U.S. for speaking tours and for meetings with church and government officials.

Social movement organizations (SMOs) in the United States and transnational social movement organizations (TSMOs) differed in their organizational capacities, issues of focus, and types of activities in which they engaged. Perhaps one of the most developed organizations in the human rights mobilizing structure in the 1970s was the National Council of Churches (NCC) Human Rights Office, which was formed in 1977 and headed by Rev. William Wipfler. Earlier, as head of the NCC's Latin America program, Wipfler befriended Perez Esquivel and provided assistance to the newly formed SERPAJ. The Office helped develop an international communications network of church workers that responded to reports of human rights abuses (Wipfler 1994). Upon hearing of a "disappearance," the Office would notify the State Department of the case, contact sympathetic members of Congress and ask them to look into the case, call the embassy of the country in which the disappearance occurred to inquire about the case, provide information to journalists about the case, and generate public action in the form of telegrams and/or telephone calls inquiring about the person who was abducted (Wipfler 1994; AIUSA 1981). The NCC Human Rights Office and similar organizations were invaluable assets to the Latin American human rights movement, and SERPAJ strove to maintain contact with them.

The growth and development of human rights groups in the United States and other countries provided important opportunities for SERPAJ and other human rights groups in Latin America. Important opportunities also developed in the U.S. government, which from 1973 to 1980 placed human rights concerns relatively high on its foreign policy agenda. In the mid-1970s new institutional opportunities emerged as Congress passed legislation tying U.S. military and economic aid, and U.S. votes in international financial institutions (e.g., the World Bank), to the human rights practices of the recipient country. With this legislation, the State Department was required to prepare annual reports on the human rights conditions of all countries receiving aid. During this period Congress also passed country-specific legislation cutting off miliary and, in some cases, economic aid. In 1977, Congress created the post of Assistant Secretary of State for Human Rights and Humanitarian Affairs, a post to which President Jimmy Carter appointed Patricia Derian, an energetic advocate of human rights.

The election of Jimmy Carter to the White House in 1977 also broadened opportunities for human rights promotion, as he appointed key civil rights activists to administrative posts. For example, Carter appointed Andrew Young, who had been a staff member of the Southern Christian Leadership Conference (SCLC) and a close associate of Martin Luther King, Jr., to the post of UN ambassador. Young, in turn, appointed to his staff a group of civil rights activists, including Brady Tyson, who was active in human rights generally and in the FOR and SERPAJ in particular. Tyson took a pioneering role at the UN in calling attention to Argentina's human rights violations (Weissbrodt and Bartolomei 1991, 1026).

Opportunities for human rights activists also expanded in some European countries during the 1970s, as several countries—such as

Norway, Holland, and Sweden—explicitly tied human rights practices to their foreign aid.

At the same time, opportunities in intergovernmental organizations were expanding. The rules of access for nongovernmental organizations (NGOs) became more open during the 1970s and 1980s, creating more institutional opportunities for groups to use IGOs like the Human Rights Commission. However, NGO statements to the Commission were restricted, and access was limited to those groups that had been given consultative status, which SERPAJ then lacked. The composition of the delegations and the individuals in IGOs also influenced the functioning of IGOs. For example, as director of the UN Human Rights Division, Dutch diplomat Theo van Boven aggressively pursued a human rights agenda.

However, political alignments of the delegations on the Human Rights Commission during the late 1970s and early 1980s blocked the Commission's work on Argentina and several other countries that seriously violated human rights.[2] Nevertheless, in February 1980 the Commission established a Working Group on Forced or Involuntary Disappearances, comprised of independent experts who diligently collected and published evidence provided by groups such as SERPAJ on disappearances in Argentina.

The Organization of American States (OAS) and the Inter-American Commission on Human Rights (IACHR) also provided opportunities for human rights activists. The IACHR actively pursued complaints of human rights violations in the region and made strong and clear recommendations in its summary reports. However, the OAS General Assembly rarely enacted these recommendations.

Despite their limitations, SERPAJ saw these IGOs as important opportunities. SERPAJ's "Orientation Booklet," a special edition of the February 1977 issue of their magazine *Paz y Justicia,* contained a model form for reporting human rights violations to the IACHR. The booklet also included the text of the ECOSOC 1503 Resolution and Resolution 1(24) of the Human Rights Commission's Subcommission for the Prevention of Discrimination and the Protection of Minorities, which outlined procedures to examine communications concerning human rights violations. Clearly, part of SERPAJ's strategy was to utilize institutional opportunities outside the repressive state as well as within it.

---

2. A major goal of the International Campaign for Human Rights 1976–1978 was to establish an independent office of UN High Commissioner on Human Rights to overcome these kinds of geopolitical machinations that constrained human rights work in the commission.

Although not formally launched in the United States, the Campaign gained many supporters in Europe and Latin America. One of the early and major supporters of the Campaign in Latin America was the Confederación Latinoamericana de Trabajadores (CLAT) [Latin American Confederation of Workers], an organization that had expressed an interest in nonviolence and had been in contact with the IFOR and SERPAJ. In Europe, the IFOR initiated and organized the Campaign,[3] known as "CHR '78" (Campaign Human Rights '78), and mobilized its network of activists to support SERPAJ (IFOR 1977, 5–7). The War Resisters International (WRI) and the British Section of the Women's International League for Peace and Freedom were among the main organizational cosponsors of CHR '78, and several prominent individuals—including Sean MacBride and Lord Noel-Baker—endorsed it. An international coordinating office was established in London, and CHR '78 national coordinating committees were established in Austria, Belgium, France, Germany, Italy, Holland, Spain, and Switzerland. National coordinators of CHR '78 were essentially the same individuals and organizations in the network of European Groups Supporting Nonviolent Initiatives in Latin America.

The Campaign in Latin America had difficulty mobilizing because of the repression there. SERPAJ's "Orientation Booklet" on the Campaign was produced during the height of repression in Argentina, at a time when eight Latin American countries—including the entire Southern Cone (Argentina, Brazil, Chile, and Uruguay)—were under military rule.[4] The booklet also included the complete text of the Universal Declaration, a model of presentation of habeas corpus, a form to record information in cases of detention or abduction, and a listing of the names and addresses of UN and OAS offices and peace and human rights groups throughout the world. Early in 1977 such information was crucial because it was unclear how widespread government-ordered disappearances were. Perez Esquivel prioritized the gathering of information on detentions and disappearances and the sharing of this information with SERPAJ's transnational contacts

3. Jim Forest, the Executive Secretary of the IFOR from 1977–1989, described the human rights activities of the IFOR in the 1970s: "IFOR's work for human rights occurs at several levels. It occurs mainly in the work of our branches in the various countries, but also in collaboration with such specialized movements as Amnesty International and the International League for Human Rights. It occurs in special efforts on behalf of member branches—particularly special campaigns for pacifists in prison for their beliefs and labors, seen recently in our work for imprisoned peace activists in Argentina and Vietnam" (Forest 1977, 4).

4. This figure does not include the military and civilian dictatorships in Central America and the Caribbean at the time.

(Acuña 1995). The risks involved in gathering this information and mobilizing for the Campaign in Argentina were great: they finally led to Perez Esquivel's arrest and detention on 4 April 1977 (H. Goss-Mayr 1993). When Perez Esquivel was imprisoned for fifteen months, which time he was tortured, and then kept under house arrest for more than a year afterwards, SERPAJ's transnational ties were pressed into action to save him and the organization.

Transnational Support for Perez Esquivel

Jim Forest, then executive director of the IFOR, was notified by SERPAJ and Jean and Hildegard Goss-Mayr of Perez-Esquivel's arrest. Forest, in turn, notified others like Tom Cornell, the program coordinator of the AFOR (Forest 1993). Marty Deming summarized the transnational strategy of the IFOR:

> The IFOR contacted the emergency list of people in support groups immediately on hearing of Adolfo's arrest. This was followed by a mailing to all support groups and friends concerned with [SERPAJ. At SERPAJ's request,] a number of letters were written to key persons in many countries to ask them to work for interventions on Adolfo's behalf at the highest levels in the government, the church, and other bodies with influence.... After consulting with several of the support groups, the IFOR designated October 4th as a day of support for nonviolent initiatives in Latin America and asked support groups and individuals to renew efforts for Adolfo's release on that day. (Deming 1977, 3)

Thus the International Campaign for Human Rights was now also becoming an international campaign to save Perez Esquivel.

At the AFOR headquarters, Cornell immediately organized public education and letter-writing initiatives on Perez Esquivel's behalf. He also helped stage demonstrations outside Argentina's UN mission in New York. In addition, he notified Ambassador Andrew Young, with whom he had worked during the civil rights movement, about Perez Esquivel's case. Young instructed Tyson to call the State Department and ask them to contact the Argentine government regarding Perez Esquivel (Cornell 1994). Fulfilling Young's request, the State Department by September 1977 had made two official inquiries to the Argentine government about Perez Esquivel.

Similar activities were organized in Europe. IFOR helped organize letter-writing campaigns, demonstrations in front of Argentine embassies, and meetings with Argentine officials in France, Germany, England, Switzerland, Austria, and the Netherlands (Deming 1993, 1977).

The transnational response to Perez Esquivel's arrest was relatively quick: As Cornell reported in *Fellowship*, statements of support for Perez Esquivel had been sent to the president of Argentina by organizations including the IFOR, Pax Christi International, WRI, Amnesty International (AI), the International League for Human Rights, The U.S. Catholic Conference, the American Friends Service Committee, and the NCC. All of these organizations had had contact with SERPAJ earlier in the 1970s, and several of them were part of the pre-SERPAJ transnational network of the 1960s and 1970s.

Soon after hearing of Perez Esquivel's arrest, Jim Forest contacted Betty Williams and Mairead Corrigan, two Irish women who were awarded the Nobel Peace Prize in 1976 for their work in Northern Ireland. Through his IFOR work, Forest knew Williams and Corrigan, and hoped they, as Nobel recipients, would nominate Perez Esquivel for the Prize to give him greater international visibility and protection.[5] Williams and Corrigan nominated him for the Prize in 1978, 1979, and 1980. The IFOR arranged a trip for Mairead Corrigan to Argentina in September of 1979, just after Perez Esquivel was released from house arrest. She spent ten days there speaking to various individuals and groups about nonviolence and human rights; she also publicly praised Perez Esquivel for his work, proclaiming that she hoped he would receive the Nobel Peace Prize for that work (*Paz y Justicia*, Oct.-Nov. 1979). When Corrigan left Argentina, she smuggled out documentation on disappearances given to her by Perez Esquivel (Corrigan Maguire 1994).

The Nobel Peace Prize: Transcending Sovereignty

The Nobel Peace Prize was awarded to a human rights activist— South African black leader Albert Lithuli—for the first time in 1960. This shift to considering human rights activists appropriate recipients of the Prize, which later allowed Williams and Corrigan to nominate Perez Esquivel, created a new international institutional opportunity for movements and activists. From 1960 to 1979, nearly one-third (6 of 17) of Nobel Peace Prizes awarded went to human rights activists or organizations.[6] In this way, an internationally famous nongovernmental institution had transcended the sovereignty of the state by bestow-

---

5. This tactic had been used once before, in the case of Carl von Ossietzky, a German pacifist imprisoned for opposing the Nazi regime. Ossietzky won the Prize in 1935, and although the receipt of the Prize did not win his freedom, it apparently saved his life and led to better treatment during his imprisonment (Abrams 1988, 125–129). In her Nobel lecture, Williams compared Ossietzky and Perez Esquivel.

6. The names and dates are: Albert Lithuli, 1960; Martin Luther King, Jr., 1964; Rene Cassin, 1968; Sean MacBride, 1974; A. Sakharov, 1975; and Amnesty International, 1977.

ing a major award to actors who use international norms to criticize their own state's behavior. The Prize brings international attention to the recipient and his or her cause, creating new opportunities for meeting with world leaders.

Contrary, perhaps, to what the Argentine military junta expected, Perez Esquivel's imprisonment did not kill the International Campaign for Human Rights but seems, in fact, to have strengthened it. The CLAT took a greater role in the Campaign; they developed SERPAJ's idea of an Assembly of the Peoples and in November 1978 held a Latin American Assembly for the Human Rights and Liberties of the Workers and the Peoples. Over sixty unions and labor confederations and over a dozen human rights groups from every country in Latin America attended the Assembly. Thirteen non-Latin American organizations sent delegates: among these were the UN Division on Human Rights (van Boven's agency), the International Labor Organization, the U.S. Catholic Conference, the Latin American Conference of Bishops, and AI. The Assembly approved the "Latin American Declaration on the Rights and Liberties of the Workers and the Peoples," in which civil and political rights and democracy were affirmed and combined with social, economic, and cultural rights and the rights of unions and workers (Latin American Confederation of Workers 1978). The Declaration became an organizing document for the CLAT, and the Assembly has become a regular CLAT event since 1978. In 1987, CLAT established a new TSMO, the Latin American Commission for the Rights and Liberties of the Workers and the Peoples. Thus, the International Campaign had one major institutional outcome, albeit a nongovernmental, though transnational, one.

Although Perez Esquivel's receipt of the Nobel Prize helped the Campaign reach some of its goals, it did not significantly advance human rights in the United Nations. A special convocation of the General Assembly was held in 1978 to commemorate the thirtieth anniversary of the Universal Declaration, but this was not structured as the Campaign had hoped. Also, no progress was made towards establishing an office of High Commissioner on Human Rights, because the proposal was tabled in committee. The Human Rights Commission did, however, organize a 1978 seminar on National and Local Institutions for the Promotion and Protection of Human Rights, which approved a series of guidelines.

The Impact of the Nobel Peace Prize

Alfred Nobel had hoped that the Nobel Peace Prize he had created would be awarded to men and women who made contributions to peace and human unity and could use the Prize and the money that accompanied it to help them in their ongoing work (Abrams 1988). In awarding the Prize to Perez Esquivel, the Nobel Committee expressed the hope that the Prize would help him with his work as it had other human rights activists who had received it (Abrams 1988; Ready et al. 1985). The Prize certainly brought attention to the situation in Argentina, even though Perez Esquivel himself was not very well known outside a small transnational network of activists.

The Prize opened many new opportunities for Perez Esquivel. On his way to Oslo to receive the Prize, he stopped in the United States to meet with Catholic bishops, members of Congress, officials from the State Department, and UN Secretary General Kurt Waldheim. He also met with Latin American foreign ministers attending an OAS meeting in which the 1979 Inter-American Commission on Human Rights report on Argentina was being discussed. After receiving the Prize, Perez Esquivel, accompanied by Jim Forest of the IFOR, visited members of Parliament and high-ranking government officials in various European countries, as well as Pope John Paul II, to whom he presented a dossier on the 442 disappeared infants and children in Argentina. The pope, who had spoken out against the repression in Argentina, presented Perez Esquivel with a papal silver medal (Forest 1993).

In Argentina the receipt of the Prize by Perez Esquivel was what Iain Guest called "the ultimate accolade for Argentina's human rights movement and the ultimate public rebuke for the junta" (Guest 1990, 238). As Guest reported:

> [I]n private the Junta's reaction was close to panic. Concluded one Foreign Ministry analysis: "The decision of the Nobel Peace committee is further proof of the intensity of the international campaign. It also creates a situation in which Argentina and the Soviet Union are placed in the same boat. Sakharov and Perez Esquivel are symbolic figures who have been projected from anonymity to international prominence by the prize. This serves to unite both governments and subject them to the same criticism." (1990, 239)

Perez Esquivel believed the Prize gave him and SERPAJ, as well as other Argentine human rights activists, some protection; nevertheless, he continued to receive death threats, and SERPAJ workers were still harassed and arrested. The Prize was awarded at an important moment: In September of 1979 the IACHR sent a delegation to Argentina to investigate human rights abuses and later issued a report very critical of the regime. The combination of the Prize and the IACHR investigation helped create an opening for the public debate of human rights in Argentina (Jelin 1987). Although segments of the Argentine press denigrated the Prize and its recipient, on 14 October 1980, two major papers, *Clarin* and *La Prensa*, ran lengthy front-page stories about Perez Esquivel and his work. Both papers devoted a great deal of space to the story, and they prominently, fairly, and accurately covered Perez Esquivel and his work and the reactions of individuals and organizations throughout the world. The *La Prensa* and *Clarin* stories included Perez Esquivel's explicit (though noninflammatory) criticisms of the regime's human rights record.

Even this mixed coverage suggested that an opening had, in fact, preceded Perez Esquivel's receipt of the Prize in order for such stories to be published, and that the event contributed further to the opening. Political scientist Guillermo O'Donnell, a prominent dissident, reports that by 1979 he felt safer from repression than he had felt earlier; among the events contributing to this change in the political situation were the IACHR visit and an increase in union activity (O'Donnell 1993). In short, the receipt of the Prize by Perez Esquivel added to the growing disintegration of the dictatorship.

The Nobel Peace Prize opened a new stage in transnational activism for SERPAJ. Transnational mobilizing structures were strengthened and expanded partly because of the Prize, and many IGO and national governmental officials became more accessible and supportive of Perez Esquivel and SERPAJ's work. The newly found fame of SERPAJ and its Coordinator General contributed to the founding in 1981 of a SERPAJ branch in Uruguay, then under a repressive regime. According to Fr. Luis Perez Aguirre, organizer and coordinator of SERPAJ-Uruguay, "the help of Adolfo Perez Esquivel after he received the Nobel Prize was decisive because it put in our reach all his international links" (Perez Aguirre 1993).

By awarding the Prize, the Nobel Committee, a nonstate international institution, transcended state sovereignty and reinforced international norms; it contributed to Argentina's growing political opening and the debate about human rights within Argentina; and it increased Perez Esquivel's and SERPAJ's access to a variety of governmental and nongovernmental actors, organizations, and resources. In short, the Nobel Committee became an unexpected, yet very important, transnational ally for the movement.

Conclusion

This study illustrates several important points concerning the dynamics of transnational social movements. First, it highlights the inadequacies of a state-centric analytic approach. SERPAJ was formed through a transnational network of activists that drew heavily on church networks. This transnational network had a major influence on the organization's capacity to survive and on the strategies and tactics it chose. With only very limited opportunities to influence the behavior of repressive states from within, SERPAJ tried to mobilize pressure from without; it gathered information on the repression and worked with its transnational contacts to inform the world about the situation in Latin America and to move states to cut off their support for repressive regimes there. The transnational network also served to mobilize transnational protest against the repression of SERPAJ members, most notably Adolfo Perez Esquivel. The receipt of the Nobel Peace Prize by Perez Esquivel illustrates how an international institution can transcend state sovereignty and help a movement that is challenging its own government. The Nobel Committee's decision in 1960 to begin awarding the Prize to human rights activists created a new international opportunity for social movements.[7]

This study of SERPAJ also shows the inadequacy of analyses that map only the number and type of SMOs and the structure of political opportunities within a single country. The number and type of like-minded SMOs in *other* countries, and the political opportunity structures in those countries, influence the context in which social movements operate. SERPAJ was able to mobilize on a transnational scale because of the existence of like-minded and supportive movement groups and changing political opportunities in a number of national political arenas.

---

7. The varying impacts on social movements of the receipt of the Nobel Peace Prize by their leaders is an area requiring further research (but see Abrams 1988). For example, it appears that Perez Esquivel's receipt of the Prize had a greater impact in Argentina than Martin Luther King, Jr.'s receipt of the Prize had in the United States. The impact of the Prize may be related to the degree of state repression, among other factors.

PART THREE

*Generating Constituencies
for Multilateral Policy*

8

MOBILIZING AROUND THE UNITED NATIONS SPECIAL SESSIONS ON DISARMAMENT

David C. Atwood

Abstract

The UN Special Sessions on Disarmament (SSDs), held in 1978, 1982, and 1988, provided opportunities for transnational mobilization around the disarmament issue and generated attempts by transnational social movement organizations (TSMOs) and other nongovernmental organizations (NGOs) to influence the preparations for these conferences and the political negotiations taking place during them. They also engaged even more nongovernmental organizations in mobilizing public opinion on nuclear disarmament. As a result, the attention of governments to nuclear disarmament was heightened, and they were pressed to acknowledge links between disarmament and other social concerns. The political organization of the conferences and differences among disarmament organizations meant that transnational social movement organizations (TSMOs) were unable to exert much direct influence on the negotiations. Nonetheless, their participation in the SSDs had important indirect consequences: First, it affected public mobilization on the issue and therefore the terms of national and intergovernmental debate; second, it resulted in political learning by TSMOs and fostered transnational cooperation among peace and disarmament organizations.

In 1995, the fiftieth anniversary of the bombing of Hiroshima and Nagasaki, the world saw renewed attention to nuclear disarmament.[1]

1. This chapter draws substantially on the author's participant-observer research at the SSDI and SSDII and as described in Atwood (1982, 1983).

A year in which the Nuclear Nonproliferation Treaty was extended indefinitely, its review mechanisms and disarmament principles strengthened, also saw unprecedented governmental and popular opposition to Chinese and French decisions to continue nuclear testing. The nuclear threat, so much a focus of the First United Nations Special Session on Disarmament (SSDI) in 1978, is still very real. But important steps have been taken in the intervening seventeen years to control nuclear and other weapons systems, turning major parts of the 1978 rhetoric into reality.

The 1978, 1982, and 1988 Special Sessions on Disarmament (SSDs) were important in setting the international agenda on disarmament and related issues. They have also been important focal points for social movement organizations in their efforts to mobilize public opinion and affect national and international political decisions related to international peace and security.

The SSDs, like the many other UN-sponsored ad hoc world conferences and special sessions of the UN General Assembly, represented attempts to expand international cooperation on a perceived global problem (Taylor 1989, 30; Weiss and Jordan 1978, 3). In 1995 alone, the World Summit for Social Development (the "Social Summit," Copenhagen), the Fourth World Conference on Women (Beijing), and the Review and Extension Conference of the Nuclear Nonproliferation Treaty, addressed increasingly urgent global concerns.

Global conferences help to publicize issues, to change dominant attitudes, and to initiate problem-solving actions, often by strengthening existing international institutions or developing new ones (Weiss and Jordan 1978, 4). In addition, conferences help raise new issues, redefine or increase the salience of existing ones, and restructure global responses to them. Thus, they often "can be the mechanism to promote the change in the agenda against the opposition of those who want to maintain the *status quo*" (Willetts 1989, 46). As such, they are important targets of social movement efforts.

The General Assembly of the United Nations regularly includes disarmament and related issues in its annual deliberations. The 1976 decision to devote a special session solely to disarmament signaled a growing concern about global arms races and the inadequacies of existing disarmament measures. The First Special Session on Disarmament focused international attention on disarmament-related matters and gave them a new sense of urgency (Jack 1977, 112–20; Groom and Guilhaudis 1989, 129–31). The Final Document of SSDI remains a benchmark for measuring international progress in this critical issue area.

Despite the good intentions and designs outlined in the Final Document of SSDI, the reintensification of the Cold War from about 1980 and new stages in the nuclear arms race contributed to the SSDs' disappointing results. Although the Second Special Session on Disarmament (SSDII) managed at least to reaffirm the directions set in the Final Document of SSDI and to endorse the establishment of a World Disarmament Campaign, the timing of the 1982 SSD was not propitious and its goals were not sufficiently clear (Groom and Guilhaudis 1989, 135). Likewise, the timing of the 1988 SSD contributed to its failure to achieve specific goals, despite wide areas of agreement achieved during the meeting and despite (or, ironically, perhaps because of) the fact that it took place in a period of Cold War thaw when genuine progress was being made in bilateral East-West arms reduction negotiations (Herby 1988, 5; Akashi 1988, 7).

Despite their disappointing results, the three SSDs nevertheless affirmed the centrality to the world community of disarmament concerns in relation to global security. As the Under-Secretary General for Disarmament Affairs commented at the end of SSDIII:

> The Third Special Session on Disarmament . . . should not be looked at as an isolated event. It was rather a chapter in the long and tortuous process of humanity's search for a more secure world. . . . It has also showed where the remaining obstacles lie. (Akashi 1988, 9; see also, on achievements of SSDII, Groom and Guilhaudis 1989, 138–39, and of SSDIII, Herby 1988, 2)

The Final Document of SSDI demonstrated another function of special sessions, namely, mobilizing public opinion on an issue (UN Document A/RES/S-10/2, July 1978, par. 129). In this sense, the SSDs were not just meetings of government representatives. The work of peace organizations and other transnational social movement organizations (TSMOs) contributed to the momentum that brought about the First Special Session on Disarmament (Jack 1977, 11). Their participation at the SSDs was an integral part of the conference process and reflected the part social movement organizations (SMOs) play in the development of international regimes and policy change.

Although the term "the peace movement" is often used to describe the collection of national and transnational organizations working on disarmament-related issues, this movement is enormously diverse.[2]

---

2. "Social movement actors" at the SSDs included a wide range of NGOs, many of them national SMOs working explicitly for peace and disarmament. Groups pursuing other goals, such as development and human rights, also participated in the conferences, as did transnationally organized SMOs. The more inclusive term NGO will thus be used here to refer to this diverse collection of actors.

The pluralism of organizations concerned with disarmament thus was an important factor conditioning their relationship to the SSDs and continues to affect efforts to organize transnationally on that issue. A second conditioning factor was the fact that states guard closely their necessary preeminence in areas related to security. This has meant that, unlike the areas of human rights or environment issues, for example, multilateral discussions and decision making about disarmament remain largely closed to nongovernmental actors. This factor limited the part nongovernmental organizations (NGOs) could play in the special sessions on disarmament and continues to qualify the work of SMOs in the field of international security. By examining closely the work of TSMOs and other NGOs at SSDI, and comparing their activities in 1978 with those at the subsequent SSDs, this analysis distills lessons about the role of TSMOs in global disarmament efforts.

Opportunities prior to Special Session I

The First UN General Assembly Special Session on Disarmament was a catalyst for efforts by hundreds of local, national, and transnational nongovernmental actors to increase their expertise, form coalitions, and try to mobilize publics and influence governments (see Atwood 1982, 42–74).

In the months leading up to SSDI, some organizations published materials to increase public awareness of disarmament issues in general and the Special Session in particular. Groups in many countries sponsored conferences and undertook a variety of other activities to engage a wider sector of the population. Of particular importance was the renewed interest in disarmament among churches in many Western countries.

Many groups also intensified protest activity to increase public pressure—particularly in the United States, Canada, Britain, the Netherlands, and Japan. Other activities sought to directly influence governmental positions at the SSD. For example, the Disarmament Working Group of the Coalition for a New Foreign and Military Policy, a Washington-based network of more than forty national religious, labor, peace, research, and social action organizations, understood that major progress on disarmament at the SSD depended on the willingness of the United State to play a positive role there. It therefore tried to influence U.S. policy through meetings with government officials and members of Congress.

The SSD also stimulated a great deal of transnational interaction among NGOs, including the formation in October 1977 of the International Mobilization for Survival (IMfS), a coalition of international and national peace and disarmament SMOs. Aimed primarily at activist organizations that used strategies of nonviolent public protest and political organizing, the IMfS sought, for many months before SSDI, to inform its constituents about actions taking place in various countries and to coordinate protest actions in the United States, Western Europe, and Japan. In addition, immediately before the SSD, many organizations around the world submitted special messages and documents to the United Nations, demonstrating public support for nuclear disarmament or providing specialized information.

Perhaps the most significant single joint international event before SSDI was the International NGO Conference on Disarmament, held in Geneva in the spring of 1978. Attended by more than 500 representatives from 85 different international nongovernmental organizations and more than 200 national organizations from 46 countries, the conference prepared formal statements on disarmament issues, increased public awareness, and encouraged NGO action for disarmament. This conference was organized by the Geneva-based Special NGO Committee for Disarmament, which, with its counterpart in New York, the NGO Committee on Disarmament, represented to the UN the interests of more than one hundred NGOs. These committees were chiefly responsible for negotiating an official NGO role and for organizing joint NGO activities before and during the SSD.

One particularly important type of NGO activity was to provide assistance to national and international officials in their preparation for the SSD. The Stanley Foundation in the United States organized three off-the-record, informal gatherings on SSD themes to give diplomats an opportunity to interact with one another and to grow in their understanding of other national perspectives outside the formal context of the UN itself. The Quaker United Nations Office in New York organized a series of informal seminars aimed at UN delegates who were not experts on disarmament, particularly those from small or poor countries. Other organizations orchestrated informational meetings between representatives of governments and arms control experts.

Activities in Special Session I

The hundreds of individuals attracted to New York in May 1978 by the Special Session on Disarmament reflected the expanded public interest and involvement in disarmament issues. Some 236 NGOs, represented by over 800 individuals, officially registered with the UN to participate in SSDI (United Nations Centre for Disarmament 1978). In addition, over 500 Japanese representatives from more than 200 regional and national Japanese organizations came as a single national NGO delegation to SSDI (*Disarmament* 1978, 76).[3] Although those numbers pale in comparison with recent world conferences, SSDI was, in terms of NGO participation, the largest such world conference of the decade (Feraru 1979, 416; 1974). In addition, many organizational representatives and individuals not registered with the UN participated in the many nongovernmental events running parallel to the SSD.

A major feature of many ad hoc world conferences both before and since SSDI has been NGO forums parallel to the IGO sessions. For a variety of reasons, however, this feature was not part of any of the Special Sessions on Disarmament. Nevertheless, NGO involvement at the SSDs had both integrated and parallel features.[4] Integrated activities were those that took place as a result of the access to the UN that was granted to organizations during the special sessions. Parallel activities were those happening outside the UN but which, nonetheless, were an important part of the nongovernmental presence.

The following typology attempts to show the range of objectives of nongovernmental integrated and parallel activities undertaken during SSDI, although some activities are part of both integrated and parallel NGO activities.

Integrated Activities

1. Getting Information—activities to better inform NGOs about disarmament-related matters and the work of SSDI.

2. Expertise / Facilitating—providing expert assistance or technical information to the UN or member states, or otherwise facilitating the work of SSDI.

3. Lobbying / Representation—urging consideration of some program or principle or communicating a particular point of view upon SSDI as a whole or upon individual member states.

Parallel Activities

1. Providing Information—educational activities to help NGOs enhance their influence at SSDI.

---

3. A large percentage of NGOs taking part in SSDI were not international organizations (i.e., those normally having consultative status with the UN) but rather were national or local groups from different parts of the world.

4. The terms "integrated" and "parallel" are borrowed from Archer (1978, 6–23). Archer also identifies a "technical/monitoring" type of involvement by NGOs at UN conferences, but this type of involvement was less applicable to NGO behavior at the Special Sessions on Disarmament because of the type of conference the Special Sessions represented. See Atwood (1982, 210–20) for an explanation of factors behind the decision not to hold a "parallel" NGO Forum at SSDI, factors that presumably were at work again in 1982 and 1988.

2. Mobilizing—generating public awareness of and support for disarmament in general and the work of SSDI in particular.

3. Coordinating—establishing, maintaining, or improving NGO peace and disarmament networks.[5]

The Integrated Role

One of the acknowledged functions of SSDI was its use as a forum for better informing the public about the problems of and prospects for disarmament and for mobilizing the public.[6] Because NGOs were seen by UN staff as important to this public opinion function, some formal role for them at the SSD was necessary. Arrangements for NGO participation at SSDI required, nonetheless, some seventeen months of negotiation between the New York NGO Committee on Disarmament and the chair of the SSDI Preparatory Committee. The role for NGOs at SSDI—if limited—was unprecedented, marking a new stage in the involvement of NGOs in the UN's disarmament work (Atwood 1982, 75–120; Jack 1977, 97–99). NGO privileges set at SSDI were extended to the 1982 and 1988 special sessions.

Representatives of organizations registered with the UN for SSDI could observe the open meetings of the General Assembly, but they were denied access to informal drafting committees, where most of the work of the Special Session took place. They were also permitted to use all the facilities normally available to NGOs regularly represented at the UN, to submit documents for indexing and display, and to attend daily briefings sponsored by the UN on issues related to the Special Session. With the exception of the special days set aside for NGOs to address the plenary of the Special Session's Ad Hoc Committee, no form of oral intervention in the work of the Special Session was allowed, a practice that continued through the next two SSDs and is a routine restriction on nongovernmental actors seeking to influence UN institutions and conferences dealing with disarmament. Despite such limitations, TSMOs and other NGOs have used the opportunities created by UN special sessions and conferences to join in intergovernmental negotiations and to bring citizen voices to those negotiations.

Officially registered representatives of local, national, and interna-

---

5. These purposes have been developed in part by adapting what earlier research by Feraru showed to be the major objectives of NGOs at ad hoc global conferences and in part on the basis of the author's own observations at SSDI and SSDII (Feraru 1974, 40; Atwood 1982).

6. For a fuller description of this "integrated" role, see Atwood (1982, 149–208).

tional NGOs often used the opportunities to participate in the Special Session to learn about global disarmament politics. Observing open sessions, they learned about the dynamics of such UN meetings. They were briefed weekly by the UN's Office of Public Information on the issues discussed at SSDI and in the closed sessions. Registered NGOs used the NGO Lounge as a place to meet, get information about the SSD program, contact members of the UN Secretariat and national missions, and order official UN documentation. This experience was probably of greatest value to organizations that had no formal relationship with the United Nations prior to SSDI.

NGOs also engaged in a range of activities to communicate their views on disarmament-related issues to UN member states. Their newly won right to submit documents to the UN for listing and display allowed NGOs from many parts of the world to bring their ideas and concerns to the attention of delegates. In all, during the months before and during SSDI, the UN Secretariat received more than 250 proposals, resolutions, and petitions, ranging from the highly detailed recommendations of the International Peace Research Association to a "Declaration of Principles, Proposals for a Treaty, and Call for Action" of the International Workshop on Disarmament in New Delhi; from a statement on "Environment and Disarmament Issues before the UN Special Session on Disarmament" by the Sierra Club Earthcare Center to an "Appeal with Petition" by member groups of the Committee of Citizens of the City and Prefecture of Hiroshima, Japan, that was signed by 268,770 individuals (UN Documents A/IN/S-1/1, 6 June 1978 to Add. 2, 30 June 1978). Although the substantive impact of these documents on the Final Document was probably slight, they broadened the nongovernmental presence at SSDI far beyond those organizations actually there.

Lobbying governments was a type of integrated action. Most governments taking part in global conferences determine their positions long before the conferences begin. Hence, although hard bargaining went into deciding the language of the Final Document, efforts to influence government positions needed to take place in national political arenas months before the SSD. Nevertheless, accredited TSMO representatives devoted much of their energies toward lobbying governments during the weeks of SSDI. They did so through informal contact in UN corridors, briefings, and visits to different missions to the UN in New York.

Much NGO lobbying sought to make national delegates aware of the presence and positions of the disarmament movement, support progressive proposals, and register opposition to particular positions. For example, early in the SSD, the Japanese NGO delegation, five hundred strong, visited all national missions to the UN urging nuclear disarmament. Representatives of the Mobilization for Survival likewise visited the missions of the nuclear powers. Other national NGOs sought meetings with their respective official delegations.

Jointly organized NGO lobbying activities included working groups on nuclear disarmament, disarmament and development, and other related problems. Some joint visits were made to national missions to the UN. However, a coordinated lobbying effort was never very well planned, and an overall strategy for influencing the course of the SSD never materialized.

The fact that SSDI was held at UN Headquarters also influenced nongovernmental lobbying. In effect, two classes of NGOs emerged: the insiders, those regularly in New York who had long worked to gain NGO access to the SSD, and the outsiders, who had come to New York to take part in the SSD. Because their regular work at the UN gave insiders the advantage of preestablished relationships with UN officials and national delegations, they had far greater access to and voice in the Special Session. Outsider groups, unfamiliar with UN operations, often had unrealistic expectations about how much lobbying they could do and how much influence they could have. This insider/outsider tension among NGOs limited their collaboration.

In fact, much of the insider NGO representation focused not on the specific disarmament-related issues under discussion at the SSD, but rather on getting language incorporated into the Final Document that would "regularize and strengthen the role of NGOs in the disarmament area" beyond simply an informational function (interview with Barrett Hollister, quoted in Atwood 1982, 172). Although it did not go as far as some had hoped, what was achieved in the Final Document's language was due in large part to the skilled lobbying of a few of the New York-based insider groups (Jack 1977, 98).

Addressing the Ad Hoc Committee of the Special Session in one of its open sessions was, symbolically, the most important integrated activity by nongovernmental actors at SSDI. The right to make oral interventions was negotiated in the course of preparations for SSD, but the difficult and politically sensitive process of deciding who would speak was left to the NGO community itself (Atwood 1982, 178–88; Jack 1977, 102–3; Hollister 1978, 1–2). A Speakers Committee, made up of members of the NGO Committees in New York and Geneva, was set up to recommend speakers to the UN. The decision to schedule speeches from different organizations, rather than to select a number of outstanding speakers to make a clearly articulated and comprehensive message to the General Assembly, illustrated the lack of unity among NGOs in 1978. Inter-NGO politics thus became stronger than considerations of how to maximize the opportunity afforded by the day' access.

Differences and rivalries between the Geneva and New York NGO committees, the major source of problems in the committee's selection process, arose partly because the Geneva and New York NGOs were then united under two distinct coalition organizations, each with its own traditions and ways of operating. But the differences also illustrate the fact that in 1978 international NGOs themselves, like the nations, were divided along Cold War lines. Since most Eastern NGOs with UN representation were then located in Geneva, rather than New York, the differences between the Geneva and New York members of the Speakers Committee were aggravated by ideological orientations.

Nevertheless, by 12 June 1978 representatives of twenty-five organizations—including the African-Asian Peoples' Solidarity Organization, the International Youth and Student Movement for the United Nations, the International Fellowship of Reconciliation, the World Veterans Federation, the World Peace Council, the Asian Buddhist Conference, and the Women's International Democratic Federation—were selected to make presentations (UN Document A/S-10/AC.1/PV.6; A/ 1–10/AC.1/PV.7, 13 June 1978). The statements were pragmatic, based in international political realities, and avoided moral posturing. Aware of the special privilege they had been given and agreeing on the goal of advancing NGOs' role in UN disarmament matters, NGO speakers avoided polemics and the temptation to lecture or accuse delegations.

Most speakers referred to the contribution their organizations sought to make. For example, the speaker for the Pugwash Conferences on Science and Human Affairs (corecipient of the Nobel Prize for Peace in 1995) reminded delegates that disarmament would be achieved only through a series of small, determined steps. He recalled that the Pugwash Conferences had introduced one of those steps, the proposal for a nuclear test ban. A number of speakers referred to the linkages between the arms race and other global problems. For example, the representative for the World Federation of Scientific Workers reminded delegates that the arms race was not only dangerous but also harmful to national economies.

Some speakers urged action in specific areas and suggested where progress might be possible. The World Association of World Federalists suggested that the nuclear powers announce a moratorium on the testing and deployment of new strategic weapons until a comprehensive test ban was ready. To varying degrees in the 1990s, nuclear powers actually adopted a similar position in the run-up to the completion of the Comprehensive Test Ban Treaty in the autumn of 1996. There were suggestions for strengthening UN disarmament and security machinery. There were specific calls for a strengthened UN/NGO relationship on disarmament. As small a gesture as it was, granting NGOs the right to address the Ad Hoc Committee demonstrated their recognized role in disarmament affairs. The symbolic value of the event outweighed the content in importance. In the development of UN/NGO relations in the field of disarmament, the NGO speech day was perhaps the most important event of SSDI.

Sharing expertise and facilitating the consideration of issues was a final feature of NGOs' integrated role at SSDI. In the relationship between nongovernmental actors and international institutions, this function is not confined to providing technical information but also involves bringing information to the attention of IGO officials or national delegations and otherwise facilitating the work of IGOs.

The large number of general interest and outsider NGOs at SSDI and the governments' self-defined negotiating positions limited NGO opportunity to provide expertise and facilitate discussion, but the Quaker United Nations Office and others organized pre-SSD conferences and seminars for diplomats that accomplished some of this task. Moreover, during the SSD, Quakers also organized informal, off-the-record seminars for members of various delegations on topics germane to the SSDI discussions. Some NGO representatives were of direct assistance to delegates, particularly those from the third world, by helping them to prepare speeches and draft language for the Final Document. Some of the documents submitted and speeches made on 12 June contained concrete proposals for arms control and disarmament measures and provided additional political and technical expertise that aided the work of SSDI.

The important contribution of expertise by peace and disarmament research institutions was recognized by the UN, which offered these organizations an additional opportunity to address the Ad Hoc Committee. On 13 June six such institutions, including the Stockholm International Peace Research Institute (SIPRI) and the Institute for World Economics and International Relations in the USSR, presented specific arms control and disarmament proposals, directly challenging delegates to take dramatic new steps (UN Document A/s-10/AC.1/PV.8, 14 June 1978).

At least five national delegations appointed representatives of NGOs and well-known arms control and disarmament experts as public members of their delegations. For instance, Nobel Prize winner Philip Noel-Baker was in the British delegation and nuclear scientist George Kistiakowsky in the U.S. one.

The Parallel Role

During the five weeks of the Special Session, NGOs engaged in a range of parallel activities.[7] Some were officially sponsored by the NGO Committee on Disarmament in New York, while many others were initiated by one or more other NGOs. The major goal of all these activities was to provide services and information to NGOs attending the Special Session and to mobilize public awareness about it and about disarmament in general. They were also, however, aimed in part at the UN and national delegations to the SSD.

The main reason that no parallel NGO forum or conference was held at SSDI was that the New York NGO Committee on Disarmament, which would have been responsible for planning such an event, lacked the organizational capacity and resources to do so. Few nongovernmental organizations had paid, full-time professional staff located at UN Headquarters, and therefore a great deal of the coalition's work fell to two member organizations, the Quaker United Nations Office and the World Conference on Religion and Peace, whose secretary-general, Homer Jack, also chaired the NGO Committee on Disarmament. Preoccupied as they were in negotiating and arranging for integrated activities, the NGO Committees in Geneva and New York chose to concentrate their efforts on publishing an NGO newspaper during the Special Session and providing a facility near the UN that NGOs could use as a focal point for their SSDI activities.

Reporting and interpreting developments for INGO constituencies was, therefore, the parallel action with the highest priority. As Ralph Levering shows (chap. 13), the most consistently successful TSMO project at UN-sponsored world conferences and special sessions probably has been the publication of an NGO newspaper. The planning for a newspaper began a year before SSDI. Differences between the Geneva and New York NGO Committees left the New York group to devote much of its energy to publishing *Disarmament Times*.

The newspaper served a vital information function. Reporting on the progress of SSDI in a depth not covered by the mainstream media, the newspaper was of use to both delegates and NGOs. Its pages also provided a daily calendar of events, meetings and activities within and outside the UN. Its interviews, guest editorials, and choice of issues covered allowed the newspaper to serve as a lobbying instrument for both NGOs and members of delegations. This was an especially important way for some of the smaller countries to make their voices heard. Its contributions led the United Nations Secretariat to

---

7. For a fuller description of this "parallel" role, see Atwood (1982, 209–307).

help distribute *Disarmanent Times* within the UN itself, a major achievement for an NGO document at that time. Moreover: *Disarmament Times* did not end with SSDI; it was also a feature of SSDII and SSDIII, and it has been in continuous publication since 1978 as an ongoing project of the New York NGO Committee on Disarmament.

Running the Disarmament Information Bureau was the other major parallel project of the NGO Committee on Disarmament. Located in a storefront directly across from the UN Secretariat, the bureau was open from a month before SSDI to the end. Its purpose was to help New Yorkers, visitors from around the world, and NGO representatives to find their way around the Special Session and to learn more about disarmament in general. The Information Bureau, along with the NGO Lounge and the Plowshare Coffee House provided NGOs with facilities that they could call their own and that increased their access to the Special Session. Here literature from NGOs, research institutes, the UN, and national governments was available, along with announcements of events and guidance on UN procedures. The location of the bureau also made it a highly visible symbol of the NGO presence. What it did not do—and this need was not really met—was to coordinate NGO action at SSDI itself.

Providing points of contact and debate outside SSDI involved a great range of activities for literally thousands of people. Two such projects —the Plowshare Coffee House and Discussion Center and the Peoples' Assembly—offered programs for NGOs and the wider public. The more successful of these, the Plowshare Coffee House, was a project of the American section of the International Fellowship of Reconciliation, and it complemented the projects of the NGO Committee on Disarmament. Plowshare was situated in the Church Center for the UN, located directly across the street from the United Nations and the home of many NGOs with "missions" at the UN. It served as a crossroads for NGOs and individuals from New York and elsewhere. Its formal program of events, which ran throughout the five weeks of the SSD, offered a "marathon teach-in on aspects of militarism and disarmament" (Maas 1978, 11). Like *Disarmament Times*, Plowshare was also a feature at SSDII and SSDIII.

The Peoples' Assembly was a series of seventeen public forums on disarmament-related themes. It was organized quite separately from any of the official NGO activities and apparently without even coordination with those planning the Plowshare program. The Peoples' Assembly was intended to symbolize a world-government presence at SSDI, and this intention reflected the agenda of one of its major backers, the World Citizens' Assembly, whose main goal was the creation of a "peoples' house" within the UN system. It promoted this agenda through the Peoples' Assembly and at other settings throughout the Special Session.

Like much of the nongovernmental participation at SSDI, this example demonstrates both a strength and a weakness of the peace and disarmament community then. The great variety of constituencies represented was a strength, but the inconsistencies in tactics and strategies of those interests were a serious weakness.

Public action was organized to mobilize public awareness of SSDI and to dramatize a popular hope that the Special Session would initiate major steps to control the global arms race. The drama and color of these actions added a dimension to SSDI quite unlike anything that had taken place at previous UN conferences. Marches, rallies, vigils, and a sit-in were organized by the Mobilization for Survival, the U.S. branch of IMfS. In order to draw maximum public attention to the Special Session, most of the Mobilization-sponsored events were timed for the first week of the Special Session when, for example, an "International Religious Convocation for Human Survival," demonstrated worldwide religious commitment to disarmament.

The major Mobilization action was the march and rally for disarmament, held on 27 May. These events drew the largest participation of all NGO-sponsored projects at SSDI. Between 15,000 and 20,000 people, including contingents from various countries, participated in a march across Manhattan and a colorful rally in Dag Hammarskjöld Plaza near the UN. Coordinated with these events in New York were demonstrations in San Francisco and a number of European capitals. Although small in scale compared to the antinuclear demonstrations that took place in the early 1980s, they were seen at the time as a positive sign of an emerging, broad public constituency on these issues.

Acts of civil disobedience, seen as critical tools of protest by some NGOs, were important forms of public action organized by NGOs seeking to influence SSDI. The Mobilization for Survival's 12 June "Sit-In for Survival," the principal such action, targeted the U.S. Mission to the UN. Over 300 people were arrested for crossing the barricades in front of the Mission, creating one of the largest single incidents of mass arrest in New York City's history. Through media coverage the event drew more public attention to the Special Session—at least in the United States—than probably any other single event, including the UN deliberations themselves.

In addition to the actions sponsored by the Mobilization, there were other public demonstrations for disarmament, including a daily "Vigil for Disarmament," organized by the Fellowship of Reconciliation. Such public actions applied nonviolent direct action to disarmament work, using SSDI as a focal point. After the 1978 Special Session, marches, rallies and other forms of public demonstrations increased, particularly in Western Europe, in campaigns for disarmament and against nuclear weapons.

Planning for joint action after the Special Session was also a feature of the parallel activities of NGOs at SSDI. For example, the International Mobilization for Survival organized a Strategy for Disarmament Conference, seeking to establish a more permanent and consultative international structure for global disarmament work. This meeting of several hundred people provided an opportunity for genuine transnational exchange, but it also showed some of the major difficulties of organizing a transnational disarmament movement. Disarmament mobilization is clearly shaped and motivated by different national experiences. Thus the issue of the neutron bomb had been a major factor in mobilizing disarmament efforts in the Netherlands, due to its possible deployment in that country, whereas for Australian organizations the questions of uranium mining and the export of uranium were more critical organizing points. Accordingly, a transnational coalition like the IMfS could seek to coordinate in a general way the actions of constituent organizations, but regional or national situations would have a great impact on the particular emphasis of any action. This reality was a significant feature of the transnational disarmament efforts in the early 1980s.

Two other inter-NGO coordinating events emerged during SSDI. One, a symposium called "NGOs: Toward SSDII," was organized by the NGO Committee on Disarmament, partly at the urging of many NGOs that were not members of the NGO Committee. The other, the "NGO Forum," was organized primarily in response to those who felt the NGO Committee on Disarmament had not done enough to bring NGOs together during the Special Session. These meetings offered an opportunity for NGOs to evaluate their performance at SSDI and look ahead. Although both succeeded in airing a great range of issues, neither contributed much to strategic planning for action after the Special Session.

These meetings revealed again the clear differences in style, orientation, and purpose among NGOs that had been apparent elsewhere during the weeks of the Special Session. In the process, the many events parallel to SSDI increased NGOs' awareness of each other, of the issues uniting and dividing them, of their weaknesses and strengths. Interaction and coordination during SSDI were thus important in strengthening the peace and disarmament movement network thereafter.

Beyond Special Session I

The upsurge in disarmament activity that took place after 1978 was due, at least in part, to the new awareness of disarmament-related issues and the international contacts resulting from SSDI. In addition, the promise of a Second Special Session on Disarmament in 1982 provided a new focal point for NGO activities. SSDII itself became a setting where an even larger number of organizations interacted and worked together than had been the case in 1978. This time, the number of officially accredited organizations grew to 450, with 3,391 persons representing these organizations (including 1,686 individuals representing Japanese national NGOs), in addition to the many thousands who took part in the large range of parallel events (United Nations Department of Public Information 1982).

NGO participation at SSDII had many of the same integrated and parallel features as SSDI but on a wider scale, representing the very large growth in public engagement for disarmament between 1978 and 1982. Perhaps the most important indicator of this increased attention to disarmament was the 12 June march and rally. Hundreds of thousands of people from across the United States and from many different countries of the world converged on New York City for a massive public demonstration—the largest in U.S. history—of support for a nuclear arms freeze and economic justice (Atwood 1983).

Although many of the factors affecting the NGO performance at SSDI also shaped SSDII, better NGO coordination of lobbying activity and better preparation on the issues for the 1982 session demonstrated that some lessons had been learned in 1978. Moreover, many organizations attending SSDII were more realistic in their expectations and demands. They saw SSDII as an opportunity not so much for international negotiation as for further mobilizing public support for disarmament and for building stronger transnational alliances. Therefore, like SSDI, the Second Special Session—despite its lack of tangible political results—may have also furthered disarmament efforts such as the Nuclear Weapons Freeze Campaign in the United States, the Campaign for Nuclear Disarmament in Britain, and other movements in parts of Western Europe.

The preconference efforts of NGOs for the Third Special Session in 1988 were less intense than had been the case in 1978 and 1982, in part perhaps because this was the third session within a few years, and also because much attention was being focused then on the thawing relations between the Soviet Union and the United States, which generated new negotiations for bilateral nuclear arms reductions. Nevertheless, SSDIII was still a focal point for much nongovernmental activity, and it attracted some 2,000 officially accredited nongovernmental organization representatives to New York (Herby 1988, 3).

TSMOs and International Disarmament Negotiations

In a narrow sense, nongovernmental activity during the First Special Session on Disarmament had little impact on the actual outcome of the meeting. Given the fact that disarmament was not an area where NGOs had much influence, this is not surprising. If, however, the Special Sessions are viewed as parts of a process, the NGO contribution was important in a number of ways.

NGOs were largely responsible for whatever public awareness of the SSDs there was. Through their various educational programs and actions around the world especially before and during Special Sessions I and II, and by means of such activities as marches and rallies, they played a vital role in building and shaping public attention to the UN events and the disarmament issues addressed there.

The actual physical presence in New York of hundreds of people from around the world was a visible and vocal reminder to government representatives that what they were or were not doing at the Special Session was being monitored and would be reported to large constituencies. NGOs, in their various publications, speeches, and discussions, increased the attention paid in the SSDs to linkages between the arms race and other issues such as development, national economic performance, and the environment. They thus contributed to ensuring that many dimensions of the disarmament issue were recognized. In short, the SSDs provided an opportunity for social movement actors to mobilize around and act in global disarmament negotiations.

Social movement actors were included in SSDI largely to the extent that they facilitated the UN's interest in raising public awareness and mobilizing public support for disarmament. To some extent, this factor offset the unwillingness of states to grant real access and influence to nongovernmental actors in security-related areas. Moreover, where nongovernmental actors were seen to have expertise of value to the UN, they were given substantial access to the decision-making process. In this respect, the special sessions showed that the effectiveness of nongovernmental actors depends on their having something to contribute and on their professionalism, credibility, and basic understanding of the system and issues. Regardless of their expertise, no social movement actors are likely to substantially shift government positions during an actual conference, although there may be opportunities to do so during preparation for conferences.

The SSDs contributed to the development of nuclear disarmament movements in many countries. They provided opportunities for networking and coordination that, although not fully utilized, helped many participants to better understand the UN system and to realize the extent of citizen disarmament efforts around the world. Mobilization around the Special Sessions contributed to broader disarmament mobilization, drawing in NGOs not previously involved in disarmament work and other social groups, such as churches and labor unions.

Post-Cold War conflicts not only call for new kinds of multilateral responses but also call attention to new disarmament challenges. In particular, these conficts have led to and been exacerbated by the proliferation of light weapons and antipersonnel weapons, which are killing thousands of people around the world. In addition, as the 1995 Review and Extension Conference on the Nuclear Nonproliferation Treaty vividly demonstrated, the tasks remaining to limit, reduce, and ultimately eliminate weapons of mass destruction are many and difficult.

Working locally, nationally, and transnationally, social movement organizations have been participants in processes aimed at meeting these challenges. The First United Nations Special Session on Disarmament illustrates the important role of issue-oriented NGOs in expanding the understanding of complex issues, posing alternatives, building public pressure on governments for action, and influencing the international climate that makes possible steps toward disarmament and the real security needs of the world community.

9

LIMITS TO TRANSNATIONALISM

The 1980s Freeze Campaign

David Cortright and Ron Pagnucco

Abstract

Why was there not a truly transnational mobilization around the nuclear freeze campaign that originated in the United States and entered intergovernmental debate in the form of a 1982 UN General Assembly resolution? Despite the massive public mobilization in the U.S., and notwithstanding the convening of three UN General Assembly special sessions on nuclear disarmament, the peace movement never converged around a cooperative transnational nuclear freeze effort, partly because of the external constraints and opportunities defined by different national political debates and contexts, such as by diverse responses to the Cold War rivalry and important differences between the U.S. and European political cultures.

Born out of local referenda and town meetings in New England, the nuclear freeze movement was propelled to national attention by 1982 referenda in which voters in California and seven other states endorsed a nonbinding resolution supporting a bilateral nuclear freeze. The philosophy and structure of the Nuclear Weapons Freeze Campaign (NWFC) were almost entirely grassroots oriented. Yet the freeze movement was concerned with international issues, and its defining moment—when nearly one million people rallied against the nuclear arms race in New York's Central Park—occurred during the Second UN Special Session on Disarmament (SSDII) in 1982. A motto of the movement became "think globally, act locally." The freeze movement sought to build a domestic disarmament constituency in the United States to achieve a U.S./Soviet halt to the testing, production, and deployment of all nuclear weapons. This attempt to combine grassroots activism and internationalism was not always successful and exposed some of the underlying tensions and weaknesses in the freeze movement.

Much attention has focused on the grassroots activism and national lobbying of the freeze movement (Cortright 1993; Meyer 1990; Solo 1988; Waller 1987). Less well known are the transnational activities of the movement and the various attempts to build international support for the freeze and link the movement to other issues. While transnational programs were never a major component of freeze movement activity, they were essential to the declared objective of the campaign: halting the international arms race.

The establishment of an international program grew from a recognition that an end to the nuclear arms race could not be achieved solely by the United States: Liaison with peace movements and governments in other countries, especially in Europe and the Soviet Union, was necessary. Transnational efforts were also part of the movement's strategy for gaining public attention, establishing political legitimacy, and building support for disarmament.

Despite its grassroots orientation, the NWFC established an international presence from its very beginning. Even before the campaign was formally established, early freeze organizers began to reach out to officials and peace movement colleagues in other countries. In 1979, Terry Provance of the American Friends Service Committee (AFSC) organized a delegation to the Soviet Union that advocated a proposal for a mutual halt to the nuclear arms race to officials at the Soviet Foreign Ministry and scholars at the Institute for U.S.A.-Canada Studies (Solo 1988, 44–45). Although Soviet officials gave no immediate response to the moratorium proposal, the delegation's experience of lobbying for the idea in Moscow encouraged the AFSC delegation to push the concept further. After the trip to Moscow, Provance, Pam Solo, and others joined with Randall Forsberg and her colleagues at the Boston Study Group to create the NWFC (Solo 1988, 113).

When the NWFC was officially founded in March 1981, an International Task Force was created to maintain contacts with peace movements outside the United States and to represent the freeze before international bodies. Some freeze organizers, such as Solo, argued that transnational work was important because the freeze movement could learn from the proposals and political perspectives of colleagues in Europe and elsewhere. It would also be valuable, she emphasized, to coordinate planning and strategy among the various peace movements (Solo 1993). Transnational cooperation was seen as especially significant for the looming fight against INF weapons (Intermediate-Range Nuclear Forces)—cruise and Pershing II missiles in the West, SS-20 missiles in the East—that came to dominate European security politics in the first half of the 1980s (Rochon 1988). Solo and Mike Jendrzejcyk of the Fellowship of Reconciliation were instrumental in persuading the NWFC to establish an international office. According to Randy Kehler, "[the NWFC] got pulled into the international arena more than initiating it. . . . The very size and visibility of the Freeze Campaign meant that people were contacting us from other countries, wanting to know what we were doing" (Kehler 1993). Kehler also believed that it was important for the freeze movement to "establish relationships and broaden our vision to include a global disarmament perspective" (Kehler 1993).

Although the NWFC adopted an international program, "an internationalist perspective never flourished in the decision-making committees of the freeze" (Solo 1988, 114). This shortcoming was, in Solo's view, a principal cause of the U.S. movement's inability to challenge the INF weapons more effectively and accounted for its fundamental political weakness, an inability to break out of conventional Cold War politics.

If an international perspective had been internalized, . . . the freeze would have been better able to differentiate the realities of U.S.-Soviet conflict from the sources and uses of cold war rhetoric to domesticate the movement. The movement might have been better equipped to deal with the [INF] missile deployment issue and with the political opportunities that greater U.S.-European cooperation would have offered. Lacking an international program, the freeze was implicitly saying to itself, and to other movements, that it thought it could stop the arms race without challenging the Cold War. (Solo 1993)

The movement invoked the bilateral nature of the freeze proposal to prove that the movement was equally critical of the Soviet Union for perpetuating the arms race. Bilateralism began to function as a shield against a more structural critique of the Cold War global system, enabling the movement to sidestep the problem that the superpowers' relationship posed for disarmament efforts. Avoiding this problem, however, only reinforced in the movement an excessive focus on weapons hardware—to the neglect of systemic problems—and enmeshed the freeze idea in the trap of arms-control-as-usual (Solo 1988, 114).

At the United Nations

The largest public manifestation of nuclear freeze support—indeed, the largest peace rally ever held on American soil—took place on 12 June 1982 in conjunction with the Second UN Special Session on Disarmament. Giving voice to the massive public concern about nuclear war, the rally was also an international event, with delegations participating from Japan, the Soviet Union, many of the nations of Western Europe, Zambia, Bangladesh, and many other countries. At first glance, the sponsorship of such a rally at a UN Special Session on Disarmament (SSD) seems only natural. What better venue for generating public pressure for disarmament? However, an attempt to mobilize mass participation at the First UN Special Session on Disarmament in New York in May 1978 had yielded only modest results (see chap. 8). In 1982 it was not the UN per se, or even the Special Session on Disarmament, that captured the public imagination. One million people rallied in New York because of the growing fear of nuclear war—and the deeply urgent feeling, shared by millions of others, that something had to be done to pull the world back from the brink of nuclear confrontation.

The events at SSDII inevitably focused attention on the UN as an institution. As chapter 8 demonstrates, such meetings can play an important role in building new international regimes and thus become important venues for social movement groups to press for global change. Traditionally, the role of the UN in the field of disarmament has been quite limited. Although the UN has maintained a Committee on Disarmament for decades and has sponsored several major initiatives—most notably, the Nuclear Non-Proliferation Treaty (NPT)—it has been unable to exert significant influence on nuclear policy.

It is not surprising, then, that the arms control policies of the United States and the Soviet Union were conducted in a bilateral context, with little or no role for the UN In the 1970s, as the nuclear arsenals on both sides multiplied, nations within the nonaligned movement began to call for a renewed commitment to disarmament and for a more significant UN effort to restrain the nuclear danger. The result was the First Special Session on Disarmament (SSDI) in 1978, the largest UN meeting ever held on disarmament (Rotblat 1993, 27). The SSDI final document contained strong language committing the signatory nations, including the nuclear powers, to disarmament. It acknowledged that "[t]he most effective guarantee against the danger of nuclear war and the use of nuclear weapons is nuclear disarmament and the complete elimination of nuclear weapons" (Rotblat 1993, 27–28).

Although the United States and the Soviet Union signed the First Special Session declaration, their actions belied their words. The direction of U.S. and Soviet policy was not toward disarmament but toward greater arms competition and Cold War hostility. Both sides continued to build new and ever more dangerous weapons systems. When the Second Special Session on Disarmament was convened, the atmosphere was far less hopeful, and little came of the meetings.

Nevertheless, SSDII was marked by a significant degree of citizen involvement in UN proceedings and greater public pressure for disarmament. A dramatic reversal of roles between governments and citizen groups occurred between the first and the second SSD. At the 1978 gathering, governments took the initiative, and citizens were only somewhat mobilized on the issue. By 1982 governments were largely immobilized, as the ever more dangerous and costly arms race careened out of control, while an aroused citizenry in the United States, Europe, and elsewhere became more active and focused in demanding progress toward arms reduction.

The International Task Force of the freeze mounted a major effort to lobby for the freeze resolution inside the UN General Assembly. A special three-person staff was hired to bring the resolution before the Assembly and to coordinate and assist efforts by other citizen groups. Between mid-April 1982 and December of that year, the task force staff distributed copies of the freeze proposal and supporting documentation to all 157 national missions to the UN, interviewed and met with groups of delegates, wrote and conferred with U.S. and Soviet negotiators, and provided information and support for other citizen groups.

Two different nuclear freeze resolutions were introduced into the Assembly: one sponsored by Mexico and Sweden, with cosponsorship from Columbia and Ecuador; the other by India, with support from the German Democratic Republic, Liberia, and Mali. The Mexican-Swedish proposal was closest to the language of the U.S. NWFC. It called for the United States and the Soviet Union "to proclaim, either through simultaneous unilateral declarations or through a joint resolution, an immediate nuclear arms freeze" as a first step toward comprehensive disarmament (Nuclear Weapons Freeze Campaign 1982, 17). The resolution also called for a comprehensive test ban, the complete cessation of the manufacture of nuclear weapons and their delivery systems, a ban on further deployment of weapons and delivery vehicles, and a cessation of the production of fissionable materials. It advanced an initial five-year bilateral freeze, to be extended "in case other nations join in such a freeze, as the General Assembly expects them to do" (Cohen 1983, 14).

The Indian proposal was more limited, calling for a multilateral freeze on only the production of nuclear weapons and fissionable materials. In December of 1982, the General Assembly passed both nonbinding measures by large margins. The United States and most Western nations opposed both resolutions, although Greece voted in favor, and Denmark and Iceland abstained. The Soviet bloc and the nonaligned nations voted in favor. China abstained on the Indian proposal and voted no on the Mexican-Swedish resolution.

The UN votes on the freeze were significant because a large majority of the world's governments openly supported a comprehensive halt to the nuclear arms race. The UN debate also had public relations value, as it helped focus public and government attention on the nuclear arms race and the freeze movement's proposal for ending it (Solo 1993). The impact was especially important in several Western European countries. Denmark abstained because freeze supporters in the Danish parliament, representing the majority, threatened to turn the UN decision into a vote of confidence and thereby potentially topple the government. In the Netherlands, members of Parliament debated whether to force the government to change its negative vote on the freeze; and a motion to this effect lost by just three votes. A similar drama unfolded in Norway, where legislators opposed to the government's decision to side with the United States threatened a political crisis over the vote (Cohen 1983, 14, 21).

Perhaps the greatest impact of the UN debate was in the arena of public opinion. The General Assembly vote was one more in an extensive series of national and international indications of widespread public support for a halt to the arms race. The December votes came soon after state and local elections in the United States in which 18 million people, a quarter of the electorate, had voted on nuclear freeze referenda, with 60 percent in favor (Cortright 1993, 17–22). The UN votes came at a time when hundreds of organizations and professional associations and prominent political leaders were endorsing the freeze. Taking the issue to the UN was a logical extension of the strategy of getting mayors, educators, physicians, and state governments to support the freeze (Solo 1993). It was part of a mounting tidal wave of public opinion that sought to convince political leaders in Washington and Moscow that the people of the world wanted an end to the arms race and progress toward nuclear disarmament.

After this successful opening effort at the UN, the NWFC disbanded the International Task Force staff and turned its attention toward grassroots organizing and congressional lobbying in the United States. Although the NWFC hired an international coordinator in 1983, it no longer maintained a UN presence.[1]

Solo regretted that the NWFC did not maintain a permanent pres-

---

1. This did not mean that the entire movement gave up on UN activity. For instance, Parliamentarians for World Order, an early supporter of the freeze, worked closely with the NWFC during the General Assembly debate, using its extensive network of contacts among members of parliament in twenty-eight countries to win support for the freeze resolutions and to introduce the freeze proposal into the legislatures of countries such as Australia, Canada, India, Italy, Kenya, Nigeria, and the United Kingdom (Duece 1983, 9).

ence at the UN, although she acknowledges the time and resource constraints that led to the decision (Solo 1993). Late 1982 was also a time when the freeze faced severe red-baiting attacks from the Reagan administration, which charged that the campaign was Soviet-inspired (see Donner 1982). In response, movement leaders sought to concentrate more on strengthening their grassroots constituency and political legitimacy at home. Similarly, the growing push in late 1982 and early 1983 to get the freeze resolution passed in the U.S. Congress narrowed and "nationalized" the movement's framing of the freeze. But the movement's failure to follow up on its UN activities constituted a missed opportunity. The campaign turned its back on an institution that had overwhelmingly supported the freeze, abandoned a major forum for influencing world public opinion, and did not fully utilize an opportunity to work for institutional innovations.

Cooperation with the West European Peace Movement

The freeze movement made considerable efforts to establish relations of dialogue and mutual support with the principal peace groups in Western Europe, including the Campaign for Nuclear Disarmament in Great Britain, the Interchurch Peace Council in Holland, and the Greens in West Germany. Cooperation with the European movements was only natural, since part of the early enthusiasm and interest in the freeze derived from the enormous mobilizations for peace then taking place in Western Europe (see Rochon 1988). The freeze gained considerable legitimacy and moral support from the peace demonstrations in Europe, which dramatized the paradox that the people supposedly being protected by NATO missiles opposed their deployment.

For all the natural affinity of the two movements, however, there were major differences between the issue-framing strategies of the NWFC and those of the European peace groups. Movement frames are interpretations of a problem involving *diagnosis*, a definition of a condition as a problem requiring action; *prognosis*, a proposed solution to that problem; and *frame resonance*, a means of "strik[ing] a responsive chord" among the people the movement seeks to mobilize (Benford 1993, 679). The NWFC differed from European peace groups in their approaches to all three of these aspects of framing.

While both movements shared a concern about the U.S.-USSR nuclear arms race, the overriding issue for the Europeans was how to block the planned deployment of ground-launched cruise and Pershing II missiles. The proposed INF deployment, approved by NATO countries in December 1979, was the principal catalyst for the huge peace mobilizations in Europe. The people of West Germany, Great

Britain, Italy, the Netherlands, and Belgium found themselves on the front line of a dangerous new escalation of nuclear firepower. It was perhaps only natural in light of the proposed deployment and the worsening Cold War tensions at the time that a extraordinary number of people on the Continent became concerned about the threat of nuclear war. A poll in West Germany in January 1980 found a startling 48 percent of the population believing that nuclear war was "probable in the next ten years" (quoted in Rochon 1988, 46). The European peace groups also shared a "non-aligned" interpretation of the arms race:

> The dominant strand of thought within the [European] peace movement [was] that the problem of the arms race is rooted in an international system composed of two superpowers who each line up their allies and prepare to confront the other. . . . Each [superpower] needs the other to justify its own domination within its bloc. A state of disarmed peace would undermine the basis of bloc cohesion and weaken the dominance of the superpowers. (Rochon 1988, 61)

The focus of the U.S. freeze movement was on the entire superpower nuclear arms race, not just missiles in Europe. Many within the NWFC opposed any kind of "single weapon" organizing—whether on the INF issue or the "Stop MX" campaign that was developing at the time—urging instead the more comprehensive approach of attempting to stop the testing, production, and development of all nuclear weapons. The objective of the freeze proposal was to stop nuclear weapons activities by the United States and the Soviet Union everywhere. Advocates of this position believed that a strong effort on the INF issue would dilute the message of the freeze by challenging just one class of missiles rather than all nuclear weapons. The freeze was "better," some argued, because it would stop new missiles not only in Europe but in Asia and throughout the world.

The frames used by the NWFC and the European groups not only had different diagnoses of the problem but also contained different prognoses. The multiparty, proportional representation electoral system in Holland and Denmark allowed the peace movements there the opportunity to influence the positions of major nonmajoritarian political parties. Because of these national political opportunity structures, the Dutch and Danish peace movements were able to have a major impact on the 1983/1984 INF debates in those countries, which resulted in governmental decisions to delay the acceptance of cruise and Pershing II missiles. The NWFC in the United States found itself in a very different electoral context and was unable to exert similar influence on the major political parties.

The sharpest difference in framing between the European and U.S. movements was on the question of bilateralism. The debate was usually muted in public, to avoid an impression of divisions within the ranks, but the difference was very real. The NWFC proposal called for a simultaneous halt to the arms race by both the U.S. and Soviet sides. The bilateral dimension of the freeze was fundamentally important to its political appeal in the United States: It allowed the movement to parry the red-baiting attacks of the Reagan administration by demonstrating a genuinely critical stance toward the Soviet Union and enabled it to work with a Congress structured to be moderate, especially in the national security arena (Pagnucco and Smith 1993). Indeed, by distancing itself from Soviet influence and by challenging Soviet as well as U.S. nuclear policies, the NWFC advanced a frame with broader resonance and could build a much wider public following than previous U.S. peace movements had enjoyed. Some critics in the United States found this emphasis on bilateralism excessive (Borosage 1983, 37–40), but the leadership of the NWFC remained firmly committed to the bilateral concept. According to Kehler, there was a concern that "to weigh in on [INF] would undercut our claim to be evenhanded in terms of the bilateral nature of the agreement" (Kehler 1993).

The frame shared by most European peace groups had a different prognosis. In the view of these groups, the superpowers had little real interest in arms control and disarmament, since East-West tensions gave them justification to dominate their respective blocs. To prevent nuclear war, Europe must break its alliances with the United States and the Soviet Union, break out of the logic of the blocs, and no longer seek security through nuclear deterrence dominated by the super powers. This view seemed to resonate with a large number of Europeans, many of whom saw the U.S. and the USSR as equally to blame for the growing nuclear tensions.

Many Europeans supported the concept of unilateral initiatives. Some groups, such as the Campaign for Nuclear Disarmament (CND) in Great Britain, openly espoused unilateral disarmament. Bilateral arms negotiations were seen as a cover for continued nuclear escalation. Bold initiatives were necessary, European activists argued, to break the cycle of the arms race and create momentum for disarmament. Independent steps would serve as confidence-building measures and create a new political dynamic that could lead to mutual arms reduction. Some within the freeze movement shared this view, believing that "independent initiatives and a bilateral freeze were not necessarily incompatible" (Solo 1993).

But the majority within the NWFC shunned unilateralism and remained committed to a bilateral approach. Not surprisingly, some with

CND were not happy with the freeze proposal. Having worked hard within their movement to build support for unilateralism, they considered the freeze proposal a weakening of their position and a potential step backward. A British freeze campaign surfaced briefly during the 1983–84 period, initially attracting support from celebrities and prominent politicians, but it was unable to compete with the substantial following enjoyed by CND and quickly dissolved (Solo 1993).[2]

The Europeans' preference for independent initiatives did not mean that they opposed the nuclear freeze or were against bilateral reductions. The West Europeans consistently called for a U.S. and Soviet halt to the arms race, opposing both NATO missiles and Soviet SS-20 weapons. But the primary emphasis in Europe was on halting the NATO missiles—unilaterally, if necessary. Intellectually it was possible to argue that the bilateral freeze and stopping INF missiles were compatible, but in practice they were separate agendas, requiring different programs and tactics. Because of these differences, the European and U.S. peace movements were unable to work together effectively to prevent the deployment of INF weapons.

Even if the freeze movement had mounted a massive campaign in the United States against the INF weapons, this probably would not have been sufficient to block deployment. Europe witnessed the largest peace demonstrations in its history in the fall of 1983, with nearly three million people marching through the streets of major capitals (Rochon 1988, 6; Cortright 1993, 127). Yet in spite of this unprecedented outpouring of opposition, which was equivalent to that which toppled communist governments in the East six years later, NATO leaders pushed ahead with the missile deployments. It is doubtful that additional pressure from people in the United States would have made a major difference. Nonetheless, by failing to mount a serious attempt to block the deployments, the NWFC disillusioned many within its own ranks and lost a critical opportunity to build transnational links with the European peace movement.

Timidity on the INF issue also contributed to the NWFC's undoing. By retreating to an increasingly narrow frame, the freeze found itself paralyzed in the face of what many considered the most critical nuclear weapons issue of the decade. As a major new escalation of the arms race proceeded in Europe, the nuclear freeze movement seemed pow-

---

2. Interestingly, the notion of the utility of unilateral initiatives was vindicated by experiences during the late 1980s. Unilateral concessions by Gorbachev in 1987 and Bush's and Gorbachev's 1991 initiatives for tactical nuclear weapons reductions were decisive steps in ending the Cold War. The easing of nuclear tensions and the transformations of the international system were thus sparked by unilateral initiatives.

erless. With the cruise and Pershing missiles arriving in Europe, hope that the arms race might be halted began to fade. The enthusiasm that initially characterized the freeze movement ebbed, and the campaign lost its focus.

Contact with the Soviet Government and Official Peace Committees

From the earliest days of the campaign, the freeze movement sought to bring the idea of a nuclear freeze to Soviet government authorities. These efforts were a logical and necessary consequence of the bilateral freeze proposal, since agreement was necessary from both Washington and Moscow. Initially Soviet officials expressed general interest in the freeze idea but made no commitments. In 1982, however, when the Strategic Arms Reduction Treat (START) negotiations opened in Geneva, the Soviet government actually adopted a modified version of the freeze proposal and offered it to U.S. officials as the official Soviet bargaining position. The Soviet plan, which was not the same as the more comprehensive proposal of the U.S. peace movement, urged that strategic armament be "frozen quantitatively . . . and that modernization be limited to the utmost" (Talbott 1984, 279).

In contrast, the NWFC proposal called for the complete end to all weapons modernization in addition to a quantitative halt. The Soviet proposal was widely regarded as merely a propaganda gesture (Talbott 1984, 279), directed more to Western publics than to the Reagan administration officials sitting across the table. Nonetheless, the Soviet decision to embrace the freeze, at least partially, was a sign of the freeze movement's wide influence. On the other hand, the Soviet gesture may have hurt the freeze movement by creating the impression among some that the freeze was a Soviet proposal.

Of the many attempts to lobby the Soviet government to take initiatives to end the arms race, perhaps the most dramatic was the joint U.S. and European peace movement delegation to the 1985 U.S.-Soviet summit in Geneva. When the Reagan-Gorbachev summit was announced, leaders of the NWFC and the Committee for a Sane Nuclear Policy (SANE) (including one of the authors) met to plan a response, which included sending a citizens' delegation to Geneva to seek meetings with Reagan and Gorbachev.[3] The goal of these efforts was to build public pressure for concrete steps to halt the arms race. The

3. About the same time, an independent U.S. group, Women for a Meaningful Summit, and representatives of European peace groups were also raising the idea of a citizen delegation.

U.S. and European groups agreed on a common strategy of raising expectations for concrete results from the summit, and they worked effectively together both at Geneva and at the Reykjavik summit the following year.

The groups also agreed to focus their demands on the call for a mutual halt to nuclear weapons testing, which was seen as an easily verifiable first step toward ending the arms race. This focus on the test ban assumed increased importance in August 1985, when Gorbachev announced that the Soviet Union would begin a unilateral moratorium on nuclear testing. Peace activists quickly recognized the importance of the Soviet action and turned their attention toward convincing the Reagan administration to reciprocate.

The SANE-Freeze delegation carried more than one million petitions on behalf of a test ban to the Geneva summit. The groups had asked Rev. Jesse Jackson to lead the delegation, and he served as spokesperson when the peace activists met with Gorbachev and other high-level Soviet officials on the first day of the summit. Jackson asked the Soviet leader to extend the test ban indefinitely, and he also challenged Gorbachev on the issue of human rights for Jews and other minorities within the Soviet Union. After Jackson and Gorbachev completed their lengthy and sometimes heated exchange, Justine Merritt spoke on behalf of Women for a Meaningful Summit. Jackson then presented the petitions to the Soviet leader, and the remarkable meeting came to an end. A similar attempt was made to meet Reagan in Geneva, but the administration spurned peace movement requests. When the SANE-Freeze delegation nonetheless insisted upon delivering the petitions, a lower level official at the U.S. embassy received the boxes and listened indifferently to Jackson's appeal for a halt to nuclear testing.

The peace movement meeting with Gorbachev received extensive international press coverage. Much of the coverage was negative, however, especially that of the *Washington Post* and the U.S. television networks. Many of the stories were critical of Jackson for supposedly upstaging and embarrassing the U.S. president. The reports mentioned Jackson's challenge to Gorbachev on human rights but not his appeal for a U.S.-Soviet testing moratorium (Hertzgaard 1989, 291). The presence of the peace groups that had sponsored the delegation and collected the petitions was hardly noted. Even Bill Moyers, the otherwise liberal commentator for CBS, criticized Jackson and the peace movement delegation for playing into Gorbachev's hands. Local news reporting was more favorable, in part because freeze groups across the United States had sponsored community events to support the efforts of the citizens' delegation in Geneva and to raise public expectations for progress at the summit, thus generating pressure on Reagan and Gorbachev for an end to the arms race.

Many other attempts were made to influence Soviet government policy, by the NWFC itself and by associated peace and arms control organizations. Marcus Raskin of the Institute for Policy Studies in Washington instituted a series of conferences with Soviet academic experts on the need for a more comprehensive disarmament policy. Admirals Eugene LaRocque and Eugene Carroll of the Center for Defense Information carried on a dialogue with Soviet leaders, first Chernenko and then Gorbachev, on the proposal for a nuclear test ban. Groups of scientists such as the Natural Resources Defense Council worked with their counterparts in the Soviet Union to establish independent verification systems for monitoring a test ban (Cortright 1993, 209–11). The impact of these initiatives is uncertain, but at least one inside observer of Soviet policy considered the influence of Western peace groups decisive. Tair Tairov, a secretary general of the Soviet-controlled World Peace Council who later left the organization and condemned it as a "Stalinist/Brezhnevite structure," told an interviewer in 1988 that the Western peace groups had a significant influence on Kremlin policy: "If it wasn't for the peace movements in the West, there would have been no new thinking.... Gorbachev would never have proclaimed the idea of a nonviolent, non-nuclear world. He knew that the world was already fertile. The peace movements created the historical arena in which he could go ahead" (Disarmament Campaigns 1989, 31).

A controversial and hotly debated aspect of this international liaison with the Soviet Union was contact with the Soviet Peace Committee and other officially approved peace councils in Eastern Europe. The NWFC, SANE, and other groups occasionally met with these groups in the United States and in Moscow, using such opportunities to encourage citizen-to-citizen dialogue and at times to criticize Soviet human rights abuses and demand greater Soviet efforts to halt the arms race. In 1984 and 1985, for example, several U.S. peace groups pressed the demand for a halt to nuclear testing through official Peace Council organizations.

Although some leaders of the freeze movement supported these efforts, others opposed such contacts, arguing that the official Peace Committees were completely dominated by Communist Party authorities and had no political independence. Intense debates over this question raged within the NWFC National Committee and Executive Committee (Kehler 1993). National Committee member Jesse Prosten, a retired vice president of the United Food and Commercial Workers and longtime labor activist, criticized those who opposed the official

Peace Councils for "caving in to McCarthyism." Others countered that cooperation with the official committees legitimated Soviet government control over these groups and made it more difficult for independent citizen initiatives to emerge in the Soviet Union. When a dissident organization, the Soviet Group to Establish Trust, sent a request through the AFSC for contact with freeze movement leaders, the issue was brought to a head. The NWFC was unable to reach consensus on the question, however, and decided not to relate formally to either the official committees or the independent dissident groups (Solo 1988, 113).

This was another area where the freeze movement differed from the European peace movement. The West European groups were strongly committed to what author Mary Kaldor called "détente from below," and they provided considerable encouragement and support to independent peace and human rights groups in the East (Kaldor 1991). But the West Europeans also maintained dialogue with the official committees in the Soviet bloc countries. The leading group in this interaction with official and unofficial groups in the East was European Nuclear Disarmament (END), in which Kaldor played an important role.

END, founded by the eminent British historian E. P. Thompson, was a transnational organization facilitating communication and coordination between peace groups in the West and human rights activists in the East. Condemning the entire Cold War system of competing blocs, END directed its challenges at both Washington and Moscow. In the West a greater commitment to peace was needed, END argued, while in the East human rights and freedom were paramount. Disarmament and democracy must be achieved together, Thompson and his colleagues asserted. Indeed, it was only through the linkage of the two that genuine peace could be attained. The philosophy of END reflected the view of Vaclav Havel, the future Czech president: "Respect for human rights is the fundamental condition and the sole genuine guarantee of true peace. . . . Lasting peace and disarmament can only be the work of free people" (Havel 1985).

Solo has criticized the NWFC's inability to follow the lead of the Europeans in relating to peace and human rights groups in the East. The decision not to work with groups in the East "revealed once again the movement's inability to address the international politics of the East-West conflict and the arms race" (Solo 1988, 113). Solo and others wanted the flexibility to relate to both official and unofficial groups, but they were unable to convince the majority, which retreated again to a narrow interpretation of the freeze mission. As a result, the freeze movement continued to operate within the constraints of the Cold

War system and became "a captive of the politics we were trying to overcome" (Solo 1993).

Conclusion

The transnational experience of the Nuclear Weapons Freeze Campaign and its limited attempts to use a major intergovernmental organization illustrate some of the difficulties of transnational activism, especially on security issues during the Cold War period. Although the NWFC did try to form a loosely structured coalition with peace groups in Europe, there were important differences in framing, goals, and ideology between European peace groups and the NWFC. The diagnosis and prognosis of the problem and the activities of the European groups were shaped by their historical, cultural, and political contexts—not only within their own countries but also within their region. Many European groups believed that their countries were pawns in a struggle between two superpowers that did not intend to disarm. Many wanted to move "beyond the blocs" and the bipolar Cold War logic to escape the domination of the superpowers.

Similarly, operating in a political context of electorally viable social democratic, socialist, and green parties, many European peace groups were free to act creatively on the left and still remain politically relevant, though they did not necessarily tie the fate of their efforts to the electoral fate of any particular party. Walter Kaltefleiter and Robert L. Pfaltzgraff noted the importance of the multiparty system to European peace movement impact: "One can . . . conclude that the greatest potential of [peace] movements seems to be in those political systems in which there is a multi-party structure. . . . This multi-party structure is . . . necessarily dependent upon fragile political coalitions" (1985, 194). Under a proportional representation electoral system, a broader range of voices and policies is represented in government than is the case in a majoritarian system like that in the United States.

The NWFC was never free to act creatively on the left, partly because of the structure of the electoral system. In the United States politicians must moderate innovative and creative policy ideas in order to build a majoritarian electoral coalition out of a diverse constituency. Creative policy ideas that must be taken seriously because they may gain a sufficient electoral backing in a system of proportional representation can be ignored in the U.S. system. Congress is a collection of moderates working under procedures that were established to prevent fast and/or drastic change and that reward status quo policy proposals. With such constraints it is not surprising that the NWFC advocated a moderate, bilateral freeze on nuclear weapons. The superpower status of the United States and four decades of Cold War rhetoric also contributed to the historical and cultural constraints on the NWFC. Thus it is not surprising that European peace groups often had a different orientation from that of the NWFC. These diverse historical, cultural, and political contexts shaped the strategies and goals of peace groups and impeded transnational cooperation.

It is also not surprising that the NWFC, working within a superpower nation in a bipolar global system, advocated a bilateral policy and did not fully exploit the multilateral processes of the UN. The NWFC successfully lobbied delegates to SSDII to support a freeze resolution, but it clearly did not strive to build a comprehensive multilateral arms control and security regime. This is unfortunate in light of the fact that peace movement actors had a new opportunity in these sessions to become more involved in the regime-building process. The NWFC's retreat from internationalism to bilateralism soon after SSDII ruled out any chance that this large coalition would transcend the Cold War logic that ultimately imprisoned it.

10

BUILDING POLITICAL WILL AFTER UNCED

EarthAction International

Jackie Smith

Abstract

Some transnational social movement organizations (TSMOs) intervene directly in intergovernmental conferences to try to influence the language of particular treaties and to help implement multilateral agreements. But many more elements of transnational movements work to educate national and local organizations and individuals about global problems and the political systems designed to address these. EarthAction is a TSMO that works to integrate its affiliate organizations into multilateral policy processes by informing them about the issues at stake and by suggesting tactics that encourage local mobilization around global issues. For example, EarthAction helped to sustain pressure on governments to adhere to declarations they made during the 1992 UN Conference on Environment and Development (UNCED). Such TSMO efforts, however subtle their results, may be critical to advancing concrete policy change to protect the environment.

Although many scientists and activists are increasingly convinced of the urgency of international action to counter many global environmental problems, national leaders often lack the political will to generate multilateral cooperation that effectively addresses these problems.[1]

1. I appreciate the extensive contribution Robert C. Johansen has made to this study of EarthAction and to my overall research on TSMOs. Thanks also to Lois Barber and Nicholas Dunlop, the International Coordinators of EarthAction, for providing me with information on their work.

Where problems are recognized, governments often prefer to take minimal steps towards their mitigation rather than to act decisively for their prevention or reversal. In democracies, one reason for such a choice is that politicians' electoral mandates lead them to think in terms of two-to six-year periods, whereas the consequences of environmental degradation may not be manifest for decades or centuries. Political leaders are, therefore, unlikely to have strong interests in supporting multilateral responses to global crises with only subtle, ambiguous, and long-term implications for their own constituencies (Pirages 1989). Nevertheless, in the past two decades, states have advanced multilateral cooperation for the environment in dramatic ways (Haas 1996; Porter and Brown 1995). Environmental transnational social movement organizations (TSMOs) have contributed to this development.

EarthAction's Mobilization to Advance UNCED Goals

Founded in 1991, EarthAction is a TSMO that mobilizes local, national, and international nongovernmental organizations (NGOs) around issues of peace, human rights, and sustainable development. Its more than 1,500 partner organizations[2] in over 140 countries are linked around common campaigns through routine mailings and telephone contacts from EarthAction's regional international offices. EarthAction attempts to make global issues matter for politicians' short-term (e.g., electoral) interests. It has sought in particular to advance the goals outlined in Agenda 21, the final declaration of the UN Conference on Environment and Development (UNCED). UNCED was held in Rio de Janiero in 1992 to address growing concerns, particularly among Northern governments, about continued environmental degradation and to reconcile these with Southern governments' urgent development needs.

Between late 1992 and early 1995, EarthAction initiated more than twenty global campaigns focused on environment, development, peace, and human rights issues. Nearly half of these campaigns sought explicitly to further goals specified in Agenda 21. EarthAction's envi-

---

2. EarthAction partners range from very large transnational groups, such as Greenpeace International, to national chapters of international organizations, such as the International Commission of Jurists-Kenya, to autonomous national SMOs and NGOs, such as the Philippine Green Forum, to local organizations, such as the U.S.-based Eagle Rock Committee for Survival. While many EarthAction partners are SMOs, a large number of them are not specifically organized for advocacy. Examples of the latter include religious orders, schools, and recreational clubs, which are among EarthAction's partners.

ronmental campaigns have aimed to generate pressure on governments to strengthen their commitments to more equitable and
sustainable development. These campaigns supported multilateral negotiations on the two major conventions that resulted from UNCED
—the biological diversity and the climate change conventions—and
EarthAction has also supported the development of the Desertification
Convention, which was another goal of the Agenda 21. EarthAction's
treaty-oriented campaigns are complemented by its efforts to support
institutional reform and treaty implementation.

EarthAction's Strategy

EarthAction works as a catalyst for global political change primarily
by building the infrastructures for a politically active, global civil society. Believing that global change will occur only when political leaders
face sufficient pressure from their constituencies, EarthAction's leadership attempts to make global issues matter for local and national elections by helping inform citizens and their legislators about global
problems and about government attempts to resolve these problems.
Providing detailed information about the timing of negotiations, the
terms of debate, and expert assessments of what is needed to resolve
a crisis, EarthAction enables partners, their members, and elected officials (parliamentarians) to become more involved in multilateral political processes than they could be otherwise. Its editorial advisories,
moreover, provide media producers with tools they need to cover
complex global issues that they may find difficult or that may not be
part of their routine reporting.

Both directly and through its network of NGOs, EarthAction also
monitors global political processes, informing partners about how and
when effective pressure can be applied. Partners that hope to influence
their government's policies on the rights of indigenous peoples, for
instance, may have been unaware of an International Labor Organization (ILO) convention on indigenous peoples' rights before receiving
EarthAction's Alert on the subject. And few citizens' organizations are
able to attend international negotiations in order to identify which
governments need to be pressed on what issues.

In addition to providing informational tools, EarthAction serves to
aggregate global environmental interests. Its communications links
with partner organizations foster communication among NGOs and
the identification of common interests and possibilities for cooperation.
In other words, EarthAction helps develop and reinforce transnational
movement frames, that is, interpretations of global environmental
problems and the steps needed to remedy them.

To develop transnationally relevant mobilizing frames, EarthAction first identifies interests and concerns that span nations and regions. Its decentralized secretariat allows EarthAction staff relatively frequent communication with partner organizations, helping it maximize human contact across its global network. Believing that "human follow-up to the Action Alert mailings is essential: people respond to people, not paper," EarthAction follows its mailings with telephone calls to portions of its partner base (EarthAction 1993a, 1).

One central goal of EarthAction's interest in aggregation work is to support the organizational capacities of partners. By providing routine updates on issues, EarthAction helps to sustain activists' momentum and to demonstrate success, however limited. Summaries of how other partners have used EarthAction materials promotes learning and tactical innovation by partners. Facilitating networking among partners, EarthAction helps to generate and reinforce transnational mobilizing frames while supporting its partners' own organization-building efforts.

Recently EarthAction has begun working more directly to cultivate communications links within its network and thereby to nurture the infrastructures of global civil society. Channeling small grants to local partners, EarthAction helps these groups heighten their visibility and develop contacts with local and regional citizens' groups, media, and parliamentarians. Partners receiving support grants translate and disseminate EarthAction materials and conduct follow-up telephone calls within the region. Because EarthAction is a worldwide organization involving people from many different national and linguistic backgrounds, such translation and local adaptation of EarthAction's campaign materials is essential. Locally based organizations are often best able to do this kind of work. This not only brings EarthAction's material to more people, but also it helps develop the capacities of the "contact" group and heightens that group's visibility as a recognized node in the EarthAction network.

EarthAction's interest aggregation and communication functions help generate enthusiasm and sustain momentum for its campaigns: Partners are encouraged by reading each Alert's message that "This alert is being sent to over 1,000 citizen groups in 129 countries which are part of the EarthAction network. . . . When you act, you are acting together with citizens from all parts of the world."[3] Partners contacted in telephone surveys repeatedly have expressed their appreciation for the work EarthAction does to show them they are not alone in their struggles (EarthAction 1994a; 1995a). As one report noted: "We hear

---

3. These numbers have changed as EarthAction's membership has grown.

repeatedly from small environment, development and peace groups around the world, 'Thanks for being there. Now we feel less isolated.' ... Alleviating both the feelings and reality of struggling in isolation is key to the sustainability of organisations that work for peace, justice and environmental protection" (EarthAction 1994b, 6).

National Arenas

EarthAction's campaigns to advance the aims of UNCED influenced national political arenas when they generated citizens' pressure upon governments to implement the conventions they signed at Rio or to take progressive positions on decisions in intergovernmental negotiations, such as those on the Convention to Combat Desertification. In some cases, EarthAction campaigns sought to generate letters from around the world urging leaders of single nations to further global agendas. Although it is often impossible to measure the impact this pressure had on national policymaking, it is clear that such pressures do make policymakers aware of citizens' concern about their foreign policy activity (cf. Knopf 1993). Although the pressure brought to bear on decisions regulating CO_2 emissions, protecting biological diversity, and curbing desertification may not have influenced policymakers at that particular time, it could be a factor in subsequent decisions.

Supporting national mobilization and action, EarthAction helps partner organizations monitor and respond to activities of their governments that are related to the international treaties and institutions EarthAction promotes. In this way it nurtures national constituencies for multilateral problem solving—constituencies that can be important to monitoring and supporting the implementation of international agreements. These constituencies, moreover, can have broad, long-term impacts on national environmental policies.

Intergovernmental Arenas

By generating transnational movement frames and mobilizing activists around specific multilateral policy decisions, EarthAction influences intergovernmental arenas by helping to harmonize national positions before negotiations begin. Facing similar pressures from activated constituents and parliamentarians, governments may be open to concessions that they would otherwise have resisted. Moreover, EarthAction's citizen action and media campaigns help generate public attention to otherwise obscure intergovernmental negotiations, thus increasing government accountability in these arenas.

Such mobilization can restrict governments' policy choices: The European anti-INF mobilization, for instance, limited the U.S. ability to deploy INF weapons in Europe (Knopf 1993, 620). But greater citizen mobilization around multilateral policies need not simply constrain government choices. In some cases, such mobilization may make it easier for governments to accept policy change. For instance, transnational pressures helped bolster Gorbachev's willingness to confront his domestic opposition by pursuing a mutual security foreign policy in the late 1980s (Risse-Kappen 1994).

Thus EarthAction's work to cultivate and mobilize support for transnational social change frames helps shape government perceptions of the costs and benefits associated with particular policy choices. By demonstrating public support for environmental agreements, EarthAction and similar groups help encourage governments (or reform-oriented elements within governments) to advance multilateral agreements rather than postpone decisions or limit commitments. For instance, EarthAction's and other TSMOs' work to prepare for the First Conference of the Parties to the Climate Change Convention appears to have helped encourage the decision of small island states to submit a proposal to strengthen that convention.

Mechanisms for conference follow-up, such as treaty review conferences, help keep global problems on political and public agendas and stimulate action to address them. The Commission on Sustainable Development, for example, was set up to review governments' progress towards the goals of Agenda 21 through annual meetings similar to those of the UN Human Rights Commission. As routine sessions for evaluating the effectiveness of multilateral agreements, such review mechanisms create regular opportunities for TSMOs to voice their concerns. But without transnational efforts like those of EarthAction to draw public attention to them, such conferences are unlikely to effectively change government practices.

Political leaders are typically preoccupied and generally disinclined to take initiatives on the issues addressed in large conference settings. But more focused, annual review meetings allow greater opportunities for action. Because environmental problems often affect states differently, some states may have a direct interest in an immediate international response while others can afford to take a wait-and-see approach. Sometimes the fact that a problem has yet to achieve political salience inhibits action because "policy makers in many countries see little reason to take difficult or costly actions to avert unknown and perhaps distant risks" (Paterson and Grubb 1992, 296). Furthermore, the public agenda is only intermittently focused on critical issues. But the political work needed to see a problem from its diagnosis to its political remedy demands months or years of perseverance. Transnational movement pressures like those promoted by EarthAction help generate consistent and sustained pressure on governments that can lead to concrete policy changes.

Several of EarthAction's campaigns broadened political options in intergovernmental arenas by promoting alternative multilateral approaches. For instance, the campaign to influence the Global Environment Facility (GEF), an intergovernmental agency that provides economic assistance to developing countries for projects to improve environmental practices, promoted an NGO role in the identification, design, and implementation of projects. This campaign also called for an information system that would allow greater public accountability. This proposal, advocated by many organizations besides EarthAction, addressed some of the concerns of Southern countries while posing less of a threat to Northern interests than proposals by the Southern Countries themselves. In another case, EarthAction's campaign promoting the ILO convention on indigenous people's rights provided an alternative means of advancing the goals of the Convention on Biological Diversity and the negotiations on a forests treaty. Arguing that the recognition of indigenous peoples' land rights would curb environmentally unsustainable development in forest regions, EarthAction's campaign helped link these seemingly different multilateral efforts.

EarthAction's broad partner base allows it to generate global action by large numbers of partner organizations that typically are focused on local or national issues to the exclusion of global ones. By monitoring multilateral negotiations, EarthAction helps empower these groups to take action in intergovernmental political arenas. Its International Steering Committee and staff are informed on legal and political issues surrounding the negotiations and are present at major intergovernmental meetings. They are thus able to answer questions raised by EarthAction partners regarding the positions of particular governments. Moreover, EarthAction's contacts with a wide range of more technically focused global lobby groups allow it to generate materials that are well researched and that offer appropriate action proposals. Established to help local and national groups become more involved in global work, EarthAction generates resources to educate activists on the major global problems and the obstacles to political progress on resolving these problems. EarthAction's presentation of background on global issues in an accessible format helps EarthAction's partners cultivate an informed constituency for global politics. This constituency, then, is better prepared to monitor governments and intergovernmental negotiations than they might be otherwise.

Transgovernmental Arenas

EarthAction's work has been strongly supported by intergovernmental officials because it so clearly supports multilateral institutional development. Each of the campaigns described above represents attempts to strengthen specific international agreements. Therefore, intergovernmental officials charged with implementing these agreements share many of EarthAction's goals. For this reason, several intergovernmental agencies, including the Intergovernmental Negotiating Committee for a Convention to Combat Desertification (INCD) and the UN Environment Programme (UNEP), have supported EarthAction's work. These intergovernmental officials see citizens' groups like EarthAction as means of working beyond governments to generate support "from below" for multilateral problem solving.

The posturing and political maneuvering that is typical of intergovernmental relations complicates cooperation. But if politicians are pressed by well-informed constituencies favoring multilateralism, they may approach the negotiating table differently. Thus, the INCD worked with EarthAction to increase governments' concern about desertification and their desire to act on the problem by generating public and media attention to the negotiations. Similarly, other UN agencies have worked with EarthAction to cultivate support for IGO work on other sustainable development issues.

EarthAction, UNCED, and Environmental Politics

Table 10.1 lists EarthAction's campaigns on each major problem in the Rio Declaration and their corresponding change targets. Although a few of EarthAction's campaigns focused on particular governments, most were efforts to bring citizen pressure on many governments in order to advance *multilateral* cooperation. Each EarthAction campaign represents an effort to nudge governments towards ever more extensive environmental cooperation. For instance, after initially publicizing efforts by governments to develop a Convention on Desertification, EarthAction shifted its strategy to press governments to sign and then ratify the agreement. The campaigns EarthAction initiated to advance Agenda 21 goals on climate change, biodiversity, and desertification are detailed below. EarthAction's activities make it an important interest aggregator, monitor, and catalyst in intergovernmental negotiations and institution building.

Although many bemoan the shortcomings of the UNCED process, the conferences and agreements it spawned helped institutionalize global environmental cooperation. The review processes institutional-

TABLE 10.1.

EarthAction Campaigns to Advance UNCED

Campaign and Date	Change Target
Climate Change Convention	
Send a Message to Clinton (12/92)	Clinton Administration Policy
Global Environment Facility (2/93)	GEF Review Decision
Climate Change and Biodiversity (6/93)	Climate Change Convention—Nat'l Implementation
Stabilize Our Climate (1/95)§‡	Climate Change Convention—Review Conference
Biological Diversity Convention	
Stop Logging Clayoquot Sound (1/93)**	Canadian Logging Policy
Global Environment Facility (2/93)	GEF Review Decision
Climate Change and Biodiversity (6/93)	Biodiversity Convention—Nat'l Implementation
Protect Diversity of Life on Earth (9/93)*	Biodiversity Convention—Nat'l Implementation
Protect the Diversity of Life (3/95)§‡†	Biodiversity Convention—Implementation *and* ILO Convention 169 (Indigenous and Tribal People's Convention—Signing & Implementation)
Desertification Convention	
Protect the Land That Feeds Us (12/93)‡	Desertification Convention—Negotiation
Desertification Negotiations (4/94)§‡	Desertification Convention—Signing
Desertification Convention (10/94)§‡	Desertification Convention—Signing

Source: From Smith 1995b.
§ Campaign included simultaneous Parliamentary Alert
‡ Campaign included simultaneous Editorial Advisory
* Represents follow-up (strategically staggered) Editorial Advisory
† International and customized, U.S. Campaign
** "Back Page" follow-up actions were taken in April and September, 1993

ized by Agenda 21 and by the Biodiversity, Climate Change, and Desertification Conventions ensure that environmental issues will be a
more routine subject of governments' attention, if not action. Environmental TSMOs like EarthAction have been important actors in this
process.

Combating Climate Change

During UNCED, 160 governments signed the Framework Convention on Climate Change, agreeing to take steps to reduce carbon diox-
ide (CO_2) emissions to 1990 levels. The agreement came into force in

March 1994, after 50 governments ratified it. The first Conference of
the Parties to the Convention met in Berlin to review the treaty in the
spring of 1995.

EarthAction worked to limit climate change with four campaigns
between 1992 and 1995. Its December 1992 campaign urged its partner
organizations around the world to send letters to Bill Clinton, then
president-elect, to advance multilateral efforts to promote peace, sustainable development, environmental protection, and human rights.
Partners were asked to advocate concrete goals in each area, including
greater reductions and strengthened multilateral monitoring of greenhouse gas emissions. The June 1993 campaign promoted progress on
both conventions signed at UNCED, advancing a more specific proposal for a protocol to the Climate Change Convention that would
reduce greenhouse gas emissions to at least 20 percent below 1990
levels.[4] EarthAction pressed leaders in developing countries to fulfil
their obligations under the convention to implement and further national and regional efforts to reduce CO_2 emissions. Mobilizing citizens, journalists, and parliamentarians to press their governments to
accept common proposals, EarthAction sought to harmonize governments' policies on emissions limits.

In the preparatory meetings before the first Conference of the Parties
in Berlin, Western governments were reluctant to introduce a protocol
that would require parties to further reduce emissions, and only late
in the process did the Alliance of Small Island States (AOSIS)—a politically weak and ecologically vulnerable group—introduce the protocol
that was considered at the Berlin "Climate Summit" (Bureau of National Affairs 1994c). AOSIS's last-minute introduction of the proposed
protocol, as well as its earlier behavior in negotiations on sustainable
development, demonstrated the alliance's apprehension about raising
costly demands that might alienate Northern governments and risk
any chance of their winning even minimal agreements. TSMOs at preparatory meetings for the Berlin Summit were frustrated that their
efforts to back the interests of AOSIS governments were continually
watered down because delegates from the small island developing
states feared pushing Northern governments too hard. Nevertheless,
when representatives from the United States and Britain asked TSMO
representatives why the small island states were sidestepping the key
issues, they found that " 'The problem was not a reluctance on the part

---

4. These commitments represented a small portion of the 60 percent cuts that the
Intergovernmental Panel on Climate Change claimed was needed to effectively control
climate change.

of Northern governments, but the timidity of island governments' " (Ally and Gollop 1993).

There is a very real tendency in international diplomacy to avoid hard issues, particularly when confronting them requires states relatively vulnerable to economic and other pressures (e.g., AOSIS) to ask much stronger states (e.g., the United States) to modify their behaviors. But without decisive action by the states most affected by environmental destruction, adequate and equitable solutions will not emerge. As one Caribbean activist complained, " '[o]ur concern is that we are running the risk of losing the moment. If [small island developing states] continue to shilly shally and don't get our act together they (Northern governments) won't take us very seriously' " (Ally and Gollop 1993). EarthAction, like other NGOs that were present at those meetings, sought to encourage and strengthen the AOSIS proposal. Its media, parliamentary, and citizen action campaigns of January 1995 were devised to bring pressure on governments as they prepared for the Berlin review conference.

EarthAction further promoted UNCED's goal of limiting climate change by supporting the restructuring of the Global Environment Facility. Designed to provide developing countries with financial resources to implement UNCED's environmental protection initiatives, the GEF was critical to both the political and practical advancement of UNCED goals. Developing countries agreed to focus on the problems deemed most urgent by the industrialized nations, including climate change and the loss of biological diversity, if, in turn, industrialized countries provided financial resources and allowed developing nations a stronger role in GEF decision making. Northern threats to reduce their already meager financial contributions to the GEF preempted strong Southern efforts to realize the promise of the GEF envisioned at UNCED. EarthAction's campaign amplified the opposition of developing states to World Bank dominance over the GEF, urging the alternative of greater citizen participation in it. EarthAction partners contacted the ministers of finance in numerous governments to press for more consultation with citizens' groups in the identification, design, and implementation of projects. They also asked political leaders to guarantee public access to information about the projects funded under the GEF. These two steps advanced calls for public accountability, which is "a time-honoured tool for dealing with bureaucratic failures" (EarthAction 1993b, 1). By promoting greater transparency in GEF decision making, EarthAction's objectives helped promote key interests of developing countries without mirroring elements of their demands that Northern governments opposed. Developing countries were unable to overcome the commanding influence of industrialized states in the short term, but they gained potential leverage through TSMO constituencies in Northern nations.

Protecting Biological Diversity

The second major agreement signed at UNCED was the Convention on Biological Diversity, which called upon its signatories to develop and advance national plans for protecting biological diversity while encouraging the transfer of technological and financial resources from Northern to Southern countries. Although lacking legally binding commitments, this convention specified concrete aspects of national conservation plans while seeking to mitigate inequalities caused by the exploitation of national resources. EarthAction's campaigns on the Biological Diversity Convention included two Action Alerts to promote this convention and the Alert, described above, on restructuring the GEF. An "Editorial Advisory" on the convention was issued just before the October 1993 meeting of the signatories. Sent to a list of reporters compiled by EarthAction, the advisory provided the international news media with background on the convention and on the problem of biological diversity. It recommended reading matter, prerecorded radio and television material, and questions to ask policymakers, in addition to notifying journalists about a media briefing and workshop to be held near the negotiation site. This editorial campaign provided critical information for the news reports of several media outlets, and it was used by World Environment News to produce a video news clip that was rebroadcast by CNN and other large networks worldwide (EarthAction 1994c, 7).

A key to reaching agreement on the Biological Diversity Convention and to its ultimate success was the commitment of Northern governments to provide financial and biotechnological support for less developed, Southern countries that lack the means to develop the biological resources within their boundaries. EarthAction sought to reinforce these redistributive commitments and to otherwise mitigate tensions between Northern and Southern governments through its campaign to strengthen the GEF. It also explicitly addressed North-South tensions in its campaign against Canadian logging policy. This EarthAction Alert argued, "[i]f affluent British Columbia is unable to save its rainforests, how can we expect other countries, under tremendous pressures of poverty and debt, to save theirs?" (EarthAction 1993c,1). Through this campaign, EarthAction focused international citizen pressure on bringing the environmental policy of a single, Northern government in line with global interests. Using a single Action Alert and two follow-up notices, EarthAction helped to bring *sustained* pressure on the Canadian government to protect its remaining forests, just as it and other Northern governments were asking Southern governments to do. An EarthAction partner in Canada, Friends of Clayoquot Sound, reported that

> [t]he Canadian Government is clearly feeling the international pressure. Last week Canada's ambassador to the UN, Arthur Campeau, said "I believe that the Clayoquot conflict has gone on far too long. It is causing us damage greater than we are prepared to admit. Abroad, Canada's envied image of world leader in protection of the environment is being eroded and replaced by one of an environmental outlaw." (quoted in EarthAction 1994b, 6)

Thus EarthAction's international citizen pressure highlighted for Canadian officials the potential international costs of the continued destruction of its forests.

EarthAction's "Forests Campaign" of March 1995 tried both to advance the formal commitments made at UNCED and to promote other initiatives to protect the earth's resources. In this campaign EarthAction used a Parliamentary Alert and Editorial Advisory in addition to the regular citizens' alert to reach government officials through their constituents, national legislators, and media. The campaign addressed the broad problem of losing plant and animal species, citing two main ways to curb further environmental destruction. Recognizing that governments were currently in the process of negotiating a Forest Convention, EarthAction pointed out that such a treaty would take years to realize and that other multilateral steps could address this increasingly urgent crisis.[5]

EarthAction emphasized the need for the 157 state signatories to the Convention on Biological Diversity to carry out their pledges to protect vanishing species and ecosystems. Partners were asked to hold their governments to their pledges to identify and protect endangered species. Moreover, believing that "[t]he indigenous people who inhabit many of the world's forests make far better forest stewards than distant bureaucrats," EarthAction promoted the rights of indigenous people to control the land they have traditionally occupied (EarthAction 1995b, 1).

The International Labor Organization's Tribal People's Convention

---

5. Governments have resisted taking action on the forests issue by relegating it to a distinct negotiating forum rather than integrating it with the Biodiversity Convention or with other international agreements.

(ILO Convention 169) protects the rights of indigenous peoples to own and control the use of their traditional land. This convention not only reaffirms indigenous peoples' territorial rights but also protects indigenous lands from destructive business and government practices. However, as an EarthAction Alert informed partners, although ILO Convention 169 promised to protect endangered forests, only seven countries had signed the convention. Northern governments, the Alert stated, should be urged to sign it, to provide financial support for indigenous peoples' efforts to protect their territorial rights,[6] and to increase their financial support of developing countries trying to implement the Convention on Biological Diversity. By relating this ILO initiative to the Convention on Biological Diversity, EarthAction helped both to advance UNCED's general aims and to link the UNCED process to other multilateral efforts.

Resisting Desertification

Also resulting from UNCED was the International Convention to Combat Desertification. Formal negotiations for the convention originated with Agenda 21, although it remained secondary in importance, behind the Conventions on Biological Diversity and Climate Change. EarthAction's campaign sought to generate more widespread awareness of and support for the Convention to Combat Desertification, as the negotiations for it proceeded.

EarthAction's first antidesertification effort was to issue an Action Alert and Editorial Advisory in December 1993 (EarthAction 1993d). These materials informed partners and journalists about the causes and consequences of global desertification and about the status of intergovernmental negotiations to address the problem. The Alert provided background information for partners interested in attending the negotiations or in becoming more involved with the Intergovernmental Negotiating Committee for a Convention to Combat Desertification (the international agency charged with organizing the negotiations and implementing their decisions) or with other NGOs. It sought to help partners influence intergovernmental negotiations at the early stages, when the form of the convention was still open for modifications. EarthAction issued toolkits on the Desertification Convention again in April and October of 1994 to increase the awareness of both the general

6. Two other EarthAction Campaigns, "Protect Indian Lands in Brazil" (EarthAction 1993d) and "Defend the Ogoni People in Nigeria" (EarthAction 1994e), sought to protect natural resources that were part of indigenous peoples' traditional lands from government encroachment, thus reinforcing these demands.

public and politicians of the issues at stake and the steps to which governments were committing themselves. EarthAction partners and parliamentarians were urged to press governments to increase financial support for efforts to combat desertification and to uphold their treaty commitments by "ensur[ing] that decisions on the . . . programmes to combat desertification and/or mitigate the effects of drought are [under]taken with the participation of . . . local communities." Throughout the treaty negotiations, governments of industrialized countries resisted increasing funds devoted to combating desertification, even though such funds were less than $1 billion per year, in contrast to what UNEP estimates is a need for between $10 and $22.4 billion annually (EarthAction 1994c, 1).

To facilitate journalists' coverage of the signing of the convention, an Editorial Advisory was sent to several thousand editorial writers around the world (EarthAction 1994b, 7). It included suggested "news hooks," local angles on the issue, a background summary of desertification and efforts to prevent it, questions journalists could ask policymakers, "key facts and quotes" to include in stories on the issue, expert sources, and a camera-ready map locating desertification problems. As a result of EarthAction's work on the Desertification Convention, numerous news stories were written that otherwise might not have been.[7] EarthAction helped draw journalists' attention to the materials by following the initial mailing with telephone calls to hundreds of writers and producers to remind them about the toolkit and to answer questions about desertification or the negotiations to combat it (EarthAction 1994b, 7).

EarthAction's staff used these calls to help journalists tailor stories on global desertification to their particular regions or locales (McKenna 1995). As a result of EarthAction's media work, National Public Radio in the United States was prompted to send a team of reporters to five African countries to produce a series of broadcasts on desertification, and major news outlets, such as the *Times* (UK), the *Independent* (UK), the Canadian Broadcasting Company, and *Berlingske Tidende* (Denmark), reported on desertification negotiations (EarthAction 1994c, 7).

Conclusions

Although the road from Rio has been disappointing because of the world's governments have failed to take more decisive environmental

---

7. This conclusion is based upon follow-up phone calls made to journalists to whom EarthAction materials were sent. Journalists were asked whether EarthAction materials influenced their decision to report on the desertification negotiations (Bernstein 1995).

action, it clearly has led to some progress. Perhaps most important, UNCED—including the preparation for the conference and the follow-up work done by EarthAction and other TSMOs—has generated increased public and governmental awareness of global environmental issues. Efforts by transnational environmental movements have helped advance transnational mobilizing frames that amplify the prominence of environmental issues on many governments' policy agendas and reinforce multilateral solutions to environmental problems (Keohane et al. 1993). Another important consequence of UNCED is the new global institutions it helped spawn, most notably, the GEF and the Commission on Sustainable Development. These institutions, although largely failing to address the core obstacle to global North/South equity concerns, have created new forums through which EarthAction and other TSMOs and NGOs can press governments to develop more environmentally sustainable policies. EarthAction's persistent work to reinforce the goals of Agenda 21 is an important part of the political processes surrounding global environmental policy. And the UNCED conference process itself provided both a focal point and political legitimacy for EarthAction's efforts.

As UNCED Secretary-General Maurice Strong observed, "Inertia is as powerful a force in human affairs as it is in the physical world" (Strong 1991, 294). As a result, the political processes structured by intergovernmental institutions are far from automatic. States typically resist infringements on their own sovereignty by intergovernmental agencies. By nurturing transnational mobilizing frames and by drawing citizen groups into multilateral decision-making processes, EarthAction nudges governments to act.

By monitoring government progress in and commitment to resolving environmental crises, EarthAction provides its partners with information they need to be active in global policy processes. In short, EarthAction's work helps articulate and focus shared interests of its partners, amplifying the needs and demands of local populations and empowering them to act on global issues. These functions of EarthAction help shape the contexts in which national, multilateral, and transgovernmental decisions are made. Specifically, such TSMO activities alter decision makers' perceptions of the costs and benefits (both political and environmental) of different policy choices.

UN conferences and review sessions provide opportunities for TSMO action, and they also represent important steps in the international community's adaptation to newly identified problems. They are used to mobilize public and official attention to issues, to develop or cultivate support for particular responses to problems, and to generate (and, increasingly, to help implement) mechanisms for ongoing problem management. TSMO participation in these events and their after-maths is, however, vital to their realization of the tasks of drawing public attention to global problems and of sustaining institutions that effectively respond to such problems. Moreover, the work of TSMOs like EarthAction can, help governments reach agreements in multi-lateral negotiations by expanding policy options, altering the political costs of multilateral cooperation, and enhancing the transparency of international negotiations and institutions. Over the long term, TSMOs' work helps improve the effectiveness and responsiveness of multilateral institutions.

PART FOUR

Targeting International Institutions

11

LIMITS TO MOBILIZATION

Environmental Policy for the European Union

Dieter Rucht

Abstract

With the evolution of the European Union (EU), the locus of environmental policies is gradually shifting to the supranational level. As a consequence, environmental social movement organizations (SMOs) have begun to reorient their strategies. This reorientation has resulted in a general tendency of movement organizations to join broad regional alliances, to strengthen EU-wide umbrella organizations, and to establish lobbying offices in Brussels. Nevertheless, the weight and impact of these efforts to influence EU environmental policy should not be overestimated. Compared to their powerful opponents, these groups have few resources. Moreover, they face a number of conditions that inhibit their influence on the EU. Finally, these groups lack the "radical flank effect" of mass mobilization and direct action that exists on the national level. These circumstances generate little optimism for a more powerful representation of environmental interests within the European Union.

Over the last few years, efforts to coordinate environmental policy on the international and supranational levels have intensified, and the locus of control in environmental policies is gradually shifting towards levels beyond the nation-state[1] (Caroll 1988; Tudyka 1988; Kimball 1992; Haas et al. 1993). This tendency seems particularly strong in

---

1. An earlier and much shorter version of this paper has been published in German (Rucht 1993a). I am grateful to Jackie Smith for her valuable comments and Kenn Kassman for editing the English version of this chapter.

situations where a group of countries has strengthened its overall political cooperation or even transferred legal competencies from national to international bodies, as is the case with the European Union (EU). As the administrative center of the EU, Brussels has clearly increased its influence in many policy domains, including that of environmental policy.

How have environmental nongovernmental organizations (NGOs) adapted to this shift of decision making from the national to the EU level? Theoretically, several options are available to them. First, following the slogan "think globally, act locally," the groups may intensify their activities on the national and subnational levels because they expect that gains made on these levels will somehow be transferred to the EU level. Such hopes are not unrealistic, as national governments still play an important role in EU decision making. Second, national environmental NGOs could try, individually, to exert a more direct impact upon the various agencies of the EU—either by intervening occasionally (for example, by sending an ad hoc delegation to inform and to lobby decision makers in a particular case), or by establishing a permanent office in Brussels. Finally, national environmental NGOs could intensify cross-national cooperation by coordinating national campaigns, supporting already existing international environmental groups, or by creating new international bodies (Rucht 1993b).

The third option seems a natural solution. It not only promises the greatest influence on EU policymaking but also appears feasible: Environmental NGOs face fewer pressures to compete directly with one another than do, for example, firms in the automobile or chemical industry. Although a global tendency towards growing cooperation and internationalization of environmental NGOs can be observed (Pearce 1991; Princen and Finger 1994; Green Globe Yearbook 1994), at least within the EU this tendency is less prominent than one might expect. Paradoxically, most groups continue to act primarily on national and subnational levels. This limitation does not necessarily indicate the groups' lack of awareness about the cross-national nature of many important environmental problems but, rather, may be related to other factors. Moreover, it is unlikely that the groups' relatively weak engagement at the EU level stems primarily from a lack of capacities and resources; organizations such as Greenpeace and the World Wide Fund for Nature operate on a global level. Hence, there must be additional reasoning that prevents many environmental NGOs from strongly engaging in EU policymaking.[2]

2. For a broader discussion of social movements' opportunities and restrictions in EU policymaking, see Marks and McAdam (1994).

Drawing from interviews[3] with representatives of international environmental NGOs, EU administrative agencies in Brussels, available documents, and other sources, this analysis describes the EU political arena faced by environmental NGOs in Brussels in order to explain the above paradox. Because of their own internal structures and an unfavorable intergovernmental institutional context, environmental NGOs face considerable difficulties.

One major problem is the heterogeneity of environmental NGOs' organizational structures, expectations, and policy styles. As far as the institutional context is concerned, the EU offers no formal channels of access and participation, and only a few jurisdictional leverage points. Above all, environmental policy in Brussels is still marginal relative to other policy domains such as agriculture, industry, and commerce. Although lip service is paid to environmental needs, administrations and interest groups in traditional policy domains continue to treat environmental concerns as a tiresome distraction. Therefore, even when environmental NGOs may influence policymakers in EU environmental agencies, policy gains are not necessarily the result.

Institutions and Relevance of EU Environmental Policy

The *Council of Ministers* clearly plays the key role in all political decision making within the EU. Although referred to in the singular, in fact the council consists of twenty-two different councils. Fundamental decisions are taken to the European Council, which includes the heads of the governments of all fifteen member states. The twenty-one Councils of Ministers are assigned to various policy areas. As a rule, the decisions of the council represent the smallest common denominator inherent in the positions of all the national governments rather than an "elevated" supranational wisdom. In political terms, the members of the council are bound to national interests and voters. Decisions are often blocked because one or two countries exert their veto power.[4] In

3. I conducted interviews in 1992 with representatives from the following Brussels-based environmental SMOs and TSMOs: Climate Action Network, Coordination Européenne des Amis de la Terre, Coordination Paysanne Européenne, EarthAction, European Environmental Bureau, Greenpeace EC-unit, World Wide Fund for Nature, and Directorate-General Environment, Nuclear Safety and Civil Protection of the EU commission. A further source of information was a meeting with Uwe Brendle and Claude Weinber, who have written about environmental groups in the EU. My research also profited from a series of interviews conducted with representatives of national environmental groups in Germany and France since 1985.

4. Since the Single European Act of 1987, the strict rule of unanimity for all decisions has been relaxed in favor of majority rule for measures regarding the Internal Market. Other measures still require unanimity.

cases of uncertainty and conflict, the national representatives of the council do not rely so much on the administration in Brussels but upon their home countries. The political will of the council is documented in numerous directives, regulations, and international treaties.[5] In fact, it is the council and not the European Parliament that basically has the legislative function. The general problem of all council decisions is that they cannot be directly implemented or enforced in the current fifteen member countries because the executive resources and enforcement powers remain in the hands of the national governments. Even when the European Court of Justice sentences a government for breaking EU regulations, the court cannot rely upon or compel member states to enforce effective sanctions (Krämer 1991).

It is a common saying that the *European Parliament* is toothless and powerless. The only relevant leverage point it has is the control over the budget of the EU. Thus, there are few concrete opportunities for the parliament to steer EU policies. Numerous attempts to strengthen the position of the EU Parliament vis-à-vis the council have either failed or resulted in only slight improvements in the parliament's competencies.[6]

The *European Commission*, which like a national government is divided into various specialized departments, primarily initiates decisions of the Council of Ministers. The leaders of the commission (seventeen commissars) are nominated by the council and (only since the Treaty of Maastricht) have to be accepted *en bloc* by the European Parliament. The basic task of the commission is to prepare and execute the council's decisions and to elaborate positions and statements of routine politics. One should note that the size of the whole EU apparatus does not exceed the size of the local administration of any large German city such as Cologne (about 16,000 employees). Moreover, according to most insiders, the public officers and civil servants in the EU Commission are, for the most part, competent and flexible experts who, contrary to popular perceptions, do not primarily defend the interests of their respective home countries but rather identify with the EU as an encompassing unit. In many cases, the commission has produced progressive and competent proposals that then have been lost in the typical bargaining among national representatives in the council.

5. Directives passed by the EU are immediately valid in all member states. In contrast, regulations and decrees on environmental policy must first be adopted by national bodies by a certain date before they are applicable (Krämer 1991).

6. The 1987 Single European Act strengthened the role of the parliament. With the 1992 Maastricht Treaty, the parliament obtained the right to reject the complete list of persons nominated as commissioners. For a detailed analysis of the competencies and problems of the European Parliament, see Schönberger (1994).

It would be wrong to conclude from this that the commission is a mere executive body with virtually no political power. An indication of the commission's growing political importance can be seen in the increase of Brussels-based political lobbyists. According to estimates, the number of lobby organizations has risen from 600 to 3,000 and the number of people seeking to lobby from 6,000 to 9,500 between 1986 and 1990 (Andersen and Eliassen 1991). In contrast to practices in countries such as the United States, these lobby groups are largely unregulated and there exists no "code of conduct." Whether lobbyists get access to the seventeen commissioners, the twenty-three director-ate-generals (a kind of governmental department) and the roughly one thousand committees of the administration is completely at the discretion of the targeted officials.

Consequently, a very heterogeneous and barely visible structure of private and public, regional and national, European and other lobbyists has emerged (Grote and Ronit 1992; Mazey and Richardson 1993; van Schendelen 1993). Some of these lobby organizations have official status and are regularly involved in formal contacts with the commission, which is their key target. An example is the *Council on Economic and Social Affairs,* with 198 members from employers, trade unions, and various other groups. Occasionally, committees of lobbying organizations, interest groups, or movement groups are invited by representatives of the commission to present their views or to give advice on specific proposals and programs. In many cases, bilateral contacts occur between individual representatives of the commission and lobbyists, advisers, and experts.

As a rule, both sides seek to maintain a working basis because—divergent interests and stands notwithstanding—they often depend on each other. Lobbyists, on the one hand, need reliable and timely information in order to influence ongoing proposals and decisions. The administration, on the other hand, often needs the expertise and goodwill of external groups to elaborate proposals that are well informed and to increase the likelihood that their proposals will be accepted. The administration is quite aware that lobbyists locked out by the commission may seek and successfully gain access to their national governments or directly to members of the council.

In October 1972 heads of EU member states officially acknowledged for the first time the need for joint environmental policy within the EU. The First Action Program was decided one year later. The most recent relevant step in this area is marked by the Fifth Action Program for Environmental Protection (1992). The aim of environmental protection is fixed in a general statement in Article 130r, chapter 1 of the EU treaty (Wilkinson 1993). Chapter 2 says that environmental protection is a task that runs across conventional policies and thus has a special status. Article 2 of the European treaty, however, places these goals beneath that of securing the common economic market.

The most important material regulations in environmental policy refer, among other things, to the protection of drinking water, seas, lakes, rivers, and species; to problems of waste disposal, chemical products, emissions (including noise); and to environmental impact assessment (see, e.g., Press and Taylor 1990; Judge 1993; Jachtenfuchs and Strubel 1992; Wilkinson 1993; Hey 1994; Holl 1994; and Zimmerman and Kahlenborn 1994). From the very beginnings until today, more than two hundred EU directives, regulations, and executive orders have been passed (Klatte 1992, 1).

The *Directorate-General Environment, Nuclear Safety, and Civil Protection* holds the overall responsibility for environmental policy within the commission. This directorate has more or less constant links to other directories, members of the European Parliament, national administrations, scientists, Brussels-based lobbyists, and other groups. As a rule, the directorate does not direct its proposals toward the general public. Instead, these are presented by the joint representatives of the commission.

The directorate's interactions with many partners usually involve long and often cumbersome processes of exchange of opinion and bargaining before decisions are made. As a result, the proposals have often become modest, vague, or both. Quite a few proposals (e.g., on energy taxes or environmental labeling) represent compromises among many divergent interests that have lost their initial boldness and clarity. Such compromises dissatisfy many who want to go further, including the bureaucrats who have initiated and helped steer this process.

Only rarely are regulations passed that are clear-cut and reflect the already achieved level of environmental protection in the most advanced member states. Observers have applied the metaphor of a convoy to illustrate the different national positions regarding environmental protection: Denmark, the Netherlands, and—in some decisions—Germany are the avant-garde.[7] Somewhere in the middle Italy, France, Belgium, and Luxembourg are following along. At the end of the convoy ride Great Britain, Greece, Spain, and Portugal. This order appears to roughly correspond to the strength and perseverance of the environmental movements in these countries. The British case is the clear exception, however, for there are very strong environmental SMOs in Great Britain (Lowe and Goyder 1983). Even so, British envi-

---

7. To this group one has certainly to add the recent newcomers Sweden, Finland, and Austria.

ronmental social movement organizations (SMOs) tend to act more moderately than their counterparts in most other EU countries (Hey and Brendle 1994).

How important and influential is environmental policy as compared to other policies in the EU? Ignoring the abundant rhetorical claims, one could use the size of the individual directories as a telling indicator. While the Directorate-General Agriculture includes several thousands of employees, there were only 350 employees in the Directorate-General Environment, Nuclear Safety and Civil Protection in 1992, and only 175 core civil servants among them. Another telling indicator is the budget, although, of course, the relevance of regulative policies can hardly be measured in strictly financial terms. Whereas agriculture represents roughly 50 percent of the overall budget, the budget for environmental matters is less than 1 percent. The marginal role of environmentalism in Brussels is also mirrored by its relative weight on the national level. As a rule, departments for environment have only modest resources. Their share of the overall budget is mostly lower than on the EU level.

Journalists reporting specifically on EU politics likewise give little weight to environmentalism, even though they may rhetorically stress its importance. There are few contacts between journalists and elites engaged in environmental affairs. In many cases, journalists know environmental NGOs only by name. What dominate mass media reporting, and thus public awareness in EU matters, are still the domains of agriculture, industry, commerce, rural development, and technology, although one should notice that "environmental policy has been the fastest growing area of EC policy." (Liefferink et al. 1993, 4)

Even most of the national environmental NGOs seem to perceive the institutions and events in Brussels as of minor importance. To be sure, in this respect there are striking differences from country to country. This neglect of attention may be gradually changing, however, as shown by the increasing presence and activities of environmental NGOs in Brussels.

Environmental Organizations in Brussels

Although some EU countries have several strong individual environmental organizations, none of these organizations has established a branch in Brussels. Instead, there are various kinds of supranational bodies. The core of these consists of four transnational social movement organizations (TSMOs): Two of them are umbrella organizations representing heterogeneous groups from EU member states; the two others are relatively homogeneous organizations.

Founded in 1974, the *European Environmental Bureau* (EEB) is the oldest institution to coordinate and represent nongovernmental groups vis-à-vis the EU (Lowe and Goyder 1983). Initially, the EEB was conceived as an intermediary organ between environmental NGOs and the EU bureaucracy. In fact, the EEB has become an umbrella organization on the EU level representing nearly all relevant environmental associations in the EU. Starting with 26 groups in 1974, the number of represented groups rose to 56 in 1984, 120 in 1992, and 160 by the end of 1994. Groups are represented not only from the 15 EU member states but also from 11 European Free Trade Association (EFTA) countries. The bureau claims to represent more than 11 million individual members in these 26 countries (EEB 1995, 39).

Despite this growth, the EEB exhibits weaknesses typically found in umbrella organizations, such as a lack of resources, a heterogeneous membership, and weak links to most member groups. Members have criticized the EEB—particularly in its early years—for its reluctance to take strong stands or engage in controversial issues. By the mid-1980s the EEB was criticized for having become an "old boys network." Since then it has gradually adopted a more conflict-oriented course. But this has been limited by internal heterogeneity and by the fact that about half of the EEB budget comes from the EU or its member states.

Whereas some environmental SMOs, both inside and outside the bureau, argue that the EEB is overly moderate, other voices, mainly coming from the EU administration, blame the bureau for sometimes going too far and for not being not "constructive." These contradictory pressures complicate the EEB's work. Furthermore, the bureau's ambition to cover virtually all relevant aspects of environmental policy is incompatible with its modest staff (four full-time staff members) and informational capacities.

The second major environmental group represented in Brussels is CEAT, the *Coordination Européene des Amis de la Terre* (the EU regional office of Friends of the Earth). CEAT represents a worldwide network of environmental NGOs from 38 countries, among them 24 in Europe. Although these groups vary considerably in their structures and priorities, the organizational structure of Friends of the Earth is more coherent than that usually found in open umbrella organizations. This relative organizational coherence results primarily from their acceptance of only one significant, fairly decentralized, and broadly oriented environmental organization per country.

The Brussels office was founded in 1985. By 1992 it included eight staff people, each working an average of two-thirds of a full-time position. Although CEAT is engaged in a broad range of thematic areas, since the early 1990s the office has focused on environmental problems in Eastern Europe. This shift of attention is also reflected by the establishment of an additional European branch in the Czech Republic. In contrast to the EEB, the national members of CEAT are more homogeneous. They tend to have a grassroots structure and to take more confrontational action than most other environmental NGOs.

Greenpeace International's international secretariat is headquartered in Amsterdam, and it established a Brussels office devoted to European environmental concerns in 1988. Greenpeace devotes comparatively few resources to its European office; in 1995 the Brussels office was run with only five staff members, compared with 120 staff in Greenpeace's German headquarters in Hamburg. This disproportionate allotment of resources probably reflects the cumbersome nature of work to influence EU policies. The kind of lobbying activity demanded by the EU structure does not fit Greenpeace's traditional strategy, which frequently includes highly symbolic, dramatic actions designed to maximize media attention and private donations (Rucht 1995). Greenpeace keeps its own trademark at the forefront. Therefore, it tends to prepare and conduct most of its actions completely autonomously, although it does not in principle reject loose forms of cooperation and increasingly participates in joint campaigns.

Greenpeace's emphasis on media-oriented activities is criticized by other groups that emphasize the more mundane, less spectacular tasks essential to environmental protection. When the Brussels office engaged in lobbying at all, it was not overly successful, with the exception of an initiative to interdict hazardous waste exports to third world countries. This relatively low success rate also has to do with the fact that Greenpeace does not closely follow the agenda set by the EU Commission but tries to follow its own issue priorities. This is reflected in the decision by Greenpeace's EC Unit to abandon its membership in the EEB because of pressure from its international office.

The *World Wide Fund for Nature* (WWF) has considerable resources and claims to have roughly four million members. The organization's central mission originally focused on protecting areas of rich wildlife and species diversity. In more recent times, however, the WWF has broadened both its range of activities and its thematic concerns. The European office of the WWF was established in 1989. With its handful of staff people, it has about the same size office as that of Greenpeace. This European branch, unlike the national chapters, concentrates primarily upon lobbying and distributing information. It is reputed to be a serious, competent, and pragmatic organization that avoids confrontational activities.

Besides these "big four," which have recently become five with the establishment of a European Office for Associations Concerned with the Protection of Birds, there are many other environmental NGOs that differ widely in organizational profile and primary emphases.

One of the most recent and also most dynamic groupings are the thematically oriented networks, chief among them the *Climate Action Network* (CAN), the *Biotechnology Network*, the *Legal Network*, and *European Youth Forest Action*. In part, these networks are not bound to the geographic area covered by the EU but include other areas or even operate on the global level, as is the case with CAN. The groups that are part of such networks are completely autonomous; however, and without the existence of efficient (though not necessarily large) offices, network communication and cooperation would not work. CAN, for example, has offices in Brussels, Africa, Southeast Asia, South Asia, and Latin America, thus linking some 160 organizations (Climate Action Network 1994). Modern means of communication, such as electronic data banks and e-mail, are particularly indispensable for these relatively small but far-reaching networks. The core of their activities is the collection and distribution of information as opposed to lobbying or mobilizing for direct actions (Roncerel 1992).

Other groups engaged in matters of environmental protection tend to be relatively small and resource-poor. One example is the *Foundation of European Nature Heritage* that was formed by groups in Germany. Another is the *Coordination Paysanne Européenne*, which combines interests of small farmers with ecological needs. Still another is the *Euro-Citizen-Action-Service*, which defends the interests of consumers and clients and teaches them techniques of successful lobbying.

Several large national environmental organizations have established a particular staff position for EU politics in their domestic offices. Unlike some national interest groups of industry or commerce, however, no single national environmental group, or even combination of groups from the same country, has established its own office in Brussels.

Contacts and cooperation among such a variety of environmental NGOs are certainly competitive in some areas and some issues, but usually are not highly conflictual. For example, the executive secretaries of the "big four" gather every six weeks or so to share experiences and to coordinate their tactics (Van Ermen 1991). In addition, a broader range of environmental and other groups occasionally meets in the so-called Forum Liaison. Overall, contacts among SMOs and TSMOs are friendly and supportive, reflecting the fact that a livable environment is a collective good whose protection does not follow the logic of a zero-sum game.

Reviewing trends over the last ten years, one sees that international umbrella organizations, homogeneous international organizations, and largely informal and loose environmental networks have increasingly gained footholds in Brussels (van der Heyden et al. 1992; Hey and Brendle 1994). These movement networks also include groups and individuals within the European Parliament. Nevertheless, the sheer number and variety of groups should not overshadow the fact that various hurdles impede environmental organizations' ability to influence the EU's environmental policy.

Limiting Factors

Environmental TSMOs targeting the EU face a number of obstacles. Some of these conditions are related to the structure and composition of the groups. Others grow from the EU political arena in which these organizations seek to act.

Scarce Resources. First, in contrast to interest groups in many other policy domains, environmental NGOs in Brussels have relatively few resources and staff. Barely thirty people are continuously working in these groups to influence EU environmental policy, a number that is dwarfed by the figures representing national staffs of even medium-sized environmental NGOs in industrialized countries. Because of this lack of personnel, not all relevant processes and decisions in the EU administration can be influenced or even closely and competently monitored by environmental NGOs, which must focus their activities on the issues that appear most urgent. The lack of resources devoted to environmental movement work in Brussels cannot be attributed simply to a scarcity of resources in national and subnational groups, but it also grows from the fact that few environmental NGOs are completely aware of the long-range and localized consequences of EU policymaking.

Absence of Direct Action. Another limitation of Brussels-based environmental NGOs is their failure to mobilize mass memberships for demonstrations or direct action.[8] Unlike in some other policy areas such as agriculture, militant protest tactics for environmental protection are virtually nonexistent in Brussels. The action repertoire of the groups is essentially limited to negotiations with officials, lobbying, declarations, expert studies, press releases, and press conferences. Therefore, environmental TSMOs in Brussels are not backed by masses of mobilized people or by the threats of mass actions that could disrupt the routine activities of decision makers. The striking absence of dem-

---

8. In contrast, these kinds of activities were much more central to the European environmental groups surveyed by Dalton (1993).

onstrations and direct action is usually explained by factors such as the spatial distance of most of the domestic groups from Brussels and the anonymity and complexity of EU decision making. This argument, however, is only a partial explanation, because it should also apply to agricultural policies, which have evoked heated farmer protests in Brussels.

EU Funding. Another problem of environmental TSMOs in Brussels stems from their dependency on EU money. Roughly 6.5 million ECU (European currency unit) was transferred to these groups in 1993 (Klatte 1992). Among the "big four" offices, only Greenpeace has deliberately renounced applying for EU money, on the grounds that environmental organizations need to remain totally independent of government agencies. Whether this flow of money reduces the critical potential of environmental NGOs is uncertain, but because EU subsidy decisions are made annually, it is reasonable to assume that environmental leaders routinely consider this factor when making program decisions. Such a possibility moderates the criticisms of some environmental NGOs towards the EU. It is probably not by chance alone that the EEB, which is pursuing the most moderate political course, is also the environmental organization that depends the most upon EU money for the financing of its operations. Thus, it seems that dependency on EU subsidies has had a moderating effect, although this effect seems to have declined in the recent years.

Heterogeneity. The heterogeneity and diversity of environmental NGOs is usually interpreted as a strategic asset. It allows for quick adaptation to new topics and challenges, an implicit division of labor, and smooth coexistence without direct competition. In addition, diversity may well be necessary to reflect different national backgrounds, social bases, goal priorities, or strategic preferences. In some cases, however, this diversity demands cumbersome and time-consuming procedures to coordinate these groups, to ally them for specific campaigns, and to avoid contradictory statements between the individual groups. Resources are wasted when groups independently invest money and human power in the same goal, such as collecting information, without sharing their findings. Finally, when environmental NGOs are unwilling or unable to take a common stance on certain issues (or are even promoting somewhat contradictory claims) this discrepancy not only appears confusing to the general public but also may serve the interests of those opposing better environmental protection.

Characteristics of the overall heterogeneity of environmental NGOs in Brussels are their differences in policy styles and level of aspiration. In spite of general agreement on goals, environmental NGOs diverge in their choices of strategies and tactics. For instance, one study found that British groups tend to be pragmatic, whereas German groups are less open to compromise (Hey and Brendle 1994). While these differences stem from organizations' adaptations to different national contexts, they clearly hinder cross-national cooperation.

Other differences in strategies and tactics result from the considerable variations in existing national standards for environmental protection. For example, environmental NGOs from Denmark and the Netherlands are highly motivated to tighten EU standards and bring them closer to what has already been achieved in their home countries.[9] In contrast, environmental NGOs from Spain, Portugal, and Greece tend to be satisfied with EU regulations that are unacceptable to other countries because even these relatively low standards represent progress from their existing domestic regulations. Such differences make it difficult for environmental NGOs in Brussels to speak with one voice.

Lack of Institutional Access. A fundamental difficulty for effective representation of environmental interests in Brussels stems from the lack of institutional embedding of environmental NGOs in EU policymaking. Environmental NGOs have no formal rights to information, no institutionalized channels of access, and no rights to participate in the decision-making process of the EU.[10] In other words, they lack the key elements of a favorable political opportunity structure (Tarrow 1983; Kitschelt 1986; Kriesi 1995).

Because, as it has been argued, direct action is hardly feasible, the environmental groups focus on lobbying even when opportunities for this strategy are largely unfavorable. Apart from an annual meeting between the environmental groups and members of the commission, communication between both sides remains completely informal and, to outsiders, opaque. This engagement in elite negotiations may contribute to the perception of some national environmental NGOs that in Brussels there is too much lobbying and not enough protest. Even litigation at the European Court of Justice is not overly promising. Although about 60 percent of all complaints brought to the court refer to environmental matters, environmental NGOs have no formal role in such litigation, and in many cases, the sentences of the Court are not enforced.

9. The fear of acquiring lower environmental standards was a strong argument against joining the EU in debates in Finland, Norway, Sweden, Austria, and Switzerland.

10. However, there are plans to establish an advisory body, the Environmental Forum, which, among other associations, would include the major environmental organizations.

Complexity of Policy Process. In addition to this lack of access to the EU polity, environmental policymaking in the EU is a complex multilevel and multiplayer game. Thus processes such as agenda setting are marked by "instability and unpredictability" (Mazey and Richardson 1992, 110). The process provides many more leverage points for those who want to block rather than to promote environmental concerns. As a rule, these players are also stronger than their environmental movement opponents.

First, the environmental department within the commission is surrounded by the more powerful departments of economy, commerce, agriculture, technology, regional development, and others. In many cases, the environmental impacts of these departments' policies are hardly considered, much less systematically assessed.

Second, in struggles between environmetal NGOs and the external power constellations their nongovernmental opponents favor the latter. The interest groups in sectors such as chemistry, pharmacy, electronics, automotive and other transport, agriculture are "armed" with large and well-equipped lobbying offices in Brussels (Platzer 1984; McLaughlin et al. 1993). For example, the agricultural sector is represented by 22 European-level organizations and a considerable number of national interest associations that have permanent representation in Brussels (Anderson and Eliassen 1991, 183). *The European Federation of Pharmaceutical Industry Associations* (EFPIA 1978) employs 20 staff and receives membership fees from 16 mostly well-funded national associations (Greenwood and Ronit 1994, 38). Even a young industry such as biotechnology has a strong European presence: The *Senior Advisory Group on Biotechnology,* for instance, represents 31 multinational enterprises, including giants like Bayer, Ciba-Geigy, Du Pont, and Hoffmann-La Roche. In contrast, the Biotechnology Network, which promotes environmental concerns has just one full-time expert in Brussels.

These quantitative asymmetries are aggravated by discrepancies in opportunities to influence the commission. Whereas the environmental NGOs' refusal to cooperate would not strongly impress the Directorate-General Environment, Nuclear Safety and Civil Protection (not to speak of other directorates), many EU executive bodies could hardly implement measures against the outspoken resistance of their corresponding (largely business) lobbies, because their operations frequently depend on their expertise. Finally, even when a relatively progressive (or nonprogressive) environmental proposal has passed the commission, one or several environmental laggards in the council can reject this proposal.

Media Obstacles. Precisely because social movements usually lack financial resources and institutional access to policymakers, they try to get the attention and support of the broader public via the mass media. Once public opinion is mobilized, policymakers can no longer ignore the issues at stake. Environmental SMOs and TSMOs targeting the EU can argue that there is hardly a truly European public to mobilize around their regional goals.

Several factors, including fragmentation along language barriers, have prevented the establishment of a European-wide attentive public (Gerhards 1993). Attention paid to aspects of environmental policymaking in the mass media of individual states does not typically lead to the emergence of a European public opinion that could directly support collective action in the EU arena. Hence, although media strategies are prominent among national environmental SMOs (see Dalton 1992, 69), they are much less central to those groups targeting the EU.

Strategies

Given this broad range of structural difficulties environmental groups face in Brussels, several questions arise: What steps can these groups take to increase their presence and power? Do they have any promising strategic options at all? Are there recent strategic opportunities that may enhance the impact of these groups?

The discussion of these questions may be simplified in terms of four strategic choices. Each choice uses a binary scheme that emphasizes specific costs and benefits. This abstract discussion ignores the variations in benefits and costs caused by different organizational structures and focuses as well as by different external constellations of power. Moreover, these choices are not mutually exclusive.

National vs. Supranational Engagement. When confronted with this question, some environmental groups respond to the growing relevance of the EU level by, for instance, creating positions for EU specialists in their national headquarters, supporting transnational coalition offices in Brussels, or playing an active part in these offices' activities. Other groups argue that the key decisions taken by the Council of Ministers were—and still are—oriented towards national interests and power constellations. Therefore, these groups try to exert pressure on their domestic governments, which then is transmitted via their countries' ministers to the relevant EU bodies. The validity of this more traditional strategy is supported by experience: First, the opportunity structures and political processes in home countries are better known, and, second, there is no need for the complicated procedures necessary to coordinate with groups from other countries.

Acting Autonomously vs. Forging Alliances. Even when environmental groups have decided to engage in political activities in Brussels, at

least the more powerful groups have to decide whether to do so alone
—for example, by sending a permanent delegate or creating an independent office—or to ally with other groups from the same country or
those from other countries. The rich and truly international organizations such as Greenpeace and WWF have their own branches in Brussels, whereas most other groups are represented, if at all, by an
umbrella organization. The obvious argument in favor of such a joint
venture is that it not only is more cost-effective but also demonstrates
regional unity. In practice, however, many environmental groups complain about the almost inevitable compromise positions that go too
far for some and not far enough for others. What then keeps these
transnational coalitions together is more a lack of resources than a
consequence of converging goals and strategies.

Lobbying vs. Mobilizing Adherents. Most environmental groups, either
for tactical reasons or because of a lack of other opportunities, focus
on lobbying. Even Greenpeace, which is known for its often disruptive
direct actions and its constant search for media attention, does considerable amounts of lobbying through its office in Brussels. Lobbying is
seen by some as a way to be viewed as a serious actor in the international political arena and as a means of obtaining otherwise unavail-
able information. But there are also highly skeptical voices. Nicholas
Dunlop, coordinator of EarthAction International,[11] argued: "Public
interest lobbyists are always outgunned." Moreover, he fears that some
groups are compromised by accepting commission subsidies. What
really impresses politicians, he believes, is the power of voters; accordingly, he promotes a grassroots mobilization strategy. But radical action is usually not viewed as a viable option by TSMOs and SMOs
operating in Brussels. Thus, they lose the threatening and disruptive
potential that is so strong and vital to environmental movements in
several EU states.

Thematically Focused vs. Generalized Engagement. Scarce resources and
a lack of personnel, together with the coexistence of a range of groups,
force environmental groups to limit their fields of engagement in order
to concentrate their energies on selected areas and issues. Even the
most powerful groups such as Greenpeace and WWF cannot cover the
full range of environmental problems. The result is a more or less
implicit division of labor which also is positively evaluated by most
of the groups and observers. The emergence of thematically focused
networks in recent years—a trend that can also be found at the na-

---

11. At the time this research was done, EarthAction operated its European regional
office in Brussels. It closed this office in part because of difficulties of navigating the EU
policy process.

tional level—is a clear indicator of specialization and diversification in environmental interest representation in Brussels.

On the other hand, although less prominent, some groups also feel a need to broaden their thematic scope, particularly when they see that their concern is intimately linked to other issues. An example of this trend is the close cooperation between several associations for bird protection that have transformed themselves into broader environmental groups. These diverging paths of specialization and generalization bring costs. The first strategy is often combined with a move towards expert activities and thus a loss of a broad and actively involved citizen mobilization. In contrast, the broadening of thematic concerns often results in a kind of superficiality and a lack of expertise that is particularly disadvantageous when complex issues are handled within the EU bureaucracies. Generally speaking, however, the trend towards specialization within and between environmental groups is irreversible in Brussels as long as close interaction with the commission is sought.

Conclusion

As in many other policy domains, environmental decision making within the EU gradually is shifting from the national to the EU levels. In reaction, nongovernmental environmental groups have begun to intensify their cooperation, to establish joint branches in Brussels, and to lobby the commission.

Both the internal and the external conditions of these groups, however, are far from ideal. From the perspective of two major approaches in social movement literature—the resource mobilization and political opportunity theories—environmental groups in Brussels face a number of problems. First, the Brussels-based groups have only modest resources. Nongovernmental interest representation on behalf of environmental concerns in the EU is basically a matter of a few political "entrepreneurs." Second, similar to the situation in national contexts, the groups in Brussels compete for scarce resources (Mazey and Richardson 1992, 125). In addition, most groups are dependent on subsidies from the EU and therefore may be vulnerable to compromise. Third, the groups are composed of extremely different structural components with diverging strategies and policy styles, making it difficult to form strong alliances.

Whereas analogous constraints also apply to most environmental groups operating on the national level, there are also a number of unfavorable conditions that are specific to (or at least more pronounced in) the EU arena. First, groups in Brussels do not have institutionally secured rights of access to the EU polity. Second, environmental policymaking at the EU level is an opaque, multilevel, and multiactor game, with many formal and informal veto powers that usually work against environmental interests. These veto opportunities are of particular relevance because of the large discrepancy between the EU countries in ideological and structural terms. In particular, the countries' standards and ambitions in environmental policy differ widely. Quite often, the pace of environmental progress is dictated by the slowest ship in the multinational convoy. Third, the weight of environmental policy relative to the more established policies in EU politics is lower than in most individual EU countries. The Directorate-General Environment, Nuclear Safety and Civil Protection is a dwarf in the shadow of several mighty giants.

Finally, and probably most important, two means that could compensate for the structural difficulties of environmental groups are absent at the EU level. In Brussels, unlike in the individual countries, moderate ways of influencing environmental politics are not reinforced with demonstrations and disruptive action. Lacking a coherent, attentive, and informed European public opinion, the bureaus of environmental groups in Brussels are cut off from the rank and file membership in individual countries. Moreover, efforts to influence environmental decisions in the EU are relatively unattractive and unspectacular, and they therefore attract little attention from the average group member and the wider public, many of whom are preoccupied with local or national issues. Thus, environmental groups in Brussels lack "power in numbers" (De Nardo 1985) as well as the opportunity to generate a "radical flank effect" (McAdam et al. 1988, 718–19), and they pose little or no threat to business as usual in the EU.

Taken together, these unfavorable conditions can explain the paradox that environmental action and cross-national cooperation in Brussels still lack pressure, comprehensiveness, and continuity, in spite of several factors that, from a first glance, should support all three. Among these supportive factors one could count a significant public awareness for environmental concerns in most EU countries, the existence of fairly strong domestic environmental groups, and the remarkable shift of environmental decision making from national levels to the EU level.

Proposals have been offered to improve this overall situation of the Brussels-based groups. It would be a serious strategic error, however, to attempt to integrate the existing organizations and networks into a unified, firm, and hierarchical organization. First, this would contradict the organic diversity of environmental NGOs and the rather different settings in which they have developed. Second, it would undermine the current advantages of group existence in a highly flex-ible "multiorganizational field" (Curtis and Zurcher 1973) that is now free from the pressures to create a rigid hierarchy of goals and strate-gies. Other proposals seek to improve the means of coordination and to restructure the umbrella organizations (Hey and Brendle 1994). But even these relatively moderate suggestions are met with skeptical or indifferent reactions by several environmental NGOs and thus would be hard to implement.

There is no ideal and easy way for environmental NGOs to achieve a profound and encompassing effect on environmental policymaking in the EU. This weakness is also felt by advocates for environmental protection within the EU administration. Ironically, these intergovern-mental organization officials worry about the strategic weakness of nongovernmental environmental organizations that usually are per-ceived by national administrations as adversaries. These public em-ployees often wish to strengthen their critics in order to bring greater pressure on EU member states to enhance the status and policy rele-vance of the EU environmental department.[12]

At present, this invitation for stronger movement pressure on EU environment policy is wishful thinking. Most of the environmental NGOs in European countries place priority on the problems in their home countries over the seemingly distant, obscure, and anonymous decision-making processes at Brussels. This priority is likely to change only when concrete experiences show that decisions and nondecisions taken in Brussels impact the environment in all parts of the EU.

12. This is also evident in national arenas. For instance, in a meeting with environ-mental groups, the Austrian environmental minister stated, "As long as you don't attack us, we cannot attack and put pressure on politicians in power. We *need* your pressure" (*Süddeutsche Zeitung*, 8 June 1988, emphasis added).

12

INTERCEDING AT THE UNITED NATIONS

The Human Right of Conscientious Objection

Michael W. Hovey

Abstract

In addition to their well-known activities "on the ground" to defend human rights, transnational social movement organizations (TSMOs) play an increasingly significant role behind the scenes to help establish human rights norms. This chapter focuses on the "intercession" of TSMOs—especially the Quakers—at the United Nations Commission on Human Rights to advance the right to be a conscientious objector. Their strategies and tactics, which have shifted with UN and global politics, are described and categorized in terms of *advocacy* and *mediation*. The major TSMO activities influencing international institutions concerned with human rights can be described in terms of six stages of intercession: raising the issue, seeking sympathetic partners, educating about the issue, working the system, facilitating agreement between disputants, and seeking consensus.

Transnational social movement organizations (TSMOs) promoting and defending human rights, such as Amnesty International or Peace Brigades International, have gained broad public recognition for their fact-finding, nonviolent accompaniment, and other activities "on the ground." But the important work of these and other TSMOs to influence international organizations behind the scenes by pressing for the establishment of human rights norms has often escaped public attention. Scholarly interest in this area has also been limited.[1] These TSMO efforts, while less dramatic, are no less significant in the overall promotion of human rights, and they deserve more attention from scholars.

Among such TSMO efforts are those in behalf of the international human right of conscientious objection to military service. This may be defined as the objection or refusal to participate in war and military service for reasons of conscience, based on religious or similar (e.g., moral, ethical, philosophical) training and belief. There are, of course, many variations and nuances to this description, and the definition of conscientious objection has itself been a matter of intense dispute.

The refusal, for reasons of conscience, to bear arms at the behest of one's government has perhaps been the quintessential conflict between the individual and the state for centuries. The primary historical experience of conscientious objectors (COs) has thus been one of persecution, which often resulted in imprisonment, voluntary or involuntary exile, and even execution (Brock 1990; Finney 1989; Helgeland et al. 1985; Kohn 1986; Zahn 1964). Only in the past two hundred years have a few nations agreed, grudgingly, to make provisions for those who feel duty-bound to follow the dictates of their conscience rather than the orders of their national leaders when summoned to perform military service (Moskos and Chambers 1993, Schlissel 1968).

Aware, however, that COs in most countries still face the same penalties their predecessors did in centuries past, TSMOs promoting human rights interceded at the United Nations on behalf of COs around the world.[2] The term "intercede" is significant here: It is meant both in the sense of lobbying or pleading on someone's behalf and in the sense of mediating in a dispute. TSMO *intercession* was instrumental in negotiating the formal recognition of the universal human right of conscientious objection to military service.

In the United Nations, TSMO efforts began in earnest in 1971 and, between 1987 and 1995, resulted in the passage of resolutions recognizing this right. The Friends World Committee for Consultation of the

1. Among the few scholarly studies are Ray and Taylor 1977; Wiseberg and Scoble 1977; Yarrow 1978; Shestack 1978; Cassese 1979; Chiang 1981; Weissbrodt 1984; Price Cohen 1990; Steiner 1991; Rodley 1991; Hannum 1992; Weiss, Forsythe, and Coate 1994.

2. In 1991, Amnesty International reported that, of sixty-six nations that had mandatory conscription, only nineteen made provision for conscientious objectors. Of these, all but two (Brazil and South Africa) are in Europe. There were no data on countries, such as the United States, that do not have conscription but provide for "in-service conscientious objection" or CO status for those who become COs after joining the armed forces voluntarily (AI 1991).

Society of Friends (Quakers) played a leading role promoting such recognition at the UN Commission on Human Rights (hereinafter, the Commission). Regional intergovernmental organizations, such as the European Commission on Human Rights and the Organization on Security and Cooperation in Europe, have also dealt with the human right of conscientious objection (Engram 1982). The scope of this chapter, however, is limited to TSMO involvement in the deliberations of the UN Commission, "the first international body empowered to promote all the human rights of all the world's peoples" (Tolley 1987, xiii).

Established in 1946, the Commission, a subsidiary body of the UN Economic and Social Council (ECOSOC), is made up of fifty-three member-states of the United Nations, elected to serve three-year terms. The job of the Commission is to promote awareness of human rights ideals, protect human rights by drafting statements that establish universally recognized norms ("standard-setting"), and implement procedures for monitoring and enforcing those norms.

Nongovernmental organizations (NGOs), including TSMOs, are permitted under Article 71 of the United Nations Charter to hold "consultative status" at the Commission. ECOSOC guidelines state that NGOs may submit reports, make oral and written interventions, and otherwise "consult" with members of the Commission during their deliberations.[3] In fact, as this analysis shows, TSMO consultations with the Commission do far more than simply provide information.

TSMOs and the United Nations

TSMOs' work for conscientious objection revealed six stages of intercession: raising the issue; seeking sympathetic partners and allies; educating about the issue; working the system; facilitating agreement between disputants; and seeking consensus. The first three stages deal primarily with the *advocacy* role of TSMOs, while the last three are

3. ECOSOC Resolution 1296 (XLIV) of 23 May 1968 delineated the arrangements for consultations with NGOs (TSMOs) and divided them into three categories—Category I, Category II, and the Roster—based on the degree to which the organization's purpose and membership reflect the interests of the United Nations. Most TSMOs fall into either Category II or the Roster. Category II NGOs "have a special competence in, and are concerned specifically with only a few of the fields of activity" of ECOSOC and have a "general international concern" with human rights "not restricted to the interests of a particular group of persons, a single nationality or the situation in a single State or restricted group of States." NGOs on the Roster do not have a broad competence in the field of human rights but "can make occasional and useful contributions to the work of the Council or its subsidiary bodies." See Cassese (1979) for more detail on these categories.

related to their role as *intermediaries*. While these six stages do not always follow in chronological order or exhaust the categories of TSMO actions, they do illustrate the breadth of TSMO roles in promoting agreements among governments.

Raising the Issue

The issue of the human right of conscientious objection was raised at the UN at least three times before 1970.[4] The topic did not find its way onto the agenda of the Commission, however, until 16 March of that year, when Eileen Egan, representative of *Pax Romana*, a TSMO of Catholic scholars, called for recognition of the right in written and oral interventions. The time was apparently ripe for consideration of the issue; the Council of Europe's Consultative Assembly had recognized the right to conscientious objection in 1967, so European members of the Commission had been primed to deal with the topic (Engram 1982). Egan reported that she felt compelled to raise the issue after having successfully lobbied the world's Catholic bishops for their approval of conscientious objection during the final session of the Second Vatican Council in 1965 (Egan 1991).

Egan's efforts during 1970 to get other TSMOs to sign her statement were unsuccessful, but not because they disagreed with the message. Duncan Wood, who then led the team of representatives at the Quaker United Nations Office (QUNO) in Geneva, stated that while he "of course" supported Egan's initiative, he felt "it would go nowhere" given the Cold War political tensions present among the Commission members (Wood 1993).

Nevertheless, when Egan made her intervention, the Saudi Arabian ambassador to the UN, Jamal Baroody, happened to be seated in the chamber and was impressed with the statement. He spoke in favor of her proposal at that time and later that year raised the issue before the General Assembly in a discussion of a draft resolution regarding "youth and respect for human rights." The General Assembly transmitted the resolution (A/C.3/L.1766/Rev.3) to the Commission, and the topic of the "human right of conscientious objection to military

4. In 1950 the Philippine government proposed, in a written intervention to the UN committee charged with drafting the International Covenant on Civil and Political Rights, that conscientious objection be considered a human right. The proposal was withdrawn due to thin support for it. Later that year the Secretary General circulated a study of the issue prepared by a TSMO, the Service Civil International, but no action was taken. In 1956 the UN itself conducted a study of conscientious objection in the context of religious discrimination; nothing came of this either (See Engram 1982, 359–99).

service" became a fixture on the agenda of the Commission (Wood 1976).

Seeking Sympathetic Partners and Allies

At the invitation of the Quakers, during 1971 a small group of TSMOs concerned with conscientious objection formed a consortium to develop a joint statement for presentation before the Commission during the debate on conscientious objection. They also contacted Theo van Boven, head of the Netherlands delegation, who was known as an ally on the issue. With his help, TSMOs succeeded in keeping the topic of conscientious objection on the Commission's agenda for the next five years (Wood 1976).

According to Wood, the TSMOs at first hoped to gain passage of a declaration[5] on the rights of conscience, or at least a request that the Sub-Commission on the Prevention of Discrimination and Protection of Minorities (an advisory body of twenty-six "experts" on human rights to the Commission) draft such a statement. Van Boven, however, suggested a more moderate approach: He drafted a resolution that simply requested the Secretary General to prepare a report on member-states' national policies and practices regarding conscientious objection and alternative civilian service. The resolution also called on the Commission to study the issue once the Secretary General's report became available. A member of the Austrian delegation, Felix Ermacora, who would become another close ally of the TSMOs, spoke in favor of van Boven's resolution.

The resolution passed by a vote of eighteen to three with seven abstentions, and the voting process itself revealed to the TSMOs where their opposition would lie: The USSR voted against the resolution, and other Soviet bloc nations abstained; Iraq and Morocco voted against the measure, while other Moslem nations abstained or voted in favor. Similarly, the floor debate preceding the vote exposed areas of disagreement among member-states. The Iraqi delegate declared conscientious objection incompatible with the Islamic faith. Some third world delegates stressed that community needs sometimes superseded individual rights. Delegates from Communist nations condemned consci-

5. Generally speaking, the Commission is responsible for drafting *conventions*, which are international treaties and thus legally binding; *declarations*, which are not legally binding, although widespread acceptance may be seen as evidence of customary international law; and *resolutions*, which are not legally binding but serve as guidance for states to use in drafting national legislation (See Tolley 1987).

entious objection as antithetical to the Soviet constitution and to Marxist doctrine.

In the years following this original debate, TSMOs continued to rely on each other as partners in the negotiations over resolutions and fostered alliances with sympathetic delegations. The Dutch and Austrian delegations, for their part, came to rely on the expertise and skill of the Quakers in both drafting resolutions and persuading other delegations to support these.

Educating about the Issue

Although it was immediately obvious that international politics would obstruct TSMOs' efforts to gain recognition of the right to be a CO, less apparent were the difficulties posed by widespread misunderstandings of conscientious objection itself. To meet this challenge, Quaker representatives cosponsored, with other TSMOs, a series of luncheon meetings at the Quaker UN offices in New York and Geneva, where various aspects of conscientious objection and strategies for advancing it as a human right were discussed. On 13 October 1971, for example, the Quakers, Pax Romana, and War Resisters International (WRI) hosted a luncheon for representatives of Amnesty International (AI), the World Student Christian Federation, the International Catholic Child Bureau, and UN member-state delegates from Venezuela, the Netherlands, New Zealand, Austria, India, the United Kingdom, Norway, the Philippines, Finland, Uruguay, Mexico, Pakistan, Nigeria, Ghana, Peru, and France. These luncheons not only provided a forum for education and strategizing but also facilitated a growing rapport between the individuals and communities represented. Such meetings were held regularly until 1989.

QUNO also sponsored several seminars, sometimes lasting an entire weekend, for interested TSMOs and member-states. In February 1980, for example, a two-day seminar was held in Geneva, assembling TSMO representatives from the Mennonite Central Committee, Christian Peace Conference, Lutheran World Federation, AI, Women's International League for Peace and Freedom, International Fellowship of Reconciliation, Service Civil International, the World Association of World Federalists, among others. Delegates Ermacora of Austria, van Boven of the Netherlands, Nyamekye of Ghana, and Beaulne, the Canadian ambassador to the Holy See, made presentations to the seminar participants.

TSMOs also provided a steady stream of briefing papers, booklets, articles, and written interventions to the Commission members on the topic of conscientious objection. Oral interventions before the Commission often addressed the particular concerns of member-states who opposed recognition of the right. TSMOs regularly pointed out, for example, that the hesitation to recognize individual rights at the expense of service to the community could be addressed by requiring alternative civilian service of those who would not accept military service.

Working the System

While working with Theo van Boven and enjoying the gradual success of his incremental approach to gaining recognition of conscientious objection as a human right, the consortium of TSMOs began to see the necessity and benefits of proceeding more gradually than some preferred. "We learned you can't take big leaps forward," said Martin MacPherson, who served as the Quaker representative in Geneva when the first and second resolutions explicitly recognizing the right were passed (1987 and 1989). "You must go step-by-step and build every year" (MacPherson 1993).

It was precisely this insight that transformed TSMOs from mere lobbyists/advocates into key actors/mediators in UN conference diplomacy. TSMOs found that discussion and debate within the Commission on Human Rights rarely, if ever, focused solely on the merits of the "human rights" argument. They realized that both internal (UN and Commission) and external (global) politics play a significant part in the proceedings at the United Nations and that their strategy and tactics would have to account for these factors.

The key global political reality with which TSMOs had to grapple, at least until the late 1980s, was the East/West, Communist versus "free world" ideological struggle (Weissbrodt 1988). Efforts to gain recognition of many human rights, including the right to be a CO, were frequently stalled or halted altogether by the Cold War.

After consultation with TSMOs in 1973, for example, van Boven offered a draft resolution (E/CN.4-/L.1256) that modestly stated that "conscientious objection to compulsory military service *involves questions* (emphasis mine) of fundamental human rights" and *"Invites* (emphasis in original) Member States . . . to provide for the right to object."

The Soviet delegate, Sergei Evdokayev, strongly opposed even this toned-down appeal for recognition of the right. First, he offered several pretexts for not considering the resolution at all, including the claim that "the Secretary General's report had reached Moscow too late for study" (see Wood 1976, 3). When this approach failed, he employed rules of procedure that allow "a motion not to consider the substance of a question [to take] priority over any substantive proposal." With the support of the Soviet Union's third world allies, a motion not to consider the resolution passed (Wood 1976).

TSMOs played a more direct part in deliberations in 1978 when the General Assembly, in Resolution 33/165, recognized the right of all persons to refuse service in military or police forces used to enforce apartheid. This victory, significant in its own right, invigorated the TSMOs in their continuing struggle to gain recognition of the right to be a CO in all cases. It also taught a valuable lesson in tactics: Rachel Brett, a QUNO staff member in Geneva, had produced a "single text" draft—i.e., an actual preliminary document for circulation—rather than simply offering suggestions to the sympathetic delegates and waiting for them to take action on their own. This time-honored and proactive negotiating tactic permitted TSMOs to establish the terms of reference for the debate that followed (Salacuse 1991).

Throughout the 1980s, David Weissbrodt, professor of law at the University of Minnesota and a longtime ally of TSMOs concerned with conscientious objection, was often called upon to provide other such drafts, which were then circulated to TSMOs and sympathetic delegates in the months before the Commission's sessions. The Quakers took "readings" on how others felt about the wording of the documents and whether they could "live with" such wording (MacPherson 1993). When everyone was assembled at the Palais des Nations in Geneva for the Commission meeting, TSMO representatives and government delegates could meet to discuss and debate already familiar statements. Ultimately, the delegation serving as chief sponsor of a draft resolution is responsible for the final decision on acceptable language, based on its contacts with other delegations. Since 1985 the Netherlands (1985, 1993, 1995) and Austria (1987, 1989) have played this sponsoring role for resolutions on the right to conscientious objection, and their task was facilitated by Quakers' work in cultivating consensus around single-text drafts.

Facilitating Agreement between Disputants

Cold War rivalries made it virtually impossible to gain support for recognition of the right of conscientious objection among Soviet bloc and allied nations. Conscientious objection was seen as a "Western" idea, overly solicitous of individual rights at the expense of the needs of the society at large. Following Mikhail S. Gorbachev's assumption of power, however, the policy of *glasnost* (openness) led to a change in how the Soviets and their allies acted in the United Nations. T. Rameshvili, the former Soviet delegate and then Russian Federation delegate to the Commission, explained that discussions he held with TSMO representatives—in particular, the Quakers and the International Commission of Jurists—about alternatives to military service helped him convince his government, first, to abstain from voting on the 1987 resolution, and, later, to support a consensus ("pass without a vote") position in 1989 and 1993 (Rameshvili 1993). Completing the transformation, the Russian Federation in 1993 became a cosponsor of the resolution for the first time (as did the United States).

In addition to providing calm and informed assurances to delegations worried about the possible effects of granting conscientious objector status to those opposed to military service, TSMOs facilitated agreement between the disputing parties by proposing or supporting changes in the resolutions' language that, while not entirely representing their own positions, were acceptable compromises.

For example, in the 1993 draft resolution, the language agreed upon at first included the following sentence in the operative paragraphs:[6]

> 2. [The Commission on Human Rights] *Affirms* that persons performing military service cannot be excluded from the right to have conscientious objections to military service.

After floor debate and the acceptance of proposed amendments made by India and France, the final product read:

> 2. [The Commission on Human Rights] *Affirms* that persons performing *compulsory* military service *should not* be excluded from the right to have conscientious objections to military service. (amended wording italicized)

The sponsoring Dutch delegation knew that these minor changes would be acceptable to the Quakers, Pax Christi International, and other TSMOs; the essential points were made, and the changes would encourage passage of the resolution by consensus. While the "final call" was up to the Dutch delegation, earlier discussions with delegates from Ireland, Austria, and the United States convinced the Dutch that these delegations would be attentive to the wishes of the TSMOs.

---

6. UN resolutions are typically divided into two sections, the preambular and operative paragraphs. Preambular paragraphs are very important in setting the tone, providing background, and establishing the legitimacy of the "actions" that are called for in the operative paragraphs.

Seeking Consensus

TSMO efforts to gain consensus on the human right of conscientious objection to military service are rooted in both philosophy and strategy. Philosophically, a "universal human right" must be recognized by all—not just a majority—if it is to be universal (Donnelly 1982). TSMOs committed to the human right of conscientious objection believe it is a right that everyone—not simply those represented by a majority vote—should be able to exercise.

Strategically, TSMOs realized that the broader the support for the right of conscientious objection, the easier it would become to promote wide acceptance of a "universal" human right that is not yet considered legally binding but is on its way toward being recognized as customary international law (Weissbrodt 1988).

In order to reach their objective, TSMOs promoted consensus on two levels: among themselves and among the governments represented on the Commission. Luncheons, seminars, and informal discussions in the coffee lounge and the corridors of the Palais des Nations helped promote understanding and consensus among TSMOs, but differences of opinion continued to surface, even as late as 1993. During the session of the Commission that year, for example, the representative of WRI strongly favored inclusion of "political beliefs" as a criterion for conscientious objection. Other TSMOs opposed this move and expressed concern that expanding the definition of conscientious objection to include partisan political positions would deflate the momentum building toward recognition of the right based on "religious, moral, or similar motives," which are less transitory (at least theoretically) than political leanings.

Promoting consensus among the member-states represented on the Commission was more difficult. An important step toward this goal came in 1982–83, when TSMOs gained members' agreement on a Commission resolution instructing the Sub-Commission on the Prevention of Discrimination and Protection of Minorities to prepare a report on "conscientious objection to military service." This document (E/CN.4/Sub.2/1983/Rev.1) came to be known as the Eide/Mubanga-Chipoya Report, named after the Sub-Commission authors, Asbjorn Eide of Norway and Chama Mubanga-Chipoya of Nigeria. TSMOs provided much of the background information and even suggested the format for the report; needless to say, they were pleased with the findings of the report and eager to see the Commission use it to guide deliberations in subsequent meetings. It provided a single source of common vocabulary on the issue—a most helpful tool in any negotiation. Together with the global political changes resulting from *glasnost* and the

end of the Cold War, this helped advance TSMOs' ultimately successful struggle to gain recognition of the universal human right of conscientious objection to military service.

Conclusion: TSMOs as Intercessors

Had the TSMOs simply contented themselves with speaking their
piece and issuing a set of demands, without regard for the Commission's formal procedures, it is doubtful that their efforts would have
succeeded. By demonstrating that they were team players, willing to
accept and abide by the formal structure of discussion, deliberation,
and debate that characterizes UN meetings, they were able to carve
out for themselves a role in intergovernmental negotiations. In so
doing, they helped generate intergovernmental consensus around
changes in human rights norms.

To gain an appreciation for the overall impact and significance of
the work of TSMOs, it is important to examine the often overlooked
efforts of a relative handful of their representatives in intergovernmental arenas such as the Human Rights Commission. Clearly, efforts at
the international institutional level can complement the more traditionally embraced activities of transnational social movement organizations, such as grassroots education and organizing, local
demonstrations, etc. Human rights and peace activists around the
world, for example, can now point to the international recognition of
the human right of conscientious objection to military service in their
local efforts to assist and defend those who refuse to perform military
service for reasons of conscience.

As the public becomes more aware of the role of TSMOs at the
United Nations—witness the interest in the NGO and TSMO participation in the Fourth World Conference on Women, held in Beijing in
September 1995—scholars should devote more attention to the work
of TSMO representatives who intercede within the halls of diplomacy
to promote international cooperation, as they continue to study those
who agitate outside those halls.

13

BROKERING THE LAW OF THE SEA TREATY

The Neptune Group

Ralph B. Levering

Abstract

Sustained social movement participation in the Third UN Conference on Law of the Sea (UNCLOS III) was limited by the duration of the conference, the complexity of the issues being negotiated, and the cost of attending its lengthy sessions. Nevertheless, two transnational social movement networks, the Ocean Education Project (OEP) and the United Methodist Law of the Sea Project (UMLSP), or the "Neptune Group," made significant contributions to international cooperation for ocean resource management. By organizing seminars for delegates, researching technical issues relevant to debates, and publishing a newspaper to help circulate ideas and information, the Neptune Group served as a catalyst and broker in the UNCLOS III negotiations. This case demonstrates that social movement actors must learn how to be effective in international negotiations, and that the success or failure of their efforts depends heavily upon the individuals representing them.

In March 1980, when the Third United Nations Conference on Law of the Sea (UNCLOS III) had been underway for more than six years with no end in sight, Richard Hudson, a New York-based world order activist, aptly observed that UNCLOS III deserved "a whole *Guiness Book of World Records* by itself" because it was "the biggest, longest, most expensive—and potentially the most important—international conference ever held"[1] (Hudson 1980, 1).

One might quibble with some of the judgments contained in these adjectives: The 1945 conference in San Francisco that founded the United Nations—and thus established the institutional framework for UNCLOS III—might well be considered more important, for example. But one cannot deny that UNCLOS III (1973–82) was extremely significant, for it established what Guilio Pontecorvo has called a "new order of the oceans" (1986). Among many other provisions, the 1982 treaty, which formally became international law in 1994, established uniform 12-mile territorial seas and 200-mile economic resource zones for coastal states, elaborated detailed rules relating to passage through straits and archipelagoes, and set up mechanisms for the peaceful resolution of disputes. State Department official Carlyle Maw's bold assessment in November 1980 has held up: "[W]hat has been accomplished [at UNCLOS III] is truly remarkable—the greatest accomplishment in the development of international law of all time" (U.S. Department of State 1980).

UNCLOS III took place, because, in Clyde Sanger's apt phrase, "[m]ost countries had something important they wanted to settle, or change" (1987, 3). Developed nations, notably the United States and the Soviet Union, were concerned that unilateral claims to ever larger offshore territorial and resource zones would hamper the global operations of their navies and fishing fleets. Developing nations, aware by 1967 that the deep seabed contained large quantities of nickel and other minerals, feared that ships from developed nations would harvest these minerals and keep the profits, thus widening the gap between rich and poor. Moreover, the "cod wars" between Great Britain and Iceland and the "tuna wars" involving the seizure of U.S. fishing vessels off the west coast of South America—both frequent by the late 1960s and early 1970s—grew out of nations' conflicting claims to ocean resources. An updated law of the sea—an international treaty specifying the rights and responsibilities of coastal nations and how the remaining vast ocean commons would be governed —clearly was needed to reverse growing tensions over the world's oceans.

UNCLOS I and II, held in 1958 and 1960, with sharply limited agendas, failed to resolve most of the increasingly urgent problems of

---

1. This chapter is based on *Citizen Action for Global Change: The Neptune Group and Law of the Sea*, coauthored with Miriam Levering (Syracuse: Syracuse Univ. Press, forthcoming). Criticisms of social movement activities targeting the Law of the Sea negotiations can be found in the conclusion of that book and in Schmidt (1989, 66–67).

ocean management. Moreover, many of the newly independent nations of the post-1945 era had not participated in them and did not endorse the limited agreements reached there. If a widely accepted ocean treaty was to be fashioned, therefore, the UN would have to invite all nations to take part and ask the conference to consider the full range of ocean issues. Despite the preference of some developed nations for a narrower agenda, the 1970 UN General Assembly resolution establishing UNCLOS III reflected the desire of the developing-nation majority for universality and comprehensiveness (Schmidt 1989, 22).

To my knowledge, social movement involvement in the relatively brief meetings of UNCLOS I and II was virtually nonexistent, but it was clearly a factor in UNCLOS III negotiations. Still, the duration of the conference, the complexity and highly technical nature of the many issues being negotiated, and the cost of attending its lengthy sessions in Caracas, Geneva, and New York discouraged sustained participation by all but the most determined social movement representatives.

At the forefront of social movement activity at UNCLOS III were two small world-order transnational social movement networks based in Washington: the Ocean Education Project (OEP), founded in January 1973, and the United Methodist Law of the Sea Project (UMLSP), founded two years later. Established to work specifically on ocean negotiations, the OEP and UMLSP more closely resemble transitory transnational social movement networks than more permanent, formal transnational social movement organizations (TSMOs). Each involved a small cadre of dedicated and well-informed activists and drew upon preexisting transnational mobilizing structures for their financial and informational resources and for political legitimacy.[2] Because they worked together to set up seminars and other programs, and because they published a newspaper, *Neptune*, featuring factual, well-researched articles on the issues facing the conference, delegates and UN officials referred to the representatives of OEP and UMLSP as the "Neptune Group." The conference's most renowned negotiator and last president, Tommy Koh of Singapore, stated a widely shared opinion when he singled out the Neptune Group in December 1982 as the social movement actor that had made by far the greatest contribution to UNCLOS III.

2. The OEP, for instance, was inspired by and had overlapping membership with the World Federalist Association, a TSMO. Most of its funding came from the American World Federalists and Quakers. The UMLSP likewise had strong religious institutional support: A working committee of the United Methodists, it benefited from the material and symbolic resources that global organization provided.

Understanding the Neptune Group

Broadly speaking, the Neptune Group arose because, throughout the twentieth century, there have been a substantial number of Americans of vision and resources (with active but less numerous counterparts in Western Europe and elsewhere) who believed that the U.S. and other democratic nations should take the lead in building a world ruled by law and orderly government to replace the international anarchy that had led, in their judgment, to the frequent, often devastating wars of modern history. Historians have labeled these members of the broader American peace movement who supported increased world governance "internationalists" or "liberal internationalists," partly to distinguish them from the pacifists who comprised the movement's other major wing (see, e.g., Chatfield 1992, 43–50).

Liberal internationalists in the U.S. helped conceptualize and champion the League of Nations during and after World War I, and they helped build public support for the United Nations during and after World War II through such Social Movement Organizations (SMOs) as the United Nations Association. Those supporting more ambitious moves toward world government—including the founder of the Ocean Education Project, Miriam Levering, and her husband and partner on law of the sea, Sam Levering—joined such organizations as the United World Federalists.[3] Since the early 1900s both liberal internationalism and pacifism strongly influenced numerous Protestant denominations, including the Leverings' Religious Society of Friends (Quakers) and the United Methodists. The Neptune Group thus grew out of both the secular and religious components of the American peace movement, particularly its liberal internationalist wing.

The major goal of movement actors participating in UNCLOS III under OEP auspices was to strengthen world governance. Lee Kimball, who worked for OEP in late 1974 and early 1975 before moving to UMLSP, succinctly stated OEP's central objective: "The Ocean Education Project is a nongovernmental group interested in seeing an effective international organization result from these Law of the Sea Conferences capable of implementing the concept of the oceans and the deep seabed beyond national jurisdiction as the 'common heritage of mankind' " (Kimball n.d.).

Although the Neptune Group never completely abandoned its ambitious goal of substantially strengthening international institutions,

---

3. In 1947, the Leverings helped to found the United World Federalists as a U.S. peace group working to promote global governance. By the 1970s the organization had grown into a transnational SMO, calling itself the World Federalist Association.

over time the more modest goal of reaching agreement on a treaty and encouraging U.S. leadership in implementing it took precedence in both OEP and UMLSP publications. And while UMLSP supported increased world law and governance, the leaders of the Methodist Project—aware of their church's strong emphasis on Christian stewardship and the American public's strong support in the 1970s for environmental protection—placed more emphasis in their publications and talks than Levering did in OEP documents on the conference's efforts to protect the ocean environment.

The daughter of a liberal Methodist minister, Levering grew up imbued with the church's social gospel teachings that human society could be improved with divine assistance, and that a person's highest calling was to help to improve it. A history major at Cornell University, she married Sam on the day she graduated in 1934. Like him, she spent much of her time between then and 1972 working for peace in Quaker groups and in secular organizations like the United World Federalists. Sixty years old when UNCLOS III first met in December 1973, she saw the conference as her last best chance to help strengthen global governance.

Levering's skill as an inspiring motivator / friend and hence an effective builder of networks of people willing to advance what they defined as a common cause was especially helpful to her work on UNCLOS III. Jim Orr, who worked on *Neptune* at Geneva, noted that Miriam's "enthusiasm and commitment are crystal clear to everybody, and I think it's infectious" (Orr 1989). Partly because of Miriam's charismatic personality and networking skills, the United Methodist offices in Washington and New York enthusiastically joined the crusade for ocean law, and dozens of young people—often working for little or no pay—devoted their summers or took time off from college or graduate school to assist her. Her charisma was also instrumental in fundraising: much of OEP's funding consisted of contributions of $100 or less from people who knew the Leverings personally and trusted that Miriam and Sam would put the money to good use. Finally, Miriam's personality and networking skills, combined with the admiration many delegates had for Quakers' longtime work for peace and social justice, helped build trust in the Neptune Group among often skeptical diplomats and UN officials at the conference.

Working primarily for the UMLSP, Kimball (along with her colleague Barbara Weaver, who headed UMLSP and did most of its fundraising and organizational work) was the backbone of its efforts both in Washington and at the conference. A full generation younger than Levering and equally committed to the success of UNCLOS III, Kimball was taking courses for her M.A. in international relations—with a strong emphasis on ocean law—when the conference began. She was highly analytic and had, she recalled, a "secular, at times cynical style" that helped her establish effective personal relationships with some of the more hard-nosed delegates and mining company representatives (Kimball 1995). She quickly developed a detailed knowledge of the substantive issues in the negotiations, especially those related to deep seabed mining. She was also extremely hardworking: editing *Neptune* and establishing close relationships with negotiators at the conference, lobbying Congress and the U.S. administration, setting up seminars for delegates and UN officials, or completing scholarly articles between sessions, she often worked eighteen-hour days promoting law of the sea.

According to both delegates and NGO colleagues, Kimball made her greatest contributions at the conference itself. State Department official Otho Eskin found her "very articulate and effective" (Eskin 1989). Edward Miles, a professor at the University of Washington who attended many UNCLOS III sessions, noted her "extraordinary access" to delegates (Miles 1990). Neptune Group colleague Arthur Paterson recalled her skill in "helping to identify a problem and bringing in outside experts" (Paterson 1989). And Tommy Koh described Kimball as "a solid pro," "very hard working," and "very tactful and discreet" (Koh 1990).

Both Levering and Kimball skillfully stretched their organizations' modest resources by forming networks with other social movement actors and with foundations, universities, and church groups to advance their cause. For instance, the Sierra Club joined OEP in sponsoring a series of programs at the session in Caracas in the summer of 1974. The Quaker UN program cosponsored numerous seminars in New York, as did Quaker House in Geneva. The United Methodist UN Program provided office space and meeting rooms in New York; the Women's International League for Peace and Freedom provided space for writing and editing *Neptune* in Geneva. Faculty from Harvard, MIT, Columbia, Penn, Bryn Mawr, and Johns Hopkins's School of Advanced International Studies cosponsored programs with the Neptune group around the northeastern United States. The Stanley Foundation also cosponsored and paid for several important seminars. Without the contributions of these and many other organizations, the Neptune Group's work would have been much more limited.

Assisting the Negotiators at UNCLOS III

At any given time, SMO and TSMO representatives pursued one of two basic strategies during UNCLOS III. The first strategy involved trying to persuade delegates of the appropriateness of particular social movement proposals: for example, the proposal by (among others) John Logue of the World Order Research Institute and Elisabeth Mann Borgese of *Pacem in Maribus* that substantial revenues from oil and natural gas extracted within 200 miles of shore be devoted to helping developing nations. The second strategy largely eschewed advocacy and focused on trying to help delegates reach agreement on a treaty.

In general, the first strategy proved ineffective and unpopular with delegates, who disliked being lectured on what the treaty ideally should contain. Delegates and UN officials became especially upset when Logue, Mann Borgese, and others persisted in advocating their ideas on revenue sharing long after it became clear that these proposals were going nowhere (Ratiner 1989; Koh 1990). The second strategy, which the Neptune Group largely pursued after 1974, quickly proved much more effective.

Like most social movement representatives interested in law of the sea, Levering started out as an advocate. In July 1973 she was an observer to a month-long meeting of diplomats and UN officials in Geneva preparing for the formal sessions of UNCLOS III that would begin that December. Advocacy was very much on Levering's mind. She sought to "convince negotiators to gain some revenues from the seabed for the international community before coastal appropriation of seabed resources foreclosed this hope." She met rebuff after rebuff: Several delegates made excuses to avoid meeting with her, and others chided her for being too idealistic. An official from the reputedly broad-minded Norwegian government was especially blunt: "If the taxpayers of Norway wanted to share oil revenue with the UN and developing countries, they would have told us." A comment by UN official David Hall made the deepest impression: "Mrs. Levering, if we can get any treaty at all, I will be happy" (M. Levering n.d.).

Levering learned in Geneva that it would be difficult to negotiate any treaty, much less one that transferred resources to the world's poorer nations. She thus began to realize that OEP's main goal should be to help the delegates reach agreement. She also learned from the dodged appointments and from the large number of sessions closed to TSMOs and other nongovernmental organizations (NGOs) that many diplomats and UN officials, angry about the moral posturing and publicity seeking of NGOs at the 1972 environmental conference in Stockholm, were cool to NGO participation in UNCLOS III.

OEP was still feeling its way at the first UNCLOS III negotiating session in Caracas, and its efforts there were amateurish: OEP and its TSMO partner, the Sierra Club, were more interested in publicizing the "right" positions on the ocean environment and in bringing in big-name speakers like Thor Heyerdahl than they were in getting to know delegates and in learning how they could be helpful to the negotiations. OEP made other mistakes, including the distribution of pamphlets opposing the unilateral seabed mining bills then being introduced in the U.S. Congress. Some delegates from other nations considered these pamphlets ethnocentric and irrelevant to their nations' positions (M. Levering n.d.).

Recognizing mistakes made at Caracas and benefiting from the addition of Lee Kimball and the UMLSP, the Neptune Group was much more effective at the subsequent session in Geneva in the spring of 1975. During the months before this session, Levering and Kimball sought advice on how they could be most helpful from diplomats they knew and from social movement actors in the U.S. and in Geneva. One result was a series of programs more focused on the state of the negotiations than had been the case in Caracas. Another was to publish regular issues of a factual newspaper, *Neptune*, that sought to improve communication among the large numbers of delegates and others who gathered at the conference. *Neptune* was inspired by *Pan* (Bread), a newspaper that had been helpful at the 1974 World Food Conference in Rome.

The Geneva session marked the emergence of what delegates began to call the "Neptune Group" as a significant player in the conference. UN officials and delegates greeted the first of *Neptune*'s six issues with considerable skepticism: UN officials permitted it to be distributed only at the documents table, and some delegates refused to take copies of the first issue that OEP and UMLSP members distributed.

Convinced by the premier issue that *Neptune* sought to help the conference through factual analysis, UN officials relented and permitted the group to distribute many of the five thousand copies of subsequent issues in coffee bars and reception areas. More importantly, members of the group observed delegates avidly reading *Neptune* both in the coffee shops and during speeches in the plenary sessions. Moreover, delegates repeatedly offered compliments, criticisms, and suggestions of what should be included. They also handed group members material to include, often anonymously, in future issues. Kimball and Levering quickly found that they were getting more articles than they had space to print and thus had to disappoint some delegates.

The issues of *Neptune* published at Geneva and at subsequent sessions of the conference reflected the approach that the group took to the negotiations in general. This approach combined sincerity with political astuteness. First and foremost, group members wanted a workable, widely accepted treaty—that is, one that necessarily would have to be based on compromise. Second, they wanted a treaty that would be as generous as possible to poorer nations and to those that had short coastlines or were landlocked. The first goal gave them credibility as realists with many Western delegates—a position that social movement representatives like Logue and Mann Borgese never achieved. The second increased their standing with delegates from the "Group of 77" (G77) developing countries, whose representatives were using UNCLOS III and other international forums to press their demands for what they called a "new international economic order" more favorable to third world nations than the existing global economic system.

After the 1975 session in Geneva, the Neptune Group's greatest contribution to the conference was the sponsoring of numerous seminars and other informal meetings to help delegates complete a treaty that most nations could accept. Some of these meetings were designed to allow delegates to meet informally with outside experts to discuss ideas that might lead to breakthroughs in the negotiations. Others, often organized with fewer outside experts and more time for small-group discussions, sought to set up situations away from the conference where the different sides in disputes among delegates could stop posturing and begin to find a solid basis for compromise. Because leading negotiators appreciated both kinds of meetings and kept asking the Neptune Group to organize more, and because Neptune Group representatives repeatedly saw ideas that emerged from the discussions appearing in the negotiating text, group members gladly devoted the enormous amount of time and effort required to organize meetings they hoped would best meet delegates' needs.

Perceptions of the seminars' usefulness to the conference was confirmed overwhelmingly both in contemporary comments and letters and in more recent interviews. A U.S. delegate saw the seminars as "both education [especially of developing nation delegates] and the opportunity . . . to explore substantive issues without regard to national positions" (Oxman 1990). Reflecting more broadly but with the seminars clearly in mind, a delegate from Mauritanias wrote Levering in 1981 "to express my deepest thanks to the group you represent for helping me and other third world delegates to understand some of the basic issues concerning the subject matter of the Conference" (Gayan 1981). A UN official commented that the seminars "served to open channels of communication which contributed to a lessening of tension and often provided new ideas which were followed up on during the formal sessions of the conference" (Werner 1985). And a West German delegate wrote Kimball that "at the meetings you arranged, we had the chance to meet delegates and other people interested in the Law of the Sea Conference, whom otherwise I at least would not have met, certainly not for such informal and agreeable discussions" (Eitel 1981).

The Neptune Group's seminars peaked in both number and effectiveness during the four years of Jimmy Carter's presidency (1977–80). Because the Carter negotiating team led by Elliot Richardson strongly supported the negotiations and encouraged the group's efforts to facilitate agreement, these were hopeful times for diplomats and pro-treaty social movement actors alike. Delegates and UN officials repeatedly asked Kimball and Levering to organize meetings at which major issues facing the conference could be discussed in an informal atmosphere. During these years the group sponsored or cosponsored at least ten major (day-long, two-day, or weekend) meetings involving outside experts and substantial time for discussion. In addition, it sponsored at least sixty shorter (usually luncheon or evening) meetings at the conference.

During the Carter and early Reagan years, most of the group's programs centered on deep seabed mining, the issue that was preventing the completion of the negotiations. Because deep seabed mining was a prospective rather than a currently operating industry, almost everything about it was uncertain. But delegates—especially ones from poorer nations—believed that they had to write detailed rules regulating seabed mining in the treaty to prevent companies from the technologically advanced nations from absorbing all the profits from such mining and possibly shutting down some of their own mining operations, thus eliminating a vital source of revenue. Moreover, most third world delegates saw the minerals on and beneath the ocean floor beyond the 200-mile economic zone as the "common heritage of mankind," not the property of those with the technology to extract them. Many delegates from developed nations, in contrast, viewed the minerals as open to extraction on the basis of traditional freedom of the seas until such time as the conference reached consensus on precisely what regulations and restrictions, if any, should be placed on seabed mining (see Schmidt 1989, 22–43).

Even without the political and legal differences on this issue between developed and developing countries and between nations with and nations without land-based mining operations, the many unanswered questions and technical uncertainties surrounding deep seabed mining complicated efforts to build new ocean law in this area. Neptune Group members, notably Kimball, thus worked tirelessly during the late 1970s and early 1980s writing detailed papers and setting up meetings on issues blocking progress in the negotiations, talking informally with delegates about their views on the disputed issues, and otherwise trying to help the conference reach consensus on seabed mining.

More than any of its other seminars, the group's programs on financial arrangements for seabed mining earned it the lasting gratitude of delegates and UN officials. In late January 1978, while the conference was not in session, the group organized a two-day seminar on financial arrangements in New York. The main attraction of this gathering was Professor J. D. Nyhart of MIT, who introduced UN officials and diplomats (including Koh and three other G77 delegates) to the MIT computer study he had directed on the profitability to seabed mining companies of operations from each mine site under either a three-metal or a four-metal recovery operation. Nyhart presented figures on expected expenses and income, and hence expected profits, under various scenarios.

At the time of this seminar, Koh, who headed the negotiating group on financial arrangements, was looking for ways to introduce credible figures into the negotiations in his group and quickly saw the potential of the MIT econometrics model. Koh subsequently went to Cambridge, where he met with Nyhart and several of his associates to learn more about the study.

Convinced that the MIT model offered the best chance to break the deadlock between developed and developing nations over financial arrangements for seabed mining, Koh asked the Neptune Group to organize an all-day seminar on the model on Saturday, 29 August, eight days after the start of the resumed seventh session in New York (21 August-15 September 1978). Koh personally made efforts to ensure that a large contingent of delegates from the G77 were among the roughly fifty people (including thirty-six delegates and three mining company representatives) attending the meeting. With financial help from the World Affairs Council of Philadelphia, the Neptune Group assembled the entire MIT team of Nyhart, Lance Antrim, and Dale Leshaw, plus James Sebenius of Harvard.

During two three-hour sessions, seminar participants listened to a thorough explanation of the model by Nyhart and his colleagues and then observed how well the MIT/Harvard team held up under a lengthy barrage of questions from critics ranging from free-market industry representatives to G77 supporters of state-run enterprises. Because most delegates' backgrounds were in law rather than in economics, much of the day was spent explaining such economic concepts as "cost model," "accounting model," "net present value," and "internal rate of return" (Neptune Group 1978).

The effectiveness with which the MIT/Harvard team presented their model was a turning point in the negotiations. For the first time there was a common base of knowledge and assumptions upon which those participating in Koh's negotiating group could work toward consensus. U.S. negotiator Ronald Katz appreciated the model's thoroughness and noted another advantage of the model: Because it was an academic study, delegates could "accept the MIT model as a basis for negotiations in a face-saving way without conceding the correctness of the point of view of their opponents" (Katz 1979, 210).

Not everyone was enthusiastic: Mining company representatives and Western officials thought the projected profits were too high, and the overall head of the negotiations on seabed mining issues, Paul Engo of Cameroon, complained that the delegates had "been dragged into adopting models and systems of calculations on fictitious data that no one, expert or magician, can make the basis of any rational determination" (Dubs 1990; Engo quoted in Katz 1979, 85). But Engo and other skeptical G77 delegates went along with Koh, partly because mining company representatives and officials from Western nations also found fault with the model, and partly because there seemed to be no other way to move toward consensus on financial arrangements. Indeed, the only major advance in the negotiations at this session was a paper Koh produced, based largely on the MIT model, that specified figures and percentages for payments from private contractors to the agency designated to supervise mining, the International Seabed Authority (ISA).

A very gratifying moment for Neptune Group members occurred at a 1978 seminar on decision making in the ISA. At the end of the meeting, Bernardo Zuleta, the UN official responsible for the conference's day-to-day operations, rose to thank the members of the group not only for putting on that day's meeting but also for the overall help that they were giving to the conference. He said that he also wanted to make amends for remarks that Kimball had overheard in Caracas: namely, that nongovernmental organizations were in the way and were backseat drivers, always calling for impossible things in this unideal world. In contrast, the Neptune Group was the kind of backseat driver who watched the map and, instead of berating the driver for getting sleepy, announced that the next rest area was three miles ahead, saying, "Let me buy you a cup of coffee." Coming from a high UN official who earlier had been highly critical, Zuleta's remarks reinforced something the group's members had known without doubt after the August seminar on financial arrangements: The Neptune Group had truly come of age as a participant in UNCLOS III (M. Levering n.d.).

After 1978 the Neptune Group continued to organize seminars as requested by Koh and other leaders of the conference. And it continued to publish *Neptune*, which frequently reported new ideas that emerged from seminars occurring between conference sessions. In addition, the group made three other valuable contributions to the conference. First, in order to build community and trust, it continued to host frequent parties and receptions at which delegates and others attending the conference could get to know each other socially. Second, in order to increase media and hence public awareness of UNCLOS III, members of the group set up press conference and media briefings, normally before and after each session; they also spent long hours briefing individual reporters from around the world on developments in the negotiations.

Third, and more directly helpful to the conference, the group was involved in a wide range of unpublicized, often confidential efforts to facilitate the negotiations. For example, several members, including Kimball and Levering, used their many contacts both inside and outside the conference to answer countless factual questions from delegates. This was an important service, because many delegates from developing nations were embarrassed at the thought of asking for information from developed countries' delegates or from mining company representatives. Kimball also produced confidential options papers for the negotiators' use and served as an informal mediator between them on possible compromise language. At the request of conference leaders, another Neptune Group member, Jim Magee, spent several months developing a computer program that produced forty-five possible voting formulas for the governing Council of the ISA. The delegates chose one of these for inclusion in the treaty.

In short, much of the group's most valuable work at the conference was done in confidential discussions with negotiators and in research undertaken for them, all designed to move the negotiations forward as rapidly as possible. As in the well-publicized seminars and *Neptune*, the group played diverse brokering roles in these more confidential settings.

Assessing the Group's Contribution

Kimball summarized four of the Neptune Group's key contributions in a letter to Koh in April 1980:

1. Bringing together constructively in a third-party [nonofficial] forum delegates, UN Secretariat members and individuals whose expertise can contribute to solving difficult LOS issues;
2. serving as a third-party source of information through the seminars and *Neptune*;

3. playing a communications facilitation role among delegates and the Secretariat through informal contacts, friendships and receptions . . .; and

4. preparation of detailed background papers and reports related to the seminar program which are used by delegates and the Secretariat alike. (Kimball 1980)

Paralleling Kimball's points, Koh identified the group's "three valuable services" in his presidential address at the 1982 signing session in Montego Bay, Jamaica:

[The Neptune Group] brought independent experts to meet with delegations, thus enabling us to have an independent source of information on technical issues. They assisted representatives from developing countries to narrow the technical gap between them and their counterparts from developed countries. They also provided us with opportunities to meet, away from the Conference, in a more relaxed atmosphere, to discuss some of the most difficult issues confronted by the Conference. (United Nations 1982)

Although *information* and *communication* describe much of what Neptune Group members did at UNCLOS III, these concepts by themselves fail to capture the essence of the group's contribution. A more helpful concept is what Kimball has sometimes called the "catalyst function," or what she and others have identified as the "honest broker" role. Kimball explained the honest broker/catalyst role:

drawing on their independent status, NGOs may be able to promote or facilitate agreement . . .; that is, they can act as a kind of "honest broker" to mediate compromises. Such meetings may also generate new ideas by bringing together individuals with varying specializations and backgrounds. This catalyst role is distinguished from the activist role . . . in that it contributes not to a particular substantive outcome but rather to the process of reaching agreement or compromise per se. The wide range of NGO contacts contributes to this ability to facilitate agreement. (Kimball 1990, 146–47)

Kimball's cogent analysis points to an important paradox in social movement effectiveness, at least at UNCLOS III. Social movement organizations and TSMOs are normally established to bring to fruition the farsighted goals of their founders and supporters. The two Neptune Group organizations fit this pattern. OEP, founded and largely funded by World Federalists and Quakers, sought international governance of ocean space as a step toward greater international authority in other areas, including armaments. The United Methodist Church began and generously funded UMLSP largely to further the biblical ideal of a more equitable sharing of the world's resources and the more modern goals of protecting the ocean environment and strengthening international law. Yet these two groups working together became the most effective social movement effort at UNCLOS III not because they stood for high-minded ideals but because, in practice, they subordinated their desire to advocate these long-term ideals to the practical goal of being as helpful as possible to the conference.

Two key lessons based on this experience may be drawn for social movement representatives working in other international negotiations. First, such representatives have to learn how to be effective in particular international negotiations—a highly challenging task that many social movement representatives either fail to undertake or flunk if they do attempt it. The fact that each new negotiation differs in significant ways from its predecessors makes becoming effective especially difficult.

Second, the success or failure of social movement efforts depends heavily on the individuals who represent them. "It is my observation that the success of an NGO turns largely upon the character of the individuals who operate it," William Stelle, a counsel for the House Merchant Marine and Fisheries Committee who followed UNCLOS III closely, wrote in 1985. "When the individuals have demonstrated proficiency in the subject matter, knowledge of the participants and experience in the process of negotiation, it is more than likely that their efforts to facilitate negotiation will be positively received, and will yield results. Suffice it to say that the converse is also true" (Stelle 1985).

In the Neptune Group's case, success depended largely on Miriam Levering's and Lee Kimball's distinctive, complementary contributions. Yet none of these contributions would have been possible if the group's leaders had not correctly gauged the challenges facing them in late 1974: the need to shift from advocating preferred outcomes to assisting the negotiators; and, in order to actually help the negotiators, the need to move beyond being generalist supporters of the conference to becoming specialists in the issues being negotiated and, equally important, in the Byzantine UNCLOS III negotiating process itself. In mapping out their own goals, contemporary social movement leaders would be wise to note that, from the perspective of late 1974, the likelihood that the Neptune Group would be able to meet these challenges was uncertain at best.

PART FIVE

Theoretical Implications

14

THE GLOBALIZATION OF
SOCIAL MOVEMENT THEORY

John D. McCarthy

Abstract

Most research on social movements is grounded in the assumption that social movements operate within state boundaries. The case studies in this book contribute to the study of social movements through their illumination of six core concepts: strategic framing processes, activist identities, mobilizing structures, resource mobilization, political opportunity structures, and repertoires of contention. From an application of these concepts to the realm of transnational social movements come suggestions for further research to increase knowledge about the transnational dimensions of social movement activity.

Western analysts increasingly employ a common set of conceptual tools in making sense of the emergence and trajectories of social movements. Strategic framing processes, activist identities, mobilizing structures, resource mobilization, political opportunity structures, and repertoires of contention are orienting concepts now routinely employed to explain the timing, spatial and social location, and success of citizens' collective efforts to bring about social change.

These tools, however, have been crafted by researchers working almost exclusively from empirical evidence about nationally focused social movements operating *within Western democracies* (McAdam et al. 1996). The essays in *Solidarity beyond the State* focus their analyses instead upon transnational social movements, providing a valuable opportunity to assess the more general utility of the above concepts, since most transnational movements include constituent groups in non-Western, nondemocratic nations and routinely seek to influence transnational as well as national and subnational authorities.

The wide use of the five orienting concepts typically depends upon a common set of assumptions about the elements and processes of social movements. Social movements are ongoing collective efforts to bring about consequential social change. They may provoke countermovements aimed at resisting or reversing such change. Movements are composed of a set of constituent elements, including activists, who devote extensive effort; constituents of groups that provide financial and other support; and adherents, people who support the goals of a movement but are not active. Movements vary in the extent to which they are composed of advocates for disadvantaged groups or of constituents who stand to benefit directly from the changes they seek.

Movements typically include social movement organizations (SMOs), which devote their principal effort toward promoting social change. There is great variation in how such groups are structured. Movements also include networks of adherents that are not formally organized. And movements may exhibit a wide variety of action elements, including—but not restricted to—mobilizing support and resources, lobbying authorities, silent vigiling, promoting violence or terrorist campaigns, and staging mass demonstrations. Because many movements seek changes on behalf of disadvantaged classes, they are especially likely to use extraordinary and/or disruptive tactics; however, movements vary greatly in the extent to which they use such tactics.

Social movements may form around chronic social cleavages such as class, religion, region, language, and ethnicity. However, as associational structures increasingly replace more traditional communal structures as the locus of personal identity, social movements are more likely to develop around emergent, socially constructed categories of shared identity and/or grievance. And they may seek broader or narrower goals. Finally, social movement dynamics are conceived as ongoing strategic interactions between movement elements and other institutions, organizations, groups, individuals within a society, and, especially, state authorities.

Strategic Framing Processes

Rooted in the work of David Snow, Robert Benford, and their colleagues (Snow et al. 1986; Snow and Benford 1988), framing has been defined as "the conscious strategic efforts by groups of people to fashion shared understandings of the world and of themselves that legitimate and motivate collective action" (McAdam et al. 1996, 6). But in doing framing work, social movement actors do not operate in cultural vacuums. Nor do their efforts typically go unopposed. Motivating frameworks are constructed out of preexisting cultural materials, and their advocacy pits activists against other, sometimes powerful social actors, including states, corporations, religious bodies and counter-movements. As a result, successfully generating a widely embraced frame often involves a lengthy contest. And, in the recent period, the role of mass media institutions is central to understanding the outcomes of these contests.

If the work of strategic framing is difficult at the national level, it is far more difficult at the transnational level, as several of the authors in this volume note. Movements attempting to construct frames that resonate in diverse cultural settings and to promote frame bridging, or the linking of new mobilizing frames with existing cultural materials, confront great obstacles. Frame bridging is so important because of the great cultural and language differences existing throughout the world. It is also difficult, because frames that resonate with diverse local personal experiences are not easily discovered. Consequently, creating a widely embraced transnational frame is likely to be a far more lengthy, extensive, and multifaceted process than it is at the national level.

The broad mobilization of a movement can occur only after much strategic framing work has already been accomplished. To understand the timing and social location of transnational mobilization, then, requires systematic comparative assessments of both successful and unsuccessful strategic framing efforts. A number of the essays in this volume take for granted the extensive and successful framing campaign—for human rights—that preceded the specific transnational movement activism they chronicle. No doubt, one of the most successful transnational framing efforts in the recent period has been the creation of a common transnational conception of human rights. The work of the Peace Brigades in Sri Lanka, chronicled by Patrick Coy (chap. 5), could have proceeded only within the context of those pervasive understandings. Similarly, the Campaign for Human Rights carried out by SERPAJ, described by Pagnucco (chap. 7), could not have been successfully launched outside of such an international consensus. Clearly, however, these campaigns contributed to the broadening and deepening of the transnational human rights frame.

Several essays focus directly upon the strategic framing efforts themselves. Hovey describes how transnational social movement organization (TSMO) activists labored to expand notions of human rights to include the right of conscientious objection within the broader human rights frame (chap. 12). Atwood describes the efforts of TSMO activists to frame nuclear disarmament and nuclear nonproliferation in order to provide the basis for broader mobilization around these questions (chap. 8). These cases demonstrate that transnational frames have emerged and have undoubtedly motivated transnational collective action. However, the case described by Cortright and Pagnucco, focusing upon the unsuccessful attempt of the nuclear freeze movement in the United States to create a transnational mobilizing frame (chap. 9), reveals the important difficulties activists face when trying to transcend national discourses in order to craft transnational frames. To better assess the conditions under which effective transnational mobilizing frames emerge, hypotheses drawn from cases such as these must be tested through systematic comparisons among two or more cases.

These several cases, including the mother of all successful transnational framing efforts—human rights—suggest proper patterns of action for effectively embedding mobilizing frames in transnational discourse. Such patterns of action include locating international forums and institutions within which to wage framing contests and then succeeding in leaving written traces of successful framing contests waged there. So in the proceedings of international conferences, in international agreements, at the United Nations, at regional institutions like the European Union (EU) and the Organization of American States (OAS), and in media discussions of them, international discourse about issues can be shaped toward activists' mobilizing frames.

To empirically assess framing campaigns, Gamson and Modigliani (1989) have fruitfully deployed the concept of issue culture—mass public discourse around a social issue—which he has shown can be systematically estimated in media coverage over time in his studies of nuclear power in the U.S. Tracking public issue cultures provides a way of evaluating how effective activists are in altering the issue frames that concern them. National media discourse has provided the evidence base for such systematic tests of strategic framing efforts in the U.S. Tracking a diverse sample of national public discourses over time would provide a glimpse of how transnational framing efforts variably penetrate national discourse. It is not so clear what equivalent transnational locations might serve as sources of media discourse, although CNN and its competitors as well as international news agencies, such as Reuters, might be usefully employed as parallel evidence sources for tracking shifts in mobilizing frames in transnational discourse. Short of more systematic attempts to chronicle the success of transnational framing efforts, little progress is likely to be made in unraveling the features that distinguish the successful framing formulas from the unsuccessful.

The essays in this volume provide the first step for further, comparative analysis of transnational framing contests and the conditions shaping their impacts. Certainly vigorous transnational issue-framing contests proceed around a wide range of issues, including global economic inequality, and many social issues, such as sexual identity and abortion. Yet none of them has achieved the pervasive hegemony of the human rights frame. To understand the success of the human rights frame requires comparing that issue framing contest with other, less successful ones. Vigorous transnational issue-framing contests proceed around a far wider array of issues than are addressed here, including global economic inequality, and many social issues, such as sexual identity and abortion. Yet none of them has achieved the pervasive hegemony of the human rights frame. To understand its success requires comparing that contest with less successful ones.

Finally, many institutional actors are deeply involved in these contests beyond TSMO activists. These include multinational corporations, multinational religious bodies, and states, among others. The narrow TSMO focus of most of the papers in this volume means that the nature of the wider framing contests and the framing fields upon which they are played remain unexamined—and are therefore background unaccounted for. This is doubly true for the role of transnational media actors themselves, almost all of which are profit-making enterprises and, as a result, have deep-seated interests in the outcomes of many framing contests. As a consequence, such analyses at the very least run the risk of seriously misunderstanding the success and failure of specific framing campaigns, for the presence or absence of powerful transnational institutional allies is of crucial importance to their outcomes, given the typical weaknesses of TSMOs.

Activists' Identities and Careers

The study of social movements at the state level has increasingly focused upon the nature and origin of activist identity on the assumption that the process of identity formation significantly shapes broader movement mobilization dynamics. This is the individual cognitive equivalent of strategic framing: As activists create mobilizing frames, there is a reciprocal process of cognitive adoption of ever more sophisticated activist identities. The essays in this volume chronicle in great detail the efforts of a wide variety of TSMO activists, but processes by which activist identities are formed are likewise important dimensions of social movement activity that future research must address.

Theorists of the origin and evolution of activist identity have pointed to both bottom-up and top-down processes. Theorists of the new social movements (NSMs) have stressed the importance of new ways of postmaterialist living that they argue give rise to the possibilities of new feminist and ecological identities, for example (Calhoun 1993; Cohen 1985). And analysts of intense activist experience have demonstrated the long-term biographical consequences of such activism (e.g., McAdam 1988). Others have described how state policies serve to create common identities. For instance, Nagel shows the relationship of a pan-native American identity to U.S. state policies that treat all Native Americans alike, despite their important economic, regional, and tribal differences (1995). And others have documented the victim identities that were facilitated by U.S. federal and state policies on crime victimization in general (Weed 1995) and on drunk driving victimization in particular (McCarthy 1994).

Each of these approaches can provide clues for thinking about how transnational activist identities emerge and are shaped and nurtured. Several of the globalization processes described by Kriesberg (chap. 1) can be expected to provide the basis for developing transnational identities, some of which may evolve into activist identities. Increasing global integration, especially through increasing personal contact across state boundaries and through transnational communication, provides individuals and communities greater opportunity to form social bonds and experiential empathy with individuals and communities around the world. However, it should not be taken for granted that these experiences will necessarily result in transnational identity formation: Such contacts may have the opposite effect, reinforcing nationalist and/or subnational identities as well as activist identities, as the presence of transnational Islamic terrorist groups illustrates. The conditions under which globalization processes produce one or another of these results is an empirical question demanding serious investigation.

The experience of activists in certain national SMOs can be expected to have important consequences for the transnationality of their self-conception. Joining Amnesty International or Greenpeace and participating, even vicariously, in their transnational efforts can be expected to provide the opportunity for members to develop a deepened appreciation for transnational solidarity among people. So, too, can involvement in movements like the U.S. sanctuary movement, which provided protection for aliens in the U.S. who faced persecution if returned to their homelands. Coutin (1993) demonstrates the transforming cognitive consequences of involvement in this movement for many U.S. citizens—what she calls the development of an "international notion of citizenship."

Nevertheless, adoption of a transnational identity does not necessarily imply transnational activism, as studies of national social movements remind us. Acting upon one's identity requires the opportunity to act. At the community level, much activism is by volunteers who take time out of their daily activities to engage in social change efforts. Beyond the local level, however, activism is far less likely to consist of volunteer efforts, but rather—and particularly in wealthy industrial societies—of paid professional activism. This should be even more the case with transnational activism, where the personal transaction costs of activism can be expected to be even higher than at the national level. It is one thing to travel to Washington, D.C., for a one-day demonstration, but another thing entirely to travel to Beijing for a conference lasting several weeks. Therefore, understanding transnational activism requires attention to transnational activist identity formation as the source of motivation for activism. It also requires understanding the more or less formal opportunities that allow committed activists to choose extended careers in transnational activism. Such an understanding leads to a consideration of mobilizing structures and the mobilization of resources, which I take up in turn.

Mobilizing Structures

Systematic observation of social movement mobilization has regularly revealed the central importance of mobilizing structures. Mobilizing structures include the more or less formally organized everyday life patterns upon which movements build collective action, ranging from religious groups and neighborhood associations to workplace cliques and friendship groups. Building upon these preexisting social relations, activists can facilitate mobilization, because they are spared the greater effort of creating new social relations and networks of communication between constituents from scratch. If such mobilizing structures are available for co-optation by activists, they may also be able to appropriate a portion of the previously pooled resources of the group, which might include equipment, communication structures, work space, and financial resources.

Many of the TSMOs described in the chapters of this book show the importance of a group's ability to draw upon preexisting institutional structures in mobilizing around issues of concern. A variety of institutions provide support structures for the TSMOs described in these essays. They include international religious bodies—the Roman Catholic Church in the case of SERPAJ, traditional peace churches and some mainstream churches in the case of groups lobbying the UN for the right of conscientious objection and for the law of the sea. It is also routine for such groups to provide a commitment of personnel and an access to technology as well as financial resources to activist campaigns like these, but the essays here could not discuss such matter in detail. Many religious groups are structured transnationally, so they provide natural infrastructural vehicles for transnational activism if their support can be garnered (Zald and McCarthy 1987). Indeed, the Society of Jesus (the Jesuits) may be an early prototype of a transnational social movement, and the transnational structure of that religious order has provided a foundation for transnational political and social activism into the modern period.

We know that modern national movements are typically built on relations and structures developed at work, at worship, in associations, and in local daily activities. Transnational movements likewise can be expected to rely upon successful co-optation of the resources of groups that make up the existing range of international nongovernmental organizations (INGOs), unless they create TSMOs by the more arduous route of building networks of relations between previously unconnected people and groups. Smith's analysis of EarthAction highlights how this TSMO emerged as a coalition of local, national, and international affiliates. The coalition structure is designed to facilitate citizens' participation in international environmental politics by channeling technical, political, and tactical information to organizations otherwise lacking such information.

It is useful to imagine all of the existing TSMOs as making up a single transnational social movement sector (TSMS). All INGOs and nongovernmental organizations (NGOs) make up the potentially co-optable associational landscape that transnational activists confront as they attempt to mobilize support. The range of INGO associational structures potentially available to activists, however, clearly does not consist of a representative aggregation of all NGO associational structures, just as national level structures do not, typically, represent the range of local community associational structures. To the extent that this is the case, local activists are unlikely to always find international infrastructures that are available—let alone co-optable—to facilitate mobilization around the substantive issues that concern them parallel to local ones. The shape of the TSMS, therefore, can be seen as an interaction of (1) the aggregate shape of transnational activists' preferences, (2) the aggregate shape of and relations among the global NGO and INGO sectors, and (3) the variable co-optability of NGOs and INGOs.

Social movements are conceived as collective, cooperative efforts at social change. Yet SMOs, it is widely noted (Wilson 1960; Zald and McCarthy 1980), also have strong incentives to compete with one another for resources, constituents, and legitimacy. Such conflict, if and when it exists, is for the most part not treated in these essays, but it is seen quite vividly in DeMars's account of interlaced cooperation and conflict between the several humanitarian organizations active during the war in the Horn of Africa. He demonstrates graphically how each TSMO was constrained by its constituent base, its perception of the conception that its base had of the limits of legitimate humanitarian action, and the direct competition between the several TSMOs within which each strategic approach was crafted. Typically, analysts of broad social movements or single SMOs have deemphasized the importance of intramovement conflict, while analysts of social movement sectors have been more likely to recognize the ambivalent incentive structure that confronts individual SMO leaders as they seek collective goals while attempting to maintain bounded organizational structures. The same dynamics should be at work among TSMOs generally, as they find themselves competing for support among individual constituents, associational structures, and institutional financial supporters such as foundations.

The level of competition can be expected to be higher in the TSMS than in national social movement sectors (SMSs), and even higher than among SMOs at the local community level. This is so because the demography of movement organizational structure appears strongly related to its geographic scope. The broader that scope, the less likely that organizations are composed of individual members, and the less likely that they depend upon the volunteer labor of constituents. Smith's evidence shows that almost 70 percent of the TSMOs she identifies are either federations of local sections or coalitions of organizations. Although we do not have equivalent comparative data across national and local levels, less systematic evidence suggests that membership-based organizations become more common as the geographic scope of coverage of an SMO narrows and the most common form at the local level is that of groups with individual, volunteer members.

Also, as the geographic scope of coverage of an individual membership group expands, the likelihood that its members have weaker links to the organization grows. This is the case because of the difficulties of building global individual-membership organizations as well as the major innovations in knitting together disparate sympathizers through modern mobilization technologies such as fundraising concerts, direct mail, and telemarketing. And while some of the most well-known TSMOs, such as Greenpeace, Friends of the Earth, and Amnesty International, are technically federations of national sections, they are, in fact, highly professionalized organizations with relatively weak links, or what I have called elsewhere (McCarthy 1987) thin ties, to their mass of individual members (Dalton 1994) upon whom they nevertheless heavily depend for financial support. Accordingly, the dynamics of interorganizational competition are likely to be quite different for these organizations than they are for TSMOs composed of coalitions of constituent organizations, the most common TSMO form (42 percent in 1993). This is because individual membership organizations must compete only for weak, low-cost commitment among masses of potential constituents while coalitions depend upon sustaining support from existing organizations or grants from foundations, both much scarcer commodities. Thus, the dynamics of interorganizational cooperation can also be expected to be different, as reflected in Smith's evidence in chapter 3 that individual membership TSMOs display the lowest network densities, or the smallest number of IGO or NGO contacts of 211 the TSMO forms (table 3.5).

National sections of TSMOs are not necessarily characterized by weak membership. The cadre structural form displayed by both Peace Brigades International and by SERPAJ, for example, consists of groups composed of a small number of highly active members who do not attempt to mobilize a mass constituency. As a result, national TSMO structures of this form are less likely to become dependent upon institutional funders.

The editors of this volume chose explicitly to focus on TSMOs as the unit of analysis rather than to adopt the concept of issue network or epistemic communities, which have proved useful in some international relations research (Sikkink 1993; Sikkink and Keck in press; P. Haas 1992). Clearly the social movement efforts described in the case studies can be analyzed from a network perspective, although conversely the network approach would also benefit from the rich, organizational level perspectives offered here. Indeed, existing research in international relations has not yet made use of the great theoretical strength of more formal network analysis (e.g., Granovetter 1973), and it still fails to account for the dynamic, often competitive interactions characterizing relations among social movement and other political actors. But applications of more systematic network theory has proved fruitful in the study of national movements and is also likely to contribute to research on transnational movements. Diani (1994) has demonstrated the potency of applying more systematic network analysis for understanding movement mobilization in his work on the Italian environmental movement. There he uses systematic evidence of linkages between Italian environmental SMOs to describe an evolving pattern of cooperative relations that look very much like the issue networks described by Sikkink. The bulk of past work on national social movement sectors (SMSs) has tended to be SMO-centric; likewise, most of the studies in this volume are TSMO-centric. Network approaches, in contrast, provide the promise of both theoretical and methodological tools to help the analyst broaden the focus from the individual TSMO in an attempt to analyze aggregated collective action. The idea of the transnational social movement industry (TSMI), introduced by Smith, Pagnucco, and Chatfield in chapter 4, is aimed at accomplishing the same aim and, in addition, shifts the focus away from the individual TSMO.

An additional issue concerning TSMO structures themselves is inspired by the neo-institutional theorists of organizations (Powell and DiMaggio 1991). They note, in general, that aspiring organizations seek social legitimacy by structuring themselves along the lines of their most highly legitimate predecessors. Others (McCarthy, Britt, and Wolfson 1991) note that similar homogenizing forces emanate from processes of formal organizational access at the national level, not unlike that of receiving formal UN status at the transnational level. At the state level in the U.S., these twin dynamics are seen to determine the structures of newly emergent movement organizations. Formal decision-making processes as well as tactical repertoires are directly affected by these processes. Many TSMOs seek formal recognition not only to gain access to UN conferences but also (and perhaps more importantly) to gain formal recognition and penetration of states, where they at least hope to deliver humanitarian aid, if not create social change. These processes of institutional isomorphism and state inducements appear as pervasive, if not more so, among the population of TSMOs as they are among national populations of SMOs.

Resource Mobilization

TSMOs must, like all national movement organizations, usually attempt to mobilize at least some labor, financial support, in-kind support, and legitimacy in order to increase their chances for survival. At the most local levels, the ratio of in-kind support and volunteer labor to financial support, as noted above, is quite high. For TSMOs the effective ratio of financial support to the other two kinds of support can be expected to be dramatically reversed because TSMOs are unable to operate exclusively with such locally based resources. As a consequence, TSMOs are more dependent upon finding stable sources of financial support in order to maintain operations than are typical local SMOs. What are the origins of the typical sources of such support? The case studies in this volume suggest that resource support for transnational SMOs include at least the following: (1) international political authorities, (2) national political authorities, (3) international religious organizations, (4) national religious organizations, (5) INGOs, (6) NGOs, (7) foundations, (8) constituent organizations, and (9) members and sympathizers. The typical forms of support are direct financial aid and in-kind aid, such as office space, temporary grants of personnel, access to communications technology and other equipment, and public support.

While movement analysts have concluded that the emergence of SMOs—and, by extension, TSMOs—is especially facilitated by the support from sources other than mass constituents (e.g., sources 1 through 7 above), it is not so clear that dependence upon such sources is related to longer-term survival of SMOs at the local community level (Edwards and McCarthy 1996). This is so because of the widely noted fickleness of outside financial supporters toward particular social change movements. Religious groups, foundations, and authorities face diverse demands from broad constituencies, and such demands necessarily change over time. As a consequence, today's hot social issue in the minds of elite sponsors may be replaced by another torrid issue that commands the media spotlight tomorrow. Institutional funding sources are thus notoriously unreliable, and—while such support may help groups to form—it is unlikely that they will serve as a stable long-term source of support for most groups. Foundations typically encourage groups to become self-sufficient after some period of initial support (usually five-year cycles). In fact, however, groups that begin dependent upon a single source of support usually find it difficult to establish other sources (Walker 1991; McCarthy and Castelli 1994), although Imig's (1996) work on how several national poor welfare groups in the U.S. during the 1980s replaced crucial state support with private sources in order to survive the efforts of the Reagan Administration to "defund the left" suggests that it is not impossible. Earlier social movements, such as the labor movement, succeeded in entrenching themselves in state structures, thus guaranteeing stable sources of financial support. Elements of the human rights movement appear to have succeeded in accomplishing a similar stable relationship with state and transnational authorities. It is not yet clear whether our understanding of these processes of institutionalization at the national level will provide useful guidelines for making sense of them at the transnational level.

Political Opportunity Structure

The concept of political opportunity structure evolved from historical scholarship on the rise of "the" social movement, or the labor/socialist movement during the nineteenth and twentieth centuries. The emergence, shape, and development of that movement is interpreted as a collective response to the development of the scope, resources, and penetration of the modern state—as national states aggregated power and resources, movements came more and more to target state authorities with demands for social change in existing societal arrangements (Tilly 1984; Tarrow 1995).

The broad idea of the centrality of the state for understanding social movements has been recently extended to account for variations in movement features between states and within states over shorter time spans. It has been employed to account for the timing of the U.S. civil rights movement (McAdam 1982), the shape and timing of the cycle of Italian protest during the 1970s (Tarrow 1989), and differences in the form and extent of the SMS in four European nations during the 1970s and 1980s (Kriesi et al. 1995), among others. A number of different accounts of the primary dimensions of political opportunity structures are relevant to understanding movement dynamics. The following list captures the dimensions common among them:

1. The relative openness or closure of the institutionalized political system.

2. The stability of that broad set of elite alignments that typically undergird a polity.

3. The presence of elite allies.

4. The state's capacity and propensity for repression. (McAdam et al. 1996, 10)

Two major emphases characterize the growing empirical work with these ideas: the dynamic, within a state, and the static, across state approaches. The first attempts to "explain the emergence of a particular social movement on the basis of changes in the institutional structure or informal power relations of a given national political system," and the second tries to account "for cross-national differences in the structure, extent, and success of comparable movements on the basis of differences in the political characteristics of nation states in which they are embedded" (McAdam, McCarthy, and Zald 1996, 3).

The most obvious extension of these ideas for thinking about transnational movements is to expect that as authority becomes increasingly vested in transnational bodies, social movements will tend to become more transnational in scope and target. This is the line of analysis pursued by Rucht in chapter 12, where he shows how the evolution of authority toward the European Union (EU) has led some national environmental movements to increasingly make EU bodies the target of their influence attempts. Marks and McAdam (1994), pursuing the same logic, note that the growth of regional transnational authorities created around threatened areas such as rivers and lakes is leading to a parallel increase of subnational mobilization within European environmental movements that is, nevertheless, transnational in substantive focus.

And while actual authority appears to be evolving toward the EU, it is not at all clear that a similar pattern of increasingly concentrated transnational authority is occurring elsewhere at the regional or at the global level. Few of the papers in this volume focus directly upon changes in the locus of authority, although many of the authors clearly assume a broad trend in the transnationalization of authority. But the capacity to make binding decisions has eluded the UN throughout most of its first fifty years, and it is clear that this capacity is not the resource controlled by intergovernmental bodies—such as the UN— that is of greatest value to transnational movements. The possibility of gaining legitimacy and increased access to global media discourse aimed at changing consciousness may be sufficient to account for the pattern of rapid growth of TSMOs described in chapter 3.

The increased likelihood that transnational activists will seek access to transnational forums may reflect these rational tactical goals, or simply the increased availability of such forums, but probably a combination of the two. That there are many forums in which TSMO activists can gain a hearing for their framing of issues is evident in this book, most particularly in the chapters by Atwood, Levering, and Hovey. Activists contribute to creating such forums, as with the UN Special Sessions on Disarmament, and then use the forums to their own purposes. Clearly the scope and strength of intergovernmental institutional forums influence the dynamics of transnational movements.

The dominant logic that guides this way of considering the impact of transnational political opportunity upon the behavior of transnational movements ignores their efforts within nations and the extent to which national political opportunity structures affect the variable likelihood of transnational activism. Koopmans's work (1995, 60–63), which compares the political level of the target of protest, suggests that national political opportunity structures are quite important in shaping the extent of protest with transnational targets. He shows that some nations (e.g., Switzerland and the Netherlands) experience a far greater proportion of protest events aimed at international targets (approximately 25 percent) than do other systems (e.g., Germany and France, with about 10 percent of protests). These differences appear strongly related to the extent of national mobilization of the third-world solidarity movement in each nation. Following this logic, comparative analyses of the role of national political opportunity structures in fostering extranational solidarity movements may be a more productive line of research for understanding the level of transnational mobilization than focusing upon the role of transnational political opportunity structures.

Repertoires of Contention

Although social movement strategies and tactics are typically seen as the somewhat independent collective initiatives of activists, social movement analysts have increasingly come to view them instead as dependent variables that are highly contingent upon framing choices (Dalton 1994), movement organizational structural configurations (McCarthy et al. 1991), and—most importantly—political opportunity structures.

Strategic repertoires can be conceived of as some mix of public education, direct aid to victims of injustice, and attempts to change structures directly (McCarthy and Wolfson 1996). A wide variety of tactics may be used to achieve each of these aims. Many analysts have defined a subclass of collective efforts as social movements by the tactics employed—movements are those efforts where unorthodox tactics are paramount. Movements can be characterized, in a more nuanced approach, by the routine mix of strategies and tactics they employ—their repertoire of contention. Recently, however, it has become clear that collective efforts that most observers would agree are social movements employ a diverse set of tactics in attempting to achieve their goals, including typically both the most orthodox tactics as well as some unorthodox ones (McCarthy, Smith, and Zald 1996). Clearly public education is one of the primary strategies that the TSMOs chronicled in this book use for attempting to bring about social change. In addition, it seems that these TSMOs rarely employ unruly or disruptive tactics. And, although Greenpeace has become widely known for its use of quite unorthodox tactics, the rate of use of even the most routine protest tactic of public demonstrations seems extremely low among TSMOs, in contrast to national SMOs. Rucht recognizes this contrast, concluding that it constitutes an important weakness for transnational movements: National movements employing a range of conventional and unruly tactics reveal that "radical flanks" of highly disruptive protesters can be of great help in advancing the aims of mass movements.

Yet it is not at all clear that the widespread impression concerning the relative paucity of transnational protest is correct. Public protests are common at the UN Headquarters in New York, and they may be more common than is widely recognized in Geneva and Brussels. Public protest is effective only if it is widely known (Lipsky 1968), and the mass media are even more crucial in bringing transnational protest to

wide public attention than they are for national or local protest. Without access to good systematic international protest event data, such as
police records or movement archives chronicling protest, we should be
especially cautious about our impressions gained from media coverage
about transnational protest. We now know a good bit about what
features of national level protests make them more likely to be the
object of media attention (Snyder and Kelly 1977; McCarthy, McPhail,
and Smith 1996). These features include distance of the media institution from the protest event as well as the size and unruliness of the
event. Given the typical commitment to nonviolence of many transnational movements and the great distances involved, it would be reasonable to predict that routine protests by transnational movements at
the UN in New York could expect precious little coverage around the
world. Of course, this claim is easily open to empirical test.

In any case, the main outlines of typical transnational repertoires of
contention are not yet clear because we lack systematic evidence about
the scope and shape of transnational protest and the transnational
social movement sector is in its adolescence—routinized repertoires of
contention emerge and become institutionalized slowly over the life of
movement sectors.

Conclusion

The recent and rapid expansion of knowledge about the dynamics
of social movements is an important result of the development of
more or less standardized methods of systematic data collection and
analysis. To the well-developed and powerful methodology of individual survey research has been added protest event analysis (Olzak 1989;
Rucht and Olemacher 1992), organizational analysis (Young et al. 1993;
Dalton 1994; Walker 1991; Minkoff 1995; McCarthy and Wolfson 1996),
and network analysis (Diani 1994). These approaches make individuals, protest events, SMOs, and networks of one or the other, respectively, the central unit of analysis. Each depends upon identifying
populations of the unit of analysis, sampling those populations, gathering systematic information about features of the sampled units, and
relating that aggregate evidence to time series or comparative evidence
of social structure, political structure, and public discourse. These
methods have been generated largely to address the main theoretical
questions raised by the conceptual tools that have provided the structure for the preceding discussion: strategic framing processes, activist
identities, mobilizing structures, resource mobilization, political opportunity structures, and repertoires of contention.

Case studies of movements and of TSMOs can be of great value, as essays in this book illustrate. They are a necessary first step in isolating the key contrasts between TSMOs and the TSMS and SMOs and SMSs. The high quality of the preceding analyses, incorporating in great measure our most useful conceptual tools, provides a enormous first step toward understanding the dynamics of transnational social movements, bringing that study into the theoretical mainstream. But if the study of transnational movements is to fully join the mainstream of social movement analysis, it must also be based upon newly generated, or aggregated, systematic evidence about the shape and extent of transnational social movements over time and across space. Once that terrain has been more sufficiently mapped, the theoretical value of case studies of TSMOs, selected according to the coordinates of that map, can be immense.

Transnational Social Movements, World Politics, and Global Governance

Chadwick F. Alger

Abstract

Mainstream international relations research has been preoccupied with states as central actors in world politics and has tended to exclude actors like those described in this volume. The cases here demonstrate how transnational social movements can mobilize transnational resources in national conflicts, generate constituencies for multilateral policy, and target international institutions to affect interstate relations. Five categories of transnational social movement activity may be identified here: creating and mobilizing global networks, participating in multilateral political arenas, facilitating interstate cooperation, acting within states, and enhancing public participation. Evidence from the preceding case studies helps illustrate how social movement actors accomplish these tasks. From an examination of the contributions of TSMOs' activities to global governance come suggestions for further research on transnational social movements and their relations to other global actors.

Mainstream international relations research still tends to assume that analysis of world politics requires different concepts and theories than politics in other settings, thereby isolating the study of world politics from the mainstreams of social science. This volume refutes that assumption and builds bridges across the chasms separating sociology and international relations research and writing.

The preoccupation of political scientists with the state, particularly those concerned with interstate relations—usually less precisely labeled as "international" relations—has inhibited their capacity to perceive realistically other actors crossing state boundaries. Sociologists, especially those in North America, have tended to limit their inquiry to behavior within societies, which are customarily assumed to have the same borders as states. Exceptions include Elise Boulding (1976), Louis Kriesberg (1982), and Robert Angell (1969), but these efforts have had little effect on the mainstream of international relations research in North America.

This volume breaches the fragmentation within political science that has retarded comprehension of a rapidly changing world. By applying insights from social movement analysis within states to social movements that cross state boundaries, this volume not only broadens understanding of social movements by abandoning limitations that territorial boundaries have imposed on inquiry but also deepens understanding of world politics.

Examining how transnational social movement organizations (TSMOs) mobilize transnational resources in domestic conflicts, generate constituencies for multilateral policy, and target international institutions, the preceding cases reveal the roles of TSMOs in linking state and local action with global political processes. Any reader must be impressed by the variety of TSMO activities, the range of activities in which they are engaged, and the diversity of issues in which they become involved. Indeed, the wide scope of transnational social movement efforts complicates this effort to evaluate the contributions of this study to the emerging body of research on transnational social movements.

TSMO Activities and Global Politics

This political scientist was overwhelmed by the diverse array of kinds of TSMO activities—some thirty—revealed in only nine case studies in this volume. In order to assess the implications of TSMO actions for global politics, I grouped these activities into five categories: Creating and mobilizing global networks, participating in multilateral political arenas, facilitating interstate cooperation, acting within states, and enhancing public participation.

Creating and Mobilizing Global Networks

All TSMOs (1) *create transnational organizations* with a headquarters, periodic meetings of representatives from a number of countries for making policy on one or more global issues, and establish secretariats

TABLE 15.1.

Activities of TSMOs Illustrated in Chapters 5 to 13

---

1. *Creating and Activating Global Networks*
    1. Create transnational organizations (7)*
    2. Gather information on local conditions through contacts around world (7)
    3. Alert global network of supporters to conditions requiring attention (7)
    4. Create emergency response network around world (5)
    5. Mobilize pressure from outside states (7)

2. *Participating in Multilateral Political Arenas*
    6. Mobilize TSMOs around issues in IGOs (8)
    7. Build TSMO coalitions (12)
    8. Raise new issues (12)
    9. Support IGO development (10)
    10. Address IGO meetings (8)
    11. Submit documents to IGO meetings (8)
    12. Improve skills in conference diplomacy (8)
    13. Increase expertise on issues (8)

3. *Facilitating Inter-state Cooperation*
    14. Prepare background papers and reports (13)
    15. Educate delegates (12)
    16. Educate representatives of states to narrow technical gap (13)
    17. Serve as third party source of information (13)
    18. Expand policy options (10)
    19. Facilitate agreement (12)
    20. Bring delegates together in third party fora (13)

4. *Acting Within States*
    21. Linking to local partners (6)
    22. Linking TSMOs with complementary skills (5)
    23. Working in state arenas to harmonize state policies (10)
    24. Humanitarian Aid (6)
    25. Development (6)
    26. Protective Accompaniment of persons in danger (5)

5. *Enhancing Public Participation*
    27. Remind government delegates that they are being watched (9)
    28. Enhance public understanding (9)
    29. Increase transparency of international negotiations and institutions (10)
    30. Link to local partners (6)
    31. Provoke public protest (9)

---

* Numbers in parenthesis indicate the chapter in which an example of this activity can be found

to implement these policies. The case of the Service for Peace and Justice in Latin America (SERPAJ) suggests that TSMOs tend to emerge out of more informal networks composed of local organizations and individuals linked through common concerns. This case study (chap. 7) illustrates how TSMOs employ these networks in implementing organizational policies.

Whether working for human rights, ecology, or some other issue, TSMOs often employ their transnational networks to (2) *gather information* on local conditions through contacts around the world. At times this effort may involve systematic monitoring of local conditions, as with the human rights infringements of military dictatorships in Latin America (chap. 7) or Sri Lanka (chap. 5). When appropriate, this information is then used to (3) *alert global networks of supporters* about conditions requiring attention. When evidence merits action, as exemplified by the emergency relief delivered in Eritrea and Tigray (chap. 6), TSMOs may (4) *create an emergency response network* around the world. When conditions limit, or make very costly, challenges within states, TSMOs may (5) *mobilize pressure from the outside,* which SERPAJ activists did in bringing international pressure against the Argentine government through the Nobel Peace Prize initiative.

Participating in Multilateral Political Arenas

Atwood's discussion (chap. 8) of the UN Special Sessions on Disarmament (SSDs) illustrates the now widespread efforts to (6) *Mobilize TSMOs around issues in intergovernmental organizations (IGOs).* This mobilization, of course, includes the regular scheduled meetings of assemblies and councils throughout the UN system and in other IGOs. As exemplified by the efforts of Quakers in working for the human right of conscientious objection (chap. 12), these efforts often include (7) *building TSMO coalitions around specific issues.* At the same time, this case revealed that TSMOs not only respond to issues placed on IGO agendas by governments and secretariats but also (8) raise new issues. TSMOs are often active in supporting the (9) *development of multilateral institutions,* as illustrated by the activities of EarthAction (chap. 10). At the same time, TSMOs have tended to push for expansion of their roles in the political processes of IGOs. Two examples are opportunities provided for TSMOs by the UN SSDs to (10) *formally address* the *Ad Hoc Committee* and (11) *submit documents for listing and display.* This case also illuminates the importance of growing TSMO participation in IGO political processes with respect to (12) *improving conference diplomacy skills* of TSMOs and (13) *increasing their expertise on issues.*

Facilitating Interstate Cooperation

TSMOs not only seek to shape the agendas and policy positions of IGO delegates and their governments but also desire to contribute to the attainment of interstate agreements in multilateral settings. Toward this end, reliable background information that documents problems and rationales for multilateral agreements may be very useful. Sometimes this is achieved through (14) *preparing background papers and reports*, as was done by the Neptune Group in the Third UN Law of the Sea Conference (UNCLOS III).

(15) *Education of delegates* may help these individuals become advocates for social movement goals. Such efforts include luncheon meetings and weekend seminars, as in the case of Quaker efforts in lobbying for the human right of conscientious objection. A special kind of education takes place in efforts to (16) *educate representatives to narrow the technical gap*. For example, efforts of the Neptune Group to enhance the technical competence of some African, Asian, and Latin American delegates with respect to certain highly technical issues regarding law of the sea.

Often movement toward interstate agreement may be inhibited not by the lack of information, but rather by a flood of contention arising from the differing viewpoints of those claiming expertise. In such cases, some trusted TSMOs, such as the Neptune Group, can serve as (17) *third-party sources of information*. Agreement may also be impossible when groups of states hold tenaciously to opposing policy options. On such occasions TSMOs can facilitate agreement by (18) *expanding policy options* to include one that may be acceptable to opposing groups, as demonstrated by EarthAction on biological diversity and climate change issues. TSMOs may also be more directly involved in playing third-party roles in IGO political processes, as the Quakers and the Neptune Group did.

Sometimes (19) *facilitating agreement* may be practiced in more informal ways—in corridors, receptions, luncheons, etc.—that are a normal part of multilateral diplomacy. Third-party roles may also be played in much more formal settings by (20) *bringing delegates together into a third-party forum*, as with the meetings for delegates, secretariat, and experts convened by the Neptune Group during the Law of the Sea Treaty negotiations.

In discussing the contributions of nongovernmental organizations (NGOs) to the creation and strengthening of international human rights norms, Ann Marie Clark developed a list of requirements for "a third-party model of norm generation" that complements this group of TSMO activities drawn from the case studies in the volume. She concludes that an organization is effective when (a) its purpose appears to be independent from one state or group's point of view; (b) it has information and expertise that states would not be likely to gather on their own; (c) it can convey a sense that its independence is a result of representativeness, either of principle or broad public opinion, or both; and (d) it invokes existing principles in a way that refers to concrete behavior and extends the reference to real or potential new cases of violation (A. M. Clark 1996, 17–18).

Acting within States

The nine case studies also reveal that the activities of TSMOs penetrate states in a diversity of ways. As humanitarian action in the Horn of Africa illustrates (chap. 6), some TSMOs reach inside states and (21) *link with local partners*. In this case, Emergency Relief Desk (ERD), a coalition of church-based donors, was able to link with local churches. ERD thus complemented War on Want (WOW), which had no natural local partners, and the International Committee of the Red Cross (ICRC), which negotiated with government and opposition leaders.

The Sri Lanka case (chap. 5) illustrates the need for the involvement of TSMOs that perform separate functions but also the value in (22) *linking TSMOs with complementary skills*. In responding to the predicament of a militant Tamil, the ICRC visited him in prison and documented his case, Amnesty International gave his predicament visibility in major daily newspapers, and Peace Brigades International offered protective accompaniment after his release from prison.

Complementary to TSMO efforts to facilitate interstate cooperation in multilateral settings are efforts to (23) *harmonize state policies through efforts in state arenas* before interstate negotiations begin. Such attempts at harmonization include the alerts sent by EarthAction to citizen groups in many countries in an effort to create national constituencies for multilateral responses to environmental problems (chap. 10).

Perhaps TSMOs are most known for their (24) *delivery of humanitarian aid*, as clearly exemplified in efforts in the Horn of Africa. This case illuminates the complexities confronted by organizations attempting to obtain needed resources, deal with governments in both recipient and donor countries, maintain relations with contending / warring parties, and conduct necessary relations with a diversity of other involved parties. Particularly illuminating are the differing definitions of "neutrality"—as *balance* by ERD, as *advocacy* by WOW, as *neutral humanitarian intermediary* by the ICRC. But here again, as in (22) above, there are indications that these differing approaches can make complementary contributions.

Local development activities of TSMOs (chap. 25) are likewise widely known, and also usefully exemplified by the Horn of Africa case. Particularly useful here is portrayal of the growing tendency to design humanitarian aid strategies that lead to sustained development rather than sustained dependency. In this case it was WOW that funded grassroots agriculture and health projects of two local consortia, making the poorest people active participants in their own economic development.

Many readers probably found (26) *protective accompaniment of persons in danger*—as practiced by Peace Brigades International in Sri Lanka— the most surprising contribution of TSMOs. In chapter 5 we learned that protective accompaniment may involve regular visits to persons deemed to be in danger, may require presence only when a person is engaged in public actions considered to be risky, or may involve constant, twenty-four-hour accompaniment. Accompaniment is necessarily complemented by regular communication with government officials, police, or paramilitary groups thought likely to harm the accompanied person.

Enhancing Public Participation

In many ways TSMOs are attempting to expand direct public involvement in the issues they seek to affect. Of course, these efforts tend to be directed toward activating people in support of the goals and policies of specific TSMOs, rather than toward broadening public participation itself. TSMOs must overcome the general problem of relative public ignorance of and disengagement from foreign policy processes and international negotiations. Most of the cases presented in this volume—such as those involving law of the sea, the environment, the right of conscientious objection—are not in the headlines. They are acted out in organizations familiar to only a few, in conferences rarely reported, which deal with issues about which most journalists have no knowledge, slight awareness, and little interest. TSMOs must confront these challenges if they are to (27) *remind government delegates that they are being watched.* This point is made specifically with respect to the UN Special Sessions on Disarmament but is obviously relevant for the other cases.

The cases here show that many TSMOs work hard to (28) *enhance public understanding.* TSMOs were responsible for whatever public awareness and understanding there was on the UN Special Sessions on Disarmament. EarthAction's global campaigns, focused on making global environmental issues matter for local and national elections, involved broad educational campaigns focused on legislators, journalists, members of environmental organizations, and the general electorate.

TSMOs face a severe challenge in (29) *increasing the transparency of international negotiations and institutions.* Chapter 11 reveals how progress on environmental policy for the European Union is hampered by the fact that the offices of TSMOs in Brussels are cut off from their rank and file membership within individual European countries. Strategies for overcoming this problem are vividly demonstrated by efforts of EarthAction (chap. 10), following the UN Conference on Environment and Development (UNCED). In the case of the Convention to Combat Desertification, EarthAction helped partners influence interstate negotiations at the early stages, issued informational toolkits on the convention, facilitated coverage by journalists, and provided background information for those interested in attending the negotiations or becoming more involved with the Intergovernmental Negotiating Committee for a Convention to Combat Decertification (INCD).

At times TSMOs can enhance public participation in transnational efforts by (30) *linking to local partners,* thereby offering participants in local organizations outlets for transnational reach. (We have already indicated in (21) above how such linking can enable TSMOs to exercise influence within states.) The Service for Peace and Justice in Latin America enabled local cadres to employ transnational contacts for informing the outside world about conditions and for mobilizing responsive support for SERPAJ goals. In another example, the International Mobilization for Survival enabled many local disarmament organizations to become part of a global effort.

Finally, TSMOs are likely to attract the most public and media attention when they offer outlets for participation by (31) *provoking public protests.* This was clearly illustrated by demonstrations targeting the UN Special Sessions on Disarmament, including those in Britain, Canada, Japan, the Netherlands, the United States, and at UN headquarters and diplomatic missions in New York City (chap. 8). Indeed, for the most part this was the only TSMO activity in connection with the SSDs that received press attention. But the use of public demonstrations, the most routine protest tactic of national social movement organizations (SMOs) appears extremely infrequent among TSMOs. If this observation is correct, we should consider whether expanding opportunities for public participation through greater use of demonstrations serves broader political change and public mobilization goals.

This inventory of TSMO activities clearly illuminates dimensions of a global political process in which most effective TSMOs must be involved. Obviously they must *create and mobilize global networks* in order to become global actors. It is equally clear that they must *partici-*

pate in multilateral political arenas. Perhaps less apparent is that, in most issues, transnational social movement success depends upon the capacity of TSMOs to facilitate *interstate cooperation.* At the same time, it is not always fully appreciated that success in these three endeavors often requires efforts to bring transnational political processes into domestic arenas, that is, *internalize multilateral politics.* It is sometimes forgotten that success over the long term necessarily requires TSMOs to *enhance public participation.* Whether the issue involves human rights, environment, development, or some other issue, sustained solutions for global problems must eventually be implemented in the human settlements of the world. And such implementations require broad public understanding and participation.

At the same time, this portrayal of activities helps illuminate the diversity of arenas in which TSMOs must be active: (a) within their own networks, (b) in multilateral politics, (c) in the cooperative interstate activities that provide supportive background for—and overlay —these conferences, (d) within states, and (e) within the various social settings where the larger public can be educated and mobilized, both within and across states. Obviously, as the Horn of Africa and Sri Lanka cases illustrate politics between nations, and politics between ethnic groups within fragmented states often enhance the challenges confronted by TSMOs. Certainly the cases in this book reveal that TSMOs are growing in their awareness of the multiple-arena challenges of success in global politics. And it is obvious that some, as the activities of EarthAction and the Neptune Group show, are becoming adept at designing multiple-arena strategies.

TSMOs and Global Governance

Despite the fact that we have covered an unusually broad field in this excursion into one aspect of global politics, one important dimension remains to be considered. As organizations such as Peace Brigades International, SERPAJ, Emergency Relief Desk, War On Want, EarthAction, and the Neptune Group attempt to advance *their* solutions to problems, what is their long-term vision of the institutions that will be needed for sustained competence to solve this problem? In other words, what is their long-term vision of global governance in their field of competence? This question must be asked because TSMOs are a key dimension of emerging global governance—alongside states, IGOs, multinational corporations (MNCs), and various *mobilizing structures* such as churches and labor. In the introduction of *NGOs, the UN and Global Governance,* Thomas G. Weiss and Leon Gordenker assert:

NGOs are omnipresent in the policy and administrative process of UN organizations; the extent of their participation has progressively deepened. The turbulent pluralism of the NGO realm has clearly brought new and unanticipated groups into the process. Without attributing either a positive or negative value to NGO activity, it can nevertheless be recognized as a factor in global governance. (1996, 44–45)

The realm covered by Weiss and Gordenker includes many TSMOs that, by definition, are striving to "change some elements of the social structure and/or reward distribution of society." (McCarthy and Zald 1977, 1217). Are these conscious of the degree to which their short-term responses to pressing problems are creating fragments of global governance with long-term consequences?

Pushing even further: To what degree are TSMOs conscious of the necessary interdependence of the global problem that is the focus of their concern with other problems. War On Want demonstrated this concern in the Horn of Africa as it attempted to build long-term development into its approach to humanitarian assistance. It is likely that many Quakers involved in pursuing conscientious objection to military service as a human right see this also as building support for a demilitarized world. No doubt many others involved in the cases in this book perceive the interdependence of problem agendas—humanitarian relief, development, disarmament, human rights, environment, law of the sea, etc. What, then, are the broader visions of global governance toward which TSMOs aspire? A highly centralized UN system or a loose network of agencies focusing on specific problems? What role will regional IGOs play? Are new institutions required for strengthening TSMO input into IGOs—such as proposals for a UN Parliamentary Assembly, or a Second Assembly for representatives of TSMOs?

Finally, how should responsibilities be divided between TSMOs and IGOs? For example, some TSMOs now complain that, because of inadequate UN financing, they are having to fulfill functions that should be the responsibility of UN secretariats, such as monitoring the fulfillment of human rights and environment treaties. The response of UN secretariat people is that limited resources prevent them from carrying out these tasks. What are alternatives for UN financing that might permit the UN to carry out these functions? While addressing her remarks only to "African development," and focusing on NGOs broadly, Isebil V. Gruhn is concerned that "the current trend of transferring development policy making and delivery into the hands of NGOs is counter productive and will weaken the international public capacity so desperately needed" (1996, 17).

The point here is not that TSMOs should consume considerable time and resources in debating their broad vision for global governance, but that they should explicitly recognize that they are obviously engaged in "experiments" in global governance and should more self-consciously be evaluating the results. As TSMOs address a specific global problem, I am urging that they engage in a continuous, self-conscious dialogue between practice and a continually developing vision of future global governance. At the same time, TSMOs should be pondering not only what kinds of holistic visions of global governance would be compatible with their goals, but also what kinds of roles TSMOs should play in these visions. It would be difficult to overemphasize how important it is for TSMOs to address these concerns: If they do not, they will abandon the field to other actors, particularly states and MNCs.

Conclusion

Applying sociological research on national social movements to analyses of transnational movements has proved useful in exploring the recent expansion of transnational social movement activity. This effort has generated several themes that seem useful in guiding further inquiry. The cases presented here provide a useful starting point, forcing us beyond the question of *whether* transnational relations exist to the more difficult question of *how* such relations affect global politics. In short, transnational social movements—according to the editors of this volume—shape global politics by mobilizing transnational resources in national conflicts, generating constituencies for multilateral policy, and targeting international institutions.

Comparative case studies are necessary to help us move beyond these rather general observations towards more systematic understandings of the conditions under which social movements effectively shape policy. Studies like that of DeMars (chap. 6) can offer considerable enlightenment by comparing the use of different strategies in the same social context. But there is also a need for comparisons across different issue areas and across multinational and national political arenas. Such comparisons would enhance insight on the significance of problem and arena differences for TSMO strategies.

No doubt each reader, whether a researcher or a participant in TSMO activity, will have an agenda of specifically what should be compared, or even what should be the focus of single case studies. The seven research suggestions that follow are intended to provoke new thinking about the relationship between TSMOs and world politics.

1. Particularly in the context of defining, and pursuing, *global* values

there is great value in comparative study of strategic *framing campaigns*. Whether the problem be threats to peace, human rights, ecological balance, development, or sustainable development, these values tend to be defined in the context of differing *local* threats. Framing campaigns must be widely responsive to threats experienced in differing contexts. What factors enhance or detract from successful transnational framing campaigns?

2. More must be known about *mobilizing structures*, what McCarthy in the preceding chapter describes as "more or less formally organized everyday life patterns upon which movements build collective action, ranging from religious groups and neighborhood associations to workplace cliques and friendship groups" (p. 249). Such structures are the soil out of which TSMOs germinate. But because most education on international relations is state-centered, most TSMO activists do not have the knowledge, or analytic tools, that would enable them to perceive and interpret "the everyday life patterns" that transcend state borders. What *mobilizing structures* are available to specific movements and their TSMOs? How, when, and why do TSMOs arise out of these *mobilizing structures?* In what ways are these *mobilizing structures* important to the continuing success of mature transnational social movements?

The Horn of Africa case (chap. 6) suggests that the type of SMO from which a TSMO emerges will influence the type of strategies it can adopt as well as its success in intervening in particular conflicts, including how successfully it can attract domestic allies. The SERPAJ case (chap. 7) indicated that successful transnational cooperation in Latin America did not emerge until Catholic organizers replaced Protestant ones: Thus, ideological foundations of TSMOs seem important.

3. More needs to be known about how TSMOs combine efforts in *domestic political opportunity structures* and *international political opportunity structures*. Is it more effective to focus relations with some kinds of states, or regimes, in their capitals and those with others in IGOs? Should the nature of the issue determine where emphasis is placed?

Helpful here would be additional comparative studies of *international political opportunity structures*, such as, Kendall Stiles's striking comparison of relations of the World Bank, the United Nations Children's Emergency Fund (UNICEF), and the United Nations Development Programme (UNDP) with "local NGOs." He notes that "the World Bank, with its strong ties to the West and to liberal economic principles, has been most reticent of the three about engaging politically mobilized Southern NGOs. UNICEF, on the other hand, has embraced an emerging advocacy role with great enthusiasm. . . . UNDP has adopted a more tentative and mixed approach" (Stiles 1996, 11).

In a plea for a broader approach to human rights campaigns, Sigrun
I. Skogly urges a broader definition of *international political opportunity
structure* that includes "international private actors" such as "international banking and transnational corporations." Skogly also implies
that the definition of *domestic political opportunity structure* should extend beyond justice departments and foreign offices, noting that "international human rights standards should be as much a concern for the
ministry of agriculture, the ministry of finance and the national bank."
(Skogly 1996, 10–12) From Skogly's insights we may conclude that,
while studies of TSMOs should certainly not ignore states—and their
IGO extensions—it would be a mistake to limit our attention to the
state's foreign policy apparatus and to limit our definition of international organizations to IGOs.

4. More should be learned about the *identities and careers of TSMO
activists.* From what kinds of backgrounds do strongly committed and
effective leaders emerge? What kinds of TSMO experiences lead to
enduring commitment? Is it better to have long-term commitment or
frequent change of leadership and infusion of new blood? In light
of problem linkage, would strategies for rotating leaders, and active
members, among different TSMOs be a good thing?

Participants in TSMOs clearly learn much through their work, particularly with respect to identifying and exploiting opportunities for
promoting change in national and multilateral political arenas. This
point has been emphasized in the context of the SSDs (chap. 8),
UNCLOS (chap. 13), and the Human Rights Commission (chap. 12).
Probably this learning is being shared among participants within specific TSMOs, but it needs to be codified in such a way that it can be
shared more widely—and evaluated by researchers.

5. What are the strategies employed in successful, transnational *resource mobilization,* including financial, volunteer labor, and in-kind
support? Is there a relationship between monetary wealth of TSMOs
and achievement of goals? What kinds of resources, from what kinds
of sources, facilitate effective, long-term operations and sustained
problem solving? For example, states—and recipients of their financial
support—are criticized by some for shifting responsibility for refugees
to IGOs and NGOs or INGOs.

Cheryl Shanks voices fears that some NGOs could become "simply
front organizations for IGOs, carrying out IGO policies with IGO
money." On the other hand, she fears that NGOs could "use IGOs and
states simply as willing check-writers," with the possible consequence
that they will "both become like states and become 'front groups'
linked to a state ideological position that they put in place" (Shanks
1996, 15–16). Shanks reminds us about the potential relationship be-

tween *resource mobilization* and the capacity of TSMOs to bring social change, alerting us to influences that might shape the direction of that change.

6. Transnational social movements represent attempts by excluded, disenfranchised groups to change fundamental structures and policies of much stronger actors. Thus, social movements typically must co-operate with other actors—both within and outside of government—to advance their goals. Research on transnational social movements must address questions about *transnational coalition building*. When are coalitions useful? How can resistance to them be overcome? What are the characteristics of successful coalitions? Are standards needed for determining when they have outlived their usefulness and should be abandoned? What procedures for ending coalitions are best able to facilitate continuing positive relations among former coalition partners?

In a similar vein, when does growth in the number of TSMOs focusing on a single issue advance common goals and when does it undermine collective efforts? Do many smaller organizations tend to engage more active and dedicated participants than a few larger ones? Is it useful to have TSMOs emerging out of different *mobilizing structures*—some with roots in religious organizations, some in labor, etc.? Does the presence of many smaller organizations offer opportunities for an effective division of labor, with specialists on specific agenda items, on specific IGOs, and even specific regions?

Fred Gale has offered a relevant example in his account of the role of "progressive NGOs" in "environmental coalitions contesting the tropical timber trade regime." He notes two major cleavages. The first divides organizations desiring within-system change and those for fundamental systemic transformation. The second divides organizations centered in the North, which tend to combine environment and human rights issues, from those centered in the South, which place greater emphasis on "a development imperative." Yet Gale concludes that the "cleavages were neither all-embracing nor all consuming" and that there has been a considerable amount of interorganizational learning (Gale 1996, 20–21). Gale's conclusion suggests that, in this case, a variety of SMOs were needed to successfully represent and articulate a diversity of interests. The International Tropical Timber Council (ITTA) provided a useful setting in which these interests could be aggregated.

A problem related to the question of how TSMOs cooperate and work in complementary ways to promote global change is that of how governments can and do seek to frustrate change efforts by, for instance, creating their own so-called NGOs—termed government

NGOs or GONGOs—to complicate efforts by TSMOs and other NGOs to reach consensus positions and to otherwise plan common strategies. Lawrence Wittner's study of the international movement against nuclear weapons, for instance, demonstrates the obstacles posed for the movement by the Soviet Union's sponsorship and control of the World Peace Council (vol. 1, 1993).

7. Research is needed to assess the kinds of TSMO strategies that have been most successful in *facilitating interstate cooperation*. What qualifications must TSMO activists have in order to effectively advance collaborative global problem solving? Where should efforts be focused —in providing third-party information, in expanding policy options, in creating third-party forums, or in changing public attitudes, values, and perceptions?

Conversely, when must social change advocates engage in more disruptive activities in order to bring their concerns onto global political agendas and effect change? The occurrence and usefulness of disruptive tactics, including public demonstrations, in transnational social movement campaigns must be better understood. Is there any difference in their usefulness in national and international settings? Is there any difference in effective methods in the two settings? How can accurate information be attained so that comparison of their use in the two settings will be valid? Does their absence in some transnational social movement campaigns signal a movement's co-optation?

Whatever the specific research question, students and scholars must place contemporary TSMOs—as they should do for other serious human efforts—in historical contexts that include both the present *and* the future. In other words, transnational movements must be seen as part of a more enduring and nurturing "quiet revolution," to recall Chatfield's metaphor at the beginning of chapter 2 (pp. 19–20). We must accept Elise Boulding's challenge to place our thinking about "global civic culture" in the "200-year present"—i.e., in the context of the entire twentieth and twenty-first centuries (Boulding 1988, 1–15). Regrettably, histories to which most people are exposed neglect this part of the story. Fuller knowledge of TSMO history will both enlighten and empower present, and future, movements.

Certainly, present application of new technologies in communication, transportation, manufacturing, marketing, and finance has presented humankind with a growing array of pressing global problems. These changes have brought with them a qualitative and quantitative change in collective social change efforts by enhancing capacities for organizing and utilizing TSMOs in response to problems. Nevertheless, it is important to know that the efforts of humankind to enlarge, and speed, their global reach extend deep into history. Movements against violations of the rights of slaves, women, workers, freedom of religion, self-determination, and peace have had rich historical experience, and the strategies that they have pursued—whether successful or unsuccessful—provide important lessons.

More generally, TSMOs must develop the capacity to be more explicit about the future world order their movements seek. Frequently unwitting architects of emerging forms of global governance, TSMOs must recognize their role and develop capacities for pondering the long-term consequences of short-term strategies. At the same time, movement participants must acquire the competence to place the governance which they are creating for *their* problem in the larger context of governance for an array of global problems. Scholars have a responsibility to assist participants in TSMOs to acquire this competence. They can help make assumptions about the future that underly TSMO actions more explicit. And they can help place the likely long-term consequences of these actions in the context of specific alternative futures for global governance.

WORKS CITED

INDEX

WORKS CITED

Abeysekera, Charles. 1992. "The Limits of Space." *Index on Censorship* 7: 28.

Abi-Saab, Georges. 1988. "Non-International Armed Conflicts." In *International Dimensions of Humanitarian Law*. Dordrecht: Martinus Nijhoff.

Abi-Saab, Rosemary. 1986. *Droit Humanitaire et Conflits Internes — Origines et Evolution de la Réglementation Internationale*. Geneva: Institut Henry Dunant.

Abrams, Irwin. 1988. *The Nobel Peace Prize and the Laureates: An Illustrated Biographical History, 1901–1987*.

Acuña, Carlos. 1995. Interview by R. Pagnucco. 15 Apr., Notre Dame, Ind.

Africa Watch. 1991. *Evil Days: 30 Years of War and Famine in Ethiopia*. An Africa Watch Report. New York: Human Rights Watch.

Akashi, Yasushi, 1988. "Is There Still Life after SSD III?" Paper presented at the National Convention of the United Nations Association of the United States of America, New York, 12 July. Mimeographed.

Ally, Terry, and Chris Gollop. 1993. "NGOs Knock Timid Approach of Small Island States." Inter Press Service, 29 Sept.

American Almanac, The. 1996. Austin, Tex.: Hoover's.

Amnesty International (AI). 1991. *Conscientious Objection to Military Service*. London: AI.

———. 1993. *Sri Lanka-Arbitrary arrests of hundreds of Tamil people*. London: AI.

———. 1994. *Sri Lanka: Balancing Human Rights and Security: Abuse of Arrest and Detention Powers in Colombo*. London: AI.

Amnesty International USA (AIUSA). 1981. *'Disappearances': A Workbook*. New York: AI USA.

Anderson, Mary B., and Peter J. Woodrow. 1989. *Rising from the Ashes: Development Strategies in Times of Disaster*. Boulder, Colo: Westview.

Andersen, S. Svein, and Kjell A. Eliassen. 1991. "European Community Lobbying." *European Journal of Political Research* 20, no. 2: 173–87.

Angell, Robert C. 1969. *Peace on the March: Transnational Participation*. New York: Van Nostrand Reinhold.

Archer, Angus. 1978. "New Forms of NGO Participation in World Conferences." In *Non-Governmental Organizations in International Cooperation for Development*, edited by Berhanykun Andemicael, 1–29. New York: United Nations Institute for Training and Research.

———. 1983. "Methods of Multilateral Management: the Interrelationship of Intergovernmental Organizations and NGOs." In *The United States, the UN and the Management of Global Change,* edited by Toby Trister Gati. New York: New York Univ. Press.

Arén, Gustav. 1978. *Evangelical Pioneers in Ethiopia: Origins of the Evangelical Church Mekane Yesus.* Stockholm, EFS Förlaget.

Asia Watch. 1993. *Halt Repatriation of Sri Lankan Tamils.* Asia Watch. New York: Human Rights Watch.

Atwood, David. 1982. "Non-Governmental Organizations and the 1978 United Nations Special Session on Disarmament." Ph.D. diss. Univ. of North Carolina, Chapel Hill.

———. 1983. "Action for Disarmament: Public Involvement and the United Nations Special Session on Disarmament." Paper presented at International Studies Association Annual Meeting, Mexico City, 7 Apr.

Bacchetta, Gian-Battista [ICRC Head Delegate in Sudan]. 1990. Interview by W. DeMars. 7 Dec., Geneva.

Benford, Robert D. 1993. "Frame Disputes within the Nuclear Disarmament Movement." *Social Forces* 71:677–701.

Bereket Habte Selassie. 1989. *Eritrea and the United Nations.* Trenton, N.J.: Red Sea Press.

Bernstein, Johanna. (EarthAction Regional Coordinator). 1995. Interview by J. Smith. Brussels, *Belgium* 23 Mar.

Bleiker, Roland. 1993. *Nonviolent Struggle and the Revolution in East Germany.* Monograph no. 6. Cambridge, Mass.: Albert Einstein Institution.

Blondel, Jean-Luc. 1987. "Getting Access to the Victims: Role and Activities of the ICRC." *Journal of Peace Research* 24: 307–14.

Bogdan, Robert C., and Sari Knoop Biklen. 1992. *Qualitative Research for Education: An Introduction to Theory and Methods.* Boston: Allyn and Bacon.

Bomberg, Elizabeth. 1993. "Policy Networks and the European Community." Paper presented at Third Biennial International Conference of the European Community Studies Association, Washington, D.C., 27–29 May.

Borosage, Robert. 1983. "The Bilateral Box." *Working Papers* (May / June): 37–40.

Boulding, Elise. 1976. *The Underside of History: A View of Women through Time.* Boulder, Colo.: Westview.

———. 1988. *Building a Global Civic Culture: Education for an Interdependent World.* New York: Teachers College, Columbia Univ.

Braunthal, Julius. 1967. *History of the International, Vol. 2, 1914–1943,* translated by Henry Collins and Kenneth Mitchell. New York: Praeger.

Briottet, Roger. 1991. Interview by W. DeMars. 30 Jan. London, U.K.

Brock, Peter. 1990. *The Quaker Peace Testimony.* Syracuse, N.Y.: Syracuse Univ. Press.

Brysk, Alison. 1990. The Political Impact of Argentina's Human Rights Movement: Social Movements, Transition and Democratization. Ph.D. diss., Stanford Univ.

———. 1992. "Acting Globally: International Relations and Indian Rights in Latin America." Paper presented at International Congress of the Latin American Studies Association; Los Angeles, Calif., Sept.

Bulathsinghala, Vincent. 1993. Interview by P. Coy. 6 Oct. Negombo, Sri Lanka.

Burstein, Paul, Rachel Einwohner, and Jocelyn Hollander. 1995. "The Success of Political Movements: A Bargaining Perspective." In *The Politics of Social Protest: Comparative Perspectives on States and Social Movements*, edited by J. Craig Jenkins and Bert Klandermans; 275–95. Minneapolis: Univ. of Minnesota Press.

Calhoun, Craig. 1993. "Nationalism and Ethnicity." *Annual Review of Sociology* 19: 211–39.

Caroll, John E., ed. 1988. *International Environmental Diplomacy: The Management and Resolution of Transnational Environmental Problems*. Cambridge: Cambridge Univ. Press.

Cassese, Antonio. 1979. "How Could Non-Governmental Organizations Use U.N. Bodies More Effectively?" *Universal Human Rights* 1, no. 4:73–80.

Chandraprema, C. A. 1991. *Sri Lanka: The Years of Terror, The JVP Insurrection 1987–1989*. Colombo, Sri Lanka: Lake House.

Chartier, Richard. 1980. "Adolfo Perez Esquivel: Behind the Man and the Prize." *Fellowship* (Dec.): 23.

———. 1984. Interview by R. Pagnucco. 28 Apr. Croton, N.Y.

Chatfield, Charles. 1969. "Pacifists and their Publics: The Politics of a Peace Movement." *Midwest Journal of Political Science* 13, no. 5: 298–312.

———. 1992. *The American Peace Movement: Ideals and Activism*. New York: Twayne.

Chiang, Pei-heng. 1981. *Non-Governmental Organizations at the United Nations: Identity, Role and Function*. New York: Praeger.

Civil Rights Movement. 1990. *The Geneva Conventions and the International Committee of the Red Cross: Their Relevance to Sri Lanka*. 3d ed. Colombo: Civil Rights Movement and Suriya Wickremasinghe.

Clark, Ann Marie. 1996. "The Contributions of Non-Governmental Organizations to the Creation and Strengthening of International Human Rights Norms." Paper presented at International Studies Association Annual Meeting, San Diego, Calif., 18–20 Apr.

Clark, Lance. 1986. *Early Warning Case Study: The 1984–85 Influx of Tigrayans into Eastern Sudan*. Working Paper no. 2. Washington, D.C.: Refugee Policy Group.

Claude, Richard Pierre, and Burns H. Weston, eds. 1992. *Human Rights in the World Community*. Philadelphia: Univ. of Pennsylvania Press.

Climate Action Network (CAN). 1994. International NGO Directory. Brussels: CAN.

Cohen, Alan. 1983. "U.N. General Assembly Adopts Nuclear Freeze Resolutions." *Freeze Newsletter* (official journal of the Nuclear Weapons Freeze Campaign) 3, no. 1 (Jan.): 14.

Cohen, Jean L. 1985. "Strategy or Identity: New Theoretical Paradigms and Contemporary Social Movements." *Social Research* 52:663–716.

Commission on Global Governance. 1995. *Our Global Neighborhood*. New York: Oxford Univ. Press.

Cooper, Sandi E. 1991. *Patriotic Pacifism: Waging War on War in Europe, 1815–1914*. New York: Oxford Univ. Press.

Corrigan Maguire, Mairead. 1994. Interview by R. Pagnucco. 1 Oct. Amsterdam.

Cortright, David. 1993. *Peace Works: The Citizen's Role in Ending the Cold War.* Boulder, Colo.: Westview.

Counterpoint. 1994. "Danish Aid and Human Rights in Sri Lanka." *Counterpoint,* Apr./May, 26–28.

Coutin, Susan Bibler. 1993. *The Culture of Protest: Religious Activism and the U.S. Sanctuary Movement.* Boulder, Colo.: Westview.

Coy, Patrick G. 1993. "Protective Accompaniment: How Peace Brigades International Secures Political Space and Human Rights Nonviolently." In *Nonviolence: Social and Psychological Issues,* edited by V. K. Kool. Latham, Md.: Univ. Press of America.

———. 1995. "Ethnicity and the Internationality of International Observers in a Post-Colonial Society." Paper presented at the biannual National Conference of Peacemaking and Conflict Resolution, Minneapolis, Minn., May 26–30.

———. 1997. "Going Where We Otherwise Would Not Have Gone: Nonviolent International Accompaniment by Peace Brigades International in Sri Lanka." Ph.D. diss., Syracuse Univ.

Curtis, Russell L., and Louis A. Zurcher. 1973. "Stable Resources of Protest Movements: The Multi-Organizational Field." *Social Forces* 52, no. 1: 53–61.

Dahrendorf, Ralf. 1959. *Class and Class Conflict in Industrial Society.* Stanford, Calif.: Stanford Univ. Press.

Dalton, Russell J. 1992. "Alliance Patterns of the European Environmental Movement." In *Green Politics II,* edited by Wolfgang Rüdig, 59–85. Edinburgh: Univ. of Edinburgh Press.

———. 1993. "Ideology and Social Movement Organizations: The European Environmental Movements." Irvine, Calif.: Unpublished paper.

———. 1994. *The Green Rainbow: Environmental Groups in Western Europe.* New Haven: Yale Univ. Press.

Davis, Calvin D. 1962. *The United States and the First Hague Peace Conference.* Ithaca.: Cornell Univ. Press.

DeMars, William. 1992. *Decade of Displacement in Ethiopia: Internally Displaced Persons and Humanitarian Response.* Washington, D.C.: Refugee Policy Group.

———. 1993. *Helping People in a People's War: Humanitarian Organizations and the Ethiopian Conflict, 1980–1988.* Ph.D. diss., Univ. of Notre Dame.

———. 1994. "Tactics of Protection: International Human Rights Organizations in the Ethiopian Conflict, 1980–1986." In *Africa, Human Rights, and the Global System,* edited by Eileen McCarthy-Arnolds, David R. Penna, and Debra Joy Cruz Sobrepeña. Westport, Conn.: Greenwood.

Deming, Marty. 1977. "Minutes: Meeting of European Groups Supporting Nonviolent Initiatives in Latin America." 1 Oct., Natoye, Belgium.

———. 1993. Telephone interview by R. Pagnucco. 22 Nov.

De Nardo, James. 1985. *Power in Numbers: The Political Strategy of Protest and Rebellion.* Princeton: Princeton Univ. Press.

Deuce, Nick. 1983. "Legislators for the Freeze." *Freeze Newsletter* (official journal of the Nuclear Weapons Freeze Campaign) 3, no. 3 (Apr.–May): 9.

Diani, Mario. 1994. *Green Networks: A Structural Analysis of the Italian Environmental Movement*. Edinburgh: Univ. of Edinburgh Press.

Disarmament Campaigns. 1989. "An Interview with Tair Tairov." *Disarmament Campaigns* (The Hague), Dec./Jan., 31.

Divine, Robert A. 1967. *Second Chance: The Triumph of Internationalism in America During World War II*. New York: Atheneum.

Donnelly, Jack. 1982. *Universal Human Rights in Theory and Practice*. Ithaca: Cornell Univ. Press.

Donner, Frank. 1982. "The Campaign to Smear the Nuclear Freeze." *Nation*, 6 Nov., 6.

Dorsey, Ellen. 1993. "Expanding the Foreign Policy Discourse." In *The Limits of State Autonomy: Societal Groups and Foreign Policy Formulation*, edited by David Skidmore and Valerie M. Hudson. Boulder, Colo.: Westview.

Douglas, James. 1975. *Parliaments Across Frontiers*. London: Her Majesty's Stationery Office.

Dubin, Martin David. 1983. "Transnational Processes in the League of Nations." *International Organization* 37, no. 3:470–93.

———. 1991. "The Red Cross Non-Governmental Health Regime and the Origins of the League of Nations Health Organization." Professional paper courtesy of the author.

———. 1993. "International Regime Theory and International Health Cooperation in the Interwar Era." Paper presented at International Studies Association Meeting, Washington, D.C., 25 Mar.

———. 1995. "The League of Nations Health Organisation." In *International Health Organizations and Movements, 1918–1939*, edited by Paul Weindling. Cambridge, England: Cambridge Univ. Press.

Dubs, Marne. 1990. Interview by R. Levering. 4 Apr.

Duffield, Mark, and John Prendergast. 1994. *Without Troops and Tanks: The Emergency Relief Desk and the Cross Border Operation into Eritrea and Tigray*. Lawrenceville, N.J.: Red Sea Press.

EarthAction. 1993a. "Minutes of the EarthAction Steering Committee Meeting, Copenhagen." Amherst and London: EarthAction.

———. 1993b. "Global Environment Facility: Let the Public In." EarthAction Alert. Amherst and London: EarthAction.

———. 1993c. "Forests: Protect Clayoquot Sound—One of Canada's Last Unspoiled Temperate Rainforests." EarthAction Alert. Amherst and London: EarthAction.

———. 1993d. "Protect the Land that Feeds Us." EarthAction Editorial Advisory. Amherst and London: EarthAction.

———. 1993e. "Protect Indian Lands in Brazil." EarthAction Alert. Amherst and London: EarthAction.

———. 1994a. "Report on 1994 Partner Survey." Amherst and London: EarthAction.

———. 1994b. "Monitoring Results and Accomplishments." Amherst and London: EarthAction.

———. 1994c. "The Desertification Convention." *EarthAction Parliamentary Alert and Editorial Advisory*. Amherst and London: EarthAction.

———. 1994d. "Defend the Ogoni People in Nigeria." EarthAction Alert. Amherst and London: EarthAction.

———. 1995a. "Responses to Partner Survey." (Feb.-Mar.). Amherst and London: EarthAction.

EarthAction. 1995b. "Protecting the Diversity of Life." EarthAction Advisory. Amherst and London: EarthAction.

Edwards, Bob, and Sam Marullo. 1995. "Organizational Mortality in a Declining Movement: The Demise of Peace Movement Organizations in the End of the Cold War Era." *American Sociological Review* 60:805–25.

Edwards, Bob, and John D. McCarthy. 1996. "The Strength of Starting from Scratch: Organizational Persistence among Local MADD Chapters, 1985–1988." Washington, D.C.: Life Cycle Institute, Catholic Univ. of America.

EEB (European Environmental Bureau). 1995. *Annual Report of Activities 1994. EEB Coordinated Action Plan 1995–1996.* Brussels.

Egan, Eileen. 1991. Interview by M. Hovey, 13 Oct., New York.

Eguren, Luis Enrique. 1994. "International Accompaniment and Protection of Human Rights." Paper presented at Pax Christi International Seminar on Inter-position, Peace Task Forces and Human Shields, Antwerp, 23–25 Nov.

Eichelberger, Clark M. 1977. *Organizing for Peace: A Personal History of the Founding of the United Nations.* New York: Harper and Row.

Eide, Asbjorn. 1986. "The Human Rights Movement and the Transformation of the International Order." *Alternatives* 11:367–402.

Eitel, G. 1981. Letter to Lee Kimball, 7 May, Miriam Levering manuscript collection, library of Guilford College, Greensboro, N.

Engram, Jonathan M. 1982. "Conscientious Objection to Military Service: A Report to the United Nations Division of Human Rights." 12 *Georgia Journal of International and Comparative Law* 3:359–399.

EPLE (Eritrean People's Liberation Front). 1985. "EPLF Statement on the ICRC." *Adulis* 1, no. 9:6–9.

Epstein, William. 1993. Presentation to International Pax Christi Meeting on Lobbying at the United Nations, 18 Oct.

ERA. 1986. "Eritrean Relief Association 1975–1985, 1985 Annual Report." Khartoum: Eritrean Relief Association.

Eskin, Otho. 1989. Interview by R. Levering, 6 Dec.

Fabre, Jean. 1974a. "Report on the Medellin Conference." 26 Mar., IFOR (International Fellowship of Reconciliation) Secretariat, Copenhagen, Denmark.

———. 1974b. "General Report on Fieldtrip in Latin America (February 21-March 20)." 25 Mar., (International Fellowship of Reconciliation) Secreatariat, Copenhagen.

———. 1974c. "Conclusions—Proposals for Future Work in Latin America." 18 Apr., IFOR Secretariat, Copenhagen.

Falk, Richard. 1992. *Explorations at the Edge of Time: The Prospects for World Order.* Philadelphia: Temple Univ. Press.

Farmer, James. 1985. *Lay Bare the Heart: An Autobiography of the Civil Rights Movement.* New York: Plume.

Feld, Werner. 1972. *Nongovernmental Forces and World Politics: A Study of Business, Labor, and Political Groups.* New York: Praeger.

Feraru, Anne Thompson. 1974. "Transnational Political Interests and the Global Environment." *International Organization* 28 (Winter): 31–60.

———. 1979. "From UNCHE to UNCSTD: Aggregate Data on Non-governmental Organizations with Observer Status at UN-Sponsored Conferences." *Transnational Associations* 31 (9):414–18.

Finnemore, Martha. 1993. "International Organizations as Teachers of Norms: The United Nations Educational, Scientific, and Cultural Organization and Science Policy." *International Organization* 47, no. 4: 565–97.

Finney, Torin R. T. 1989. *Unsung Hero of the Great War: The Life and Witness of Ben Salmon*. New York: Paulist Press.

Firebrace, James. 1991. WOW, Interiew by W. DeMars. 17 Sept., London, U.K.

Firebrace, James, and Stuart Holland. 1985. *Never Kneel Down: Drought, Development and Liberation in Eritrea*. Trenton, N.J.: Red Sea Press.

Firebrace, James, and Gayle Smith. 1982. *The Hidden Revolution: An Analysis of Social Change in Tigray (Northern Ethiopia) Based on Eyewitness Accounts*. London: War on Want.

Forest, Jim. 1993. Interview by R. Pagnucco. 15 Sept., South Bend, Ind.

Forsythe, David P. 1985. "Humanitarian Mediation by the International Committee of the Red Cross." In *International Mediation in Theory and Practice*, edited by Saadia Touval and I. William Zartman. Boulder, Colo.: Westview.

———. 1990. "Human Rights and the International Committee of the Red Cross." *Human Rights Quarterly* 12: 265–89.

———. 1993. "Choices More Ethical than Legal: The International Committee of the Red Cross and Human Rights." *Ethics and International Affairs* 7: 131–51.

Gale, Fred. 1996. "Constructing Global Civil Society Actors: An Anatomy of the Environmental Coalition Contesting the Tropical Timber Regime," International Studies Association Meeting, Paper presented at San Diego, 16–20 Apr.

Galtung, Johan. 1975. "Nonterritorial Actors and the Problem of Peace." In *On the Creation of a Just World Order*, edited by Saul H. Mendlovitz, 151–88. New York: Free Press.

———. 1988. "The Peace Movement: An Exercise in Micro-Macro Linkages." *International Social Science Journal* 117: 377–82.

Gamson, William A. 1988. "Political Discourse and Collective Action." In *From Structure to Action: Comparing Movement Participation Across Cultures*, edited by Bert Kandermans, Hanspeter Kriesi, and Sidney Tarrow, 219–44. Greenwich, Conn.: JAI Press.

———. 1990. *Strategy of Social Protest*. 2d ed. Belmont, Calif.: Wadsworth.

Gamson, William, and Antonio Modigliani. 1989. "Media Discourse and Public Opinion on Nuclear Power." *American Journal of Sociology* 95: 1–37.

Gayan, Anil. 1981. Letter to Miriam Levering, 11 May, Miriam Levering manuscript collection, library of Guilford College, Greensboro, N.C.

Gerhards, Jürgen. 1993. "Westeuropäische Integration und die Schwierigkeiten der Entstehung einer europäischen Öffentlichkeit." *Zeitschrift für Soziologie* 22, no. 2: 96–110.

Gerlach, Luther P. and Virginia H. Hine. 1970. *People, Power, Change Movements of Social Transformation*. Indianapolis: Bobbs-Merrill.

Ghebrehiwot, Berhane, 1991. ERA-UK, Interviewed by W. DeMars. 31 January, London, U.K.

Goonesekara, R. K. W. 1994. Interview by P. Coy. 31 Aug., Colombo, Sri Lanka.

Goss-Mayr, Hildegard. 1993. Letter to R. Pagnucco, 20 Aug., from Vienna, Austria.

Goss Mayr, Jean, and Hildegard. 1990. *The Gospel and the Struggle for Peace: Training Seminar in Evangelica Non-Violence and Methods of Engaging in It.* Alkmaar, The Netherlands: International Fellowship of Reconciliation.

Granovetter, Mark. 1973. "The Strength of Weak Ties." *American Journal of Sociology* 78: 1360–80.

Green Globe Yearbook of International Co-operation on Environment and Development. 1994. Edited by Helge Ole Bergesen et al. Oxford: Oxford Univ. Press.

Greenwood, Justin, and Karsten Ronit. 1994. "Interest Groups in the European Community: Newly Emerging Dynamics and Forms." *West European Politics* 17, no. 1: 31–52.

Griffin-Nolan, Ed. *Witness for Peace: A Story of Resistance.* 1991. Louisville: Westminster/John Knox Press.

Groom, A. J. R, and Jean-Francois Guilhaudis. 1989. "UNSSODS: The Quest for Structure and Norms." In *Global Issues in the United Nations' Framework,* edited by Paul Taylor and A. J. R. Groom, 116–47. New York: St. Martin's.

Grossi, Verdiana. 1994. *Le Pacifisme Européen, 1889–1914.* Brussels: Emile Bruylant, S.A.

Gruhn, Isebill V. 1996. "NGO's In Partnership with the UN: A New Fix or a New Problem for African Development?", Annual Meeting of Academic Council for the UN System (ACUNS).

Guest, Iain. 1990. *Behind the Disappearances: Argentina's Dirty War against Human Rights and the United Nations.* Philadelphia, Pa.: Univ. of Pennsylvania Press.

Haas, Ernst B. 1958. *The Uniting of Europe: Political, Social, and Economic Forces 1950–1957.* Stanford, Calif.: Stanford Univ. Press.

———. 1964. *Beyond the Nation-State: Functionalism and International Organization.* Stanford, Calf.: Stanford Univ. Press.

———. 1990. *When Knowledge Is Power: Three Models of Change in International Organizations.* Berkeley: Univ. of California Press.

Haas, Peter. 1992. "Introduction: Epistemic Communities and International Policy Coordination." *International Organization* 46: 1–35.

———. 1996. "The Future of International Environmental Governance." Paper presented at International Studies Association Annual Meeting, San Diego, Calf., 16–20 Apr.

Haas, Peter. M., Robert O. Keohane, and Marc A. Levy, eds. 1993. *Institutions for the Earth: Sources of Effective Environmental Protection.* Cambridge, Mass., and London: MIT Press.

Haggard, Stephan, and Beth A. Simmons. 1987. "Theories of International Regimes." *International Organization* 41: 491–517.

Hannum, Hurst., ed. 1992. *Guide to International Human Rights Practice.* 2d ed. Philadelphia: Univ. of Pennsylvania Press.

Havel, Vaclav. 1985. "Peace: The View From Prague." In *New York Review of Books,* 21 Nov., p. 30.

Helgeland, John, Robert J. Daly, and J. Patout Burns. 1985. *Christians and the Military: The Early Experience.* Philadelphia: Fortress.

Hendrie, Barbara. 1989. "Cross-Border Relief Operations in Eritrea and Tigray." *Disasters* 13, no. 4: 351–60.

Herby, Peter. 1988. "Missed Opportunities: The United Nations Third Special Session on Disarmament." Geneva: Quaker United Nations Office. Mimeographed.

Hertzgaard, Mark. 1989. *On Bended Knee: The Press and the Reagan Presidency.* New York: Schocken.

Hey, Christian. 1994. *Umweltpolitik in Europa. Fehler, Risiken, Chancen.* Munich: Beck.

Hey, Christian, and Uwe Brendle. 1994. *Umweltverbände und EG. Strategien, politische Kulturen und Organisationsformen.* Opladen: Westdeutscher Verlag.

Hoole, Rajan, Daya Somasundaram, K. Sritharan, and Rajani Thiranagama. 1992. *The Broken Palmyra.* Claremont, Calif.: Sri Lanka Studies Institute.

Höll, Otmar, ed. 1994. *Environmental Cooperation in Europe: The Political Dimension.* Boulder, Colo.: Westview.

Hudson, Richard. 1980. "Law of the Sea Treaty: Heading for a Showdown." *Global Report* 7: 1–4.

Huntington, Samuel. 1991. *The Third Wave: Democratization in the Late Twentieth Century.* Norman and London: Univ. of Oklahoma Press.

Hyndman, Patricia, Sabina Fernando, and Kanya Champion. 1994. "Integrity of the Person." In *Sri Lanka: State of Human Rights 1993,* edited by Law and Society Trust. Colombo, Sri Lanka: Law and Society Trust.

IFOR (International Fellowship of Reconciliation). 1977. "Campaign for Human Rights '78." *IFOR Report,* Oct., 5–7.

Imig, Doug R. 1996. *Poverty and Power: The Political Representation of Poor Americans.* Lincoln: Univ. of Nebraska Press.

Inform. 1994. *Parliamentary General Elections 1994, Special Report: Polls Related Violence.* 1994. Colombo, Sri Lanka: Inform and Movement for Free and Fair Elections, July.

International Human Rights Law Group. 1994. *Report of the International NGO Election Observer Mission to the Sri Lanka Parliamentary Elections.* Washington, D.C.: International Human Rights Law Group.

Jabhar, Zacki. 1993. "Petition in Court against EPDP Leader on Charges of Alleged Abduction." *The Island* (Colombo, Sri Lanka) 3 Mar.

Jachtenfuchs, Markus, and Michael Strübel, eds. 1992. *Environmental Policy in Europe.* Baden-Baden: Nomos.

Jack, Homer. 1977. "How the U.N. General Assembly Approved the Special Session Devoted to Disarmament." New York: World Conference on Religion and Peace.

Jacobs, Dan. 1987. *The Brutality of Nations.* New York: Knopf.

Jacobson, Harold K. 1979. *Networks of Interdependence: International Organizations and the Global Political System.* New York: Knopf.

Jansson, Kurt. 1990. "The Emergency Relief Operation: An Inside View." In *The Ethiopian Famine*, edited by Kurt Jansson, Michael Harris, and Angela Penrose. 2d ed. London: Zed Books.

Jayaweera, Neville. 1991. "The Human Rights Dimentions." *Economic Review*, 31: 8–9.

Jelin, Elizabeth. 1987. "The movement: Eclipsed by Democracy?" *NACLA Report on the Americas* 21: 28–36, 39.

Johnston, Hank, and Bert Klandermans, eds. 1995. *Social Movements and Culture*. Minneapolis: Univ. of Minnesota Press.

Jones, Dorothy V. 1991. *Code of Peace: Ethics and Security in the World of the Warlord States*. Chicago: Univ. of Chicago Press.

Judge, Anthony J. N. 1978. "International Institutions: Diversity, Borderline Cases, Functional Substitutes and Possible Alternatives." In *International Organization: A Conceptual Approach*, edited by Paul Taylor and A. J. R. Groom, 28–83. London: Francis Pinter Ltd.

————. 1993. Letter to Jackie Smith on data collection process for the *Yearbook of International Organizations*. Brussels, 16 Nov. 1993.

Judge, Anthony J. N., and Kjell Skjelsbaek. 1975. "Transnational Associations and Their Functions." In *Functionalism: Theory and Practice in International Relations*, edited by A. J. R. Gordon and Paul Taylor, 190–224. New York: Crane, Russak.

Judge, David, ed. 1993. *A Green Dimension for the European Community: Political Issues and Processes*. London: Frank Cass.

Kaldor, Mary. 1991. "Taking the Democratic Way," *Nation*, 22 April.

Kaltefleiter, Walter, and Robert L. Pfaltzgraff. 1985. "Towards a Comparative Analysis of the Peace Movements." In *The Peace Movements in Europe and the United States*, edited by Walter Kaltefleiter and Robert L. Pfaltzgraff. New York: St Martin's.

Kandasamay, Neelakandar. Interview at Colombo, Sri Lanka, Oct. 5, 1993.

Karl, Terry Lynn, and Philippe C. Schmitter, 1994. "Democratization around the Globe: Opportunities and Risks." In *World Security*, edited by M. T. Klare and D. C. Thomas, 43–62. New York: St. Martin's.

Katz, Ronald. 1979. "Financial Arrangements for Seabed Mining Companies: An NIEO Case Study." *Journal of World Trade Law* 13:202–22.

Keck, Margaret, and Kathryn Sikkink. 1994. "International Issue Networks in the Environment and Human Rights." Paper presented at Workshop on International Institutions and Transnational Social Movement Organizations, Kroc Institute for International Peace Studies, Univ. of Notre Dame, 18–20 Apr.

Kehler, Randy. Interview by D. Cortright. 24 Sept. (telephone interview)

Kent, Randolph C. 1989. "The United Nations Disaster Relief and Preparedness Role in Ethiopia: An Evaluation of the UN Emergency Prevention and Preparedness Group, 1987–1989." UNEPPG, Addis Ababa. Photocopy.

Keohane, Robert. 1977. *Power and Interdependence: World Politics in Transition*. Boston: Little, Brown.

————. 1984. *After Hegemony: Cooperation and Discord in the World Political Economy*. Princeton: Princeton Univ. Press.

Keohane, Robert, and Joseph Nye. 1972. "Transnational Relations and World Politics: An Introduction." In *Transnational Relations and World Politics*, edited by Robert Keohane and Joseph Nye, ix-xxvii. Cambridge: Harvard Univ. Press.

Keohane, Robert O., Peter M. Haas, and Marc A. Levy. 1993. "The Effectiveness of International Environmental Institutions." In *Institutions for the Earth: Sources of Effective International Environmental Protection*, edited by Peter Haas, Robert Keohane, and Marc Levy, 3–24. Cambridge: MIT Press.

Kimball, Lee A. 1980. Letter to Tommy Koh, 11 Apr. In Miriam Levering manuscript collection, library of Guilford College, Greensboro, N.C.

———. 1990. "The Role of Non-Governmental Organizations in the Implementation of the 1982 LOS Convention" In Alfred H.A. Soons, ed., Implementation of the Law of the Sea Convention Through International Institutions Law of the Sea Institute, Noordwijk aan Zee: the Netherlands. pp. 139–61.

———. 1992. *Forging International Agreement: Strengthening Inter-Governmental Institutions for Environment and Development*. Washington, D.C.: World Resources Institute.

———. 1995. Letter to Ralph Levering, 3 Jan. In Miriam Levering manuscript collection, library of Guilford College, Greensboro, N.C.

———. N.d. [Jan. 1975?]. Letter to Cyril Ritchie. Miriam Levering manuscript collection, library of Guilford College, Greensboro, N.C.

Kinane, Ed. 1995. Telephone interview by P. Coy. 28 Apr.

Kitschelt, Herbert. 1986. "Political Opportunity Structures and Political Protest: Anti-Nuclear Movements in Four Democracies." *British Journal of Political Science* 16: 57–85.

Klatte, Ernst R. 1992. "Enforcement of EC Environmental Legislation: The Role of Citizens and Citizens' Groups. Paper prepared for the International Conference on Environmental Enforcement," Budapest, 22–25 Sept.

———. 1992. Consultant of the EC Commission Interview by D. Rucht. Brussels, 17 Sept.

Kleidman, Robert. 1993. *Organizing for Peace: Neutrality, the Test Ban and the Freeze*. Syracuse: Syracuse Univ. Press.

Knopf, Jeffrey W. 1993. "Beyond Two-Level Games: Domestic-International Interaction in the Intermediate-Range Nuclear Forces Negotiations." *International Organization* 47:599–628.

Koh, Tommy. 1990. Interview by R. Levering. 11 Apr.

Kohn, Stephen M. 1986. *Jailed for Peace: The History of American Draft Law Violators, 1658–1985*. Westport, Conn. Greenwood.

Kooijmans, Peter H. 1991. "In the Shadowland between Civil War and Civil Strife: Some Reflections on the Standard-Setting Process." In *Humanitarian Law of Armed Conflict: Challenges Ahead*, edited by Astrid J. M. Delissen and Gerard J. Tanya. Dordrecht: Martinus Nijhoff.

Koopmans, Ruud. 1995. *Democracy from Below: New Social Movements and the Political System in West Germany*. Boulder, Colo.: Westview.

Krämer, Ludwig. 1991. "Participation of Environmental Organisations in the Activities of the EEC." In *Participation and Litigation Rights of Environmental Associations in Europe: Current Legal Situation and Practical Experience*, edited by Martin Führ and Gerhard Roller, 129–38. Frankfurtam Main: Peter Lang.

Krasner, Stephen D. 1983. "Structural Causes and Regime Consequences." In *International Regimes*, edited by Stephen D. Krasner, 1–22. Ithaca: Cornell Univ. Press.

Kriesberg, Louis. 1960. "German Businessmen and Union Leaders and the Schuman Plan." *Social Science* 35 (Apr.): 114–21.

———. 1972. "International Nongovernmental Organizations and Transnational Integration." *International Associations* 24, no. 11: 520–25.

———. 1982. *Social Conflicts*. 2d ed. Englewood Cliffs, N.J.: Prentice-Hall.

Kriesberg, Louis, and David R. Segal, eds. 1992. *Social Movements, Conflicts and Change*, vol. 14, *The Transformation of European Communist Societies*. Greenwich, Conn: JAI Press.

Kriesi, Hanspeter. 1995. "The Political Opportunity Structure of New Social Movements: Its Impact on Their Mobilization" In *The Politics of Social Protest: Comparative Perspectives on States and Social Movements*, edited by J. Craig Jenkins and Bert Klandermans, 167–89. Minneapolis: Univ. of Minnesota Press.

Kriesi, Hanspeter, Ruud Koopmans, Jan Willem Duyvendak, and Marco G. Giugni, eds. 1995. *New Social Movements in Western Europe: A Comparative Analysis*. Minneapolis: Univ. of Minnesota Press.

Kuehl, Warren F. 1969. *Seeking World Order: The United States and International Organization to 1920*. Nashville: Vanderbilt Univ. Press.

Küng, Ruedi. [ICRC Head Delegate in Sudan 1985–1986] 1991. Interview by W. DeMars. 25 June, Berne, Switzerland.

Lador-Lederer, J. J. 1963. *International Non-Governmental Organizations*. Leyden: A. W. Sythoff.

Latané, John H., ed. 1932. *Development of the League of Nations Idea: Documents and Correspondence of Theodore Marburg*. 2 vols. New York: Macmillan.

Latin American Confederation of Workers. 1978. *Carta Latinoamericana de los Derechos y Libertades de Los Trabajadores y de Los Pueblos*. Caracas, Venezuela: Latin American Confederation of Workers.

Leatherman, Janie. 1993. "Conflict Transformation in the CSCE: Learning and Institutionalization." *Cooperation and Conflict* 28, no. 4: 403–31.

Leatherman, Janie, Ron Pagnucco, and Jackie Smith. 1993. *International Institutions and Transnational Social Movement Organizations: Challenging the State in a Three-Level Game of Global Transformation*. Working Paper Series, South Bend: Kroc Institute for International Peace Studies.

Lederach, John Paul. 1995. *Preparing for Peace: Conflict Transformation Across Cultures*. Syracuse: Syracuse Univ. Press.

Levering, Miriam. n.d. Unpublished memoirs. Miriam Levering manuscript collection, librabry of Guilford College, Greensboro, N.C.

Levering, Ralph, and Miriam Levering. 1997. *Brokering Ocean Law, Building World Order: The Neptune Group of NGOs and UNCLOS III, 1972–1982*. Syracuse: Syracuse Univ. Press.

Liefferink, Duncan J., Philip D. Lowe and Arthur P. J. Mol. 1993. "The Environment and the European Community: The Analysis of Political Integration."

In *European Integration and Environmental Policy,* edited by J. Duncan Liefferink, Philip D. Lowe and Arthur P. J. Mol, 1–15. London and New York: Belhaven.

Lipsky, Micheal. 1968. "Protest as a Political Resource." *American Political Science Review* 62: 1144–58.

Livezey, Lowell. 1989. "U.S. Religious Organizations and the International Human Rights Movement." *Human Rights Quarterly* 11:14–81.

Lowe, Philip, and Jane Goyder. 1983. *Environmental Groups in Politics.* London/ Boston/Sidney: Allan and Unwin.

Luard, Evan. 1977. *International Agencies: The Emerging Framework of Interdependence.* New York: Royal Institute of International Affairs.

Lyons, F. S. L. 1963. *Internationalism in Europe, 1815–1914.* Leyden: A. W. Sythoff.

MacPherson, Martin. 1993. Interview by M. Hovey. 21 Feb., West Sussex, England.

MacQuarrie, Barbara. 1993. "Reflections on Nonpartisanship in the Work of PBI." 11 pp. Unpublished.

Mahony, Liam, and Luis Enrique Eguren. 1997. *Unarmed Bodyguards: Case Studies in Protective International Accompaniment.* West Hartford, Conn.: Kumarian Press.

Mander, Linden A. 1964. *Foundations of Modern World Society.* Stanford: Stanford Univ. Press.

Mansbach, Richard, and John Vasquez. 1980. *In Search of Theory: A New Paradigm for Global Politics.* New York: Columbia Univ. Press.

Marks, Gary, and Doug McAdam. 1994. "Social Movements and the Changing Structure of Political Opportunity in the European Community." Unpublished paper.

Mazey, Sonia, and Jeremy Richardson. 1992. "Environmental Groups and the EC: Challenges and Opportunities." *Environmental Politics* 1, no. 4: 109–28.

McAdam, Doug. 1982. *Political Processes and the Development of Black Insurgency.* Chicago: Univ. of Chicago Press.

———. 1988. *Freedom Summer.* New York: Oxford Univ. Press.

McAdam, Doug, John D. McCarthy, and Mayer Zald. 1988. "Social Movements." In *Handbook of Sociology,* edited by Neil Smelser, 695–738. Newbury Park, Calif.: Sage.

McAdam, Doug, John D. McCarthy, and Mayer Zald. 1996. "Introduction: Opportunities, Mobilizing Structures, and Framing Processes—Toward a Synthetic, Comparative Perspective on Social Movements." In *Comparative Perspectives on Social Movements: Political Opportunities, Mobilizing Structures, and Cultural Framings,* edited by Doug McAdam, John D. McCarthy, and Mayer Zald, 1–22. New York: Cambridge Univ. Press.

McCarthy, John D. 1994. "The Interaction of Grass-roots Activists and State Actors in the Production of an Anti-Drunk Driving Media Attention Cycle." In *From Ideology to Identity in Contemporary Social Movements,* edited by Joseph Gusfield, Hank Johnston, and Enrique Laraña. Philadelphia: Temple Univ. Press.

————. 1996. "Mobilizing Structures: Constraints and Opportunities in Adopting, Adapting and Inventing." In *Comparative Perspectives on Social Movements: Political Opportunities, Mobilizing Structures, and Cultural Framings,* edited by Doug McAdam, John McCarthy, and Mayer Zald, [PAGES] 141–151. New York, NY: Cambridge Univ. Press.

McCarthy, John D., and Jim Castelli. 1994. *Working for Justice: The Campaign for Human Development and Poor Empowerment Groups.* Washington, D.C.: Life Cycle Institute, Catholic Univ. of America.

McCarthy, John D., and Mark Wolfson. 1992. "Consensus Movements, Conflict Movements, and the Cooptation of Civic and State Infrastructures." In *Frontiers in Social Movement Theory,* edited by Aldon Morris and Carol McClurg Mueller, 273–300. New Haven: Yale Univ. Press.

————. 1996. "National Federating Structure and Local Resource Mobilization: The Case of the Early Drunk Driving Movement." *American Sociological Review* 61: 1070–1088.

McCarthy, John D., and Mayer N. Zald. 1973. *The Trend of Social Movements in America: Professionalization and Resource Mobilization.* Morristown, N.J.: General Learning Press.

————. 1977. "Resource Mobilization in Social Movements: A Partial Theory." *American Journal of Sociology* 82: 1212–41.

McCarthy, John D., David Britt, and Mark Wolfson. 1991. "The Institutional Channelling of Social Movements in the Modern State." In *Research in Social Movements, Conflict and Change* 13:45–76. Greenwich, Conn: JAI.

McCarthy, John D., Clark McPhail, and Jackie Smith. 1996. "Images of Protest: Dimensions of Selection Bias in Media Coverage of Washington Demonstrations, 1982 and 1991." *American Sociological Review* 61: 478–99.

McCarthy, John D., Jackie Smith, and Mayer Zald. 1996. "Accessing Media, Electoral and Government Agendas." In *Comparative Perspectives on Social Movements: Political Opportunities, Mobilizing Structures, and Cultural Framings,* edited by Doug McAdam, John McCarthy, and Mayer Zald, 291–311. New York: Cambridge Univ. Press.

McCarthy, Ronald M., and Christopher Kruegler. 1993. *Toward Research and Theory Building in the Study of Nonviolent Action.* Monograph no. 7. Cambridge, Mass.: Albert Einstein Institution.

McKenna, Ian. 1995. [EarthAction staff member] Interview by J. Smith. Amherst, Mass., 6 Feb.

McLaughlin, Andrew, William Maloney, and A. Grant Jordan. 1993. "Corporate Lobbying in the European Community." *Journal of Common Market Studies* 30, no. 2: 191–212.

McManus, Phil, and Gerald Schlabach, eds. 1991. *Relentless Persistence: Nonviolent Action in Latin America.* Santa Cruz, Calif.: New Society Publishers.

McPhail, Clark, and Charles W. Tucker. 1968. "Interest Group Activities and the Public Opinion Process: A Case Study of a Liquor Referendum." *South Carolina Law Review* 20: 749–64.

Melucci, Alberto. 1989. *Nomads of the Present: Social Movements and Individual Needs in Contemporary Society,* edited by John Kean and Paul Mier. Philadelphia: Temple Univ. Press.

Meyer, David S. 1994. "Political Opportunity and Nested Institutions." Paper presented at Midwest Political Science Association Meetings, Chicago, 14 Apr.

Miles, Edward. 1990. Interview by R. Levering, 26 Feb., Washington, D.C.

Minkoff, Deborah. 1995. *Organizing for Equality: The Evolution of Women's and Racial Ethnic Organizations in America, 1955–1985*. New Brunswick, N.J.: Rutgers Univ. Press.

Mitrany, David. 1966. A Working Peace System. Chicago: Quadrangle Books.

——. 1975. *The Functional Theory of Politics*. New York: St. Martin's.

Morrison, Stephen J. 1992. "Ethiopia Charts a New Course." *Journal of Democracy* 3, no. 3: 125–37.

Moskos, Charles, and John Whiteclay Chambers II, eds. 1993. *The New Conscientious Objection: From Sacred to Secular Resistance*. New York: Oxford Univ. Press.

Muzaffar, Chandra. 1992. "Human Rights Re-Examined." *Lanka Guardian*, 15 Sept., 17–19 Sept.

Nagel, Joane. 1996. *American Indian Ethnic Renewal: Red Power and the Resurgence of Identity and Culture*. New York: Oxford Univ. Press.

Newman, Frank, and David Weissbrodt. 1990. *International Human Rights*. Cincinnati: Anderson.

Nicod, Vincent [ICRC Staff]. 1990. Interview by W. DeMars. 7 Dec., Geneva.

Nissan, Elizabeth. 1993 Interview by P. Coy. 22 Oct., London.

Nuclear Weapons Freeze Campaign. 1982. *Freeze Newsletter:* (official journal of the Nuclear Weapons Freeze Campaign) 2, no. 6, Aug./Sept.

O'Donnell, Guillermo, and Philippe C. Schmitter. 1986. *Transitions from Authoritarian Rule: Tentative Conclusions*. Baltimore: Johns Hopkins Univ. Press.

Oberschall, Anthony. 1980. "Loosely Structured Collective Conflict: A Theory and an Application." *Research in Social Movements, Conflict and Change* 3: 45–68.

Oberst, Robert C. 1994. "The Political and Social Impact of War on the Eastern Province of Sri Lanka." Paper presented at 23rd Annual Conference on South Asia, Madison, Wis., 4–6 Nov.

Oliver, Pam. 1989. "Bringing the Crowd Back In: The Nonorganizational Elements of Social Movements." In *Research in Social Movements, Conflicts and Change*, edited by Louis Kriesberg, 11:1–30 Greenwich, Conn.: JAI.

Olson, Mancur. 1968. *The Logic of Collective Action*. Cambridge: Harvard Univ. Press.

Olzak, Susan. 1989. "Analysis of Events in the Study of Collective Action." *Annual Review of Sociology* 15:119–41.

Orr, Jim. 1989. Interview by M. Levering, 6 Dec. In Miriam Levering manuscript collection, library of Guilford College, Greensboro, N.C.

Oxman, Bernard. 1990. Interview by M. Levering, 26 Feb. In Miriam Levering manuscript collection, library of Guilford College, Greensboro, N.C.

Pagnucco, Ron. 1995. "The Comparative Study of Social Movements and Democratization: Political Interactionist and Political Process Approaches." *Research in Social Movements, Conflict and Change*, 18:145–184. Greenwhich, Conn.: JAI.

Pagnucco, Ron, and John D. McCarthy. 1992. "Advocating Nonviolent Direct Action in Latin America: The Antecedents and Emergence of SERPAJ." In *Religion and Politics in Comparative Perspective,* edited by B. Misztal and A. Shupe, 125–147. Westport, Conn.: Praeger.

Pagnucco, Ron, and Jackie Smith. 1993. "The Role of the Peace Movement in the Formulation of U.S. Foreign Policy." *Peace and Change* 18: 157–81.

Pateman, Roy. 1994. "Eritrea Takes the World Stage." *Current History* 93 (May):228–31.

Paterson, Arthur. 1989. Interview by R. Levering, 3 Oct., Washington, D.C.

Paterson, Matthew, and Michael Grubb. 1992. "The International Politics of Climate Change." *International Affairs* 68:293–310.

Pearce, Fred. 1991. *Green Warriors: The People and the Politics behind the Environmental Revolution.* London: Bodley Head.

Pegg, Carl H. 1983. *Evolution of the European Idea, 1914–1932.* Chapel Hill: Univ. of North Carolina Press.

Pentz, Michael J., and Gillian Slovo. 1981. "The Political Significance of Pugwash." In *Knowledge and Power in a Global Society,* edited by William M. Evan, 175–203 Beverly Hills/London/New Delhi: Sage.

Perera, Aloy. 1994. "Canons of decency and good taste violated." *The Island,* 3 Aug., 1, 2.

Perez Aguirre, Fr. Luis. 1993. Letter to R. Pagnucco, 15 Dec.

Perez Esquivel, Adolfo. 1977. "Gira Internacional del Coordinador para America Latina, Adolfo Perez Esquivel." *Paz y Justicia* 5–6 (Mar.-Apr.):7–9.

———. 1983. *Christ in a Poncho.* Maryknoll, N.Y.: Orbis.

Pirages, Dennis. 1989. *Global Technopolitics: The International Politics of Technology and Resources.* Pacific Grove, Calif.: Brooks/Cole.

Platzer, Hans-Wolfgang. 1984. *Unternehmensverbände in der EG — ihre nationale und transnationale Organisation und Politik.* Kehl am Rhein/Strassburg: Engel Verlag.

Pontecorvo, Guilio, ed. 1986. *The New Order of the Oceans.* New York: Columbia Univ. Press.

Porter, Gareth, and Janet Welsh Brown. 1995. *Global Environmental Politics.* 2d ed. Boulder, Colo.: Westview.

Potter, Pittman B. 1934. *The League of Nations and Other International Organizations.* Geneva Special Studies, vol. 5, no. 6. Geneva: Geneva Research Center.

Powell, Walter W., and Paul J. DiMaggio, eds. 1991. *The New Institutionalism in Organizational Analysis.* Chicago: Univ. of Chicago Press.

Press, Alison, and Catherine Taylor. 1990. *Europe and the Environment: The European Community and Environmental Policy.* London: Industrial Society Press.

Price Cohen, Cynthia. 1990. "The Role of Non-Governmental Organizations in the Drafting of the Convention on the Rights of the Child." *Human Rights Quarterly* 12: 137–47.

Princen, Thomas, and Matthias Finger. 1994. *Environmental NGOs in World Politics.* London and New York: Routledge.

Putnam, Robert D. 1988. "Diplomacy and Domestic Politics: The Logic of Two-Level Games." *International Organization* 42: 427–60.

Quizon, Antonio B. 1991. "Organizing an Asian Regional Coalition to Promote Sustainable Development." In *Earth Summit: Conversations with Architects of an Ecologically Sustainable Future,* edited by Stephen D. Lerner, 205–10. Bolinas, Calif.: Common Knowledge Press.

Rameshvili, T. 1993. Interview by M. Hovey, 8 Mar., Geneva.

Ratiner, Leigh. 1989. Interview by R. Levering, 5 Dec., Washington, D.C.

Ray, Philip L., Jr., and J. Sherrod Taylor. 1977. "The Role of Non-Governmental Organizations in Implementing Human Rights in Latin America." *Georgia Journal of International and Comparative Law* 7:477–506.

Ready, Timothy, Brady Tyson, and Ron Pagnucco. 1985. "The Impact of the Nobel Peace Prize on the Work of Adolfo Perez Esquivel." Paper presented at the International Studies Association annual meeting, Washington, D.C. 6 Mar.

REST (Relief Society of Tigray). 1986. "Annual Report." Khartoum: Relief Society of Tigray.

Reinsch, Paul S. 1911. *Public International Unions: Their Work and Organization.* Boston: Ginn and Co., for the World Peace Foundation.

Ridgeway, George L. 1938. *Merchants of Peace: Twenty Years of Business Diplomacy Through the International Chamber of Commerce, 1919–1938.* New York: Columbia Univ. Press.

———. 1959. *Merchants of Peace: The History of the International Chamber of Commerce.* Boston: Little, Brown.

Riedmatten, de, Léon. [ICRC head delegate in Ethiopia, 1983–1985] 1990. Interview by W. DeMars. 19 Dec., Sion, Switzerland.

Risse-Kappen, Thomas. 1995a. "Bringing Transnational Relations Back In: Non-State Actors, Domestic Structures, and International Institutions" In *Bringing Transnational Relations Back In: Non-State Actors, Domestic Structures and International Institutions,* edited by Thomas Risse-Kappen, 3–33. New York: Cambridge Univ. Press.

———. 1995b. *Bringing Transnational Relations Back In: Non-State Actors, Domestic Structures and International Institutions.* New York: Cambridge Univ. Press.

Robins, Dorothy B. 1971. *Experiment in Democracy: The Story of U. S. Citizen Organization in Forging the Charter of the United Nations.* New York: Parkside Press.

Rochon, Thomas. 1988. *Mobilizing for Peace: The Antinuclear Movements in Western Europe.* Princeton: Princeton Univ. Press.

Rodley, Nigel S. 1991. "The Work of Non-Governmental Organizations in the World-Wide Promotion and Protection of Human Rights." *Bulletin of Human Rights* 90, no. 1. New York: United Nations Publications.

Roncerel, Annie. 1992. "Needs, Challenges and Opportunities for Environmental Action: The Case of Climate Action Network." Paper presented at The New Europe Conference: Opportunities for Foundations, Paris, 9 July.

Rosenau, James N. 1990. *Turbulence in World Politics.* Princeton: Princeton Univ. Press.

Ross, Edward A. 1920. *The Principles of Sociology.* New York: Century.

Rotblat, Joseph. 1993. "Past Attempts to Abolish Nuclear Weapons." In *A*

Nuclear-Weapon-Free World: Desirable? Feasible?, edited by Joseph Rotblat, Jack Steinberger, and Bhalchandra Udgaonkar. Boulder, Colo.: Westview.

Rucht, Dieter. 1993a. " 'Think Globally, Act Locally'? Needs, Forms and Problems of Cross-National Environmental Groups." In *European Integration and Environmental Policy*, edited by J. Duncan Liefferink, Philip D. Lowe, and Arthur P. J. Mol, 75–95. London and New York: Belhaven.

———. 1993b. "Umweltpolitische Interessenvertretung gegenüber Organen der EG: Ansatzpunkte, Struktur und Probleme." In *Lebensverhältnisse und Konflikte im neuen Europa*, edited by Bernhard Schäfers, 568–75. Frankfurt am Main: Campus.

———. 1995. "Ecological Protest as Calculated Law-breaking: Greenpeace and Earth First! in a Comparative Perspective." In *Green Politics III*, edited by Wolfgang Rüdig, 66–89. Edinburgh: Univ. of Edinburgh Press.

———. 1996. "The Impact of National Contexts on Social Movement Structures: A Cross-Movement and Cross-National Comparison." In *Comparative Perspectives on Social Movements: Political Opportunities, Mobilizing Structures and Cultural Framings*, edited by Doug McAdam, John McCarthy, and Mayer Zald, 185–204. New York: Cambridge Univ. Press.

Rucht, Dieter, and Thomas Ohlemacher. 1992. "Protest Event Data: Uses and Perspectives." In *Studying Collective Action*, edited by Mario Diani and Ron Eyerman, 76–106. Newbury Park, Calif.: Sage.

Salacuse, Jeswald W. 1991. "Your Draft or Mine?" In *Negotiation Theory and Practice*, edited by J. William Breslin and Jeffrey Rubin, 337–41. Cambridge: Program on Negotiation at Harvard Law School.

Sanders, Phyllis. 1978. "An Interview with Adolfo Perez Esquivel." *IFOR Report*, Dec., 3–7.

Sanger, Clyde. 1987. *Ordering the Oceans: The Making of the Law of the Sea.* Toronto: Univ. of Toronto Press.

Schlissel, Lillian. 1968. *Conscience in America: A Documentary History of Conscientious Objection in America, 1757–1967.* New York: E. P. Dutton.

Schmidt, Markus G. 1989. *Common Heritage or Common Burden?* New York: Oxford Univ. Press.

Schönberger, Peter. 1994. *Hauptsache Europa. Perspektiven für das Europäische Parlament.* Berlin: Duncker & Humblot.

Scoble, Harry, M., and Laurie S. Wiseberg. 1974. "Human Rights and Amnesty International." *Annals of the American Academy of Social and Political Science* 413: 11–26.

Scott, James Brown. 1909. *The Hague Peace Conferences of 1899 and 1907.* Vol. 2. Baltimore: Johns Hopkins Univ. Press.

Selvakumar, Tharmalingem. 1993. Interview by P. Coy, 5 Aug., Colombo, Sri Lanka.

Shanks, Cheryl. 1996. "NGOs: A Refuge for States?" Annual Meeting of the Academic Council on the UN System (ACUNS), Turin, Italy, 24–26 June.

Sharp, Gene. 1973. *The Politics of Nonviolent Action: Power and Struggle.* Vol. 1. Boston: Porter Sargent, 1973.

Shelley, Louise I. 1989. "Human Rights as an International Issue." *Annals of the American Academy of Social and Political Science* 506: 42–56.

Shepherd, Jack. 1975. *The Politics of Starvation.* Washington, D.C.: Carnegie Endowment for International Peace.

Shestack, Jerome J. 1978. "Sisyphus Endures: The International Human Rights NGO." *New York School of Law Review* 24: 89–123.

Sikkink, Kathryn. 1986. "Codes of Conduct for Transnational Corporations: The Case of the WHO/UNICEF Code." *International Organization* 40: 815–40.

———. 1993. "Human Rights, Principled Issue-Networks, and Sovereignty in Latin America." *International Organization* 47: 412–41.

Sikkink, Kathryn, and Margaret Keck. In press. *Activists Beyond Borders: Transnational Networks in International Politics.* Ithaca, N.Y.: Cornell Univ. Press.

Sitkoff, Harvard. 1981. *The Struggle for Black Equality.* New York: Hill and Wang.

Sivard, Ruth Leger. 1996. *World Military and Social Expenditures.* Leesburg, Virginia: WMSE Publications.

Skjelsbaek, Kjell. 1971. "The Growth of International Non-Governmental Organizations in the Twentieth Century." *International Organization* 25: 420–42.

Sklar, Holly, edited 1980. *Trilateralism.* Boston: South End Press.

Skogly, Sigrun I. 1996. "Moving Human Rights out of Geneva: The Need for a Comprehensive Approach to International Human Rights Law," Paper presented at International Studies Association Annual Meeting, Washington D.C., 1–3 Apr.

Sloan, John W. 1984. "State Repression and Enforcement Terrorism in Latin America." In *The State as Terrorist: The Dynamics of Governmental Violence and Repression,* edited by Michael Stohl and George A. Lopez. Westport, Conn.: Greenwood.

Smith, Gayle. 1990. Interview by W. DeMars. 17 Aug., Washington, D.C.

Smith, Jackie. 1995a. "Transnational Political Processes and the Human Rights Movement." In *Research in Social Movements, Conflict and Change,* edited by Louis Kriesberg, Michael Dobkowski, and Isidor Walliman, 18: 185–220. Greenwood Conn.: JAI.

Smith, Jackie. 1995b. "Organizing Global Action: Transnational Social Movements and World Politics." Ph.D. diss., Univ. of Notre Dame.

Smith, Jackie, Ron Pagnucco, and Winnie Romeril. 1994. "Transnational Social Movement Organizations in the Global Political Arena." *Voluntas* 5: 121–54.

Snow, David, and Robert Benford. 1988. "Ideology, Frame Resonance, and Participant Mobilization." *International Social Movements Research* 1:197–217.

Snow, David, E. B. Rochford, S. Warden, and Robert Benford. 1986. "Frame Alignment Processes, Micromobilization and Movement Participation." *American Sociological Review* 51: 464–81.

Snyder, David, and W. R. Kelly. 1977. "Conflict Intensity, Media Sensitivity and the Validity of Newspaper Data." *American Sociological Review* 42:105–23.

Solo, Pam. 1988. *From Protest to Policy: Beyond the Freeze to Common Security.* Cambridge, Mass.: Ballinger.

———. 1993. Telephone Interview by D. Cortright. 20 Sept.

Speeckaert, G. P. 1951. Un siècle d'Expositions Universelles, leur influence sur les congrès internationaux. *Bulletin ONG Brussels,* October.

———. 1957. *Les 1,978 Organisations Internationales Fondées depuis le Congrès de Vienne.* Brussels: Union of International Associations, doc. no. 5.

Stanley Foundation. 1994. *The UN System and NGOs: New Relationships for a New Era?* Muscatine, Iowa: Stanley Foundation.

Staggenborg, Suzanne. 1986. "Coalition Work in the Pro-Choice Movement: Organizational and Environmental Opportunities and Obstacles." *Social Problems* 33: 374–89.

Steiner, Henry J. 1991. *Diverse Partners: Non-Governmental Organizations and the Human Rights Movement.* Cambridge: Harvard Law School Human Rights Program and Human Rights Internet.

Stelle, William 1985. Letter to Lee Kimball, 11 Feb. 1985. In Miriam Levering manuscript collection, library of Guilford College, Greensboro, N.C.

Stephenson, Carolyn M. 1995. "Women's International Non-Governmental Organizations at the United Nations." In *Women, Politics and the United Nations,* edited by Ann Winslow. New York: Greenwood.

Stiles, Kendall. 1996. "International Organizations and Civil Society." Paper presented at International Studies Association Annual Meeting, San Diego, 16–20 Apr.

Stokes, Gale. 1993. *The Walls Came Tumbling Down: The Collapse of Communism in Eastern Europe.* New York: Oxford Univ. Press.

Streek, Wolfgang, and Philippe Schmitter. 1991. "From National Corporatism to Transnational Pluralism: Organized Interests in the Single European Market." *Politics and Society* 19: 133–64.

Strong, Maurice. 1991. "ECO '92: Critical Challenges and Global Solutions." *Journal of International Affairs* 44: 287–300.

Talbott, Strobe. 1984. *Deadly Gambits: The Reagan Administration and the Stalemate in Nuclear Arms Control.* New York: Knopf.

Tarrow, Sydney. 1983. *Struggling to Reform: Social Movements and Social Change During Cycles of Protest.* Western Societies Program, Occasional Paper no. 15. Center for International Studies, Cornell University.

———. 1988. "National Politics and Collective Action." *Annual Review of Sociology* 14:421–40.

———. 1989. *Democracy and Disorder. Protest and Politics in Italy, 1965–1975.* New York: Oxford Univ. Press.

———. 1995. *Power in Movement: Social Movements, Collective Action and Politics.* New York: Cambridge Univ. Press.

Taylor, Paul. 1975. "Introduction." In *The Functional Theory of Politics,* edited by David Mitrany, ix–xxv. New York: St. Martin's.

———. 1989. "The Origins and Institutional Setting of the UN Special Conferences." In *Global Issues in the United Nations' Framework,* edited by Paul Taylor and A. J. R. Groom, 7–34. New York: St. Martin's.

———. 1991. "The European Community and the State: Assumptions, Theories and Propositions." *Review of International Studies* 17: 109–25.

Taylor, Philip. 1984. *Nonstate Actors in International Politics.* Boulder, Colo., and London: Westview.

Tereke, Gebru. 1990. "Continuity and Discontinuity in Peasant Mobilization:

The Cases of Bale and Tigray." In *The Political Economy of Ethiopia,* edited by Marina Ottaway. New York: Praeger.

Thomas, Dan. 1994. "The Helsinki Movement: International Norms, Social Mobilization in Eastern Europe, and Policy Change in the United States." Paper presented at Workshop on International Institutions and Transnational Social Movement Organizations, Kroc Institute for International Peace Studies, Univ. of Notre Dame, 18–20 Apr.

Tilly, Charles. 1964. *Big Structures, Large Processes, Huge Comparisons.* New York: Russell Sage Foundation.

——. 1984. "Social Movements and National Politics." In *Statemaking and Social Movements: Essays in History and Theory,* edited by Charls Bright and Susan Harding. Ann Arbor: Univ. of Michigan Press.

Tolley, Howard, Jr. 1987. *The U.N. Commission on Human Rights.* Boulder, Colo.: Westview Press.

Traugott, Mark, ed. 1995. *Repertoires and Cycles of Collective Action.* Durham, N.C.: Duke Univ. Press.

TTAC (Tigray Transport and Agriculture Consortium). 1987. "Tigray Transport and Agriculture Consortium." London: War On Want.

Tudyka, Kurt P. 1988. *Umweltpolitik in Ost-und Westeuropa.* Opladen: Leske and Budrich.

Union of International Associations. 1983, 1988, 1993, 1995. *Yearbook of International Organizations.* Brussels: UAI.

United Nations. 1982. "Statement by President of Law of Sea Conference at Opening Meeting of Montego Bay Session," United Nations Press Release, SEA/MP/Rev.1 (6 Dec.), pp. 3, 4–5.

United States Department of State. 1980. Transcript of Meeting of the Public Advisory Committee on the Law of the Sea, 13 Nov 1980. Miriam Levering manuscript collection, library of Guilford College, Greensboro, N.C.

UN Working Group on Disappearances. 1992. *Report on the Visit to Sri Lanka of the Members of the Working Group on Enforced and Involuntary Disappearances, October 7–8, 1991.* United Nations Commission on Human Rights, 8 Jan.

USAID. 1987. "Final Disaster Report: Ethiopia Drought/Famine FY 1985–1986." Addis Ababa: USAID.

UTHR. 1992. *Sri Lanka: Human Rights and the Issues of War and Peace.* University Teachers for Human Rights (Jaffna), August, Briefing 1.

van Boven, Theo C. 1984. "Protection of Human Rights through the UN System." In *Guide to International Human Rights Practice,* ed. Hurst Hannum. Philadelphia: Univ. of Pennsylvania Press.

van der Heijden, Hein-Anton, Ruud Koopmans, and Marco G. Guigni. 1992. "The West European Environmental Movement." *Research in Social Movements, Conflicts and Change,* supplement 2:1–40.

Van der Linden, W. H. 1987. *The International Peace Movement, 1815–1874.* Amsterdam: Tilleul Publications.

Van Ermen, Raymond. 1991. Relations among Environmental NGO's and Networks at the EEC Level. Brussels. Mimeographed.

van Schendelen, Marinus P. C. M., ed. 1993. *National Public and Private EC Lobbying*. Aldershot: Dartmouth, U.K.

Veiga, Raul. 1985. *Las Organizaciones de Derechos Humanos*. Buenos Aires: Centro Editor de America Latina.

Walker, Jack L. 1991. *Mobilizing Interest Groups in America: Patrons, Professions, and Social Movements*. Ann Arbor: Univ. of Michigan Press.

Walker, R. B. J. 1988. *One World, Many Worlds: Struggles for a Just World Peace*. Boulder, Colo.: Lynne Rienner.

Wallace, Michael D., and J. David Singer. 1970. "Intergovernmental Organizations in the Global System, 1815–1964: A Quantitative Description." *International Organization* 24: 239–87.

Waller, Douglas. 1987. *Congress and the Nuclear Freeze*. Amherst: Univ. of Massachusetts Press.

Wank, Solomon. 1988. "The Austrian Peace Movement and the Habsburg Ruling Elite, 1906–1914." In *Peace Movements and Political Cultures*, edited by Charles Chatfield and Peter van den Dungen, 40–63. Knoxville: Univ. of Tennessee Press.

Wapner, Paul. 1995. "Politics beyond the State: Environmental Activism and World Civic Politics." In *World Politics* 47:311–40.

Wasantha, Ben. 1993. Interview by P. Coy. 13 Oct., Kelaniya, Sri Lanka.

Weber, Thomas. 1993. "From Maude Royden's Peace Army to the Gulf Peace Team: An Assessment of Unarmed Interpositionary Peace Forces." *Journal of Peace Research* 30:45–64.

Weed, Frank. 1995. *The Certainty of Justice: Reform in the Crime Victim Movement*. New York: Aldine de Gruyter.

Weiss, Thomas G., and Leon Gordenker. 1996. *NGOs, the UN and Global Governance*. Boulder, Colo.: Lynne Rienner.

Weiss, Thomas G., and Robert S. Jordan. 1976. *The World Food Conference and Global Problem-Solving*. New York: Praeger.

Weiss, Thomas G., David P. Forsythe, and Roger A. Coate. 1994. *The United Nations and Changing World Politics*. Boulder, Colo.: Westview.

Weissbrodt, David. 1982. "International Trial Observers." *Stanford Journal of International Law* 18: 240–53.

————. 1984. "The Contribution of International Nongovernmental Organizations to the Protection of Human Rights." In *Human Rights in International Law*, edited by T. Meron, 405–38. New York: Clarendon Press.

————. 1988. "The United Nations Commission on Human Rights Confirms Conscientious Objection to Military Service as a Human Right." *Netherlands International Law Review* 35:53–72.

Weissbrodt, David, and Maria Luisa Bartolomei. 1991. "The Effectiveness of International Human Rights Pressures: The Case of Argentina, 1976–1983." *Minnesota Law Review* 75:1009–35.

Weissbrodt, David, and James McCarthy. 1981. "Fact-Finding by International Nongovernmental Organizations." *Virginia Journal of International Law* 22: 1–89.

Werner, Mitchell. 1985. Letter to Lee Kimball, 6 Feb. In Miriam Levering manuscript collection, library of Guilford College, Greensboro, N.C.

Weston, Burns. 1985. "A Korean Odyssey." *Advocate,* 33–37.

White, Lyman C. 1933. *The Structure of Private International Organizations.* Philadelphia: George S. Ferguson.

———. 1951. *International Non-Governmental Organizations: Their Purposes, Methods, and Accomplishments.* New Brunswick, N.J.: Rutgers Univ. Press.

Wilkinson, David. 1993. "Environment: The Implications for the EC's Environment Policy of the Treaty of the European Union." *Journal of Environmental Law* 4, no.2:219–33.

Willetts, Peter. 1982a. "Pressure Groups as Transnational Actors." In *Pressure Groups in the Global System: The Transnational Relations of Issue-Oriented Non-Governmental Organizations,* edited by Peter Willet, 1–27. New York: St. Martin's.

———. 1982b. "The Impact of Promotional Pressure Groups on Global Politics." In *Pressure Groups in the Global System: The Transnational Relations of Issue-Oriented, Non-Governmental Organizations,* edited by Peter Willets, 179–200. New York: St. Martin's Press.

———, ed. 1996. *The Conscience of the World: The Influence of NGOs in the United Nations System.* London: C. Hurst.

Wiltfang, Gregory L., and Doug McAdam. 1991. "The Costs and Risks of Social Activism: A Study of Sanctuary Movement Activism." *Social Forces* 69: 987–1010.

Wipfler, Rev. William. 1994. Telephone interview by R. Pagnucco. 15 Mar., from East Rockaway, N.Y.

Wiseberg, Laurie S. 1991. "Protecting Human Rights Activists and NGOs: What More Can Be Done?" *Human Rights Quarterly* 13: 524–44.

———. 1992. "Human Rights Nongovernmental Organizations." In *Human Rights in the World Community,* edited by Richard Pierre Claude and Burns H. Weston, 372–83. Philadelphia: Univ. of Pennsylvania Press.

Wiseberg, Laurie S., and Harry M. Scoble. 1977. "The International League for Human Rights: The Strategy of a Human Rights NGO." *Georgia Journal of International and Comparative Law* 7:289–313.

Wittner, Lawrence. 1997. *Resisting the Bomb: A History of the World Nuclear Disarmament Movement, 1954–1970.* Vol. 2, *The Struggle against the Bomb.* Stanford: Stanford Univ. Press.

Wood, Duncan. 1976. "Discussion of the Question of Conscientious Objection to Military Service in the Commission on Human Rights: A Summary, 1970–1976." *QUNO Newsletter* (supplement), 16 Dec.

Yarrow, C. H. Mike. 1978. *Quaker Experiences in International Conciliation.* New Haven: Yale Univ. Press.

Young, Dennis R. 1991. "The Structural Imperatives of International Advocacy Associations." *Human Relations* 44: 921–41.

Young, Dennis R., Neil Bania, and Darlyne Bailey. 1993. "The Structure of National Nonprofit Associations, Survey Results." Toronto: Association for Research on Nonprofit Organizations and Voluntary Action.

Young, Oran R. 1989. "The Politics of International Regime Formation: Managing Natural Resources and the Environment." *International Organization* 43: 349–75.

Zahn, Gordon C. 1964. *In Solitary Witness: The Life and Death of Franz Jaegerstaet-ter.* Springfield, Ill.: Templegate Press.

Zald, Mayer N., and John D. McCarthy. 1980. "Social Movement Industries: Competition and Cooperation Among Movement Organizations." In *Research in Social Movements, Conflict and Change,* edited by Louis Kriesberg, 1–20. Greenwich, Conn.: JAI.

———. 1987. "Religious Groups as Crucibles of Social Movements." In *Social Movements in an Organizational Society,* edited by Mayer Zald and John D. McCarthy, 67–95. New Brunswick, N.J.: Transaction.

Zimmermann, Klaus W., and Walter Kahlenborn. 1994. *Umweltföderalismus. Einheit und Einheitlichkeit in Deutschland und Europa.* Berlin: Sigma.

Zunes, Stephen. 1994. "Unarmed Insurrections against Authoritarian Governments in the Third World: A New Kind of Revolution." *Third World Quarterly* 15: 403–26.

INDEX

Syracuse Studies on Peace and Conflict Resolution
Harriet Hyman Alonso, Charles Chatfield, and Louis Kriesberg, *Series Editors*

Other titles in the series include:

An American Ordeal: The Antiwar Movement of the Vietnam Era. Charles DeBenedetti; Charles Chatfield, assisting author

Bertha von Suttner: A Life for Peace. Brigitte Hamann

Building a Global Civic Culture: Education for an Interdependent World. Elise Boulding

Cooperative Security: Reducing Third World Wars. I. William Zartman and Victor A. Kremenyuk, eds.

The Eagle and the Dove: The American Peace Movement and United States Foreign Policy, 1900–1922. John Whiteclay Chambers II

An Energy Field More Intense Than War: The Nonviolent Tradition and American Literature. Michael True

From Warfare to Party Politics: The Critical Transition to Civilian Control. Ralph M. Goldman

Gandhi's Peace Army: The Shanti Sena and Unarmed Peacekeeping. Thomas Weber

Gender and the Israeli-Palestinian Conflict: The Politics of Women's Resistance. Simona Sharoni

The Genoa Conference: European Diplomacy, 1921–1922. Carole Fink

Give Peace a Chance: Exploring the Vietnam Antiwar Movement. Melvin Small and William D. Hoover, eds.

Human Rights in the West Bank and Gaza. Ilan Peleg

Interactive Conflict Resolution. Ronald J. Fisher

Intractable Conflicts and Their Transformation. Louis Kriesberg, Terrell A. Northrup, and Stuart J. Thorson, eds.

Israel, Jordan and the Peace Process. Yehuda Lukacs

Israeli Pacifist: The Life of Joseph Abileah. Anthony Bing

Mark Twain's Weapons of Satire: Anti-imperialist Writings on the Philippine-American War. Mark Twain; Jim Zwick, ed.

One Woman's Passion for Peace and Freedom: The Life of Mildred Scott Olmsted. Margaret Hope Bacon

Organizing for Peace: Neutrality, the Test Ban, and the Freeze. Robert Kleidman

Peace as a Women's Issue: A History of the U.S. Movement for World Peace and Women's Rights. Harriet Hyman Alonso

Peace/Mir: An Anthology of Historic Alternatives to War. Charles Chatfield and Ruzanna Ilukhina, volume editors

Plowing My Own Furrow. Howard W. Moore

Polite Protesters: The American Peace Movement of the 1980s. John Lofland

Preparing for Peace: Conflict Transformation Across Cultures. John Paul Lederach

The Road to Greenham Common: Feminism and Anti-Militarism in Britain since 1820. Jill Liddington

Sexism and the War System. Betty A. Reardon

Timing the De-escalation of International Conflicts. Louis Kriesberg and Stuart Thorson, eds.

Virginia Woolf and War: Fiction, Reality, and Myth. Mark Hussey, ed.

The Women and the Warriors: The U.S. Section of the Women's International League for Peace and Freedom, 1915–1946. Carrie Foster

Women's Peace Union and the Outlawry of War, 1921–1942. Harriet Hyman Alonso